ELEMENTS
OF
MACHINE
LEARNING

The Morgan Kaufmann Series in Machine Learning
Edited by Pat Langley

Machine learning studies the mechanisms through which intelligent systems improve their performance over time. Research on this topic explores learning in many different domains, employs a variety of methods, and aims for quite different goals, but the field is held together by its concerns with computational mechanisms for learning. The *Morgan Kaufmann Series in Machine Learning* includes monographs and edited volumes that report progress in this area from a wide variety of perspectives. The series is produced in cooperation with the Institute for the Study of Learning and Expertise, a nonprofit corporation devoted to research on machine learning.

Elements of Machine Learning
By Pat Langley

C4.5: Programs for Machine Learning
By J. Ross Quinlan

Machine Learning Methods for Planning
Edited by Steven Minton

Concept Formation: Knowledge and Experience in Unsupervised Learning
Edited by Douglas H. Fisher, Jr., Michael J. Pazzani, and Pat Langley

Computational Models of Scientific Discovery and Theory Formation
Edited by Jeff Shrager and Pat Langley

Readings in Machine Learning
Edited by Jude W. Shavlik and Thomas G. Dieterich

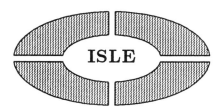

Elements of Machine Learning

Pat Langley

Institute for the Study of
Learning and Expertise

and

Stanford University

Morgan Kaufmann Publishers, Inc.
San Francisco, California

Sponsoring Editor   *Michael B. Morgan*
Production Manager   *Yonie Overton*
Production Editor   *Elisabeth Beller*
Cover Designer   *Ross Carron Design (based on series design by Jo Jackson)*
Copyeditor   *Jeff Van Bueren*
Proofreader   *Ken DellaPenta*
Printer   *Courier Corporation*

This book has been author-typeset using LaTeX.

Cover art is from *The Celtic Art Source Book* by Courtney Davis, © 1988,
and is reproduced with permission from Cassell Publishers, London, England.

Morgan Kaufmann Publishers, Inc.
Editorial and Sales Office
340 Pine Street, Sixth Floor
San Francisco, CA 94104-3205
USA
Telephone 415/392-2665
Facsimile 415/982-2665
Internet mkp@mkp.com
Web site http://mkp.com

Library of Congress Cataloging-in-Publication Data is available for this book.
ISBN 1-55860-301-8

Table of Contents

Preface

Machine learning is a science of the artificial. The field's main objects of study are artifacts, specifically algorithms that improve their performance with experience. The goals of this book are to introduce readers to techniques designed to acquire knowledge in this manner and to provide a framework for understanding relationships among such methods.

There seemed little point in writing a text that simply reflected the main paradigms within the machine learning community. I might easily have written chapters on decision-tree induction, neural networks, case-based learning, genetic algorithms, and analytic methods. However, surveys of these approaches are already available in the literature, and reiterating their content would ignore many underlying similarities among existing methods. Worse, such a text would reinforce existing divisions that are too often based on notational and rhetorical differences rather than on substantive ones.

Instead, I aimed for an organization that would cut across the standard paradigm boundaries, in an attempt to cast the field in a new, and hopefully more rational, light. My intent was to describe the space of learning algorithms, including not only those that appear regularly in the literature, but also those that have received less attention. Such a "periodic table" of learning methods, even if incomplete, could serve both to clarify previous results and to suggest new directions for learning research.

The resulting organization, as reflected in the following pages, builds on a central tenet of modern work on machine learning: that one cannot study learning in the absence of assumptions about how the acquired knowledge is described, how it is structured in memory, or how it is used. As a result, concerns about representation, organization, and performance occupy a primary role in the book's composition.

In particular, after an overview that covers the basic issues in machine learning, the text describes some simple learning methods that incorporate restrictive assumptions about representation, specifically that one can represent knowledge as logical conjunctions (Chapter 2), threshold units (Chapter 3), or simple competitive concepts (Chapter 4). The book then turns to a variety of techniques that organize such descriptions into larger memory structures, including decision lists (Chapter 5), inference networks (Chapter 6), and concept hierarchies (Chapter 7). Because the organization of knowledge is orthogonal to representation of the components, these chapters draw on each of the approaches described in Chapters 2 through 5. A number of extensions to these basic techniques appear in Chapter 8.

Most learning methods are designed to deal with static structures, but some work, especially that concerned with natural language and problem solving, focuses instead on structures that describe change over time. For this reason, the final three substantive chapters explore the acquisition of state-transition networks (Chapter 9), search-control knowledge (Chapter 10), and macro-operators (Chapter 11). These distinctions also cut across those made in earlier chapters, and although much of the work on this topic assumes a logical representation, other formalisms are also covered. The closing chapter discusses some methodological issues in machine learning and its relationship to other fields.

I have done my best to present the material clearly and without unnecessary formalism. Because some precision is necessary, I have used a common pseudocode language to state the various algorithms, but I have tempered this approach with illustrative examples of various methods' behavior on a few simple domains that cross chapter boundaries. I have also aimed for consistency in style and organization across the chapters. In each case, I have attempted to give a clear specification of both the learning task and the performance task that have driven research on the algorithms under examination. Finally, I typically consider issues of representation, organization, and performance before turning to the learning algorithms themselves, because (as argued above) one cannot understand the latter in the absence of the former.

Despite my carefully nontraditional organization, some readers may prefer to focus initially on the best-known learning algorithms and work outward from there. Rest assured, they will find descriptions of standard methods for learning logical decision lists (Section 5.2), inducing univariate decision trees (Section 7.2), altering weights in neural networks (Section 6.4), nearest neighbor methods (Section 5.6), genetic algorithms (Section 5.7), and explanation-based learning (Section 6.3). Most treatments are relatively independent of earlier material, so that a particular ordering should not be essential to understanding. Readers will also note that I have named most algorithms with mnemonic, three-letter abbreviations to distinguish them from particular software described in research papers; to clarify their origin, I have concluded each chapter with a brief history of the subject area and with pointers to the literature.

Machine learning is a large and evolving field, and although I have attempted to provide broad coverage, readers will undoubtedly detect important omissions. When I started work on this book in the late 1980s, research in the area focused on the induction of logical rules and related descriptions. As a result, this paradigm receives somewhat more attention than approaches that have come to be included under the term "machine learning" in more recent years, such as neural networks, genetic algorithms, case-based methods, and probabilistic techniques. This problem will arise in any survey of such a dynamic field.

There is also a noticeable lack of attention to issues of evaluation. Computational learning theory plays a significant role in the literature, yet the book does not incorporate results from this area, as most formal analyses are worst-case in nature and their practical importance remains unclear. Neither does the book discuss specific experimental results, as most empirical studies of learning algorithms focus on real-world domains with unknown characteristics. When there is general agreement among researchers, I have tried to characterize the behavior of different algorithms under various conditions. However, more informed conclusions must await additional studies that are designed to evaluate the strengths and limitations of alternative learning methods.

Regardless of these limitations, I believe that the current volume covers a majority of the problems of concern to machine learning researchers and the methods developed to address them. Moreover, I believe that it places a rational framework on the work to date which makes cross-paradigm connections that are typically downplayed in the literature. Without doubt, future work will suggest revisions and improvements to this framework, but if this text and its organization play some role in that process, and if they help the next generation of researchers to better understand the underlying unity of their field, they will have served their purpose.

I could never have finished this book without the support and faith of many people. The writing was spread across many places. I started the project at the University of California, Irvine, where Dennis Kibler, Doug Fisher, Jeff Schlimmer, Randy Jones, David Aha, and many others greatly influenced my view of the field. Work on the book continued at NASA Ames Research Center, which provided another supportive environment until some unfortunate conflicts interfered. Wayne Iba, John Allen, Kevin Thompson, Steven Minton, Wray Buntine, and Kathleen McKusick each provided technical and moral support during at least some of that period.

Having to leave NASA Ames in 1992 delayed the project, but I was able to continue writing during a one-year visit to Siemens Corporate Research, where Steve Hanson, George Drastal, Bharat Rao, Chris Darken, Geoff Towell, and others further altered my perspectives. During this time, Jeff Schlimmer, Doug Fisher, Paul Utgoff, Russ Greiner, Glenn Iba, and Stan Matwin provided useful comments on a draft of the text, as did Eliot Moss somewhat later. In 1994 I moved to the Institute for the Study of Learning and Expertise and to Stanford University, where Nils Nilsson, David Rumelhart, Jerome Friedman, Jeff Shrager, and other members of the local machine learning community provided an enlightening and supportive environment. Stephanie Sage stood by me throughout this period, giving both emotional and intellectual support. I might never have made it through some of the darker hours without her help, or without the music of Susan Udell to bolster my spirits.

A number of funding agencies supported me during the writing effort, including the Office of Naval Research (Grant Nos. N00014-84-K-0345, N00014-85-K-0373, N00014-94-1-0505, and N00014-94-1-0746), the Army Research Institute (Contract No. MD 903-85-C-0324), the Air Force Office of Scientific Research (Grant No. F49620-94-1-0118), and the Advanced Research Projects Agency. Alan Meyrowitz, Susan Chipman, Judith Orasanu, Abraham Waksman, Robert Powell, and Teresa McMullen supported my research in this period. Michael Morgan was patient and supportive during the lengthy writing process, and his associates at Morgan Kaufmann Publishers provided invaluable support in producing the final book. Clearly, I could never have finished *Elements of Machine Learning* without help from many directions, and if I have overlooked anyone's contribution, it is only because so many different people have been involved.

CHAPTER 1

An Overview of
Machine Learning

The ability to learn is one of the central features of intelligence, which makes it an important concern for both cognitive psychology and artificial intelligence (AI). The field of *machine learning*, which crosses these disciplines, studies the computational processes that underlie learning in both humans and machines. This book is about the science of machine learning and the progress this field has made since its inception over three decades ago.

Despite its separate identity, there are two important senses in which machine learning is an integral part of these larger fields. First, learning researchers cannot ignore issues of knowledge representation, memory organization, and performance, which are central concerns for AI and cognitive science. Second, learning can occur in any domain requiring intelligence, whether the basic task involves diagnosis, planning, natural language, motor control, or something else again. Thus, one can view machine learning as less a subfield of AI and cognitive science than as one paradigm for research and development.

In this chapter we present an overview of the issues that arise in the study of machine learning. We begin by giving some background about the field as a whole. After this, we consider various aspects of learning, including the environment in which it occurs; the representation, organization, and use of knowledge; and the nature of the learning mechanisms themselves. Finally, we review the major paradigms that have emerged within the machine learning community and the underlying similarities that cut across them.

1.1 The science of machine learning

Before delving into the details of our topic, we should first offer some broad observations about the overall field. Below we present a brief history of the discipline's development, and then review the goals that motivate researchers to study machine learning. After this, we present a framework for machine learning that serves as an organization for the later sections in the chapter.

1.1.1 Historical perspectives on machine learning

Before turning to the current state of machine learning research, let us set the stage by reviewing the history of the field. The interest in computational approaches to learning dates back to the beginnings of artificial intelligence and cognitive science in the mid-1950s. Diversity in both tasks and methods characterized research from the outset, with work including topics such as game playing, letter recognition, abstract concepts, and verbal memory. Learning was viewed as a central feature of intelligent systems, and work on both learning and performance was concerned with developing general mechanisms for cognition, perception, and action.

In the middle 1960s, both AI researchers and psychologists realized the importance of domain knowledge, which led to construction of the first knowledge-intensive systems. However, learning researchers continued to focus on general, domain-independent methods, with most work applied to perceptual domains. Eventually, pattern recognition and artificial intelligence separated into two distinct fields. The gap widened further as many researchers in pattern recognition began to emphasize algorithmic, numerical methods that contrasted sharply with the heuristic, symbolic methods associated with the AI paradigm.

During this period, most AI researchers avoided issues of learning while they attempted to understand the role of knowledge in intelligent behavior. Research on knowledge representation, natural language, and expert systems dominated this era. However, some work on learning continued in the background, incorporating the representations and heuristic methods that had become central to artificial intelligence. Some work on concept learning and language acquisition also occurred during this period.

In the late 1970s, a new interest in machine learning emerged within AI and grew rapidly over the course of a few years. Some research in this area was motivated by a frustration with the encyclopedic flavor and domain-specific emphasis of expert systems, as learning offered a return to general principles. Others were excited by the prospect of automating the acquisition of domain-specific knowledge bases, and still others hoped to model human learning. Research on concept induction and language acquisition continued, but this was joined by work on machine discovery and learning in problem solving. Many new methods were proposed, and a renewed interest in neural networks emerged, bringing back techniques that had been abandoned by AI years earlier.

Machine learning continued to branch out during the 1980s, with work extending to planning, diagnosis, design, and control. Researchers became more serious about the real-world potential of learning algorithms, and a number of successful fielded applications showed that the technology could have an impact on industry. The field also placed itself on much firmer methodological grounds, with systematic experimentation on common data sets and precise theoretical analysis becoming the norm rather than the exception. A variety of robust software packages also spread throughout the community, leading to careful comparative studies and a greater tendency to build on previous systems.

When the first workshop on machine learning took place at Carnegie Mellon University in 1980, only 30 participants were present. The field has grown rapidly since then, and it now boasts collected volumes on both general and specialized topics, a refereed journal, and an annual conference that attracts some 300 participants. The number of papers on learning published in conference proceedings and journals has increased dramatically, and the number of PhD-level researchers in the area continues to grow. Machine learning has emerged as a central concern of the AI and cognitive science communities, as most researchers have come to acknowledge the central role of learning in intelligence.

1.1.2 Goals and accomplishments of machine learning

The field of machine learning is united by a concern with learning, but researchers focus on this problem for quite different reasons. Although authors seldom make their goals explicit, the literature suggests four basic aims, each with its own methodological perspectives, its own approaches to evaluation, and its own success stories.

One goal involves modeling the mechanisms that underlie human learning. In this *psychological* framework, researchers develop learning algorithms that are generally consistent with knowledge of the human cognitive architecture and that are also designed to explain specific observed learning behaviors. This approach has produced a wide range of computational models that account for phenomena in many domains, including problem solving, natural language, perception, and motor control. Some models explain behavior at a qualitative level, whereas others fit the error rates and reaction times of human subjects. Such simulations have more than theoretical interest; because they make predictions about learning behavior, they hold potential for aiding the design of instructional materials for use in education.

Another group of researchers takes an *empirical* approach to the study of machine learning. The aim here is to discover general principles that relate the characteristics of learning algorithms, and of the domain in which they operate, to learning behavior. The standard approach involves running experiments that vary either the algorithm or the domain, and then observing the impact of this manipulation on learning. Some studies compare different classes of learning method, whereas others examine slight variations of a single algorithm; some experiments consider behavior in natural domains, whereas others systematically vary the characteristics of synthetic domains. Experimental studies of machine learning have produced a wide range of empirical generalizations about alternative methods that have suggested areas of weakness, ideas for improved algorithms, and sources of task difficulty.

A different group, also concerned with general principles, treats machine learning as an area of *mathematical* study. The goal of such computational learning theorists is to formulate and prove theorems about the tractability of entire classes of learning problems and algorithms designed to solve those problems. Here the typical approach involves defining some learning problem, conjecturing that it can or cannot be solved with a reasonable number of training cases, and then proving that the conjecture holds under very general conditions. Whereas the empirical approach borrows experimental techniques from physics and psychology, this mathematical approach borrows tools and concepts from theoretical computer science and statistics. Computational learning theory has generated many insightful and surprising theorems about the relative difficulty of learning tasks and methods for solving them.

A final group of researchers take an *applications* approach to machine learning, with the primary aim of using machine learning on real-world problems. Most fielded applications of artificial intelligence rely on expert systems, which often require person-years to develop and debug their extensive domain-specific knowledge bases. Because machine learning can transform training data into knowledge, it holds the potential for automating the process of knowledge acquisition. Here the typical steps involve a developer formulating an interesting problem in terms of machine learning, designing a representation for training cases and learned knowledge, collecting the training data, using machine learning to generate a knowledge base, and then working with users to field the resulting knowledge-based system. This approach has led to fielded applications of machine learning in diagnosis, process control, scheduling, and other areas.

A central thread that holds these approaches together is a concern with the development, understanding, and evaluation of learning *algorithms*. If machine learning is a science, then it is clearly a science of algorithms. For this reason, algorithms for machine learning occupy the central place in the following chapters. We will seldom refer to specific psychological models, empirical studies, mathematical theorems, or fielded applications. Rather, our emphasis will be on the variety of algorithms that researchers have developed and on the relations among them.

1.1.3 A framework for machine learning

Many readers will want a clear, unambiguous definition of learning. Unfortunately, any attempt to draw a fixed boundary around so broad a concept is doomed to failure, as would be attempts to define 'life' or 'love'. One can certainly generate a precise formal definition, but others can always find intuitive examples that fall outside the specified conditions or find counterexamples that fall within them.

Instead, we will proceed with a practical definition that, although somewhat ambiguous, still constrains the topic under study. Thus, we will state that:

> *Learning* is the improvement of performance in some environment through the acquisition of knowledge resulting from experience in that environment.

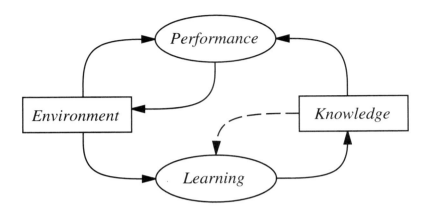

Figure 1-1. The interactions among learning, performance, knowledge, and the environment. The dashed line indicates an optional link.

This has the form of a formal definition, but closer inspection reveals that four of the terms – *performance*, *environment*, *knowledge*, and *experience* – are themselves rather vague.[1] We view this as an advantage rather than a limitation.

For example, performance suggests some quantitative measure of behavior on a task, but one can measure many aspects of behavior, such as accuracy, efficiency, and even understanding. An environment supposes an external setting with some regularity, but this may be external to the learning and performance systems while still being inside the overall system. Knowledge suggests some type of internal data structure, but this can take any form one cares to imagine. Experience requires some mental processing, but this can focus on perceptual input, motor output, or even internal traces. The notion of improvement is more clear cut, involving some desirable change in the measure of performance. However, one might want to replace 'improvement' with 'change', since human learning sometimes leads to decrements in performance.

The most important feature of this definition is its claim that learning cannot be described in isolation. A learner always finds itself in some environment, about which it attempts to learn. The learner is always linked to some knowledge base from which it can draw and in which it

---

1. Some have proposed similar definitions that focus on performance improvement on a population of tasks, whereas others have suggested alternative definitions that emphasize the acquisition of knowledge. Our formulation attempts to incorporate both ideas.

can store its acquired knowledge. The learner always attempts to improve the behavior of some performance element, which is affected only indirectly through the knowledge base it uses to control its interactions with the environment. Figure 1-1 illustrates the relations among these components.

We believe this formulation is sufficiently broad to cover all the examples of learning covered in the following pages, yet constrained enough to rule out the behavior of many existing AI systems and computational models of human cognition. The definition also covers some behaviors that we will not consider, such as the simple storage of facts in memory. Few people would argue that memorization is not learning, but neither would they find it very interesting. The reason is that, unlike other forms of learning, it does not involve *induction* beyond the training experiences to novel test cases drawn from the same environment. Nearly all research on machine learning deals with some form of induction, and we will emphasize this issue in the chapters that follow. In the remainder of the current chapter, we examine the components of a learning system in more detail, beginning with the nature of the environment.

1.2 Nature of the environment

As we have seen, learning always occurs in the context of some environment. Here we examine four aspects of the environment, including the performance task, the amount of supervision, the manner of presentation, and the regularity of the domain.

1.2.1 Performance tasks and measures

Learning involves improvement in performance, and thus learning cannot occur in the absence of some performance task. One can partition such tasks along many different lines; a simple scheme involves the distinction among perception, cognition, and action. More commonly, the AI literature emphasizes division into more specific areas such as natural language, design, diagnosis, vision, speech, reasoning, planning, and motor control. Machine learning has roles to play in each area, and we will not attempt to detail them all here.

Within the literature on machine learning, a more important distinction concerns whether one uses the learned knowledge for one-step classification and prediction or for some form of multi-step inference or problem solving. Most research has focused on the former performance task, and we will devote Chapters 2 through 8 to such classification learning. Moreover, we will see in Chapters 9 through 11 that techniques developed for classification tasks can often be adapted to learn knowledge for use in multi-step problem solving.

We should also consider the measure of performance that learning aims to improve. Typically, the goal of classification learners is to increase the accuracy of the performance system, whereas the goal of problem-solving learners is to increase their efficiency. However, one can also measure and attempt to improve the efficiency of one-step classification; conversely, in Chapter 10 we show one scheme for reducing efficiency increases to changes in accuracy.

1.2.2 Supervised and unsupervised learning

Another dimension that influences learning is the degree of supervision. In some cases, a tutor or domain expert gives the learner direct feedback about the appropriateness of its performance. Such *supervised learning* problems contrast sharply with *unsupervised learning* tasks, in which this feedback is absent. The vast majority of research in machine learning has dealt with supervised tasks, and we focus on this topic in Chapters 2 through 7. However, in Chapter 8 we will see that many methods designed for supervised problems can be adapted to unsupervised ones.

Both of these tasks can arise in learning for either classification or problem solving. For classification problems, the supervised task assumes that each training instance includes an attribute that specifies the class of that instance,[2] and the goal is to induce a concept description that accurately predicts this attribute. There is less agreement on the goal of unsupervised learning, but one can define analogous prediction tasks over the entire set of attributes.

In problem-solving tasks, supervised learning occurs when a tutor suggests the correct step at each point in the search or reasoning process; systems that operate on such feedback are sometimes referred to as *learning apprentices*. However, most work on learning in problem solving has dealt with unsupervised tasks, in which the agent must distin-

---

2. In classification domains, the task of supervised learning is sometimes called *learning from examples*.

guish desirable actions from undesirable ones on its own. This subtask has been called the *credit assignment* problem, since the learner must identify the decisions responsible for success or failure of its problem-solving efforts. As we discuss in Chapter 10, once the learner has dealt with this issue, it can draw directly on supervised methods for classification learning to acquire problem-solving knowledge.

1.2.3 Online and offline learning tasks

Yet another aspect of the environment concerns the manner in which training cases are given to the learner. We will say that *offline* learning occurs when all instances are presented simultaneously. We can contrast such induction tasks with *online* settings, in which the instances are presented one at a time. Intermediate schemes are also possible, in which the learner encounters one set of instances, followed by another set, and so on.

Many of the learning tasks confronting humans appear to be online in nature, if only because people exist in a temporal world and thus experience events in sequence. However, in some cases humans are confronted with a mass of precollected data, such as a scientist might encounter when coming to a new area. Thus, both forms of task model situations that occur in realistic situations and both have a role to play in a complete theory of machine learning. Nevertheless, most research has emphasized offline learning problems, so we will devote most of our examples in later chapters to them.

1.2.4 Regularity of the environment

A final factor that affects learning relates to the regularity of the environment.[3] One can identify four different but related environmental factors that can influence the difficulty of learning. The most obvious aspect of the environment is the complexity of the target knowledge that must be acquired. This might relate to the complexity of concept descriptions in a classification domain, to the structure of the problem space in a problem-solving domain, or to the form of the grammar in a linguistic domain. For example, a concept that involves many features or conditions might be harder to learn than one that involves fewer.

---

3. This 'environment' need not be external. For instance, a problem solver may improve its behavior based entirely on its internal experience with solving problems.

A second important factor concerns the number of irrelevant features or attributes. If the environment contains many such features, the learning system can have difficulty distinguishing them from the relevant features that it should use in making predictions. Many learning algorithms, especially the methods we examine in Chapter 2, explicitly address the problem of feature selection, but in Chapter 8 we consider this problem in more general terms.

A third issue is the amount of noise in the environment. This can take on two forms in supervised learning tasks. *Class noise* involves the corruption of supervised feedback, so that the learner is given incorrect feedback. In contrast, *attribute noise* involves corruption of the instance description itself; thus, an attribute's value may be replaced or shifted. Increased amounts of noise tend to make learning more difficult overall, but we discuss techniques for mitigating this effect in Chapter 8. A related issue involves the consistency of the environment over time. In some cases, a learned concept may suddenly cease to be valid, though it may retain partial overlap with the new situation. Such cases of *concept drift* can be difficult to distinguish from noise.

The literature contains some studies, both experimental and theoretical, of these factors' effect on behavior, but additional work along these lines is clearly needed. We should note that 'environmental' factors are never entirely a function of the environment. Clearly, the complexity of a target concept also depends partly on one's language for representing concepts, and what appears as noise or drift to one learning system may appear noise-free and unchanging to another that can observe additional features. Thus, any results along these lines must refer to the relation between the environment and the representation of that environment, to which we now turn.

1.3 Nature of representation and performance

Both learning and performance rely on the ability to represent knowledge. Below we discuss some issues relevant to the representation of experience (the input to learning) and to the representation and organization of acquired knowledge (the output of learning). However, because the effect of knowledge cannot be separated from the processes that use it, we integrate our discussion of learned knowledge with aspects of the performance component.

1.3.1 Representing experience

As we noted in Section 1.1.3, one must be able to represent experiences before one can acquire knowledge based on those experiences. We will limit our attention to representing instances of some concept, as much of the work in machine learning has focused on such experiences.

The simplest approach employs *Boolean* or *binary* features, with each instance specifying the presence or absence of a feature. For example, suppose a patient can exhibit three possible symptoms – hairiness, a tendency to howl, and ravening hunger. We can represent a patient having the first and third symptoms, but not the second, as the set {`hairy`, `¬howl`, `hungry`}. An equivalent representation uses *bit vectors*, which use position in a list to index features, with a 1 indicating the feature's presence and a 0 indicating its absence. Thus, the vector 1 0 1 describes the hairy, non-howling, hungry patient from above.

A slightly more sophisticated formalism describes each instance as a set of *nominal attributes*, which are similar to Boolean features but allow more than two mutually exclusive values. For example, this framework would let one replace the second feature above with a `sound` attribute that can take the values `howl`, `speak`, or `cluck`. Although one can always transform a nominal representation into a Boolean formalism, this does not mean the latter representation is either efficient or convenient. If the values of an attribute are mutually exclusive, then a Boolean encoding can specify some instances that never actually occur.

Numeric attributes that take on real, integral, or even ordinal values are also possible. For example, one might describe the length of a patient's hair, the amplitude of her howls, and the ferocity of her hunger. We will use numeric domains for many of our examples because they can be easily visualized. Given k numeric attributes, one can represent any given instance as a point in a k-dimensional space, with the attributes defining the axes. We will sometimes refer to this as the *instance space*. Note that feature vectors can be viewed as a special case of a numeric encoding in which the values are limited to 0 and 1. For this reason, many learning methods that work on numeric representations can be easily adapted to featural encodings and vice versa.

Although features and attributes are sufficient for many domains, some tasks are inherently relational in nature and require more sophisticated formalisms. For example, consider a scenario that involves three blocks and a table, and a particular instance in which blocks A and B rest on the table and in which block C rests on A. We can describe this situation as a set of *relational literals*: (on A table), (on B table), (on C A), (clear C), and (clear B). Each literal describes a separate aspect of the situation, but the number of such literals will differ for different instances.

Relational languages subsume featural, nominal, and numeric schemes. Note that the clear predicate takes a single argument, making it equivalent to a Boolean feature, and literals such as (length A 2.5) can specify numeric quantities of objects. However, this increased representational power comes at a cost: one can view relational instances as complex graph structures, and learning from such structures involves the solution of complex graph-matching problems. For this reason, most work in machine learning draws on simpler representations, and we will focus on them in this book, although we examine relational methods in Chapter 8.

1.3.2 Extensional and intensional concept representations

Just as a learning system must represent the experience that leads to learning, it must also represent the knowledge that learning produces. A naive approach to representation would simply list all observed instances of a concept, using the instance language for the domain. However, such *extensional* definitions of concepts have certain undesirable features. Some domains contain an infinite number of instances, making them impossible to list by extension. However, even in finite domains, the extensional approach can summarize previous experience but it cannot predict that unseen instances will be members of the concept.

A more sophisticated approach involves formulating some description of the concept for use in distinguishing between positive and negative instances. Not only is such an *intensional* definition more compact; it can also be used to classify novel instances. However, this approach introduces some new problems. We must decide on a representation, or *concept description language*, for the intensional definition. Also, we must decide on some interface between the languages used for describing concepts and for describing instances; that is, we must find some way to use the intensional description to classify instances.

This second problem leads to the notion of an *interpreter* or *matcher*, which constitutes a primitive performance component. Given an instance description and one or more concept descriptions, the interpreter must decide to which concepts (if any) the instance belongs. Thus, the interpreter can be used to transform an intensional definition into an extensional one, simply by applying it to all possible instances. In other words, we have:

$$\text{Intension} + \text{Interpreter} = \text{Extension} \ .$$

Although one would never use this relationship in practice, the extensional view remains useful for characterizing the behavior of learning algorithms and we will invoke it in later chapters. In particular, we will often refer to the extension of each concept in the instance space as its *decision region* and to the surfaces between their extensions as *decision boundaries*. We can use these geometric notations to show the predictions that an intensional description and interpreter would make on unseen test instances.

1.3.3 Interpretation of conceptual knowledge

We can divide interpreters for intensional concept descriptions into three broad classes. The *logical* approach assumes that concepts are represented as logical combinations of features or attribute values and that the interpreter carries out an 'all or none' matching process. For example, one might represent the concept of a disease as the conjunction of certain symptoms, and classify a patient as having that disease only if all those symptoms are present. As we will see in Chapter 2, such methods generate decision boundaries that are parallel to the axes of the instance space.

The *threshold* approach retains some characteristics of the logical framework, but the interpreter carries out a *partial* matching process, in which only some aspects of the intensional description must match. This requires that one specify some threshold that determines an acceptable degree of match. This may be stated in terms of an absolute number of matched features (an 'm-of-n' function), as a percentage of matched components, or as a numeric combination of features that are weighted by their importance. For instance, we might diagnose a patient as having a disease if any three of five symptoms are present, or we might count some symptoms as more diagnostic than others. As we discuss in Chapter 3, an individual threshold unit creates a single decision boundary in the instance space, with its shape determined by the details of the interpreter.

The *competitive* framework has much in common with the threshold approach. Again the interpreter carries out partial matching, so that not all aspects of the intensional description must match the instance description. However, rather than using a threshold to determine an acceptable match, it computes the degree of match for alternative concepts and selects the best competitor. For example, given two diseases that each have five associated symptoms, we might select the disease that has the most symptoms in common with those observed for a given patient. As explained in Chapter 4, competitive methods can produce up to one decision boundary for each pair of intensional descriptions, with the exact shape determined by the interpreter.

The best-match notion has important implications for the relation between intensional and extensional definitions. Both the logical and threshold methods determine the extension of a concept based entirely on its intensional description, independent of those descriptions associated with other concepts. In the competitive framework, the extension of a concept is a joint function of the intensional descriptions of all competing concepts. Thus, the 'meaning' of a concept is 'context sensitive' rather than 'context independent.' This gives competitive concepts a quite different flavor from those of the other two frameworks.

The machine learning literature tends to associate certain representational formalisms with certain interpretive methods. Logical interpreters are often used to process simple sets of features or tests, whereas threshold interpreters are often used when attributes have associated weights. However, probabilistic representations also associate numeric information with attributes, yet they are typically used in combination with competitive interpreters. Instance-based formalisms, which store training cases in memory, are typically processed in a competitive manner, but they can also be combined with logical and threshold interpreters.[4]

We believe that the interpretive process is a central issue in machine learning, and that its importance far outweighs the differences in representational formalisms often emphasized in the literature. An intensional representation has no meaning (i.e., no extension) without some associated interpreter, and different interpreters can yield different

---

4. At first glance, an instance-based formalism appears to be equivalent to a purely extensional framework, but the interpreter lets one use stored cases to move beyond the data and make predictions about unseen cases.

meanings for the same representation. For this reason, we have organized Chapters 2, 3, and 4 around the three approaches to interpretation discussed above.

1.3.4 The organization of knowledge

Early work on machine learning focused on the induction of simple concepts, for which individual conjunctions, single threshold units, or sets of competitive descriptions were sufficient. However, more challenging induction tasks require combinations of such descriptions, which in turn requires some *organization* of learned knowledge. Machine learning research has typically used one of three broad classes of organizational design. These structures share the crucial feature of *modularity*, which lets a learning system acquire each piece of knowledge in relative independence of others.

One common organization stores units in a *decision list*. As we will see in Chapter 5, the descriptions in such a knowledge structure are ordered, causing the performance system to consider earlier before later ones. Although usually associated with logical formalisms, decision lists can also be used to organize threshold units. In some variants, the units are stored not in an ordered list but in a mutually exclusive set. This approach is especially appropriate for organizing competitive units, but one can also use it with other representational schemes.

A second framework for organizing learned knowledge is the *inference network*. As we discuss in Chapter 6, these structures take the form of a tree or directed graph. The extension of each node N in an inference network is influenced by its connections to the nodes below N, and evidence for these defining nodes provides evidence for N. Thus, a set of Horn clauses specifies an AND/OR graph in which each head symbol corresponds to a logical OR and each clause corresponds to a logical AND. However, inference networks are not limited to logical representations any more than decision lists. Multilayer neural networks and Bayesian influence diagrams also constitute important types of inference networks, despite their use of different interpreters.

A third widely used organizational scheme, described in Chapter 7, is the *concept hierarchy*. These knowledge structures also take the form of a tree or directed graph, but their semantics are quite different from those for inference networks. In this case, each node corresponds to a concept and its associated intensional description. More abstract or general nodes occur higher in the hierarchy, whereas more specific ones occur at lower levels. The best-known forms of concept hierarchies are *decision trees* and *discrimination networks*, which typically use a logical matching scheme to sort experiences downward through memory. However, one can use hierarchies to organize any type of intensional description and in conjunction with any type of interpreter.

The above frameworks are designed to organize knowledge about static objects, but many tasks involve reasoning about change over time and some machine learning research has dealt with structures designed for such problems. For example, *state-transition networks* specify a set of possible states and transitions among them, along with descriptions or constraints on each. In Chapter 9 we will see that this scheme is typically used for natural language processing, whereas Chapters 10 and 11 focus on two additional frameworks – *search-control rules* and *macro-operators* – that are more commonly used in problem solving and planning domains.

1.4 Nature of the learning component

Now that we have covered the preliminaries, we can finally turn to issues that directly involve learning. We first consider the learning task in terms of search, then turn to some methods for constraining the search process. After this, we examine the distinction between incremental and nonincremental learning.

1.4.1 Learning as heuristic search

The notion of *search* has played a central role in artificial intelligence, and it has also had an important impact on machine learning. Typically, formulations of the search metaphor specify a set of possible states, a set of operators for transforming those states, and some procedure for applying those operators to search the space. We have already dealt with knowledge states in the previous section, during our discussion of concept representations. Thus, we will focus here on operators and search mechanisms.

Some research in machine learning draws on the fact that generality imposes a partial ordering on the space of intensional concept descriptions. For any given representation/interpreter combination, one can specify a lattice with a set of most general descriptions at the top, a set of most specific descriptions at the bottom, and descriptions of intermediate generality in the middle. This generality ordering imposes a structure on the space of concept descriptions that one can use to organize the search process.

For example, if one's concept description language consists of logical conjunctions, then adding a single feature or test to the current description produces a new description that is more specific, in that its extension is a subset of the initial concept. Similarly, removing a feature or test produces a more general concept description with strictly greater extension. With a threshold interpreter, modifying a single weight or threshold has similar effects, although most operators used within this framework alter multiple parameters at a time, producing a description that is neither more specific nor more general than the original one, but simply different from it.

Other learning operators take two or more concept descriptions and combine them in some manner. For example, one such approach generates a new description that takes some features or tests from one parent and the rest from the other parent. Yet other operators, designed for relational languages that allow descriptions of different sizes, compose the parents into more complex structures that retain all the literals in the parents. All of these operators act on individual concept descriptions rather than the organization of memory, but methods for altering organization typically use them as primitive steps, as we will see in Chapters 5 through 8.

In addition to states and operators, a learning system requires some procedure that applies the operators to search the state space. Any such procedure must take a position on four basic issues: where to start the search, how to organize the search, how to evaluate alternative states, and when to terminate the process. Induction methods that assume a logical interpreter, which tend to employ the generality ordering discussed above, typically start from either the most general or most specific possible state. Other schemes, including most threshold methods, start from states of intermediate generality, which they often select randomly.

In principle, one can use any search technique to explore the space of concept descriptions, from exhaustive methods like breadth-first and depth-first search to more heuristic ones. Although we will see examples of both approaches, the size of most spaces strongly recommends heuristic methods, which give up guarantees of optimality in return for tractability. In fact, the vast majority of induction algorithms do not even rely on sophisticated techniques like best-first search, but rather use simple greedy or hill-climbing methods, which appear to work well in many domains. In terms of evaluation, all induction methods emphasize ability to perform well on the training data, but many also take into account other factors to augment their decisions.

Finally, the issue of termination is more subtle than it seems at first glance. Many incremental methods never truly halt, as they continue to process instances as long as they encounter them. For nonincremental schemes, the simplest method is to continue the search until no further progress occurs or until the method finds a description that is entirely consistent with the training data. However, this naive approach can produce descriptions that *overfit*, in that they do well on the training data but poorly on novel test cases. Chapter 8 discusses this issue and some common responses.

1.4.2 Constraining search through bias

Machine learning must address the *problem of induction*, which states that generalizing from any set of observations is never logically justified, since there always exist many hypotheses that could account for the observed data. One trivial hypothesis is simply the disjunction of the observations. This is not the sort of knowledge structure one typically desires from a learning method, but without some additional constraints there is no reason to rank it below the alternatives.

Clearly, a learning system must somehow limit or direct its search through the space of possible knowledge structures. The machine learning literature often refers to this as the *bias* of the system.[5] One important form of constraint, known as *representational bias*, restricts the space of possible structures by limiting the concept description language. We will see examples of such bias in Chapters 2, 3, and 4, when we consider logical conjunctions, single threshold units, and simple competitive descriptions. These biases are quite different, but all greatly constrain the space of possible concept descriptions.

---

5. This concept bears only a loose connection to the statistical notion of bias.

We can clarify the idea of representational bias by recalling the distinction between representations for instances and concepts. Consider an instance language with k Boolean features, which implicitly defines a space of 2^k possible instances. The instance space in turn specifies a space of possible two-way partitions, each of which corresponds to a potential concept. For our Boolean domain, there are 2^{2^k} such partitions, a sizable number even when k is small. A restricted language for concepts can reduce this set considerably; for example, there exist only 3^k logical conjunctions and $2^{O(n^2)}$ concepts that one can describe with a linear threshold unit.

A more flexible approach incorporates the notion of *search bias*, which considers all possible concept descriptions but examines some earlier than others in the search process. For example, an algorithm for inducing logical conjunctions might prefer simpler hypotheses to more complex ones and thus consider concept descriptions with fewer tests before ones with more tests. In some cases, these preferences are encoded into an explicit evaluation metric, whereas in others they are embodied in the structure of the search algorithm itself.

Another source of bias is the background knowledge[6] available to the learning system. For instance, inference rules may let one rewrite experience in a different language that simplifies the induction task, as we will see in Chapter 6. Providing the basic organization for a multilayer inference network gives a similar effect. Compositional approaches often take advantage of prior knowledge in the form of domain operators or inference rules. As with representational and search bias, background knowledge can strongly direct the course of learning, although the form and use of this knowledge can vary widely.

1.4.3 Incremental and nonincremental learning

In Section 1.2.3, we distinguished between offline learning tasks, in which many instances are presented together, and online tasks, in which they are given one at a time. A similar distinction holds for learning algorithms, which can either process many training instances at once, in a *nonincremental* manner, or handle them one at a time, in an *incremental* fashion.

---

6. Of course, representational and search bias are forms of knowledge. Here we use 'knowledge' to indicate explicit data structures on which the learner can build or to which it can link new structures.

Although incremental methods lend themselves to online tasks and nonincremental approaches seem most appropriate for offline problems, it is important to keep these two issues separate. One can adapt a nonincremental method to an online learning task by retaining previous training cases in memory, adding each new instance to this set, and rerunning the algorithm each time on the extended set. Similarly, one can use an incremental method for an offline learning task by iteratively running it through the same training set many times.

Clearly, then, the surface behavior of a learning algorithm cannot determine its incrementality. A more precise notion involves the number of previous instances the method can reprocess during each learning step. We will say an algorithm is *incremental in degree k* if, when given online data, it reprocesses at most k previous cases after encountering each training instance, and that the algorithm is *nonincremental* if it reprocesses all earlier instances.

Both approaches to learning have their advantages. Nonincremental methods can collect statistics about all training cases, giving them more information on which to base their decisions. On the other hand, incremental methods would seem to be more efficient for large data sets. Because they tend to closely integrate learning and performance, incremental methods also seem more appropriate in modeling human behavior and in autonomous agents. Machine learning has actively explored both frameworks, and we will see examples of each in chapters to come.

1.5 Five paradigms for machine learning

Machine learning is a diverse field that is held together by a common set of goals and similar evaluation methodologies. Despite these similarities, researchers in machine learning tend to associate themselves with one or another of five main paradigms, which differ in their basic assumptions about representation, performance methods, and learning algorithms. One can question whether this division benefits the field, and there are certainly cases where differences of notation and rhetoric have obscured important underlying similarities. Nevertheless, because most researchers themselves make these distinctions, we will review them briefly.

One major paradigm, often termed *neural networks*, represents knowledge as a multilayer network of threshold units that spreads activation from input nodes through internal units to output nodes. Weights on the links determine how much activation is passed on in each case. The activations of output nodes can be translated into numeric predictions or discrete decisions about the class of the input. The neural net framework typically attempts to improve the accuracy of classification or prediction by modifying the weights on the links. The typical learning algorithm carries out a hill-climbing search through the space of weights, modifying them in an attempt to minimize the errors that the network makes on training data.

A second framework, known as *instance-based* or *case-based* learning, represents knowledge in terms of specific cases or experiences and relies on flexible matching methods to retrieve these cases and apply them to new situations. One common approach simply finds the stored case nearest (according to some distance metric) to the current situation, then uses it for classification or prediction. The typical case-based learning method simply stores training instances in memory; generalization occurs at retrieval time, with the power residing in the indexing scheme, the similarity metric used to identify relevant cases, and the method for adapting cases to new situations.

Genetic algorithms constitute a third paradigm within machine learning. This framework typically represents acquired knowledge as a set of Boolean or binary features, which are sometimes used as the conditions and actions of rules. The most common interpreter for this knowledge employs a logical matching process, using strengths associated with rules to resolve conflicts. In some cases, a production-system architecture lets rules apply in sequence, producing multi-step behavior. The standard learning operators in genetic algorithms generate new candidate rules from parents that have high strengths, where strength reflects some measure of performance on training cases. In effect, genetic methods carry out a parallel hill-climbing search, retaining a set of competing and sometimes complementary descriptions in memory.

A fourth paradigm, which we will call *rule induction*, employs condition-action rules, decision trees, or similar logical knowledge structures. Here the performance element sorts instances down the branches of the decision tree or finds the first rule whose conditions match the instance, typically using a logical matching process. Information about classes or predictions are stored in the action sides of the rules or the leaves of the tree. Learning algorithms in the rule-induction framework usually carry out a greedy search through the space of decision trees or rule sets, using a statistical evaluation function to select attributes to incorporate into the knowledge structure. Most methods partition the training data recursively into disjoint sets, attempting to summarize each set as a conjunction of logical conditions.

A final approach, sometimes termed *analytic* learning, also represents knowledge as rules in logical form but typically employs a performance system that uses search to solve multi-step problems. A common technique is to represent knowledge as inference rules, then to phrase problems as theorems and to search for proofs. Learning mechanisms in this framework use background knowledge to construct proofs or explanations of experience, then compile the proofs into more complex rules that can solve similar problems either with less search or in a single step. Most work on analytic learning has focused on improving the efficiency of the search process, but some has dealt with improving accuracy on classification tasks.

The reasons for the distinct identities of these paradigms are more historical than scientific. The different communities have their origins in different traditions, and they rely on different basic metaphors. For instance, proponents of neural networks emphasize analogies to neurobiology, case-based researchers to human memory, students of genetic algorithms to evolution, specialists in rule induction to heuristic search, and backers of analytic methods to reasoning in formal logic.

However, recent experimental comparisons between different learning methods have helped break down these boundaries, as has the increasing tendency to describe the results of learning in terms of decision boundaries in the instance space. Many researchers now agree that neural networks are no more "subsymbolic" than logical rules (although they may produce quite different decision boundaries), that analytic methods are not guaranteed to learn from fewer instances than rule-induction methods (although they do in some cases), and that logical rules need not be more easily understood by domain experts than other representations (although they are in some domains). Hybrid methods that cross paradigm boundaries are also increasingly common. Such convergence is the sign of a balanced and maturing field, and we hope this book will further contribute to this encouraging trend.

1.6 Summary of the chapter

In this chapter we presented an overview of machine learning, a field that cuts across the broader areas of artificial intelligence and cognitive science. We saw that interest in machine learning dates back to the early days of these disciplines but that only in the last decade has effort devoted to the topic grown to major proportions. We noted that researchers evaluate learning work from four different perspectives – psychological, empirical, theoretical, and applications. We also proposed a definition of learning as improvement in performance, through the acquisition of knowledge, that results from experience in an environment.

We examined aspects of the environment that influence the learning process, including whether the performance task involves classification or multi-step problem solving, whether the training data are supervised or unsupervised, and whether the learner encounters instances in an online or offline fashion. Still other aspects of the environment include complexity of the target knowledge, the number of irrelevant features, the amount of noise, and the presence of concept drift.

We found that the representation, organization, and use of knowledge also affect learning. We noted four alternative representations for experience – Boolean features, nominal attributes, numeric attributes, and relational literals. We also considered three basic approaches to interpreting learned knowledge – logical, threshold, and competitive matching of intensional concept descriptions. And we described three alternative schemes for organizing such descriptions into larger knowledge structures – decision lists, inference networks, and concept hierarchies.

We used the metaphor of heuristic search to consider design decisions that arise in the development of learning algorithms. We noted a variety of operators that one can use to search the space of knowledge structures, some involving modification of single descriptions and others that combine descriptions. We found that some learning methods start with very specific hypotheses, others with general ones, and still others with random descriptions. And we noted that despite the many search schemes available to machine learning researchers, nearly all work relies on simple greedy or hill-climbing methods.

Finally, we reviewed five basic paradigms – neural networks, instance-based methods, genetic algorithms, rule induction, and analytic methods – that dominate the literature on machine learning. Although we acknowledged important differences among these approaches to induction, we argued that they have more in common than typical articles suggest, and we noted recent progress in understanding the relations among them.

Historical and bibliographical remarks

Although research on machine learning has taken place since the earliest days of artificial intelligence and cognitive science, it has only viewed itself as a distinct field since around 1980, when the first workshop on the topic occurred. The collection by Michalski, Carbonell, and Mitchell (1983) includes work from that period, and the successor volume (Michalski, Carbonell, & Mitchell, 1986) reports results from the second meeting in 1983. Proceedings of the annual conference on machine learning date from 1987, and the journal *Machine Learning* has appeared continuously since 1986. Both sources provide a representative sample of research in this active field.

Numerous overviews of machine learning have been published over the years, and their changing content reflects the evolving nature of the discipline. Dietterich, London, Clarkson, and Dromey (1982), Carbonell, Michalski, and Mitchell (1983), Langley and Carbonell (1984, 1987b), Dietterich (1989), and Schlimmer and Langley (1992) all provide careful surveys of the area, but from different perspectives. Shavlik and Dietterich (1990) contains an excellent collection of papers on machine learning, some classical and others more recent, along with insightful commentary.

Many of the central concepts in machine learning have a long history. Hume (1748) describes the problem of induction, and theories of learning have occupied a central place in psychology for many decades (Langley & Simon, 1981; Bower, 1981). Simon and Lea (1974) first characterized rule induction in terms of heuristic search, although Mitchell (1982) popularized this idea within the learning community. Mitchell (1980) introduced the notion of inductive bias, while Rendell (1986a) distinguished between representational and search bias. The problem of overfitting has concerned statisticians for many years, but Breiman, Friedman, Olshen, and Stone (1984) and Quinlan (1986) introduced this issue to the machine learning community.

Some of the learning paradigms have their own avenues of publication in addition to the mainstream literature on machine learning. Annual proceedings of meetings on neural networks, genetic algorithms, and case-based reasoning contain many papers on learning from these perspectives, although they also address other issues, and journals like *Neural Computation*, *International Journal of Neural Systems*, and *Adaptive Systems* have much the same flavor. Texts in these areas by Hertz, Palmer, and Krogh (1991), Goldberg (1990), and Kolodner (1993) are also available, along with numerous collected volumes on each topic. Research in the rule induction and analytic paradigms lack separate treatment of this sort, but only because historically they have played a more central role in the machine learning literature.

The above publications emphasize empirical approaches to the study of learning, but they also contain some papers from the psychological and mathematical perspectives. The journal *Machine Learning* publishes special issues on both areas, while proceedings of the annual conferences on cognitive science and computational learning theory contain additional papers. Anderson (1981c), Rumelhart and McClelland (1986), and Klahr, Langley, and Neches (1987) contain chapters on computational models of human learning, while texts on computational learning theory come from Natarajan (1991) and from Kearns and Vazirani (1994). Reports on applications of machine learning are less common, but Allen (1994), Goldberg (1994), Widrow, Rumelhart, and Lehr (1994), and Langley and Simon (in press) review successful applications for a variety of paradigms.

CHAPTER 2

The Induction of
Logical Conjunctions

In Chapter 1 we examined three basic approaches to representing and interpreting conceptual knowledge. The most familiar of these involved logical definitions, which use an 'all or none' match to determine the membership of instances. In this chapter we consider the special case of *logical conjunctions*, which represent concepts as the 'and' of some simple tests. Much of the early work in machine learning focused on the induction of such concepts, and many algorithms for more challenging tasks build upon methods devised for this simpler task. Thus, we will go into some detail about a range of techniques, since they will prove useful in later chapters.

We begin by discussing some general issues in the induction of logical conjunctions, and then turn to some nonincremental algorithms for addressing this task, focusing first on exhaustive methods and then on techniques that use heuristics to constrain search. Next we turn to incremental approaches to the same problem, again presenting both nonheuristic methods and heuristic variants. Finally, we examine the use of genetic algorithms for logical induction, which organize their search along quite different lines from other methods.

2.1 General issues in logical induction

Before examining particular algorithms for the induction of logical conjunctions, we should briefly consider some issues that cut across the various approaches. First we review the representational and performance assumptions that underlie work in this paradigm. After this we present a more precise statement of the induction task in terms of inputs and outputs. Finally, we consider the partial ordering that exists among concepts and their logical descriptions, which plays a central role in most of the learning methods we examine in this chapter.

2.1.1 Representation and use of logical conjunctions

The induction algorithms described in this chapter are designed to find a conjunctive description for a single concept C that covers positive instances of C and that fails to cover negative instances. They represent a concept as a logical conjunction of Boolean features, values of nominal attributes, limits on the values of numeric attributes, or some combination of them.[1] We will refer to each component of such a conjunction as a *condition* or a *test*.

One can use the resulting concept description D to classify new instances by matching D against the instance description. Briefly, if the instance matches all conditions in the concept description, it is labeled as a positive instance of the concept C; otherwise it is labeled as negative. This all-or-none flavor is central to the methods we will consider in this chapter, and it has important implications for the learning algorithms themselves.

These representational and performance assumptions combine to produce decision boundaries that enclose singly connected regions of the instance space; that is, for any pair of positive instances, there exists a path that traverses only other positive instances. Moreover, these regions take the form of single hyperrectangles with surfaces orthogonal to the axes of relevant attributes and parallel to the axes of irrelevant ones. For these reasons, methods that induce logical conjunctions are sometimes described as using an *orthogonal rectangle* bias, whereas others have used the term *axis parallel* bias. This idea is best seen with some examples.

Consider a nominal domain that involves three attributes for describing the appearance of cells – the number of `tails` (`one` or `two`), the `color` of the cell body (`dark` or `light`), and the number of `nuclei` (`one` or `two`). In some later examples, we will include a fourth attribute involving the thickness of the cell `wall`, which can be `thick` or `thin`. Figure 2-1 (a) shows one cell taken from a patient with the dreaded disease

---

1. The same framework also applies to relational descriptions, but we delay their discussion until Chapter 8.

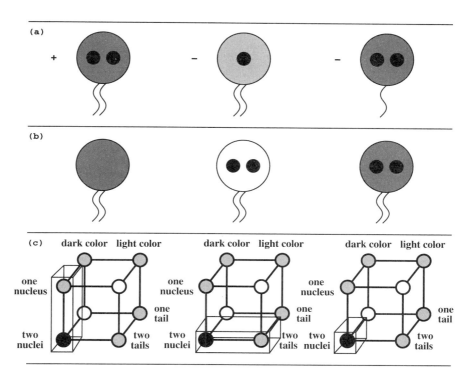

Figure 2-1. Example of a nominal domain involving cells with three attributes, showing (a) one positive (+) and two negative (-) training instances, (b) three logical conjunctions that match the positives but not the negatives, and (c) the axis parallel decision boundaries that each conjunction produces in the instance space.

LETHARGIA (a positive instance of this concept), along with two cells taken from a healthy person (negative instances). For example, the positive case has `two nuclei`, `two tails`, and a `dark color`, whereas the first negative case has `one nucleus`, `two tails`, and a `light color`.

Figure 2-1 (b) graphically depicts three conjunctions that, when combined with a logical matcher, are consistent with these instances, with missing features indicating that they play no role in the description. For example, the abstract cell on the left, which has no `nuclei`, corresponds to the conjunction `two tails` ∧ `dark color`. Similarly, the central cell, which has no `color`, specifies the conjunction `two nuclei` ∧ `two tails`. The rightmost description, which includes all three of the attributes, indicates the very specific conjunction `two nuclei` ∧ `two tails` ∧ `dark color`.

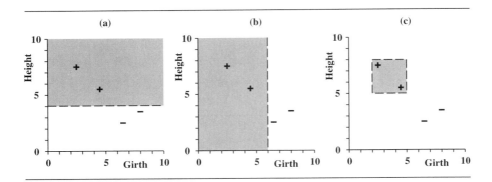

Figure 2-2. Positive and negative instances in a numeric domain involving two attributes, a person's `height` and `girth`. The most general logical conjunctions consistent with the training data, specified in terms of rectangular decision boundaries, appear in (a) and (b), whereas (c) depicts the most specific consistent conjunction.

Because each attribute in the cell domain has two possible values, they are effectively Boolean features. Thus, we can draw the instance space as a cube, with each axis representing a feature and each vertex representing a particular instance. Figure 2-1 (c) uses this notation to show the hyperrectangles that correspond to the logical conjunctions in (b). This clearly shows that all three conjunctions cover the positive instance (the dark vertex) but not the negative instances (white vertices), and also shows that they make different predictions about unseen cases (gray vertices). For instance, the second and third conjunctions classify a cell with **one nucleus**, **two tails**, and a **dark color** as negative, whereas the first conjunction predicts a positive label. Given the observed data alone, there is no reason to prefer any one of these descriptions over the others.

Now let us consider a second domain that involves two numeric dimensions, say `height` and `girth`, along with a concept description language that allows only conditions of the form (> height x), (> girth x), (< height x), and (< girth x), where x is a specific integer. Thus, a logical conjunction for this domain will contain between zero and four such conditions. Figure 2-2 depicts two positive instances (+) and two negatives (−) from this domain, along with the decision boundaries for three conjunctions that, when interpreted by a logical matcher, cover the former but not the latter. In particular, (a) shows one of the two most general conjunctions of this sort, and (b) shows the second alternative, which is no more general than the other. In contrast, (c) depicts the most specific logical conjunction consistent with the given instances. As in the nominal domain, decision boundaries take the form of rectangles with each side parallel to some axis in the instance space.

2.1.2 The task of inducing logical conjunctions

Now that we have described the representation and use of logical conjunctions, we can formulate the task of their induction from experience:

- *Given*: A set of positive training instances for the class C;
- *Given*: A set of negative training instances for the class C;
- *Find*: A logical conjunction that, to the extent possible, correctly classifies novel test cases.

To restate, algorithms that address this task receive as input a set of positive and negative instances for some class. In response, they must generate an intensional description – stated as a logical conjunction – for use in classifying future instances.

This learning task assumes that one can actually describe, or at least approximate, the concept using a conjunction of simple conditions, such as those we saw in Figures 2-1 and 2-2. This in turn assumes that the language for describing concepts includes all relevant terms. Note that the goal is *not* necessarily to find a conjunction that perfectly partitions the training cases into positive and negative instances, but to induce a description that accurately classifies novel instances. Some early work on machine learning took the former view, as do some of the methods we examine later in the chapter. However, such methods encounter difficulties in domains that contain noise or in those for which a conjunction only approximates the target concept.

One can use a simple trick to extend the above scheme to multiclass induction, which requires one to learn descriptions for a set of N concepts rather than for a single concept. For each class C, one treats all instances of the other $N-1$ classes as negative instances of C. Thus, one repeats the basic induction task N times, once for each class. However, this approach can produce descriptions that do not match (and thus fail to classify) some instances and that all match (and thus conflict) on other instances. We will return to this issue in Chapter 5, but for now we will restrict our attention to the induction of single conjunctive concepts.

2.1.3 Partial ordering of classes and concepts

As we saw in Chapter 1, the space of possible conceptual classes is partially ordered by generality. That is, if class A includes all the instances of class B, along with other instances as well, then A is strictly more general than B. This space is bounded at one extreme by the most general class possible, which contains all possible instances, and at the other by the set of most specific classes, which contain one instance apiece.

This partial ordering plays an important role in most methods for inducing logical concept descriptions. The reason is that, given such a concept representation, there is typically a direct relation between the relative generality of two classes and their relative concept descriptions. For example, given a simple conjunctive language for concepts, dropping a nominal condition from concept A's description produces a strictly more general concept, whereas adding a nominal condition to A produces a more specific concept. The same holds for conditions that involve numeric attributes, although one can also increase generality by extending a numeric range or decrease it by restricting such a range.

This simple relation between the 'syntax' and 'semantics' of logical concepts provides two benefits. First, it suggests some obvious operators for moving through the space of concept descriptions, as we will see shortly. Second, it means that the partial ordering on extensional classes carries over to concept descriptions, and one can use this ordering to constrain and organize the search for useful concepts. With the exception of genetic algorithms, which we discuss at the end of the chapter, nearly all research on the induction of logical concepts has taken advantage of this insight.

2.2 Nonincremental induction of logical conjunctions

Given a generality ordering on the space of concept descriptions, two obvious search organizations suggest themselves – one can move from general descriptions to specific ones or from specific descriptions to more general ones. In this section we focus on a nonincremental approach to logical concept induction that carries out exhaustive breadth-first search in one direction and then we briefly consider an analogous algorithm that operates in the opposite direction. In closing, we discuss some drawbacks of such exhaustive methods.

2.2.1 The EGS algorithm

We will begin our study of logical induction with a nonincremental method that carries out a general to specific search through the space of concept descriptions. Table 2-1 presents pseudocode for the EGS (exhaustive general-to-specific) algorithm, which is provided at the outset with a set of positive instances (which the induced description should cover) and a set of negative instances (which it should not). In addition, the recursive algorithm inputs a set of concept descriptions that cover all of the positives and none of the negatives; this set is initially empty but tends to grow with the depth of recursion. EGS also carries along a set of overly general descriptions, which cover all positive cases but also some negatives. This set is initialized to contain a single 'null' description with no conditions, which covers all training instances.

The algorithm carries out a breadth-first search through the space of concept descriptions. At each level of the search (i.e., each level of the recursion), EGS considers all specializations of overly general descriptions that involve the addition of one condition. For a nominal attribute not already used in the description, this involves generating one alternative condition for each value of that attribute. For a numeric attribute, one can generate a minimal specialization by iterating through all integer values, then stopping upon reaching an integer that excludes a positive instance. This iteration begins with the lowest observed attribute value for < tests and with the highest value for > tests.[2]

For each such specialized description H, EGS checks to ensure that H still covers all known positive instances. If not, the algorithm drops this description from consideration as overly specific, which also effectively removes all of its descendants in the space of hypotheses, since it will never consider them (unless it reaches them by another path). For each remaining description H not rejected in this manner, EGS checks to see whether H still covers any of the negative instances. If not, the method adds H to its set of consistent descriptions (which it carries along as it continues its search). If a description still covers some negative instances, EGS adds it to the set of overly general descriptions for the current level, which it then specializes further.

---

2. We assume the learner has access to the information needed to generate these specializations – the names of features and their possible values. If this information is not provided by the user, a system can generate it by examining all of the training instances.

Table 2-1. The EGS algorithm: Nonincremental general-to-specific breadth-first search for logical conjunctions.

```
Inputs:  PSET is the set of positive instances.
         NSET is the set of negative instances.
         CSET is a set of consistent descriptions.
         HSET is a set of overly general descriptions.
Output:  The set of most general logical conjunctions
         that are consistent with the training data.

Top-level call:  EGS(PSET, NSET, { }, {{ }})

Procedure EGS(PSET, NSET, CSET, HSET)

For each description H in HSET,
    If H does not match all members of PSET,
    Then remove H from HSET.
    If H does not match any members of NSET,
    Then remove H from HSET and add H to CSET.
If HSET is empty,
Then return CSET.
Else let NEWSET be the empty set.
    For each description H in HSET,
    Let SPECS be all one-condition specializations of H that
        fail to match more negative instances than does H.
    For each description S in SPECS,
        If CSET contains no description more general than S,
        Then add S to NEWSET.
    Return EGS(PSET, NSET, CSET, NEWSET).
```

This process continues until the algorithm reaches a level at which the set of overly general descriptions is empty. At this point, it returns the set of consistent descriptions as summaries of the instances it was given as input. Each of these descriptions is guaranteed to cover all of the positive instances and none of the negatives. Moreover, EGS will find the set of all most general descriptions that are consistent with the training data. Other consistent descriptions may exist in the space of conjunctive descriptions, but they will be more specific than at least one of the induced descriptions. Thus, the logical conjunctions generated by EGS include only those attributes that are necessary for discriminating between positive and negative instances of the concept.

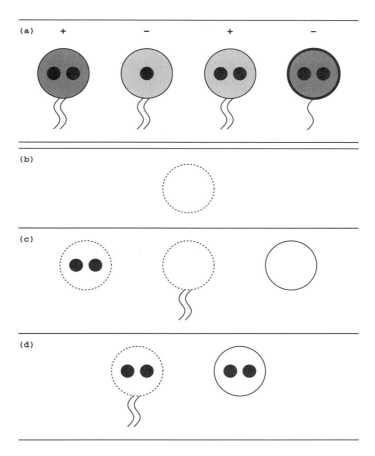

Figure 2-3. Descriptions considered by the EGS algorithm in a nominal domain involving four attributes, given the training instances in (a), at (b) the first level of search, (c) the second level, and (d) the third level.

2.2.2 Examples of EGS in operation

To further clarify the nature of the algorithm, let us consider its behavior on some training instances from the four-attribute cell domain shown in Figure 2-3 (a). EGS begins with the most general description possible, in this case depicted by the featureless cell in (b). The next level of search, in Figure 2-3 (c), shows three hypotheses that provide some improvement over the initial description, in that each eliminates matches on one of the two negative instances. One such description indicates that the cell must have `two nuclei`, another specifies `two tails`, and the third refers to a `thin wall`. Other descriptions also specialize the initial one, but fail to cover both positive instances, and thus are rejected.

At the final level of search, EGS has arrived at two descriptions that cover both positive instances but neither negative instance. These are specializations of descriptions at the previous level; one specifies that the cell must have `two nuclei` and `two tails`, whereas the other requires `two nuclei` and a `thin wall`. The algorithm cannot further discriminate between these competitors with the data available, and the set of overly general descriptions is empty, so EGS returns both as its result.

Figure 2-4 presents an example of EGS's operation in the numeric height/girth domain, in this case involving two positive and three negative instances. As before, the initial hypothesis set contains only one description, the most general possible, and again the next level of the search tree includes three specializations, each of which happens to eliminate one negative instance. Note that one of these places an upper limit on `height`, whereas another places a lower limit on the same dimension.

The third level of the search also contains three hypotheses, each of which contains two conditions that rule out two of the negative training instances. Moreover, each is a specialization of two descriptions at the previous level. The fourth and final level contains a single hypothesis that includes all three conditions mentioned in the previous level, and thus is a specialization of all descriptions at that level. Because this hypothesis covers both positive instances and none of the negatives, and because the set of overly general descriptions is empty, EGS halts and returns it as the result. This example is somewhat misleading in that one can obtain the same result by following a single path through the space of descriptions. However, the algorithm is designed to find *all* maximally general logical conjunctions.

2.2.3 Drawbacks of exhaustive methods

Despite its simplicity, one can easily identify some major drawbacks of the EGS technique, the most obvious involving its computational complexity. Even in purely Boolean domains, the worst-case size of the hypothesis set grows rapidly with the number of features. We can ignore the degenerate case in which all instances are negative, but we cannot ignore situations in which many features are relevant, leading to training sets containing only a few positive instances, with negatives for

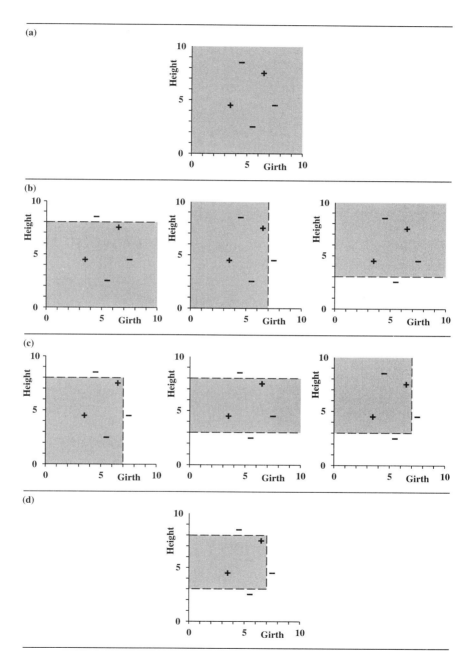

Figure 2-4. Descriptions considered by the EGS algorithm in the numeric height/girth domain at (a) the first level of search, (b) the second level, (c) the third level, and (d) the final level.

the remainder. In such domains, given k relevant Boolean features, the hypothesis set can grow to size $\binom{k}{\frac{k}{2}}$. The algorithm reaches this point halfway to the correct description, after which the set decreases in size until the end of the run. The basic problem is that EGS carries out an exhaustive breadth-first search and thus is a captive of the exponential growth that typifies such methods.

The EGS algorithm aims to find the most general possible concept descriptions, but there is no inherent reason for this inductive bias. An alternative, the ESG (exhaustive specific-to-general) method, finds the most specific logical conjunction consistent with the training data. For the data in Figure 2-3, this is the conjunction `two nuclei` $\wedge$ `two tails` $\wedge$ `thin wall`, which is strictly more specific than both descriptions generated by EGS. The ESG algorithm has some clear computational advantages over the general-to-specific technique. In attribute-value domains, ESG simply computes the most specific description without any need for search; in fact, it does not even examine the negative instances, since they do not affect the outcome. For each Boolean feature or nominal attribute, the method finds the value shared by all positive training instances; for each numeric attribute, it simply finds the minimum and maximum values.

Provided that there exists a logical conjunction consistent with the training data, the ESG technique will find the maximally specific description without the need for search. However, as we discuss in Chapter 8, these advantages disappear in relational domains, where ESG requires both search and negative instances. Moreover, a belief in Occam's razor has led many researchers to prefer induction methods that favor general descriptions over more specific ones that cover the same training data. Thus, although the ESG algorithm suffers less from combinatorial problems than EGS, it does not provide a general solution.

Another limitation of both methods lies in their inability to handle situations in which no logical conjunction is consistent with the training data. In noisy domains, even one mislabeled class or feature can seriously derail either technique in its search for consistent descriptions. For example, if the second negative instance in Figure 2-3 had been mistakenly labeled positive, EGS would have produced the single overly general description `two nuclei`. In some cases the effect of noise can be even worse, causing the method to eliminate all hypotheses from consideration. Similar problems arise in domains where the target concept is nearly but not perfectly described by a logical conjunction. These problems suggest the need for more robust algorithms that make weaker assumptions about the nature of the training data.

2.3 Heuristic induction of logical conjunctions

Heuristic approaches to concept induction hold promise for overcoming some disadvantages of the EGS and ESG algorithms. Rather than carrying out a breadth-first search through the space of concept descriptions, heuristic methods carry out more selective searches that, in many cases, find satisfactory solutions while considering only a fraction of the space. In this section we focus on *beam search*, a control structure that retains a fixed number of alternatives at each level of the search, using an evaluation function to select the best ones. We will see examples of other heuristic approaches later in the chapter. As before, we first examine search from general to specific descriptions, then briefly consider a specific to general organization.

2.3.1 The HGS algorithm

Table 2-2 presents pseudocode for the HGS (heuristic general-to-specific) algorithm, a more selective analog of the EGS technique. Like its exhaustive relative, this method accepts as input sets of positive and negative instances, along with two sets of concept descriptions, one initialized to the empty set and the other to a set containing a single 'null' description with no conditions. However, HGS interprets these last two inputs differently from EGS, with the first (CLOSED-SET) specifying candidate descriptions that cannot be improved by further specialization and the second (HSET) indicating descriptions that might still be improved. The two algorithms also differ in the details of their search processes.

At each level of its search, HGS considers all specializations of descriptions in HSET that involve the addition of one condition. For each such specialized description S, HGS uses an evaluation function to measure S's degree of fit to the training data. If the score for S is greater than the score for its parent H, the algorithm adds the hypothesis S to a set of new descriptions (OPEN-SET) that it should consider for further specialization later. If none of the specializations of H score better than their parent, then HGS adds H to CLOSED-SET, since it cannot be improved further.

Table 2-2. The HGS algorithm: Nonincremental beam search for a logical conjunction, directed by an evaluation function Score.

```
Inputs: PSET is the set of positive instances.
        NSET is the set of negative instances.
        CLOSED-SET is a set of locally optimal descriptions.
        OPEN-SET is a set of unspecialized descriptions.
Output: A logical conjunction that matches most of PSET
            and that does not match most of NSET.
Params: Beam-Size is the number of descriptions in memory.

Top-level call:  HGS(PSET, NSET, { }, {{ }})

Procedure HGS(PSET, NSET, CLOSED-SET, HSET)

Let OPEN-SET be the empty set.
For each description H in HSET,
    Let SPECS be all one-condition specializations of H.
    Let NEW-SET be the empty set.
    For each specialized description S in SPECS,
        If Score(S, PSET, NSET) > Score(H, PSET, NSET),
        Then add S to NEW-SET.
    If NEW-SET is empty,
    Then add the description H to CLOSED-SET.
    Else for each description S in NEW-SET,
        Add S to OPEN-SET.
        For each description C in CLOSED-SET,
            If S is at least as specific as C,
            Then if Score(C,PSET,NSET) > Score(S,PSET,NSET),
                Then remove S from OPEN-SET.
                Else remove C from CLOSED-SET.
If OPEN-SET is empty,
Then return the highest-scoring member of CLOSED-SET.
Else let BEST-SET be the Beam-Size highest-scoring
        members of the union of OPEN-SET and CLOSED-SET.
    Let CLOSED-SET be the members of CLOSED-SET in BEST-SET.
    Let OPEN-SET be the members of OPEN-SET in BEST-SET.
    Return HGS(PSET, NSET, CLOSED-SET, OPEN-SET).
```

After considering all specializations of the descriptions in HSET, the algorithm checks to see whether any of them have scored better than their parents. If not, HGS simply returns the parent description with the highest score; otherwise, it continues its search. However, before continuing to the next level, the algorithm must first reduce its hypothesis set to manageable size. To this end, HGS selects the Beam-Size highest-scoring members of CLOSED-SET and OPEN-SET, then calls itself recursively, with the reduced OPEN-SET taking on the role of HSET. The algorithm removes other candidates from memory, even if they might ultimately lead to useful descriptions; thus, it trades off optimality for constrained search.

The descriptions generated by HGS are *not* guaranteed to cover all positive instances and no negative instances, nor would this be desirable in domains where the data contain noise or can only be approximated by a logical conjunction. Nor are the descriptions it generates guaranteed to be minimal, in that some strictly more general descriptions may exist down a rejected branch that would have given a better score. These are the prices paid for carrying out an efficient heuristic search rather than an intractable exhaustive one, and experimental studies suggest that, in many domains, such heuristic methods work well despite their superficial drawbacks.

2.3.2 Heuristic evaluation of descriptions

The behavior of HGS depends heavily on the choice of the evaluation function Score. As shown in Table 2-2, this function takes three arguments – the description being evaluated, the set of positive instances, and the set of negative instances. In general, the function's score should increase both with the number P_c of the positive instances covered and with the number $N_{\bar{c}}$ of negatives *not* covered. A good metric should also take into account the total number of positive instances P and negative instances N.

One simple measure that satisfies both of these constraints uses the expression

$$\frac{P_c + N_{\bar{c}}}{P + N} \quad ,$$

which ranges between 0 (when no positives and all negatives are covered) and 1 (when all positives and no negatives are covered). This ratio measures the overall classification accuracy on the training data.

More sophisticated approaches invoke statistical or information theoretic measures, but even a simple measure like $P_c + N_{\bar{c}}$ (the number of covered positives plus the number of uncovered negatives) provides significant direction to the HGS algorithm.

We should briefly consider the relation between the EGS and HGS algorithms. Suppose we measure the score for a description by $(P_c + N_{\bar{c}})/(P + N)$, as suggested above, and set the `Beam-Size` to infinity. In this case, the heuristic method simulates the exhaustive EGS algorithm, searching for all minimal concept descriptions that cover all positive instances and none of the negative instances. In other words, EGS can be viewed as a special case of HGS that results from extreme settings of the latter's parameters. Another important special case occurs when `Beam-Size` is set to 1, which causes HGS to behave as a *greedy* method that selects the single best hypothesis at each level of the search.

2.3.3 The HSG algorithm

Although HGS begins with general descriptions and moves toward more specific ones as needed, one can also carry out heuristic search in the opposite direction using a heuristic specific-to-general method (HSG). However, because this algorithm does not assume there exists a conjunctive target concept consistent with the training data, it lacks the advantages that the simpler ESG method has over the exhaustive EGS. To handle more realistic induction problems, HSG must use the same techniques as HGS – a beam search directed by an evaluation function over both positive and negative instances.

Naturally, the HSG algorithm differs from HGS in its initialization, in the direction of search, and in the characteristics of the resulting descriptions. The new method begins with one of the most specific possible descriptions, each of which corresponds directly to a positive training instance. HSG selects one of these instances (say at random) as its *seed*, which it uses to generate the initial hypothesis from which to start its specific-to-general search.

As in HGS, the new scheme carries along an `OPEN SET` of hypotheses, but in this case the descriptions are not general enough. Thus, each step through the hypothesis space involves generalizing an overly specific description by dropping or generalizing a single condition, rather than by specialization. HSG uses an evaluation metric to order descriptions in terms of their fit to the training data, selects the best `Beam-Size` of these, and iterates. Again, the method halts when generalizing the hypotheses in OPEN SET produces no higher-scoring descriptions than their parents, in which case it returns the best of those parents.

Like HGS, the HSG algorithm has a constant memory cost. This means search remains under control, but that it will not always generate the optimal descriptions for a given data set. The technique should be relatively robust with respect to noise and target concepts that are only approximately conjunctive. An important exception involves the seed used to initialize search. If this positive instance has been mislabeled or falls outside the target region, HSG will find a description that covers this instance but few other positive cases of the concept. One response is to run the algorithm multiple times with different seeds; another is to select a seed that falls near the central tendency of the positive instances.

2.4 Incremental induction of logical conjunctions

In Chapter 1 we argued that, in some situations, incremental learning has advantages over nonincremental methods. To this end, we now turn to incremental approaches to the induction of logical conjunctions. As in the nonincremental case, one can search the concept space from general to specific or vice versa. In this section we focus on the first approach, then briefly consider a specific-to-general scheme and some methods that combine both ideas. In each case, we assume a breadth-first search organization, since that is the simplest for tutorial purposes. We also assume that the goal is to induce concept descriptions that cover all of the positive training instances but none of the negatives, although in closing we discuss some drawbacks of this approach.

2.4.1 The IGS algorithm

Table 2-3 presents pseudocode for IGS, an incremental general-to-specific method for the induction of logical conjunctions. The algorithm processes training cases one at a time, retaining a set of hypotheses that cover all the positive instances it has seen so far but none of the observed negative instances. The method initializes this set to one containing the most general possible description.

Upon encountering a new negative instance, IGS checks each description to determine if it covers the instance. If so, the method abandons

Table 2-3. The IGS algorithm: Incremental general-to-specific search for a conjunctive concept description.

```
Inputs: ISET is the set of classified training instances.
Output: The set of most general logical conjunctions
        that are consistent with the training data.

Procedure IGS(ISET)

Let G be the most general possible description.
Let the set of current hypotheses HSET be {G}.
Let the set of processed positives PSET be the empty set.
For each instance I in ISET,
    If I is a negative instance,
    Then for each hypothesis H in HSET that matches I,
              Delete H from HSET.
              Find the set GSET of most general specializations
                  of H that will not match I.
              Let HSET be the union of HSET and GSET.
              For each hypothesis H in HSET,
                  If HSET contains a G more specific than H,
                  Then remove H from HSET.
              For each hypothesis H in HSET,
                  If PSET contains an instance
                      that H fails to match,
                  Then remove H from HSET.
              If HSET is empty, then return the empty set.
    Else if I is a positive instance,
         Then add I to the set PSET.
              For each hypothesis H in HSET,
                  If H fails to match I,
                  Then remove H from HSET.
              If HSET is empty, then return the empty set.
Return HSET.
```

---

the offending hypothesis (since it is overly general) and replaces this description with all minimally more specific variants that fail to cover the instance. However, it abandons any descriptions that fail to cover any positive instances it has seen in the past, as well as any descriptions that are strictly more general than others in the hypothesis set.

The learning algorithm takes quite different actions upon encountering a new positive instance. In such a case, IGS deletes all current hypotheses that *fail* to cover the instance (since they are overly specific). This cycle continues until the algorithm runs out of instances or until the hypothesis set becomes empty, indicating that no descriptions are consistent with the training data. In general, the IGS algorithm uses negative instances to drive the generation of candidate descriptions, and it uses positive instances to winnow the resulting set.

To summarize, IGS produces more specific descriptions when negative instances require this action and eliminates hypotheses when positive instances are not matched. No learning occurs when correct predictions are made, since the existing descriptions are performing as desired. The algorithm has no explicit means for deciding when it has acquired a 'final' concept definition, but at each point it will have in memory the most specific hypotheses that account for the data so far. Note that the algorithm must retain and reprocess an explicit list of positive examples, making it truly incremental only in its processing of negative instances.

2.4.2 An example of IGS in operation

As an example, let us consider IGS's behavior on the set of instances we presented earlier for the cell domain. Figure 2-5 shows the training instances in the order presented, along with the hypothesis set that results after the algorithm processes each one. As noted above, IGS begins with the most general description possible, in this case an abstract cell body with no features specified. After this initialization, the algorithm processes the first positive training instance, which leaves the hypothesis set unaltered (since it is correctly matched by the only member).

The next training instance is negative and, since the initial hypothesis matches this case, IGS must make it more specific. There are two ways to accomplish this and still cover the positive instance.[3] The first involves adding the condition `two nuclei`; the other involves adding the constraint `dark color`. Note that these descriptions are no more specific than necessary to avoid matching the negative instance.

Suppose the algorithm next encounters the second positive instance shown in Figure 2-5 (c). Because the hypothesis `two nuclei` matches

---

3. In some cases, there exists only one way to generate a more specific hypothesis. Negative instances that lead to this fortuitous situation are termed *near misses*. However, one cannot usually rely on their occurrence, so IGS can learn from 'far misses' as well, albeit converging on the ultimate concept description more slowly.

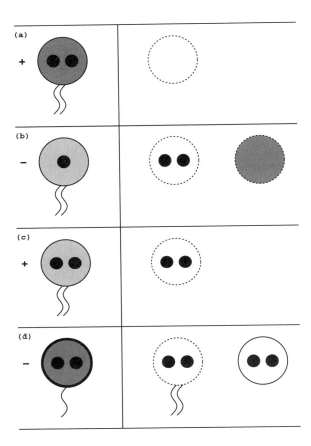

Figure 2-5. Descriptions considered by the IGS algorithm in the cell domain after (a) an initial positive instance, (b) an initial negative instance, (c) a second positive instance, and (d) a second negative instance. Instances are shown on the left, with the resulting set of hypotheses on the right.

this instance, IGS retains it in the set of descriptions. However, the other description, `dark color`, fails to match the instance, and thus is abandoned. Upon seeing a second negative instance, the algorithm finds that its remaining hypothesis matches this cell, and thus is still overly general. As a result, it generates two specializations that match neither negative instance but that match both positive cases. The first of these states that the cell must have `two nuclei` and `two tails`, whereas the other claims the cell must have `two nuclei` and a `thin wall`. Both descriptions are consistent with existing observations, although the algorithm would continue to make revisions if provided with new data.

2.4.3 The ISG algorithm

Now let us consider some other methods for the incremental induction of logical conjunctions. The ISG algorithm differs from IGS in that it carries out a specific-to-general search, but the basic structures of the two methods are quite similar. This technique also retains a set of descriptions that are consistent with the instances it has seen, but it initializes the hypothesis set to the first positive training instance.

Upon encountering a new positive instance, ISG checks each description to determine if it covers the instance. If not, the method deletes the offending hypothesis (since it is overly specific) and replaces it with all minimally more general variants that cover the instance. As we noted in Section 2.2.3, only one such description exists in nominal and numeric domains, but more than one can occur with relational languages. ISG also abandons any descriptions that cover any known negative instances, as well as any descriptions that are strictly more specific than others in the hypothesis set.

In contrast, when ISG encounters a new negative instance, it simply deletes all hypotheses that cover the instance. The algorithm takes this step for the same reason it removes new descriptions that cover previous negatives: search always moves from specific to general, so overly general descriptions cannot be corrected and must be abandoned. This overall cycle, in which ISG uses positive instances to generate descriptions and negative instances to eliminate them, continues until the algorithm stops receiving instances or until the hypothesis set becomes empty, indicating that no descriptions are consistent with the training data.

2.4.4 Bidirectional search techniques

One can also combine the specific-to-general and the general-to-specific approaches for searching the space of logical conjunctions. In one such scheme, either generalization or specialization acts as the primary induction operator, with the other giving the effect of backtracking when an hypothesis has gone too far in the primary direction. However, this approach makes less sense within an exhaustive search framework than it does within a heuristic one, like the one we describe in Section 2.5.

A second alternative, known as the *version space* algorithm, directly combines aspects of the IGS and ISG methods. This algorithm retains two sets of descriptions, one containing the most specific set of descriptions that cover the data (S) and the other containing the most general set of such descriptions (G). These correspond to the sets retained by the ISG and IGS methods, respectively. The version space algorithm invokes a subroutine very similar to ISG to update the S set. In particular, when the method encounters a new positive instance that is not covered by any element of the S set, it replaces that element with one or more generalizations that do match the instance. Similarly, when any element of the G set matches a new negative instance, the version space technique uses a subroutine very similar to IGS to produce more specific versions of that element.

One notable difference is that the learner no longer need retain either positive or negative instances. The S set takes on the role of positive data in constraining search, whereas the G set takes on the role of negative instances. Rather than eliminating descriptions that fail to cover any positive instances, the modified IGS subroutine removes any member of the G set that is more specific than all members of S. Similarly, the modified ISG routine does not delete hypotheses that match any negative instance; instead, it removes any description in S that is more general than all elements in G. Thus, this approach is fully incremental in the sense that it need never reprocess any training instance.

The version space approach has two other interesting features. First, if the S and G sets converge on a single concept description, one knows that the induction task has been completed. Second, although the elements of S and G have identical forms to the descriptions we discussed for the IGS and ISG methods, their interpretation is rather different. Rather than representing hypotheses directly, members of the S and G sets act as *boundaries* on the space of descriptions that are consistent with the data. As the algorithm observes more instances, these boundaries become more constraining, until eventually they eliminate all but one logical conjunction. Basically, the version space method embodies a *least commitment* view of induction, in contrast to the state-space search view we have emphasized throughout the chapter.

2.4.5 Comments on incremental exhaustive methods

The methods we have discussed in this section provide insights into the incremental induction of logical conjuncts, and thus are useful for tutorial purposes. However, they suffer the same drawbacks as the exhaustive algorithms we considered in Section 2.2, making them unsuitable for many applied induction tasks.

We have seen that the IGS, ISG, and version space techniques process only one instance at a time, and that the latter method in particular does not store or reprocess any training cases. However, this statement is misleading, for all three algorithms must retain in memory all descriptions that are consistent with instances seen to date. In some domains, the size of these hypothesis sets can grow exponentially with the number of training instances, although certain training orders can minimize this effect. Hence, one cannot argue that such exhaustive methods are efficient in either space or time, even though they require little or no reprocessing of the instances themselves.

The three algorithms also encounter major difficulties when noise is present and when a conjunction only approximates the target concept. The source of this problem is their concern with finding descriptions that match all positive instances and none of the negative instances. A negative instance that is mislabeled as positive (one form of class noise) will cause ISG to produce overly general descriptions and it can lead IGS to eliminate a legitimate candidate. Similarly, a mislabeled positive instance will cause IGS to generate overly specific descriptions and it can force ISG to remove a perfectly acceptable hypothesis.

Because it uses both methods as subroutines, the version space algorithm suffers from class noise in all of these ways. The effect of attribute noise is different but still considerable. Extensions of the basic algorithm to handle limited amounts of class noise and bounded attribute noise in numeric domains lead to increases in the S and G sets, which may already be very large. In general, one should avoid exhaustive methods such as IGS, ISG, and version spaces when the training data contain noise and when the target concept is not perfectly conjunctive.

2.5 Incremental hill climbing for logical conjunctions

One goal of incremental approaches is to minimize the processing needed for each new training instance, and another is to reduce memory requirements. Yet we have seen that exhaustive approaches to incremental induction can be expensive on both fronts, even when they store and reprocess few instances. Fortunately, the incremental framework supports another alternative that is more efficient and also more consistent with theories of human learning. Rather than retaining a set of competing hypotheses in memory, the learner retains a single hypothesis and (potentially) refines this tentative description after each training instance.

We will refer to this general approach as *incremental hill climbing*, because of its similarity to the well-known search technique. In this section we examine the potential of this approach and consider one incremental hill-climbing method for the induction of logical conjunctions.

2.5.1 Learning as incremental hill climbing

Hill climbing is a classic AI search method in which one applies all possible operators, compares the resulting states using an evaluation function, selects the best state, and iterates until no more progress occurs. There are many variants on the basic algorithm, but these do not concern us here. The main advantage of hill climbing is its low memory requirement; because there are never more than a few states in memory, it sidesteps the high memory costs associated with search-intensive methods.

At each point in learning, an incremental hill-climbing algorithm retains only one knowledge structure, even though this structure may itself be quite complex.[4] Thus, hill-climbing learners cannot carry out a breadth-first search or a beam search through the space of descriptions, nor can they carry out explicit backtracking. They can only move 'forward', revising their single knowledge structure in the light of new experience.

The most important difference between hill-climbing learners and their traditional cousins lies in the role of input. Incremental learning algorithms are driven by new instances, and in the case of incremental hill-climbing methods, each step through the hypothesis space occurs in response to (and takes into account) some new experience. In other words, the learner does not move through the space of descriptions until it obtains a new datum. This mitigates some well-known drawbacks of hill climbing, such as the tendency to halt at local optima and a dependence on step size.

Recall that hill-climbing methods search an n-dimensional space over which some function f is defined. This function determines the shape of an n-dimensional surface, and the agent attempts to find that point with the highest f score. In traditional hill-climbing approaches, the function

---

4. We do not require that an incremental hill-climbing learner have an explicit evaluation function, or even that it carry out a one-step lookahead. One can replace this approach with a strong generator that computes the successor state from a new input, such as an observed instance.

f is static and thus the shape of the surface is constant. In systems that learn through incremental hill climbing, each new instance changes the form of f (the function used to evaluate alternative descriptions) and modifies the contours of the surface. Like H. A. Simon's wandering ant, the learner's behavior is controlled by the shape of its world. However, the hills and valleys of the hill-climbing learner's space are constantly changing as it gathers more information, altering the path it follows. This feature makes it unclear whether the limitations of traditional hill-climbing methods still hold in the context of incremental learning.

However, this dependence on new instances to control the search process also makes memory-limited learning methods sensitive to the order of instance presentation. Initial nonrepresentative data may lead a learning system astray, and one would like it to recover when later data point the way to the correct knowledge structure. Thus, some researchers have argued for the importance of *bidirectional* learning operators that can reverse the effects of previous learning should new instances suggest the need. Such operators can give incremental hill-climbing learners the effect of backtracking search without the memory required by true backtracking. Of course, the success of this approach remains an empirical question, but it shows enough promise for closer inspection.

2.5.2 The IHC algorithm

Table 2-4 summarizes an algorithm for incremental hill climbing (IHC) through the space of logical conjunctions. For each training instance I, this method checks to determine whether its current description H misclassifies I. If the classification is correct, then it takes no action, which means that it retains H as the current hypothesis. If an error occurs, IHC generates all minimal revisions to H that correct the mistake, then uses an evaluation function to rank the competitors on the last K training cases, which it has retained in memory. The algorithm selects the best-scoring description H' and, if H' fares as well or better than H on the stored instances, makes H' the new hypothesis. Finally, IHC removes the oldest stored training case and stores the new one.[5] This process continues as long as training instances are available.

---

5. Another scheme would replace the current K training cases with an entirely new set of instances. This would decrease reprocessing of instances but might slow the overall learning rate.

Table 2-4. The IHC algorithm: Incremental hill climbing for a logical conjunction, directed by an evaluation function Score.

```
Inputs: ISET is a set of classified training instances.
Output: A logical conjunction.
Params: K is the number of instances retained in memory.

Procedure IHC(ISET)

Let H be the result of Initialize-Hypothesis.
For each training instance I in ISET,
    Let KSET be the sequence of K instances ending with I.
    If I is a positive instance,
    Then if H does not match I,
        Then let SSET be the set of most specific
                    generalizations of H that match I.
    Else (when I is a negative instance) if H matches I,
        Then let GSET be the set of most general
                    specializations of H that do not match I.
    For each member M of SSET or GSET, compute Score(M, KSET).
    Let H′ be the member of SSET or GSET with the best score.
    If Score(H′, KSET) ≥ Score(H, KSET),
        Then let H be H′.
Return the hypothesis H.
```

The algorithm responds differently to errors that involve negative and positive instances. If the current hypothesis H misclassifies a negative training case as positive, then IHC concludes that H is overly general and generates a set of minimally specific descriptions that do not match the instance. In contrast, if H misclassifies a positive instance as negative, the algorithm decides that its hypothesis H is overly specific and produces a set of minimally more general descriptions that match the instance. Thus, IHC carries out a bidirectional search through the space of logical conjunctions, with the direction of movement determined by the type of error.

The table does not specify mechanisms for generating revised descriptions, but they are basically the same as those discussed in Section 2.2.1. Producing a minimal generalization is straightforward. For nominal attributes, one simply removes those conditions from the current hypothesis H not shared by the positive instance. For numeric attributes, one extends numeric thresholds in H just enough to include the training case. As we have seen, for nominal and numeric representations, there is only one such generalization. However, the pseudocode allows for more than one minimal generalization, as can occur in the relational domains we discuss in Chapter 8.

The situation for generating specializations is more complicated. Even in nominal and numeric domains, there will typically be more than one minimal specialization; moreover, the current hypothesis H does not contain the information needed to generate this set. As we saw in Section 2.2.1, there are two basic responses. First, one can provide the learning algorithm with knowledge of attributes and their possible values, which it can then use to specialize H. Second, one can retain a positive training instance (say the most recent one), and use differences between this case and the misclassified negative instance to generate more specific variants of the hypothesis.

The pseudocode in Table 2-4 also neglects to mention the scheme for initializing the description. Obviously, one could set the initial H to the first positive instance, as in the ISG algorithm. Alternatively, one could initialize it to the most general possible description, as in the IGS method. Given knowledge of attribute values or predicates, one could even generate a random description and use this as the initial hypothesis. Different approaches would alter the number of training instances needed to reach the target concept but, at least in noise-free domains, should not affect the end result.

2.5.3 An example of IHC in operation

Figure 2-6 portrays the behavior of the IHC algorithm in response to a sequence of training instances, the same ones used in our previous examples but in a different order and with one repetition. The figure shows the descriptions considered after each training instance, along with their scores on the evaluation function from Section 2.3, $(P_c + N_{\bar{c}})/(P + N)$, for the three most recent instances. We assume the method begins with the most general hypothesis possible, a cell with no features specified.

Because the first instance is positive and this description matches it, IHC takes no action except to store the instance for future reference. The initial hypothesis also matches the second training case, but this one is negative. As a result, the algorithm considers four more specific descriptions, each with one additional condition, that do not match the

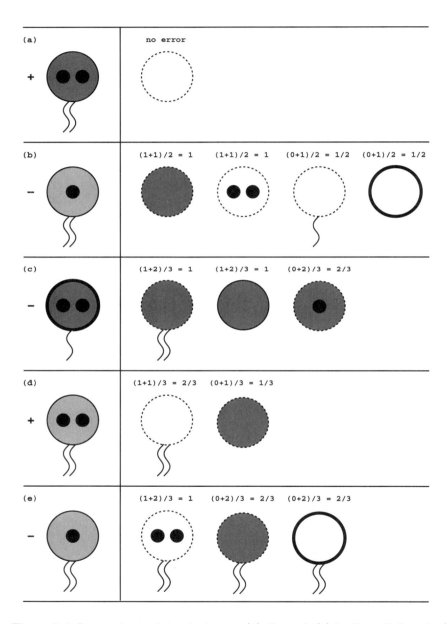

Figure 2-6. Successive training instances (a) through (e) in the cell domain (on the left) and the descriptions generated by the IHC algorithm in response (on the right), along with their scores on the evaluation function $(P_c+N_{\bar{c}})/(P+N)$, based on the current and previous two instances. The figure assumes that, in each case, IHC selects the highest-scoring (left-most) hypothesis for further consideration.

instance. IHC also computes the scores of these revised descriptions on the current and previous training instance. The best revisions are **dark color** and **two nuclei**, each with scores of $\frac{1+1}{1+1} = 1$. This score is at least as good as the score for the current hypothesis ($\frac{1}{2}$), so IHC selects one at random, say the first, as its new hypothesis.

The third instance, which is also negative, reveals that the revised description is still overly general. This time there are only three minimal specializations that do not match the training case. Two of these descriptions correctly classify both the current and the previous two instances, giving them the score $\frac{1+2}{1+2} = 1$. Since the scores for these descriptions equal that for the current hypothesis, IHC selects one at random, say **dark color** $\wedge$ **two tails**, and uses it to replace the current hypothesis.

However, the new description immediately encounters problems on the next positive instance, which it fails to match. Of the two minimally more general hypotheses, only one matches the new training case. This description, **two tails**, has the score $\frac{1+1}{1+2} = \frac{2}{3}$ on the current and previous two instances. This score is the same as that for the current hypothesis, so again IHC goes with the revised description. In addition, it replaces the previously stored positive instance with the current one, for use in future decisions.

The algorithm does not have long to wait before it puts this case to use, finding that the next instance is negative but still matches the description. Actually, this is identical to the second instance in the training sequence, although IHC does not realize it because of its limited memory. This time, the best hypothesis, **two tails** $\wedge$ **two nuclei**, has the score $\frac{1+2}{1+2} = 1$, which is better than for the current description. After replacing the latter with the former, IHC also revises its store of training cases. Given additional instances, the algorithm would continue to revise its hypothesis until it ceased to make errors in classification.

2.5.4 Comments on incremental hill climbing

As we noted earlier, the most obvious advantages of incremental hill climbing are its low requirements for memory and processing. The approach considers only one hypothesis, and it stores and reexamines a constant number of training instances for use in directing the learning process. This compares favorably to the exponential number of descriptions generated by incremental exhaustive algorithms, and even to the constant number of hypotheses and entire training set stored and processed by nonincremental beam search methods.

Naturally, there are prices to be paid for this advantage. We have already mentioned the sensitivity of incremental hill-climbing methods to training order. In addition, such methods typically need more training instances to arrive at the target concept than their more search-intensive relatives. We saw a simple example of this effect in Figure 2-6, where the IHC algorithm required five training instances to induce one of the same concepts that the EGS and IGS algorithms found with only four instances.

Nevertheless, despite the constraints they place on memory and search, incremental hill-climbing methods are robust along a variety of dimensions, in some cases precisely because they cannot maintain consistency with the observed training cases. The incorporation of bidirectional operators contributes to their capabilities, since such operators let the learner simulate backtracking by reversing poor decisions that were based on nonrepresentative training samples.

For those concerned with such issues, the IHC algorithm is guaranteed to converge on a conjunctive target concept, and to retain that description once generated, provided the training instances are sampled randomly with replacement and that they are free of noise. The method will not know when it has completed learning, but humans – the most robust learning systems known – typically do not know this either. Also, IHC is less sensitive to noise than the exhaustive methods, partly because it has limited memory of previous instances and does not attempt to formulate a description that is consistent with all of the training data.

2.6 Genetic algorithms for logical concept induction

The methods we examined earlier in this chapter, which grew out of the tradition of state-space search, all rely directly on the partial ordering by generality that we discussed in Section 2.1.3. Thus, each step these methods take through the hypothesis space involves making an existing description either more specific or more general. However, another important class of methods, known as *genetic algorithms*, come from a different tradition and carry out a very different kind of search. Genetic algorithms have found uses in many disciplines besides machine learning, and even within this field they are not limited to conjunctive induction. However, because they typically operate with logical representations, we will discuss them here.

2.6.1 Genetic representations and operators

Research on genetic algorithms was inspired by an analogy with the theory of evolution, and the basic representation and operators reflect this history. Thus, most work in this paradigm represents knowledge as strings of symbols that correspond loosely to chromosomes. For example, the instance `two nuclei`, `two tails`, `thin wall`, `dark color` might be represented as the bit vector `1 1 0 1`, with ones and zeros indicating the presence or absence of Boolean features. Similarly, a logical conjunction might be represented as `1 * 0 *`, where the symbol `*` specifies a wild card that matches against either 1 or 0. Such an abstract description specifies a hyper-rectangular region in the instance space, just as does the equivalent expression `two nuclei` ∧ `thin wall`. A common representation for numeric attributes involves transformation into a base two integer, which one then encodes as a bit string.

The evolutionary metaphor extends to the learning operators typically used in such methods. Thus, the simplest genetic operator – *mutation* – randomly replaces one value in a string with another. In the case of logical conjunctions, this can mean replacing a specific attribute value with a wild card (giving a more general description), replacing a wild card with a specific attribute value (giving a more specific description), or replacing one value of an attribute with another (giving a different one at the same level of generality). Typical genetic algorithms do not rely heavily on mutation, using it mainly as a backup to preserve 'genetic diversity' in the population.

A more important operator – *crossover* – also comes from genetic theory, but has a more complex effect. When applied to two strings, A and B, the crossover operator randomly selects a place to split both descriptions, then links the left part of A with the right part of B to form a new description, and links the left part of B with the right part of A to create another. The two resulting strings have some features from each of their parents.

In some situations, the order of features has a clear meaning, but for others (e.g., Boolean features) the order is arbitrary. In the latter

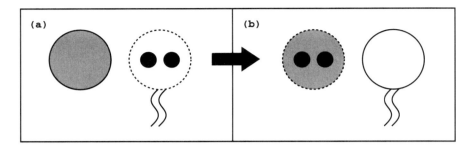

Figure 2-7. An example of crossover's effect in the cell domain. When applied to the two descriptions in (a), the operator produces two new descriptions like those in (b) that include some attribute values from each of the original ones.

case, one can use a variant of crossover that operates on unordered sets of attribute-value pairs by randomly selecting a subset of the attributes and switching their values. Figure 2-7 depicts an example of this scheme in the four-attribute cell domain, in which both the inputs and outputs are conjunctions of two attribute-value pairs.

The crossover operator has some important differences from the specialization and generalization operators we described earlier in the chapter. As we have seen, this operator accepts two descriptions as input rather than one. More important, unlike the other methods we have seen, it makes no use of the partial ordering on the hypothesis space. The resulting descriptions need be neither more nor less general than their parents, since they have aspects of each. Thus, genetic algorithms that incorporate crossover move through the hypothesis space in a quite different manner than the other methods we have described. Nevertheless, experimental studies have repeatedly shown that this approach can lead to useful descriptions.

2.6.2 Search control in genetic algorithms

Table 2-5 shows the basic control structure for a simple genetic algorithm (GA) adapted for use in the induction of logical conjunctions. Basically, the algorithm carries out a form of beam search using the genetic operators discussed above. Initialization involves creating an hypothesis set of `Beam-Size` random entries from the space of possible descriptions. The idea here is to begin search from a representative sample of the description space, so as to decrease the likelihood of halting at a local optimum.

Table 2-5. The GA algorithm: Genetic search for a logical concept description, directed by an evaluation function Score.

```
Inputs: PSET is the set of positive instances.
        NSET is the set of negative instances.

Params: Beam-Size is the overall size of the hypothesis set.
        Cycles is the desired number of iterations.
        Pmutate is the probability of mutated attribute values.

Procedure GA(PSET, NSET)
Let HSET be a set of Beam-Size randomly generated descriptions.
Let CYCLE-COUNT be Cycles.
While CYCLE-COUNT is greater than zero,
      Let TOTAL be zero.
      For each description H in HSET,
          Let S_H be Score(H, PSET, NSET).
          Add S_H to TOTAL.
      Let NEWSET be the empty set.
      Let CHILD-COUNT be Beam-Size.
      While CHILD-COUNT is greater than zero,
            Select hypotheses P and Q from HSET with
                probabilities S_P/TOTAL and S_Q/TOTAL.
            Randomly select a crossover point.
            Apply crossover to P and Q, giving R and S.
            Add hypotheses R and S to NEWSET.
            Decrement CHILD-COUNT by two.
      For each description H in NEWSET,
          For each feature F in H,
          Randomly replace F with probability Pmutate.
      Let HSET be NEWSET.
      Decrement CYCLE-COUNT by one.
Return the member of HSET with the best score.
```

On each cycle, GA uses an evaluation function to measure the quality of the current descriptions with respect to the training data, giving each competitor an associated score. The method then uses the crossover operator to generate Beam-Size successors. In each case, it selects two descriptions as parents, drawing them at random from the hypothesis set with probability in direct proportion to their relative scores. That is, if S_H is the score for hypothesis H and TOTAL is the summed score over all hypotheses, then the probability that a new description will have H as one of its parents is S_H/TOTAL. If H occurs k times in the current set, this probability effectively becomes $k \cdot S_H$/TOTAL.

For each pair of parents, the crossover operator selects a crossover point (or set of attributes), generates two new descriptions, and adds them to its set of revised hypotheses. GA then mutates each feature in each description with some (low) probability. The algorithm evaluates each of the resulting set of descriptions on the training data in turn, creates yet another set of children, and so on, continuing the specified number of iterations.

In many ways, the beam search carried out by genetic algorithms is similar to the mechanisms posited in biological theories of natural selection, and the terminology used in work on this topic reflects the similarity. Papers commonly refer to Beam-Size as the *population size*, to the evaluation metric as the *fitness* function, to the number of *generations* that have occurred, and to the *offspring* in a given population. The scheme for determining the number of children as a probabilistic function of scores corresponds roughly to the idea of survival of the fittest.

The table does not give details about the nature of the evaluation metric, but GA can use any function that reflects accuracy on the training set. Given a conjunctive target concept and a measure like $(P_c + N_{\bar{c}})/(P + N)$ from Section 2.3, the algorithm will tend to converge on a hypothesis set that contains Beam-Size copies of a single description (or slight variations) after sufficient generations have passed. Because GA does not use the generality/specificity ordering to bias its search, this description may be the most specific one that covers the training data, the most general one, or somewhere in between. If simplicity is a concern, one can use a metric that explicitly incorporates this factor.

2.6.3 Comments on genetic algorithms

One can easily alter genetic algorithms to let them process training instances incrementally. Rather than evaluating each generation on the entire training set, one computes fitness scores on the last k instances, with this set being updated after a given number of generations have passed. However, this scheme is best viewed as a form of incremental beam search, rather than as incremental hill climbing.

In terms of robustness, the GA method shares many characteristics with other beam search algorithms for logical induction. Thus, GA should be able to handle noisy training data, as well as target concepts that are only approximated by logical conjunctions. The algorithm is quite tractable in terms of computation time, but it is not guaranteed to converge on an optimal target description.

Again, we should emphasize that, in adapting genetic search to the task of inducing logical conjunctions, we have made many simplifying assumptions. The GA method shown in Table 2-5 conveys the basic ideas underlying genetic algorithms, but such techniques are not restricted to conjunctive induction, nor even to machine learning. We will return to them in later chapters in quite different contexts.

2.7 Summary of the chapter

In this chapter we considered the induction of logical conjunctions. We saw that, combined with an all-or-none matcher, such descriptions produce decision boundaries that are parallel to some of the axes in the instance space. We also found that the space of conjunctive descriptions is partially ordered by generality, and that most methods for inducing them from experience make use of this ordering.

Our discussion of induction techniques focused first on nonincremental methods that use the entire training set to direct search through the hypothesis space. For example, the EGS algorithm carries out a constrained breadth-first search from general to specific descriptions, using negative instances to eliminate entire branches of the search tree. The ESG algorithm instead employs a specific-to-general search organization, using positive training cases to constrain its decisions. These two methods differ in their inductive bias, with the former preferring more general conjunctions and the latter preferring more specific ones. However, we found that such exhaustive methods have a number of drawbacks, including their insistence on noise-free data and, in some domains, an exponential growth in memory.

In response, we examined heuristic approaches to logical concept induction, focusing on the HGS algorithm. This method carries out a beam search through the description space, using an evaluation function that measures fit to the training data to select the best hypotheses at each level. Like EGS, the HGS method moves from general to specific descriptions, but we also briefly examined a complementary algorithm, HSG, that operates in the opposite direction. Neither method is guaranteed to find the best description as measured by the evaluation metric, but we found that they are more robust than the exhaustive schemes in the presence of noise and target concepts that violate the conjunctive assumption.

We then turned to incremental techniques for the same task. The IGS algorithm operates in much the same manner as EGS, except that each step through the hypothesis space is driven by a single negative training case, with positive instances being used to remove overly specific descriptions. We also considered ISG, which moves in the specific-to-general direction, and two approaches to bidirectional search. Although these methods are incremental in the sense that they reprocess few instances, they suffer from the same problem of exponential memory growth as the EGS and ESG algorithms, and thus violate the spirit of incremental learning.

We found that incremental hill-climbing methods such as the IHC algorithm come closer to this ideal. By considering only one hypothesis at a time and retaining only a few instances in memory, such methods guard against high memory costs. In return, they may suffer from order effects and require more training cases to reach the same target concept, although this drawback can be partially offset by the use of bidirectional learning operators that let the hill climber simulate the effects of backtracking.

Finally, we examined genetic approaches to logical induction, which are based on an analogy with evolutionary theory rather than state-space search. Genetic algorithms retain a fixed-size population of descriptions in each generation, effectively carrying out a beam search through the hypothesis space, using an evaluation function to select promising paths. The primary difference between methods like GA and techniques like HGS and IHC is that genetic algorithms do not take much advantage of the partial ordering on conjunctive descriptions. Instead, they rely on operators like crossover that produce quite different effects from those given by generalization and specialization operators.

Exercises

1. Show the logical expressions for the maximally general conjunctions that are consistent with the training cases (-, 0.5, 0.5), (-, 0.8, 2.4), (+, 1.8, 1.6), (-, 0.7, 2.2), and (-, 2.4, 2.2), which take the form (class, girth, height). Draw the decision regions corresponding to each of these expressions. Now show the expressions for all maximally specific conjunctions consistent with these data, along with their decision regions. Assume an integral description language that allows tests like (< height 5) but not ones like (< height 5.5).

2. Trace the behavior of the EGS algorithm (Section 2.2.1) on the training instances:

class	tails	nuclei	color	wall
+	two	two	dark	thin
-	two	two	light	thin
-	two	one	light	thin
-	one	two	dark	thick
-	two	two	dark	thick

   Give the values of the arguments CSET, HSET, and SPECS on each recursive call of the algorithm.

3. Apply the HGS algorithm (Section 2.3.1) to the data in Exercise 2, using the evaluation function $P_c/P + N_{\bar{c}}/N$, rather than $(P_c + N_{\bar{c}})/(P + N)$. Trace the algorithm's behavior, showing values for the arguments CLOSED-SET, HSET, and SPECS on each recursive call, as well as any evaluation scores computed. How does the behavior of HGS compare with that of EGS on these data?

4. Trace the behavior of the IGS algorithm (Section 2.4.1) on the numeric data in Figure 2-4, showing values for the variables I, HSET, and GSET after processing each training case in ISET. Verify that this method produces the same final hypotheses as the EGS algorithm.

5. Write pseudocode for the ISG algorithm (Section 2.4.3), using Table 2-3 as a model. Trace ISG's behavior on the training data (+, 2.0, 2.0), (-, 3.0, 1.0), (+, 5.0, 4.0), (+, 3.0, 4.0), (+, 4.0, 5.0). For each instance I, show the values of the variables HSET and GSET (or their counterparts in your pseudocode).

6. Assume that the IHC algorithm (Section 2.5.2) observes the four training instances (+, 1.7, 2.2), (-, 2.4, 0.5), (-, 1.2,1.7), (+, 2.6, 2.1), which take the form (class, girth, height). Further suppose that the first two instances have led IHC to set the hypothesis H to (< girth 2), that the parameter $k = 3$, and that the description language allows only integer tests. Show the values of the variables GSET, SSET, H, and H', along with any scores computed, when the algorithm processes each of the last two instances.

7. Assume a string representation for hypotheses over the cell domain that takes the form (tails color nuclei wall), making the two candidates in Figure 2-7 (a) become (* dark * thin) and (two * two *), where * represents the absence of a test for the attribute in that position. The two hypotheses in Figure 2-7 (b) illustrate one possible way of applying the crossover operator (Section 2.6.1). Show the results of the other crossovers that are possible (taking the string position into account) for the two hypotheses in Figure 2-7 (a).

Historical and bibliographical remarks

Research on the induction of logical conjunctions occupied a central position in the early machine learning literature, particularly during the 1970s. Although Bruner, Goodnow, and Austin (1956) outlined the basic idea, Winston (1975) was the first to implement and popularize a version of the specific-to-general ISG algorithm. His system used a depth-first search strategy, but both Vere (1975) and Hayes-Roth and McDermott (1978) report breadth-first versions of the same approach. Mitchell (1977) extended this framework, introducing the idea of a version space bounded by S and G sets, generated by a candidate elimination algorithm that combined the ISG and IGS methods in a bidirectional manner. He also did much to popularize the notion of learning as search through a space of hypotheses (Mitchell, 1982).

Langley, Gennari, and Iba (1987) first proposed incremental hill climbing as a general framework for learning. Iba, Wogulis, and Langley (1988) adapted this idea to inducing logical concepts, while Anderson and Kline (1979) and Langley (1987) described similar schemes that rely on incremental beam search. However, none of these researchers limited their attention to conjunctive concepts. By 1980, work in the logical framework had started to focus on the induction of more complex structures, but the new techniques still incorporated as subroutines the methods developed earlier for simple conjunctions.

Nonincremental methods for logical induction emerged from a different line of research than did incremental ones. Here there was no early emphasis on exhaustive methods like the ESG and EGS algorithms (which we introduced only for tutorial purposes). The INDUCE system (Michalski, 1980) carries out an HGS-like general-to-specific search for conjunctive descriptions, and later programs like AQ11 (Michalski & Chilausky, 1980) and CN2 (Clark & Niblett, 1989) incorporate this technique as a subroutine to aid the induction of more complex logical concepts.

Genetic algorithms were first proposed by Holland (1975), and there now exists a large literature on their use in both learning and optimization. Proceedings of annual conferences have been published since 1985 to report current results, and special issues of the journal *Machine Learning* serve a similar function. Booker, Goldberg, and Holland (1989) review a particular approach to genetic learning, and Goldberg's (1990) text gives broader coverage of this area. Examples of genetic methods for supervised concept induction can be found in Wilson (1987) and in De Jong and Spears (1991).

CHAPTER 3

The Induction of Threshold Concepts

The logical formalism we considered in the previous chapter is not the only approach to representing conceptual knowledge. In this chapter, we consider an alternative framework that relies on *threshold* concepts. The representational bias of such descriptions differs from that of logical descriptions, making them suitable for different domains.

Much of the work on threshold concepts has occurred within the 'connectionist' or 'neural network' paradigm, which typically uses a network notation to describe acquired knowledge, based on an analogy to structures in the brain. For the sake of unity, we will instead use notations similar to those from earlier chapters. Despite the differences between threshold and logical concepts, we will find that there are also some important similarities.

In the following sections we consider methods for acquiring three broad classes of threshold descriptions from training data – criteria tables, linear threshold units, and spherical threshold units. First we consider these descriptions themselves, along with some generic issues that arise in their use and acquisition. We then examine algorithms for inducing each type of concept from supervised training data.

3.1 General issues for threshold concepts

As we explained in Chapter 1, threshold concepts provide a more flexible representation of knowledge than logical formalisms. The key lies in partial matching, an approach to classification that assigns instances to a class even when only some of the features in the class description are present. For this to occur, the degree of match must exceed some *thresh-*

old, from which derives our name for this scheme. However, there exist many variations on this basic approach to representation, performance, and learning.

3.1.1 Representation and use of criteria tables

The simplest form of threshold description is known as a *criteria table* or an *m-of-n concept*. Such a description includes a set of n Boolean features[1] and an integral threshold m that falls between 1 and n. The conjunction of n features is often referred to as a *prototype*, suggesting a point in the instance space, although it can extend over an entire region of the space when irrelevant features are present. This region serves as the central tendency of the *m-of-n* concept.

For example, consider the description 2 of {¬one-nucleus, ¬one-tail, thick-wall} for the dreaded disease lycanthropy from the cell domain. This description states that, if any two of the three Boolean features ¬one-nucleus, ¬one-tail, or thick-wall are present in a particular cell, then it constitutes a positive instance of the concept. Such descriptions can vary in either the features included in their prototype or in their threshold value. Criteria tables have found wide use within the medical community in diagnosis of disease.

One can rewrite an *m-of-n* description as a simple linear combination rule. In this example, we have

If ¬one-nucleus + ¬one-tail + thick-wall $\geq$ 2, then lycanthropy.

This notation clarifies the performance component associated with such summaries. Briefly, one counts the number of features in the prototype that are present in the instance and, if the sum equals or exceeds the threshold, one labels it as a member of the concept. In this case, a patient having two or more of the specified symptoms would be classified as lycanthropic, whereas those with one or zero symptoms would not.

Note that criteria tables can represent conjunction and disjunction as special cases, with *n-of-n* indicating a conjunction of n features and *1-of-n* specifying a disjunction of n features. However, the scheme is not limited to these extremes in that it can represent intermediate concepts

---

1. One can extend the method to incorporate internal disjunctions of nominal attributes and ranges of numeric attributes, but one can then treat these as Boolean features in turn.

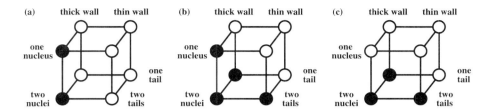

Figure 3-1. Extensional definitions of (a) a conjunctive concept, (b) the criteria table for the concept `lycanthropy`, and (c) a linear threshold unit. Note that (a) can be represented as a 2-of-2 concept but that (b) cannot be described as a conjunction. Similarly, (b) can be described as a linear threshold unit with integral weights, but (c) cannot be handled by such a criteria table.

as well. Figures 3-1 (a) and (b) depict this relationship, with the former showing the extension for the conjunction ¬`one-tail` ∧ `thick-wall`, which can be stated as a 2-of-2 concept, and with the latter showing the extension for `lycanthropy`, which cannot be stated in conjunctive terms.

3.1.2 Representation and use of linear threshold units

Figure 3-1 also makes it clear that there exist some simple concepts that neither conjunctions nor criteria tables can represent. One natural way to handle this larger class is to allow weights on each feature, representing degrees of relevance. For example, the combination

    If −1 one-nucleus + −1 one-tail + −2 thick-wall ≥ −1.5,
    then lycanthropy ,

produces the extension shown in Figure 3-1 (c), which one cannot express as any *m*-of-*n* description. To classify an instance, one multiplies each observed attribute by its weight, sums the products, and sees if the result exceeds the threshold. Such weighted combinations are often called *linear threshold units* or LTUs, but other names include *perceptrons* and *threshold logic units*.

Clearly, one can view any criteria table as a special case of a linear threshold unit in which all weights are either 1 or −1. But an arbitrary LTU can characterize *any* extensional definition that can be separated by a single hyperplane drawn through the instance space, with the weights specifying the orientation of the hyperplane and the threshold giving its location along a perpendicular. For this reason, target concepts that can be represented by linear units are often referred to as being *linearly separable*.

The representational ability of linear threshold units becomes even more clear in numeric domains. Figure 3-2 (a) shows the extension of an LTU for the height/girth domain from the previous chapter. In this case, the combination rule can be stated as

If 1.0 height + −2.2 girth ≥ 0.5, then thin .

In words, this description specifies that a person is `thin` if her `height` minus 2.2 times her `girth` is greater than or equal to 0.5. Algebra lets one transform this statement into the relation `height` ≥ 2.2 `girth` + 0.5, which clarifies the label `thin`.

The simplest linear units assume a 'hard' threshold that acts as a step function to predict 1 (for positive cases) and either 0 or −1 (for negatives). However, they can also predict continuous functions of the observed attributes. Sigmoid functions, which give a smooth transition rather than a step function, are often used to obtain this effect. One commonly used technique calculates the weighted sum $s = \sum_k w_k v_k$ of the observed attribute values v_k, then combines this term with the threshold θ in the logistic function

$$\frac{1}{1 + e^{\theta - s}}$$

to determine a predicted value anywhere between 0 and 1. However, because the classification task still requires an all-or-none decision, LTU-related performance methods typically label an instance as positive if the predicted value is 0.5 or greater.

3.1.3 Representation and use of spherical threshold units

Criteria tables and linear threshold units produce very similar decision boundaries in Boolean domains, although we have seen that the latter subsume the former. However, LTUs do not produce clear prototypes when used in numeric domains, since their extension is unbounded. To generate such an effect, one must move to a different type of threshold description. Figure 3-2 (b) shows the extension of a sample spherical unit that can be stated as

If $\sqrt{(\text{height} - 5.6)^2 + (\text{girth} - 2.5)^2} \leq 1.5$, then normal ,

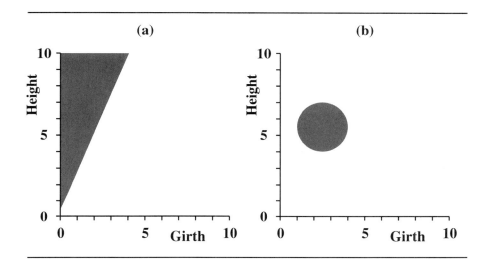

Figure 3-2. Extensional definitions of (a) a linear threshold unit and (b) a spherical threshold unit in the numeric domain of girth and height. The former covers an open region, bounded on one side by a linear equation and on the other only by the limits of the instance space; the latter covers a local region bounded by a spherical equation.

which produces a hypersphere in the instance space. Here the constant associated with each attribute specifies the location of the hypersphere's center along that dimension, whereas the threshold indicates its radius. In this case, any person whose height and girth fall within the given circle would be classified as normal in size.

As with LTUs, one can adapt spherical units to incorporate a sigmoid transformation, so that they predict continuous functions of the input attributes rather than a step function. In this case, we compute the Euclidean distance between an instance and the unit's center as $d = \sqrt{\sum_k (v_k - c_k)^2}$, where v_k is the observed value of attribute k and c_k is the center on that dimension. If we let r be the radius of the hypersphere, then the output of the unit is

$$\frac{1}{1 + e^{r-d}} \quad ,$$

which varies between 0, for an instance that falls at the unit's center, and 1, for an instance that lies infinitely far away. Again, we can transform such a prediction into a classification decision by labeling an instance as positive if the predicted value is 0.5 or less, if we want positives to fall within the sphere, or the opposite, if want them to fall outside.

An alternative approach to achieving a smooth spherical bias involves the use of a Gaussian expression

$$e^{-d/\sigma^2} \quad ,$$

where d is again the distance between an instance and the sphere's center but where σ corresponds to the standard deviation for the Gaussian. Such a description is sometimes called a *radial basis function* or a *localized receptive field*. Gaussian units are often used to predict a numeric output, but they can also be used for classification by predicting a positive instance if the above expression is less than σ.

One can extend the representational power of spherical units by allowing additional terms in the combination rule. Hyperspheres give equal weight to each attribute, which may cause the `normal` rule above to include some thin and plump people that one would like to exclude. One response is to use combinations that produce hyperellipses with axes of different lengths. This requires one additional parameter for each attribute, provided that one is willing to assume that each axis parallels some axis in the instance space. More general hyperellipses that violate this assumption require even more parameters to specify the higher-order interactions among attributes. Similarly, one can extend LTUs to produce nonlinear boundaries on open extensions by introducing quadratic, cubic, and higher-order terms. We will not focus on such extensions in this chapter, but they do provide added representational power to the threshold framework.

3.1.4 Induction of threshold concepts as search

The learning task for threshold concepts is analogous to that for logical ones: given training cases and their associated classes, generate an intensional threshold description that correctly assigns class names to new test cases. As before, one can view this task in terms of search through the space of concept descriptions, constrained both by the training data and by any bias embedded in the inductive algorithm. However, the nature of threshold concepts leads to some interesting differences from the logical framework on this dimension.

One distinction lies in the nature of the operators for moving through the concept space. As we will see in later sections, the use of partial matching means that, even for simple threshold concepts, the addition of features produces more general descriptions rather than more specific ones, since it provides more options for exceeding the threshold. Moreover, the reliance on a threshold introduces new types of learning operators that are concerned with determining its setting. In general, increasing a threshold leads to a more specific concept, whereas decreasing it produces a more general one. In schemes that use linear threshold units, increasing (decreasing) the weight on a single attribute gives greater (less) generality.[2]

Thus, for many threshold concepts there exists a partial ordering by generality much like that for logical concepts, although the larger size of the hypothesis space makes exhaustive search even less plausible than for conjunctive schemes. The partial ordering is most easily seen with criteria tables, since their threshold and weights are effectively discrete. In this case, the partial ordering is a proper superset of that for logical conjunctions, in that each such conjunction can be cast as an m-of-n concept but not vice versa. In Boolean domains, there is a clear partial ordering even for linear threshold units. The situation is more complex for numeric domains, in that arbitrarily small weight changes are possible, but this does not keep logical methods from taking advantage of the partial ordering idea to organize search.

Nevertheless, the vast majority of research on induction of threshold concepts ignores this partial ordering. Instead, it relies primarily on *gradient descent* methods to search the description space. Gradient descent is a special form of incremental hill climbing that uses a difference equation to compute a revised description from the current hypothesis H and H's behavior on a training instance. Typically, the difference equation is closely linked to an explicit criterion that one is trying to minimize, such as the number of errors in classification or the mean squared error in prediction. In most situations, one determines the difference equation by taking the derivative of the criterion expression with respect to the quantity one wants to minimize. We will see examples of specific difference equations in Sections 3.3 and 3.4.

For now, the important point is that most work in this framework incrementally applies such an equation after each training case, letting

---

2. Altering the weights on spherical units does not map onto the generality spectrum, since they indicate the central tendency of the unit rather than degrees of relevance.

it gradually converge on some global or local optimum in the space of threshold descriptions. Although such gradient descent methods are inherently incremental, algorithms for inducing threshold concepts often invoke them repeatedly on the training set to mimic the effects of nonincremental processing. Each such pass through the training set is often referred to as an *epoch*. Most such techniques also include a *gain factor*, which influences the size of the step taken through the weight space. We will see other approaches to learning in this framework, but gradient descent of the above sort predominates.

3.2 Induction of criteria tables

Criteria tables are the simplest form of threshold unit, making them a natural place to start our examination of the induction process. In this section, we consider algorithms for inducing such m-of-n concepts from training data. We will focus on nominal attributes and Boolean features, although the basic approach can be extended to numeric domains.

3.2.1 Simple threshold modification

We will begin by focusing on domains that involve only r relevant features and no irrelevant ones. In such cases, we can partition the task of inducing criteria tables into two components: determining the prototype and selecting an appropriate threshold between 1 and r (inclusive). The *threshold revision* (TR) algorithm takes advantage of this division. Given all the training instances, TR first finds the modal (most frequent) value for each attribute, then uses the resulting set P as the prototype. Earlier we noted that the space of criteria tables is ordered by generality. Thus, the algorithm can start with either the most specific possible m-of-n concept, r of P, or the most general one, 1 of P.

In the first scheme, which we will call TRG (for *threshold revision/ general*), the only learning operator involves decreasing the threshold by 1, producing a more general hypothesis. In the second method, TRS (for *threshold revision/specific*), the only operator increases the threshold by 1, generating a more specific hypothesis. Although the overall space is only partially ordered, the subset of hypotheses that differ only in their thresholds is totally ordered; as a result, neither strategy requires any real search. TRG and TRS simply continue generalizing or specializing until the quality of the hypothesis fails to improve on some criterion.

Incremental versions of both schemes are also possible. Here one initializes the prototype to the first positive instance, but revises it as new instances alter the modal values for the class. After each new training case, one also considers both increasing and decreasing the threshold, moving to the resulting hypothesis only if such an action provides some improvement on the training data on hand (e.g., the most recent k instances). This algorithm continues to revise its prototype and threshold as long as new training cases suggest improved descriptions.

3.2.2 Feature selection and threshold modification

The above methods are only sufficient to induce criteria tables when all attributes are relevant. In more realistic situations, only r out of n features are relevant, and search is needed to find the target concept. In such cases, simple threshold modifications do not produce minimal changes in concept descriptions. Thus, one must replace the learning operator with more conservative ones. First let us consider a nonincremental, specific-to-general algorithm, HCT, for the heuristic induction of criteria tables, as summarized by the pseudocode in Table 3-1.

There exist two operators that generate minimally more general criteria tables from an existing hypothesis. We will assume that ¬one-tail and thick-wall are part of the prototype, which HCT determines using modal values as in the TR method. The first operator simultaneously removes a feature and lowers the threshold by one. For example, given the current hypothesis 2 of {¬one-nucleus, ¬one-tail, thick-wall}, this operator generates three alternatives: 1 of {¬one-nucleus, ¬one-tail}, 1 of {¬one-nucleus, thick-wall}, and 1 of {¬one-tail, thick-wall}. The second operator holds the threshold constant but introduces a new feature. For example, given the current hypothesis 1 of {¬one-nucleus}, it generates the two successors 1 of {¬one-nucleus, ¬one-tail} and 1 of {¬one-nucleus, thick-wall}.

At any given stage in the search process, the HCT algorithm must evaluate the competitors according to some criterion. In small, noise-free domains, one might simply eliminate hypotheses that cover any negative training instances, as in the ESG method from Chapter 2. If the hypothesis space is large or if noise may be present, then one must use some heuristic search method, directed by an evaluation function, as described in the previous chapter. As the table shows, HCT uses a form of beam search, retaining only the best hypotheses at each level.

Table 3-1. The HCT algorithm: Heuristic induction of criteria tables using
beam search, starting with the most specific possible hypothesis and moving
toward more general ones. Replacing the initial hypothesis and the operators
produces general-to-specific search.

```
Inputs: PSET is the set of positive instances.
        NSET is the set of negative instances.
        A set of nominal attributes ATTS.
Output: A criteria table for classifying new instances.

Procedure HCT(PSET, NSET, ATTS).

Let the prototype P be the set of most common values
    in PSET for each of the attributes in ATTS.
Let the initial threshold T be the size of ATTS.
Let the initial hypothesis set HSET be {[T of P]}.
Return HCT-Aux(PSET, NSET, P, { }, HSET).

Procedure HCT-Aux(PSET, NSET, P, CLOSED-SET, HSET).

Let OPEN-SET be the empty set.
For each description H in HSET,
    Let SPECS be CT-Specialize(H, P).
    Let NEW-SET be the empty set.
    For each specialized description S in SPECS,
        If Score(S, PSET, NSET) > Score(H, PSET, NSET),
        Then add the description S to NEW-SET.
    If NEW-SET is empty,
    Then add the description H to CLOSED-SET.
    Else for each description S in NEW-SET,
        Add S to OPEN-SET.
If OPEN-SET is empty,
Then return the highest-scoring member of CLOSED-SET.
Else let BEST-SET be the Beam-Size highest-scoring
        members of the union of OPEN-SET and CLOSED-SET.
    Let CLOSED-SET be the members of CLOSED-SET in BEST-SET.
    Let OPEN-SET be the members of OPEN-SET in BEST-SET.
    Return HCT-Aux(PSET, NSET, P, CLOSED-SET, OPEN-SET).
```

A similar scheme organizes search from general to specific hypotheses. In this framework, one learning operator simultaneously adds a feature and increases the threshold by 1, whereas the other retains the current threshold and removes an existing feature. Again, this assumes that the method has computed a plausible prototype at the outset, from which the first operator draws features. In small, noise-free domains, one can eliminate any alternative that fails to cover a positive training case, but again, more realistic problems require heuristic search directed by an evaluation function.

A third viable approach searches from the simplest criteria tables, which occur in the middle of the generality ordering, toward the most complex ones, which occur at the extremes of specificity and generality. Thus, this method's initial hypothesis has the form 1 of {F}, where the term F may be any of the known features or their negation. For example, for the cell domain, this approach might initialize the hypothesis to be 1 of {¬one-nucleus} or 1 of {thick-wall}. One can select the initial feature from a prototype computed at the outset, as in the other techniques, or one can use an evaluation function to select the feature that best discriminates between classes.

This simple-to-complex approach requires some form of bidirectional search using a combination of operators from the above methods. For example, the operators 'add feature/maintain threshold' and 'add feature/increase threshold' are sufficient to generate all criteria tables, starting from any one of the simplest descriptions. The converse pair, 'remove feature/ lower threshold' and 'remove feature/maintain threshold', can also reach any hypothesis within the space. Using all four operators in conjunction may also help with some evaluation functions. Bidirectional use of operators is also necessary in incremental hill-climbing variants that process only a subset of the training data at a time.

Although the simplest methods for inducing criteria tables assume that attributes are nominal or Boolean, one can extend them to handle numeric attributes. One approach, which we consider in Section 3.4, relies on restating the criteria table in terms of spherical threshold units, then searching the resulting weight space. Another scheme, based on analogy with logical induction methods, introduces > and < tests into the concept representation, then searches through the set of possible values to determine the best such test for each attribute.

3.3 Induction of linear threshold units

As noted in Section 3.1, linear threshold units move beyond criteria tables in that they allow nonintegral weights on attributes, thus supporting degrees of relevance. Determination of these weights requires some different learning algorithms from those we have yet considered.

3.3.1 The perceptron revision method

Now let us consider the more common incremental approaches to inducing linear threshold units. The earliest algorithm of this sort, which we will call the *perceptron revision method* (PRM), retains a single LTU in memory and processes one instance at a time. As shown in Table 3-2, the method retains the current hypothesis if it correctly classifies a training case, but classification errors lead to changes in weights. In particular, we have

$$\Delta w_i = \eta v_i$$

as the change in the weight on attribute i when the misclassified instance is positive and

$$\Delta w_i = -\eta v_i$$

when the instance is negative, where v_i is the value of attribute i in the training case and $\eta > 0$ is a gain factor. Thus, each weight w_i is changed in proportion to the attribute value v_i, with the type of error determining the direction of change. This includes the weight corresponding to the threshold, which is treated as a special attribute that always has the value 1.

Figure 3-3 traces the behavior of this induction algorithm on four training cases from the height/girth domain. The PRM method can start with any combination of weights, but these are typically randomly set to small, nonzero values. Here we assume the initial hypothesis

$$1.0 \text{ height} + -2.0 \text{ girth} \geq 1.5 \text{ ,}$$

which is near the target concept (to keep things simple). The line in Figure 3-3 (a) shows the decision boundary produced by this description, with the region for positive instances on the left. We will also use $\eta = 0.04$ as our gain factor, which leads to rapid learning for this example, and we will assume that the algorithm processes training cases in the order (2.0, 5.0), (2.5, 5.0), (1.75, 6.0), and (3.0, 6.25).

Table 3-2. The perceptron revision method (PRM): Incremental induction of linear threshold units using gradient descent search.

```
Inputs:  A hypothesized linear threshold unit H.
         A set of classified training instances ISET.
         A set of attributes ATTS used in the instances.
Output:  A revised linear threshold unit.
Params:  A gain term η that determines revision rate.

Procedure PRM(H, ISET, ATTS).

For each training instance I in ISET,
    Let C be the observed class of instance I.
    Let P be the class hypothesis H predicts for I.
    If P is negative and C is positive,
    Then let the sign of the change S be 1.
    Else if P is positive and C is negative,
        Then let the sign of the change S be −1.
    If predicted class P differs from observed class C,
    Then for each attribute A in ATTS,
            Let W be the weight for A in H.
            Let V be the value of A in instance I.
            Add the product S × η × V to W in H.
        Add the product S × η to the threshold in H.
 Return the revised hypothesis H.
```

Figure 3-3 (b) shows that the initial LTU misclassifies the first training instance (marked with a rectangle), which in turn leads to weight modifications. Using the expression above, we obtain $\Delta w = 0.04 \times 1.0 = 0.04$ as the weight change for the threshold, $\Delta w = 0.04 \times 2.0 = 0.08$ for **girth**, and $\Delta w = 0.04 \times 5.0 = 0.2$ for **height**. Adding these quantities to the original LTU gives the revised hypothesis

$$1.2 \text{ height} + -1.92 \text{ girth} \geq 1.54 \ .$$

The solid line in Figure 3-3 (b) shows the decision boundary produced by this threshold unit. From this one can also see that it correctly classifies the second and third training cases, (2.5, 5.0) and (1.75, 6.0), as negative and positive instances, respectively. Thus, no learning takes place when the algorithm processes them.

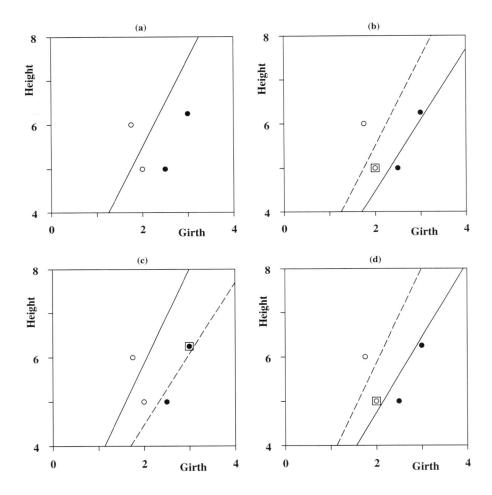

Figure 3-3. Behavioral trace of the perceptron learning algorithm on two positive (white) and two negative (black) training cases from the height/girth domain. The initial LTU in (a) misclassifies the first instance, (2.0, 5.0), as negative, producing the revised decision boundary in (b). This correctly labels the instances processed next, (2.5, 5.0) and (1.75, 6.0), but it mislabels (3.0, 6.25) as positive, giving the revised regions in (c). Finally, a second error on (2.0, 5.0) gives the LTU in (d), which correctly classifies all the training data.

However, as Figure 3-3 (c) shows, the final instance, (3.0, 6.25), is classified as positive rather than negative, initiating further changes. This time, the modifications are $0.04 \times 1.0 = 0.04$ for the threshold, $0.04 \times 3.0 = 0.12$ for `girth`, and $0.04 \times 6.25 = 0.25$ for `height`, but they are subtracted from the current weights rather than added. The result is the revised threshold unit

$$0.95 \text{ height} + -2.04 \text{ girth} \geq 1.5 \ ,$$

which gives the solid decision boundary shown in Figure 3-3 (c). Clearly, even when the algorithm has processed all of the training cases, the resulting threshold unit may not correctly classify them, since the changes introduced may have been small or since later alterations may have offset earlier ones.

For this reason, although the PRM algorithm for perceptron learning is inherently incremental, it is typically run through the entire training set multiple times to mimic a nonincremental method. In this example, the LTU from Figure 3-3 (c) has overcompensated and again misclassifies the first training instance, (2.0, 5.0), labeling it as negative rather than positive. This time the revised hypothesis is

$$1.15 \text{ height} + -1.96 \text{ girth} \geq 1.54 \ ,$$

as shown by the solid line in Figure 3-3 (d). Fortunately, this description correctly classifies the other three instances. Thus, if one runs the algorithm through the data a third time, it will make no errors, having arrived at an LTU that completely separates the classes.

Table 3-3 presents pseudocode for a higher-level algorithm that calls on PRM repeatedly until no errors occur on the training data or until it exceeds a user-specified number of iterations. This method is sometimes called the *perceptron convergence procedure* (PCP) because, if the training set is linearly separable, it is guaranteed to converge in a finite number of iterations on an LTU that makes no errors on these data.

Of course, linear threshold units may provide useful approximations even when the target concepts (and probably the training data) are not linearly separable. Also, the presence of noise can make the training set nonseparable even when this assumption holds for the target concept. In such cases, one can still run the PCP algorithm, but it needs a halting criterion other than the absence of errors on the training data. One method halts PCP when it detects repeated sets of weights, which

Table 3-3. The perceptron convergence procedure (PCP): Nonincremental induction of linear threshold units by applying PRM iteratively to the training set until it produces an LTU that makes no errors.

```
Inputs:  A set of classified training instances ISET.
         A set of attributes ATTS used in the instances.
Output:  A linear threshold unit for classifying new instances.
Params:  A gain term η that determines revision rate.
         The maximum number of iterations Maximum-Iterations.

Procedure PCP(ISET, ATTS).

Let H be an LTU with random weights between −1 and 1.
Let COUNT be Maximum-Iterations.
Repeat until COUNT is zero:
    Let NO-ERRORS be True.
    For each instance I in ISET,
        If H incorrectly classifies I,
        Then let NO-ERRORS be False.
    If NO-ERRORS is True,
    Then return the hypothesis H.
    Else decrement COUNT by one.
        Let H be PRM(H, ISET, ATTS).
Return the hypothesis H.
```

---

are guaranteed to arise on nonseparable training data. However, this requires that one retain multiple descriptions in memory, and an easier scheme simply halts training after a specified number of iterations, as shown in Table 3-3.

The rate of convergence is significantly affected by the gain term η, which controls the size of steps through the hypothesis space. Small values lead to overly conservative behavior, with each learning event producing only a fraction of the weight change needed to remove the offending error. On the other hand, large values lead to overshooting, with weight changes tending to undo corrections made by earlier ones. One response is to start with a high setting for η and gradually reduce it as learning proceeds. There also exist schemes that determine η adaptively for each training case, selecting a setting that is just sufficient to produce a correct classification on the current instance.

3.3.2 The LMS procedure

The perceptron learning method assumes a hard threshold that predicts a positive instance if exceeded and a negative one otherwise. However, one can adapt the method to handle soft boundaries like those produced by the logistic function we discussed in Section 3.2.1. Here the goal is to learn an LTU that predicts a numeric value between 0 and 1, which corresponds to the negative and positive class, respectively.

One widely used modification method, known as the *least mean square* or *LMS* algorithm, computes

$$\Delta w_i = \eta \delta v_i$$

as the change in the weight on attribute i, where v_i is the value of attribute i, $\eta > 0$ is a gain factor, and

$$\delta = p(1 - p)(o - p)$$

is an error term that incorporates the observed value o and the predicted value p for the training case. One can view this scheme as a generalization of the perceptron updating rule, in which δ is either 1 or -1. Thus, the amount of weight change depends not only on the attribute values but also on the amount of error.

The name of the LMS algorithm derives from the fact that it converges on a linear threshold unit that minimizes the mean squared error between the desired and generated output, even when the training data are not linearly separable. In fact, one can obtain the δ term by taking the derivative of this error quantity with respect to the weights. As a result, asymptotically it produces LTUs that tend to split the training instances more evenly than the perceptron method. Thus, the two learning methods have different inductive biases that, in some cases, produce quite different predictions on novel test cases.

Although one can iteratively invoke the LMS difference equation from within an algorithm like PCP, individual instances can produce changes in different directions, which can lead to large oscillations in the weights and slow learning. Another approach, shown in Table 3-4, computes the error and proposed weight changes to the current LTU for each instance, then sums these changes and uses the result to modify the LTU. Another scheme for reducing oscillation, also represented in the table, introduces a 'momentum' term into the update rule. The new equation,

$$\Delta w_i(n) = \eta \delta v_i + \alpha \Delta w_i(n - 1) \quad ,$$

Table 3-4. The least mean square (LMS) algorithm: Induction of linear threshold units using gradient descent, with the aim of minimizing the mean squared error between predictions and observations. LMS assumes that the value for the threshold term is always 1.

```
Inputs: A set of classified training instances ISET.
        A set of attributes ATTS used in the instances.
Output: A linear threshold unit for classifying new instances.
Params: A gain term η that determines revision rate.
        A momentum term α that reduces oscillation.
        The maximum number of iterations Maximum-Iterations.
        The minimum acceptable error Minimum-Error.

Procedure LMS(ISET, ATTS).

Let H be an LTU with random weights between −0.5 and 0.5.
For each attribute A in ATTS, let Δ_A be zero.
Let COUNT be Maximum-Iterations.
Repeat until COUNT is zero:
    Let TOTAL-ERROR be zero.
    For each instance I in ISET,
        Let O_I be the observed quantity for instance I.
        Let P_I be the quantity that H predicts for I.
        Add the error (O_I − P_I)² to TOTAL-ERROR.
    If TOTAL-ERROR is less than Minimum-Error,
    Then return the hypothesis H.
    Else for each attribute A in ATTS,
            Let GRADIENT be zero.
            For each instance I in ISET,
                Let δ be P_I · (1 − P_I) · (O_I − P_I).
                Let V be the value of A in instance I.
                Add η · δ · V to GRADIENT.
            Let Δ_A be GRADIENT + (α · Δ_A).
            Let W be the weight for A in H.
            Add Δ_A to W in H.
        Decrement COUNT by one.
Return the hypothesis H.
```

takes into account previous weight changes, although they are multiplied by a factor, $0 < \alpha < 1$, that gives them successively less influence. Also note that, because LMS focuses on reducing quantitative errors rather than eliminating misclassifications, the perceptron halting criterion does not apply. Instead, one typically iterates through the training set either a specified number of times or until the error reaches a low enough level.

Let us examine the behavior of the LMS algorithm on the same training data as in Section 3.3.1. We assume that the gain term ν is 0.4, the momentum term α is 0.9, and the initial LTU is

$$0.1 \text{ height} + -0.2 \text{ girth} \geq 0.15 \text{ ,}$$

which produces a decision boundary identical to that in the perceptron example. The mean squared error is 0.922 for this linear threshold unit.

After its first pass through the training set, LMS produces the revised hypothesis

$$0.119 \text{ height} + -0.27 \text{ girth} \geq 0.156 \text{ ,}$$

which gives an error of 0.898 and has moved in roughly the right direction. The next iteration gives the LTU

$$0.193 \text{ height} + -0.384 \text{ girth} \geq 0.174 \text{ ,}$$

which has a further reduced error 0.853 and which correctly classifies the entire training set.

However, the halting criterion for LMS differs from that for the PCP method, and the current algorithm cycles through the data again, producing

$$0.235 \text{ height} + -0.57 \text{ girth} \geq 0.189 \text{ .}$$

Although the mean squared error has decreased again to 0.796, the new LTU actually misclassifies one of the training cases. However, this misclassification is soon remedied on the next round, which gives

$$0.382 \text{ height} + -0.76 \text{ girth} \geq 0.225 \text{ ,}$$

a description that has 0.736 as its mean squared error. Nor does the algorithm halt at this point, but future iterations produce LTUs that correctly classify the training data as they gradually converge on one that minimizes the error.

3.3.3 Iterative weight perturbation

Although most work on the induction of linear threshold units has relied on gradient descent methods like PRM and LMS, other approaches are possible. For example, one can discretize the weight space and use any search method, such as the genetic algorithm from Chapter 2, to explore alternative LTUs. Here we consider one alternative scheme that uses the entire training set to revise weights one at a time.

Recall that the decision boundary generated by an LTU takes the form of a hyperplane,

$$\sum_{i=1}^{d}(w_i x_i) - w_0 = 0 \quad ,$$

where w_0 is the threshold, w_i is the weight for attribute a_i, and x_i is the value of an instance on that attribute. However, few instances actually lie on this hyperplane, and for a given instance j, we can define

$$\sum_{i=0}^{d} w_i x_{ij} = V_j$$

as the perpendicular distance of point j from the hyperplane, where x_{ij} is the value of j on attribute i and where the value x_{0j} is always -1. If V_j is greater than 0, the LTU will classify j as positive, whereas a negative score will result in a negative label. We would like to find a set of weights that produces the greatest number of correct signs for these V scores.

We can also define an analogous term for a particular attribute a_k,

$$(\sum_{i \neq k} w_i x_{ij})/x_{kj} = U_{kj} \quad ,$$

which also assigns a scalar to the instance j. In this case, the LTU will classify j as positive if the weight w_k, which we specifically omitted from the expression, is less than U_{kj} and label it as negative otherwise. Effectively, this lets us determine the effect on accuracy of varying w_k while holding the other weights constant. Given n training instances, we can arrange the U_{kj} values in order of decreasing size, consider settings for w_k that fall between adjacent U values, and select the setting that gives the best classification results on the training data.

Table 3-5. The IWP algorithm: Induction of linear threshold units through iterative perturbation of each attribute's weight, which continues until no further improvements occur in fit to the training data.

```
Inputs: A set of classified training instances ISET.
        A set of attributes ATTS used in the instances.
Output: A linear threshold unit for classifying new instances.
Params: The maximum number of iterations Maximum-Iterations.

Procedure IWP(ISET, ATTS).

Let H be an LTU with random weights between −1 and 1.
Let BEST be the hypothesis H.
Let COUNT be Maximum-Iterations.
Repeat until COUNT is zero:
    For each attribute K in ATTS,
        For each instance J in ISET,
            Compute Uₖⱼ using H and J.
        Place the Uₖⱼ values in decreasing order.
        For each adjacent pair of U values,
            Let Wₖ' be the average of the pair.
            Let H' be H with Wₖ replaced by Wₖ'.
            Compute Score(H', ISET).
        Let H be the LTU with the highest score.
    If Score(H, ISET) is one,
    Then return the hypothesis H.
    Else if Score(H, ISET) ≤ Score(BEST, ISET),
        Then let BEST be the hypothesis H.
        Decrement COUNT by one.
Return the hypothesis BEST.
```

Table 3-5 presents pseudocode for IWP (iterative weight perturbation), a method that iteratively perturbs the weights for each attribute in turn, in each case using the U_{kj} values to determine the best weight for attribute a_k. If the resulting weight vector correctly classifies all training cases, then IWP halts; otherwise it runs through the attribute set a second time, a third, and so on until it exceeds a user-specified number of cycles. Because a revised LTU may have a lower score than its predecessor, IWP retains the best description generated so far, which it returns if it cannot find one that perfectly splits the two classes.

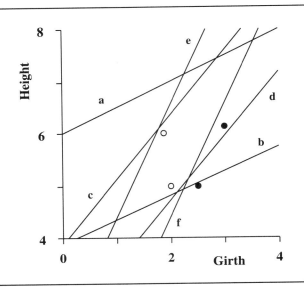

Figure 3-4. Decision boundaries generated by the IWP algorithm, starting with (a) the initial LTU, `1.0 height + −0.5 girth ≥ 6.0`, and ending with (f) a description that correctly classifies the training data, `1.0 height + −2.156 girth ≥ 2.36`. White circles depict positive instances and black circles indicate negative ones.

Figure 3-4 shows the behavior of this algorithm in the height/girth domain, starting with the threshold description

$$1.0 \ \texttt{height} + −0.5 \ \texttt{girth} \geq 6.0$$

(labeled 'a' in the figure) on the same training data as in Section 3.3.1. We assume that the algorithm first revises the threshold and then the weight for **girth**, leaving the weight for **height** unchanged, since we have one degree of freedom.

As can be seen, the first modification moves the intercept of the decision boundary but leaves the slope unmodified. Two of the five choices give the highest score 0.75, one of which produces the LTU

$$1.0 \ \texttt{height} + −0.5 \ \texttt{girth} \geq 3.875 \ ,$$

shown as 'b' in the figure. The second revision alters the decision boundary's slope but not its intercept. Again, two choices give the highest score 0.5 (lower than the previous round), one of which is

$$1.0 \; \texttt{height} + -1.224 \; \texttt{girth} \geq 3.875 \; ,$$

shown as 'c' in the figure. Future iterations alter the threshold to 2.245 and the `girth` weight to -2.156, with accuracies 0.75 and 0.5, respectively. Finally, the next threshold revision leads to

$$1.0 \; \texttt{height} + -2.156 \; \texttt{girth} \geq 0.236 \; ,$$

shown as 'f' in the figure. This LTU correctly classifies the entire training set, which leads the algorithm to halt.

Like many hill-climbing methods, IWP can get caught in local optima. For this reason, some versions include a strategy of randomly perturbing the entire weight vector when the fit ceases to improve, then resuming the iterative search process from this new hypothesis. Another response to this problem involves starting from many different, randomly generated starting vectors, running IWP or a related method for each, and selecting the best result.

3.4 Induction of spherical threshold units

Now let us consider the induction of spherical threshold units. The main approaches to this learning task are closely related to those for the other representational schemes we have considered in this chapter already, and we will focus on these relations in our discussion.

3.4.1 Spherical induction through state-space search

As we have seen, spherical threshold units have much in common with criteria tables, in that they extend the notion of prototypes to numeric domains. The parameters c_i in such units specify the center of a sphere, and thus constitute a prototypical (even if unobserved) instance. Similarly, one can use the threshold to specify the radius of the sphere, the continuous version of m in an m-of-n concept.

Thus, one obvious method for inducing spherical units is nearly identical to the TR algorithm for simple threshold modification that we described in Section 3.2.1. First one computes the mean value (rather than the mode) for each attribute over the set of positive training cases. The resulting means become the w_i parameters for the spherical unit, which defines the prototype of the concept. Next one gradually alters the radius of the hypersphere, moving either from the prototype outward (specific to general) or from the largest possible radius inward (general to specific). In the first case, threshold modification halts when the hypersphere covers all positive cases; in the latter, it stops when the unit ceases to cover any negative instances.

Again, this approach assumes that all attributes are relevant, but the HCT algorithm from Section 3.2.2 also readily adapts to spherical units. The partial ordering on this hypothesis space is more complex, but there clearly exist operators for altering the radius (described in the previous paragraph) and for adding attributes to the unit or removing them.[3] One can select among alternative actions using some reasonable evaluation metric, and one can organize search with any of the heuristic methods we have seen in earlier chapters. Incremental hill-climbing versions of this scheme are also possible, provided one allows bidirectional operators for recovering from early decisions that generate poor hypotheses.

3.4.2 Spherical induction through gradient descent

Although spherical threshold units are similar to criteria tables in their use of prototypes, they are analogous to linear threshold units in their use of nonintegral weights. The basic versions of both frameworks require $a + 1$ numeric weights, one for each of a attributes and one for the threshold. Taken together, these weights determine the position and extent of the region covered by the concept.

Given this analogy, it seems natural to adapt algorithms for inducing linear threshold units to handle spherical ones. For example, one could use the IWP method from Section 3.3.3, which would iteratively perturb first the radius and then the weights that determine the unit's center, continuing until no further improvement occurs. Alternatively, one could construct a variant of the PCP algorithm from Section 3.3.1, which would revise all weights together when a classification error occurs but leave them unchanged otherwise, continuing in this manner until arriving at a spherical unit that correctly labels the entire set of training instances.

One can also modify the LMS algorithm to induce spherical threshold units. In particular, suppose that we assume a spherical sigmoid function, as described in Section 3.1.3, for which we want to determine

---

3. A 'spherical' unit that omits some attributes actually produces a hypercylinder that extends throughout the instance space along the irrelevant dimensions.

weights that minimize the mean squared error on the training data. Given this learning task, an appropriate update method computes

$$\Delta c_i = \eta \; \delta \; \sqrt{d} \; (v_i - c_i)$$

for each center weight c_i, and calculates

$$\Delta r = \eta \; \delta$$

as the change in the weight that determines the radius. In these expressions, d is the Euclidean distance between the instance and the spherical unit's center, $\eta > 0$ is a gain factor, and $\delta = p \; (1 - p)(o - p)$ is an error term based on p, the predicted value for the instance, and o, its observed value. The first expression moves the center of the hypersphere, whereas the second alters its radius.

Let us consider the behavior of this adapted LMS algorithm, with η set to 2 and momentum set to 0, on four positive and four negative training cases from the height/girth domain. The initial spherical unit, with center at $(1.0, 7.0)$ and radius 1.0, covers one positive and one negative instance, but none of the other training data, giving 2.272 as the mean squared error. The difference equations produce a revised threshold unit with center at $(2.052, 5.948)$ and radius 1.547, with 1.502 as its error; this decision boundary includes all of the instances, negative as well as positive. The third spherical unit has nearly the same center weights, $(2.054, 5.946)$, but a reduced radius of 0.996, giving 1.367 as the error. This description correctly labels all the training data, but it seems a bit off center. The fourth description, with center at $(2.021, 5.979)$ and radius 1.076, reduces the error to 1.361, after which further iterations produce only minor changes to the weights.

3.5 Summary of the chapter

In this chapter we discussed the induction of threshold concepts. When interpreted by a partial matcher, such descriptions produce decision boundaries that are quite different from those generated by logical conjunctions. We studied three types of threshold concepts – criteria tables, linear threshold units, and spherical units – each of which introduces a different representational bias into the induction process.

We found that techniques for inducing criteria tables, or m-of-n concepts, have much in common with those for conjunctions, since one can use a partial ordering on the space of concept descriptions to constrain search. We introduced this idea with a simple algorithm that changes only the threshold on an m-of-n concept, then turned to a more sophisticated algorithm, HCT, that also includes an operator for identifying relevant features. The space of criteria tables includes concept descriptions that do not exist within the conjunctive space, and thus requires both types of operator to move through it.

We examined three algorithms for inducing linear threshold units. Most work in this area relies on gradient descent, a form of hill climbing that uses prediction errors to compute the change in weights. One version of this idea, the perceptron revision method, increases or decreases weights depending on the form of error, whereas the least mean square method computes the amount of change based on the difference between the actual and predicted values. We saw that the latter method can be invoked either incrementally or nonincrementally, but that even incremental versions are typically run over the training set repeatedly until they produce the desired output. We also saw that gradient descent is not the only approach to inducing linear threshold units. One such algorithm, iterative weight perturbation, determines the best setting for each weight in turn, producing a quite different style of search through the space of weights that describe an LTU.

Spherical threshold units combine features of both criteria tables and linear units. One can adapt the HCT algorithm directly to this representational formalism to induce descriptions with spherical or cylindrical decision boundaries of varying radius. Alternatively, one can adapt the PCP and LMS algorithms to carry out gradient descent search to find the best center and radius for a spherical unit. The most appropriate algorithm, like the most appropriate type of threshold concept, will depend largely on the domain.

Exercises

1. Using the cell notation from Figure 3-1, draw the extensional definitions for a conjunctive concept with three relevant features, a 1-of-3 concept, and a linear threshold concept than cannot be cast in either conjunctive or m-of-n terms. Show the weights and threshold for the latter concept.

2. Trace the behavior of the TRS algorithm (Section 3.2.1) on the eight instances depicted in Figure 3-1 (b), showing the evaluation score

(accuracy on the training set) for each hypothesis considered during the search process. Do the same for the TRG algorithm from the same section.

3. Trace the behavior of the HCT algorithm (Section 3.2.2) on the data from Exercise 2, using a beam size of 1 and showing the hypotheses considered at each step and their evaluation score (accuracy on the training set).

4. Alter the training instances in Figure 3-3 so that the top two cases are positive and the bottom two are negative. Starting with the same initial weights as in the figure, trace the behavior of the PRM algorithm (Section 3.3.1) on one pass through the training data, showing the weights and the decision boundary after each step.

5. Trace the behavior of the LMS algorithm (Section 3.3.2) on one pass through the training data from Exercise 4, starting with the same initial weights as in that problem. Again, show the weights and the decision boundary after processing each instance.

6. Show the weights generated at each step of the IWP algorithm (Section 3.3.3) on the training data from Exercise 4. Assume that the method first revises the threshold and then the weight for `girth`, as in Figure 3-4. Run the algorithm for two iterations, showing the scores for each possible weight change on each step.

7. Adapt the PRM algorithm to work with spherical units, and trace its behavior on one pass through the training data from Exercise 1, starting with a spherical unit having its (`girth`, `height`) center at (1.0, 6.0) and 1.0 as its radius.

8. Adapt the IWP algorithm to operate on spherical units, and trace its behavior on two passes through the weights, using the training data and initial weights from Exercise 7.

Historical and bibliographical remarks

The computational study of threshold concepts goes back at least to Rosenblatt's (1958, 1962) work on perceptron learning and to Widrow and Hoff's (1960) development of the LMS procedure. Nilsson (1965) provides an excellent review of related work through the mid-1960s, whereas Duda and Hart (1973) report on slightly later developments. Minsky and Papert's (1967) analysis of linear threshold units is held to be widely responsible for discouraging work on neural networks until the resurgence of interest during the 1980s, after development of the extended methods we discuss in later chapters. Much more recently, Mooney, Shavlik, Towell, and Gove (1989) have shown that even simple methods like PCP perform quite well in many domains, although researchers now typically focus on more sophisticated techniques.

Breiman, Friedman, Olshen, and Stone (1984) first described the IWP algorithm for determining weights on threshold units, which they used as a subroutine in constructing multivariate decision trees (see Chapter 7), and Murthy, Kasif, Salzberg, and Beigel (1993) have explored related methods in a similar context. We did not discuss linear discriminant analysis (Fisher, 1936), another class of methods for finding linear splits, that is widely used in statistics. Work on spherical units, such as that by Moody and Darken (1991) and Kruschke (1992), has typically been done within the framework of multilayer inference networks (see Chapter 6).

Criteria tables have their origin in medicine, where they are commonly used to diagnose diseases. Spackman (1988) first introduced them to the machine learning literature, but they have received little attention there except for work by Murphy and Pazzani (1991), Baffles and Mooney (1993), and a few others. We introduced them here not because they are historically important but because they provide a useful transition between logical and threshold approaches to induction.

CHAPTER 4

The Induction of
Competitive Concepts

In the first chapter we argued that competitive concepts differ from both the logical and threshold schemes in relying on a best-match interpreter. Here we consider some instantiations of this approach, which originated within the field of pattern recognition and has only recently been adopted by the machine learning community. The representational power of competitive concepts is similar to that of threshold concepts, and one can even adapt threshold formalisms to operate in a best-match fashion, but we will not consider them here.

Instead, we will focus on two broad approaches to the induction of competitive concepts. The first involves the storage of specific instances or prototypes in memory, whereas the second forms abstract descriptions cast as probabilistic summaries. In each case, we initially consider generic issues in the representation and use of such concepts, then introduce some induction methods that operate on these representations.

The task confronting competitive induction methods is much the same as that we have considered in earlier chapters. Given a set of preclassified training instances, they must find some intensional description – in this case a set of prototypes or probabilistic summaries – that correctly classifies novel test instances. Note the use of the plural here. Unlike the logical and threshold frameworks, competitive schemes cannot represent concepts in isolation; the extension of a concept depends not only on its own description but on that of others as well. For this reason, competitive learning methods always acquire multiple concepts rather than individual ones.

The typical learning operator for competitive methods involves the computation of an average over the training instances. The resulting description specifies the central tendency of the instances that produced it. Typically, averaging does not lead to strictly more general or more specific concepts; its effect is more akin to the parameter setting used with threshold concepts. However, even the latter can be usefully viewed in terms of search through a space of concept descriptions.

In contrast, most mechanisms used for the induction of competitive concepts are so simple that the search metaphor hardly seems appropriate. Some variations process one instance at a time, and these constitute examples of incremental hill-climbing methods in that they retain a single summary description in memory and carry out no explicit backtracking. However, they are not driven by errors; the actions taken by the learner are independent of whether the performance element makes the correct classification. For this reason, incremental versions typically produce the same results as nonincremental ones; there are no effects of training order.

4.1 Instance-based learning

As we mentioned above, one approach to inducing competitive concepts diverges from the methods we examined in previous chapters by storing specific instances rather than abstract descriptions. There exist a variety of learning algorithms that follow this basic approach. When applied to classification tasks, as we examine in this chapter, they are usually called *instance-based* or *nearest neighbor* methods. Here we will examine only the simplest form of these methods, but we will encounter more sophisticated versions in Chapter 5. When used for problem solving and related tasks, they are more commonly referred to as *case-based* or *analogical* methods, which we discuss in Chapters 9 and 10.

4.1.1 The representation and use of prototypes

As usual, we will first address issues of representation and performance before turning to the learning methods themselves. Instance-based methods represent each concept description in terms of *prototypes*, which are simply conjunctions of attribute-value pairs. In Chapter 5, we will see versions of this scheme that represent each class with multiple prototypes, but here we will restrict our attention to representations that allow only one prototype per class.

The instance-based approach is most easily visualized for domains that involve numeric attributes, so we will use one of these for our examples. Figure 4-1 (a) depicts prototypes for two classes in the numeric domain from previous chapters, which involves the **height** and **girth** of a person. Class **A** has an average **height** of 5 feet and an average **girth** of 6 feet. In contrast, the **height** of class **B** is 8 feet and its **girth** is 3 feet. The prototypes include no information about the distribution of these dimensions; they store only specific values.

Because they use the same representational language as instances, it is easy to confuse such prototypes with extensional definitions. However, they are just as much intensional definitions as the logical and threshold concepts in previous chapters, and one must combine them with a well-specified interpreter to determine their extension and decision boundaries.

Using prototypes for classification is a three-step process. Given a new instance I, one first computes its distance from each prototype. For numeric domains, this is often the Euclidean distance in the space of instances defined by the domain's attributes. Thus, the distance between an instance x and prototype p is

$$\sqrt{\sum_{i=1}^{a}(p_i - x_i)^2} \quad ,$$

where a is the number of attributes. For nominal domains, one would typically use a variant on the Hamming distance, in which the distance varies inversely with the number of features that agree in two instances. In some cases, researchers instead refer to the *similarity* between two instances, which is usually just the inverse of their distance. Researchers have explored a variety of metrics for use in calculating distance.

After computing the distance between the instance and each description, one uses the result to classify the instance. The simplest scheme simply predicts the class associated with the nearest prototype. For example, suppose we encounter a person we would like to assign to class **A** or **B** in Figure 4-1 (a), and whose **height** is 6 feet and **girth** is 2 feet. This description's Euclidean distance to the **A** prototype is 2.24, whereas the distance to the **B** summary is 4.12. Thus, one would assign the person to the closer **A** class.

The figure shows the decision boundary formed by the two prototypes. All instances closer to the **A** prototype fall into its decision region,

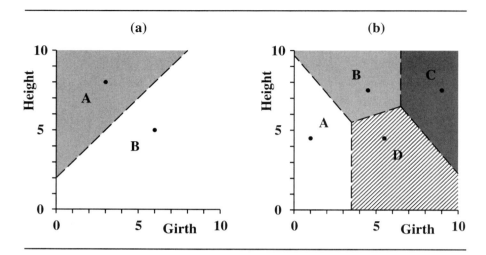

Figure 4-1. Prototypes (black points) and decision boundaries (dashed lines) for (a) a two-class domain and (b) a four-class domain.

whereas all instances closer to B (including our example) contribute to its decision region. Figure 4-1 (b) presents a more general situation that involves four classes. In general, there will exist one such decision boundary for each pair of classes C_1 and C_2, with each point on the hyperplane being equidistant from the prototypes for C_1 and C_2. Thus, k classes lead to $k(k-1)/2$ hyperplanes, although some of these will have no effect on classification. In our four-class example, only five of the six potential boundaries appear, since the boundary between A and C is redundant.

Clearly, classification to the nearest prototype gives an effect very similar to that of the linear threshold units we considered in the previous chapter. In fact, there exists a straightforward mapping from a prototype representation to a linear threshold unit. For two classes a and b, the decision boundary between these classes can be described by the linear threshold unit

$$(p_{a,1} - p_{b,1})x_1 + \ldots + (p_{a,i} - p_{b,i})x_i > \frac{1}{2}\sum_j (p_{b,j}^2 - p_{a,j}^2) \quad ,$$

where $p_{k,j}$ is the value of the prototype for class k on attribute x_j and the term on the right side of the inequality is the threshold term. For example, the prototypes in Figure 4-1 (a) give us

$$(6 - 3)\,\texttt{girth} + (5 - 8)\,\texttt{height} > \frac{1}{2} \cdot [(36 + 25) - (9 + 64)] \quad,$$

which we can rewrite as the inequality

$$3 \cdot \texttt{girth} - 3 \cdot \texttt{height} > -6 \quad.$$

Instances meeting this constraint[1] are assigned to class B, with others going to A. In the multi-class case, one must check all pairs of inequalities that separate the classes, then assign the instance to the one for which it satisfies all threshold expressions.

The above mapping holds for numeric domains, but it does not tell the full story. In Boolean and attribute-value domains, instance-based methods typically use non-Euclidean measures of distance, which makes the relation to linear threshold units less clear. But in all cases, the combination of prototypes with a competitive matching scheme produces decision boundaries that divide the instance space into convex regions, as seen in our examples.

4.1.2 An instance-averaging method

Perhaps the simplest algorithm for learning competitive concept descriptions relies on a process that averages the training instances to find the prototype for each class. Thus, to determine the value p_i for a prototype along numeric attribute i, one computes

$$p_i = \frac{1}{n} \sum_{j=1}^{n} x_{ij} \quad,$$

where x_{ij} is the value on attribute i of the jth of n instances of a given class. For reasons we will discover, this technique is uncommon, but it provides a good introduction to methods for the induction of competitive concepts.

An incremental variant of this algorithm begins with no prototypes in memory. Upon encountering an instance for a novel class, it simply stores that instance in memory along with the associated class. When it observes a new instance in the same class, the method averages the

---

1. Dividing this expression by 3 gives a line with slope 1 and intercept of 2, which accurately describes the decision boundary in the figure.

description for the instance into the prototype. In particular, for each numeric attribute i, the change in the prototype's value is

$$\Delta p_i = \frac{x_i - p_i}{n + 1} \quad ,$$

where p_i is the stored value, x_i is the observed value, and n is the number of cases encountered for the class before the new instance. Thus, the incremental-averaging algorithm must store the instance count in addition to the average, even though the performance component uses only the latter. If some instances omit the values of certain attributes, then it must store different counts for each.

Figure 4-2 (a) shows the prototypes and decision boundaries for two classes, A and B, along with a training instance for the former. If we assume that the A prototype is based on two instances, then Figure 4-2 (b) depicts the revised prototype that results from averaging the new case into the description for the A class. The computation is straight-forward: the new average for **height** is $8.0 + \frac{9.5-8.0}{3} = 8.5$, whereas the new average for **girth** is $3.5 + \frac{6.5-3.5}{3} = 4.5$. Furthermore, the count for this class would be incremented to 3. The extension of the B class has changed even though its intensional description has remained unaltered; as we noted earlier, the extension of a competitive concept C is a function not only of C's description, but also of its competitors'.

For nominal attributes, the prototypical value is simply the modal value, i.e., the one that occurs most frequently for a given class. Thus, the incremental version of instance averaging must retain even more statistics for nominal features, keeping counts for each possible value. This lets it replace the current modal value with another if the latter's count comes to exceed that for the former. For example, given the training instances **dark thin**, **dark thick**, and **light thick**, the modal values would be **dark** and **thick**. However, this could change if later instances contain the values **light** or **thin**.

In terms of efficiency and elegance, it is difficult to imagine an induction algorithm that is superior to the instance-averaging method. However, this comes at a severe cost in representational and learning power. As we have seen, the decision boundaries that the method implicitly constructs are equivalent to those formed by linear threshold units, and our discussion in Chapter 3 noted the representational limits of single hyperplanes. Briefly, they can handle concepts that are linearly separable and they can approximate concepts that cover contiguous regions of

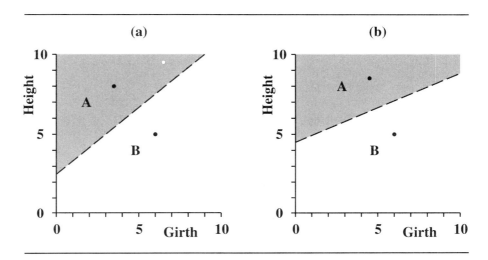

Figure 4-2. Prototypes (black points) and decision boundary (dashed line) for two classes, A and B, (a) before averaging a training instance for class A (white point), and (b) the modified prototype and decision boundaries after averaging. This example assumes that the A prototype in (a) is based on two instances.

the instance space, but they cannot produce the decision regions needed for concepts that are not singly connected. Nevertheless, hyperplanes give surprisingly accurate results on many classification tasks, despite their simplicity.

Yet the ability to *represent* arbitrary hyperplanes does not translate into an ability to *learn* such decision boundaries. The hyperplanes constructed by the instance-averaging method are completely determined by the average values observed for each class. Unlike the perceptron learning algorithm, it cannot alter weights and thresholds in response to errors; one can only hope that the 'weights' produced by the averaging process will form a useful decision boundary between the classes. Although the literature reports no experimental results on this method, it seems unlikely that its behavior would compare favorably to even such simple methods as the PCP or LMS algorithms.

4.1.3 An attribute-weighting method

One drawback of the instance-averaging method is its treatment of all attributes as equivalent. This can cause problems if different attributes involve different measurement scales (e.g., feet and miles) or even if they only have different ranges of values. One can easily sidestep these issues by noting the minimum and maximum values for each attribute, then normalizing the values to fall between 0 and 1. Incremental versions of this technique have some sensitivity to training order, but the basic idea seems sound.

However, the underlying problem with simple instance averaging runs deeper. In many domains, only some attributes are relevant to the target concept, but even with normalization, each attribute has the same importance in the distance computation used in the classification decision. Thus, a test instance might match the prototype for the correct class well on the relevant attributes but be assigned to the prototype for another class because it happens to match the latter well on irrelevant attributes. Learning can eventually correct such problems, but only after the method has observed many additional training instances.

Figure 4-3 (a) illustrates this problem in a variant of the height/girth domain in which only **girth** is relevant. The figure shows three training instances for each of two classes, the prototype that they produce for each class, and the decision boundary that results, given a Euclidean distance metric. Because the prototype for class **A** happens to be greater on the **height** dimension than the prototype for class **B**, the learned boundary diverges considerably from the target boundary. Moreover, the prototypes actually misclassify some of the training instances. Such problems tend to disappear with larger training sets, since they are more likely to contain representative samples, but it gets worse with increasing numbers of irrelevant attributes.

One response to this problem is to modify the distance metric used during classification so that it gives different weights w_i to each attribute A_i, producing the revised distance metric

$$\sqrt{\sum_i w_i (p_i - x_i)^2} \quad ,$$

where x_i is the value of the test instance on attribute i and p_i is a prototype's value on the same attribute. This metric gives the effect of shrinking the instance space more along some dimensions than others. For example, assigning **height** a weight very close to 0 would cause the classification process to effectively ignore this attribute, giving a decision boundary that is nearly parallel to the irrelevant axis.

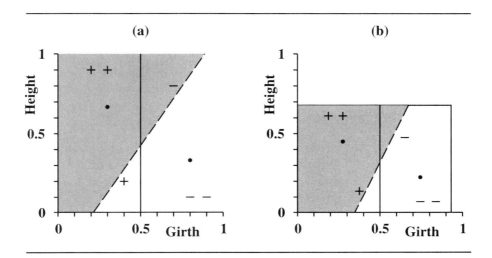

Figure 4-3. Training instances (+ and −), prototypes (black points), and decision boundaries (dashed line) for two classes, (a) using equal weights on the `height` and `girth` attributes and (b) giving the weight 0.68 to `height` and 0.93 to `girth`. The effect of weighting reduces the range of values differently for each attribute, thus altering the slope of the decision boundary. The target boundary (solid line) is parallel to the axis of the irrelevant attribute `height`.

Naturally, one would like to learn an appropriate set of weights from the training data. A simple scheme of this sort uses the equation

$$w_i = 1 \; - \; \frac{1}{n} \sum_{k=1}^{c} \sum_{j=1}^{n_k} |p_{ki} - x_{ji}|$$

to determine the weight w_i, where n is the total number of training instances, n_k is the number of training instances for class k, p_{ki} is the value for the prototype for class k on attribute i, and x_{ji} is the normalized value of the jth instance on that attribute. Given the normalized training data in Figure 4-3 (a), this expression produces the modified weights 0.68 for `height` and 0.93 for `girth`. Figure 4-3 (b) shows the resulting decision boundary, which is closer to the target boundary and which correctly classifies all of the training instances.

Many alternative methods exist for modifying the weights used during instance-based classification. For example, some incremental algorithms modify weights only on the basis of misclassified training instances.

Also, one can easily adapt the scheme described above to determine separate weights for each class, and one can also take into account the relative frequency of each class. We will soon see that both ideas play a central role in another approach to inducing competitive concepts.

4.2 Learning probabilistic concept descriptions

Probabilistic approaches to induction are somewhat more complex than instance-based ones, but they also have a firmer foundation in mathematics. The basic framework is similar in spirit to the instance-averaging method we discussed in Section 4.1.2, except that it incorporates information about the *distribution* of classes and their attribute values, and the induction process estimates this distributional information from training cases. Below we examine the representation, use, and acquisition of such probabilistic summaries.

4.2.1 Probabilistic representation and classification

Like the methods we considered in the previous section, the basic probabilistic scheme associates a single description with each class, but it stores probabilistic information about the class rather than a prototype. In particular, each description has an associated class probability or base rate, $p(C_k)$, which specifies the prior probability that one will observe a member of class C_k. Each description also has an associated set of conditional probabilities, specifying a probability distribution for each attribute.

In nominal and Boolean domains, one typically stores a discrete probability distribution for each attribute in a description. Each $p(v_j|C_k)$ term specifies the probability of value v_j, given an instance of concept C_k. In numeric domains, one must represent a *continuous* probability distribution for each attribute. This requires that one assume some general form or model, typically the normal distribution. Conveniently, a given normal curve can be represented entirely in terms of its mean μ and its variance σ^2. Moreover, the probability for any given numeric value v can be easily determined from

$$\frac{1}{\sqrt{2\pi\sigma^2}}e^{-(v-\mu)^2/2\sigma^2} \quad ,$$

which is the probability density function for the normal distribution.

To classify a new instance I, one can apply Bayes' theorem to determine the probability of each class C_i given the instance,

$$p(C_i|I) = \frac{p(C_i)p(I|C_i)}{p(I)} \quad .$$

However, since I is simply a conjunction of j values, we can expand this to the expression

$$p(C_i|\bigwedge v_j) = \frac{p(C_i)p(\bigwedge v_j|C_i)}{\sum_k p(\bigwedge v_j|C_k)p(C_k)} \quad ,$$

where the denominator sums over all classes and where $p(C_i|\bigwedge v_j)$ is the probability that the instance I is a member of class C_i given value v_j. After calculating this probability for each description, one assigns the instance to the class with the highest probability. A performance system that uses this approach is generally known as a *Bayesian classifier*.

However, in order to make the above expression operational, one must still specify how to compute the term $p(\bigwedge v_j|C_k)$. Most versions of Bayesian classifiers assume independence of attributes, which lets one calculate $p(C_i|I)$ using the equality

$$p(\bigwedge v_j|C_k) = \prod_j p(v_j|C_k) \quad ,$$

where the values $p(v_j|C_k)$ represent the conditional probabilities stored with each class. This approach is sometimes called a *simple* or *naive* Bayesian classifier. Although it seems unlikely that the independence assumption is perfectly satisfied in natural domains, the extent to which a Bayesian classifier's behavior depends on this assumption remains an open issue.

Consider the probabilistic summaries from the three-attribute cell domain depicted in Figure 4-4 (a). The healthy and virulent classes have equal base rates of $\frac{1}{2}$, but their attribute distributions are quite different. The conditional probability of observing one nucleus in a healthy cell is $\frac{2}{3}$, whereas the conditional probability for two nuclei is only $\frac{1}{3}$. The odds are also 2 to 1 that a healthy cell will have one tail rather than two tails, and that it will have light color rather than dark color. The probability distributions for the virulent class are exactly inverted, with two nuclei expected $\frac{2}{3}$ of the time, one nucleus in only $\frac{1}{3}$ of the cases, and so forth.

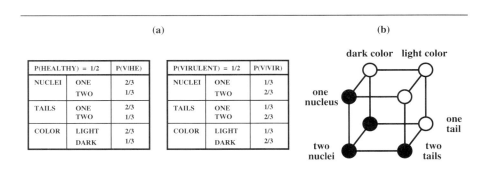

Figure 4-4. (a) Probabilistic summaries for the classes `healthy` and `virulent` from the three-attribute cell domain. (b) The decision regions produced by these summaries in combination with a simple Bayesian classifier that assumes attributes are independent, with white circles indicating `healthy` cells and black ones `virulent` cells.

Now consider the calculations involved in classifying a new cell that has `one tail`, `one nucleus`, and `light color`. If the Bayesian classifier makes the independence assumption, then for each class it finds the conditional probabilities for each observed value, and multiplies them by each other and by the base rate. For the `healthy` class, this gives $\frac{2}{3} \times \frac{2}{3} \times \frac{2}{3} \times \frac{1}{2} = \frac{4}{27}$; for the `virulent` class, it instead gives $\frac{1}{3} \times \frac{1}{3} \times \frac{1}{3} \times \frac{1}{2} = \frac{1}{54}$. The sum of these two products is $\frac{1}{6}$, and dividing each by this amount gives a probability of $\frac{8}{9}$ that the cell is `healthy` and only $\frac{1}{9}$ that it is `virulent`. The Bayesian classifier selects the more likely of these two as its prediction, which makes sense, since the instance perfectly matches the modal values for the `healthy` class.

Figure 4-4 (b) shows the decision regions produced by a Bayesian classifier for these two probabilistic summaries, which looks suspiciously like those we saw in Chapter 3. In fact, for domains that involve Boolean features, there exists a direct mapping from the Bayesian classifier representation to an equivalent linear threshold unit. In particular, the weight w_i for a given attribute i is computed as

$$w_i = \log \left[\frac{p(x_i|C)(1 - p(x_i|\bar{C}))}{p(x_i|\bar{C})(1 - p(x_i|C))} \right] \quad ,$$

where $p(x_i|C)$ is the probability of feature x_i given the class C and $p(x_i|\bar{C})$ is the probability of that feature given the other class, and the threshold w_0 for the linear unit becomes

$$w_0 = \log\left[\frac{p(C)}{1-p(C)}\right] + \sum_{j=1}^{i} \log\left[\frac{1-p(x_i|C)}{1-p(x_i|\bar{C})}\right] \quad .$$

Note that, in this framework, the base rate comes into play only in the threshold term, which makes intuitive sense. A generalized version of this mapping holds for multi-class induction tasks, which Bayesian classifiers can also handle.

However, it would be wrong to state that the probabilistic scheme has exactly the same representational power as linear threshold units, for they can produce quite different effects in numeric domains. Figure 4-5 illustrates the variety of decision regions that can emerge with Bayesian classifiers when one assumes that, in addition to being independent, the attributes are normally distributed. For example, Figure 4-5 (a) shows a situation in which the variances for one class are smaller than those for another on both attributes. Bayes' rule dictates that an instance I near the mean of the tighter class is more likely to come from this class, but for more distant instances, the probability of the other class is higher. The result is an elliptical decision region for the tighter class.

Another effect occurs when the classes have different variances on one attribute but the same on another, as in Figure 4-5 (b). Here the outcome is a parabolic decision region for the tighter class, since instances to the right of the two means are always more likely to come from that class. In some cases, a Bayesian classifier can even produce decision regions that are not singly connected, as in Figures 4-5 (c) and (d). Here one class has less variance on one attribute, whereas the other class is tighter on the second. The result here depends on the placement of the means, giving a hyperbolic region in one case and an hourglass-shaped region in the other.

4.2.2 Induction of naive Bayesian classifiers

Learning in Bayesian classifiers is a simple matter, very similar to the instance-averaging process we described earlier. The basic process can operate either incrementally or nonincrementally, but since the order of training instances has no effect on learning, the results are identical. The simplest implementation increments a count each time it encounters a new instance, along with a separate count for a class each time it is given an instance of that class. Together, these counts let the classifier estimate $p(C_k)$ for each class C_k.

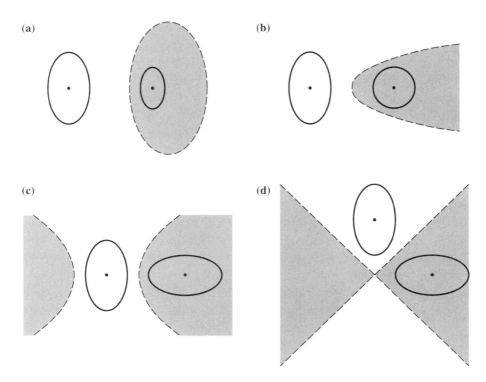

Figure 4-5. Forms of decision regions that a Bayesian classifier can produce for the two-class case in a two-attribute numeric domain, if one assumes that the attributes are independent and normally distributed. Different means (shown by dots) and variances (shown by ellipses that indicate constant probability density) can produce: (a) an elliptical region; (b) a parabolic region; (c) hyperbolic regions; and (d) hourglass regions. After Duda and Hart (1973).

In addition, for each instance of a class that has a given nominal value, the algorithm updates a count for that class-value pair. Together with the second count, this lets the classifier estimate $p(v_j|C_k)$. For each numeric attribute, the method retains and revises two quantities, the sum and the sum of squares, which let it compute the mean and variance for a normal curve that it uses to find $p(v_j|C_k)$. In domains that can have missing attributes, one must include a fourth count for each class-attribute pair.

For example, suppose the probabilistic summaries in Figure 4-4 (a) are based on three training instances for each class. Given a new **healthy** cell that has **one tail**, **one nucleus**, and **light color**, the Bayesian classifier would increment its overall count, its class count, and its count for each observed value. The resulting description for `healthy`, expressed in ratios, would include a base rate of $\frac{4}{7}$ and conditional probabilities of $\frac{3}{4}$ for `one tail`, `one nucleus`, and `light color`. The probabilities for alternative values would decrease to $\frac{1}{4}$, just as the base rate for `virulent` would lower to $\frac{3}{7}$. Taken together, these changes can affect the decision boundary and thus the classes to which cases are assigned.

The effects of learning are more complex in numeric domains. For example, observing enough instances near the mean of the rightmost class in Figure 4-5 (a) can reduce the variance enough to transform the decision region from an ellipse to the parabola in (b). Similarly, seeing enough instances that diverge from this mean along the horizontal attribute can transform (a) into the hyperbolic decision region in (c), whereas enough observations of the leftmost class above its mean can lead regions like those in (a) to evolve into ones like those in (d). Such phase changes can greatly affect the accuracy of the induced Bayesian classifier.

In some cases, the training data may produce a 0 for a base rate or a conditional probability. Since the classification decision involves multiplication, this overwhelms the effects of other factors. One way to avoid this problem is to replace 0 entries with $\frac{1}{n}$, where n is the number of training examples. When the Bayesian classifier has observed few instances, this gives a conditional probability that is relatively high, but if the class or value still does not appear after many training cases, the $\frac{1}{n}$ factor causes the estimate to approach 0.

Another response to this issue, more in accordance with Bayesian principles, is to initialize the class descriptions based on 'prior' probabilities. If the user has expectations about the base rates, conditional probabilities, or means and variances, he can set these at the outset. Lacking such knowledge, one can use 'uninformed priors' to initialize the probabilistic summaries. For example, given three classes, it seems reasonable, lacking other information, that they will each occur $\frac{1}{3}$ of the time; similarly, given a Boolean feature, one might assume $\frac{1}{2}$ as its conditional probability.

The use of priors forces one to decide how much influence to give them relative to the observations. A widespread solution assigns a constant α_j to each value v_j of a nominal attribute, then uses the expression

$$P(v_j|C_k) = \frac{c_j + a_j}{n_k + \sum_i \alpha_i} \quad ,$$

where c_j is the number of instances of class C_k in which value v_j has appeared, n_k is the number in which the attribute has occurred, and the sum occurs over values of the attribute. A common ploy involves setting all α_j to 1, which gives the prior probabilities the same influence as a single training instance. Analogous techniques exist for numeric attributes.

4.2.3 Comments on Bayesian classifiers

We have seen that the simple Bayesian classifier relies on two important assumptions. First, it posits that one can characterize each class with a single probabilistic description. In Boolean domains, this is equivalent to assuming linear separability, although the story is more complex for nominal and numeric attributes. Nevertheless, like perceptrons and simple instance-averaging methods, Bayesian classifiers are typically limited to learning classes that occupy contiguous regions of the instance space. In the next chapter, we will consider methods that move beyond this limitation.

Second, the simple Bayesian classifier also assumes independence of the attributes, which can cause problems on data like those in Figure 4-6 from the four-attribute cell domain. In this case, two attributes (color and thickness) are perfectly correlated and thus redundant; this is one extreme form of attribute dependence. Given only the features nuclei, tails, and color, a simple Bayesian classifier can induce a set of descriptions for the two classes that successfully label the training set; these descriptions predict virulent if any two of three attribute values are present. However, if the instances are equally likely, the algorithm cannot manage this feat when all four attributes are included. Effectively, the redundancy of color and thickness gives these features more influence than they deserve, causing the learned descriptions to classify the second training case as virulent rather than healthy, and no amount of training can overcome this error.

One alternative to the independence assumption stores the conditional probabilities for combinations of attribute-value pairs. In principle, given a attributes, one could estimate all a-way combinations of values, thus ensuring independence of 'features'. However, this is equiv-

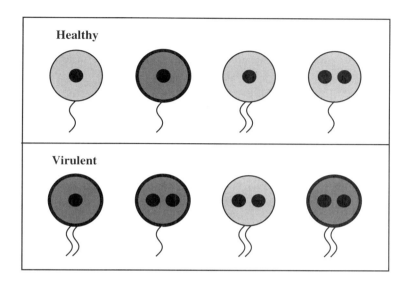

Figure 4-6. Training cases involving four attributes, two of which are redundant. These instances cannot be fully discriminated by a simple Bayesian classifier, which labels the second `healthy` cell as `virulent` after learning.

alent to storing the conditional probability for *every possible instance*. Even independent of its storage requirements, such a scheme (sometimes called an *optimal* Bayesian classifier) is impractical because it requires implausible numbers of observations to estimate parameters. In Chapter 6, we consider a more selective approach to using higher-order features in probabilistic induction.

The two strong assumptions that underlie the simple Bayesian classifier have given it a poor reputation, but the implications of these assumptions for behavior on real-world domains remain an open question. The literature contains results for Bayesian classifiers on natural domains, where one would expect neither assumption to hold, that are comparable to those obtained for the more sophisticated methods we consider in later chapters. Moreover, the probabilistic representation and classification procedure of Bayesian classifiers should make them inherently robust in noisy domains, and also should give them an ability to discriminate relevant attributes from irrelevant ones. We hope that future research will better determine how this algorithm fares under different conditions.

4.3 Summary of the chapter

In this chapter we explored methods for inducing two generic classes of competitive concepts. These approaches share a number of basic ideas: maintaining a single description for each class, using a best-match interpreter to classify instances, and employing some form of averaging during the induction process. The resulting decision boundaries are very similar to those formed with linear threshold units, and in many cases there exists a simple mapping from one representation to the other.

The first competitive approach – instance-based learning – represents each class as a prototype or central tendency, and assigns an instance to the class having the prototype that is nearest according to some distance measure. Such methods typically induce the prototype for a class through simple averaging of the descriptions for training cases of that class. However, this approach does not scale well to domains that involve many irrelevant attributes, and in response we considered an alternative scheme that learns weights on attributes for use in the distance metric.

The second approach we examined – the Bayesian classifier – represents each class in terms of probability distributions, including information about the base rates and conditional probabilities. The performance component uses Bayes' rule to compute the probability of each class given an instance description, typically assuming that attributes are independent, and assigns the instance to the most likely class. The learning algorithm simply updates the distributional information by incrementing counts for classes and for attribute values observed in the training instances. Thus, Bayesian classifiers also learn weights on attributes, although these have clear probabilistic semantics.

Both instance-based and probabilistic algorithms can operate either incrementally or nonincrementally, the former constituting examples of incremental hill-climbing methods. Although simple in nature, these techniques produce respectable results on many domains, and they provide another basis for more sophisticated algorithms that can use them as subroutines, as we will see in the next chapter.

Exercises

1. Use the instance-averaging method (Section 4.1.2) to compute the prototypes for the training data in Figure 3-4 from Chapter 3. Draw the positions of these prototypes and the decision boundaries that they produce. Also show the decision boundaries that would occur if each of the four instances were prototypes for a separate class.

2. Transform the first pair of prototype descriptions from Exercise 1 into a single linear threshold unit, as described in Section 4.1.1.

3. Use the attribute-weighting method from Section 4.1.3 to alter the distance metric for the data in Exercise 1. State the weight found for each attribute and compute the distance of both prototypes from a test case with 3.0 `girth` and 5.0 `height`. Draw the warped instance space, as in Figure 4-3 (b), and the revised decision boundary.

4. Show the probabilistic summaries induced by a naive Bayesian classifier from the eight instances in Figure 3-1 (a) from Chapter 3. Show the instances that the resulting summaries classify correctly and incorrectly. Also show the probability calculations involved in classifying the instance `two tails`, `one nucleus`, and `thick wall`. Repeat this process for the instances in Figure 3-1 (c).

5. Treat the attributes in Exercise 4 as Boolean features, and transform each set of probabilistic summaries generated there into an equivalent linear threshold unit, as described in Section 4.2.1.

6. Compute the means and variances produced by a naive Bayesian classifier on the numeric training data in Figure 3-4. Draw the means and the approximate decision boundary that results. Explain why this boundary differs from those found in the first two exercises.

Historical and bibliographical remarks

The induction of competitive concepts has long been studied in the fields of pattern recognition and statistics, and general treatments can be found in Nilsson (1965) and in Duda and Hart (1973). They have also played a role in cognitive psychology, where they have served as models of human concept learning. Reviews of these exemplar (instance-based) and independent cue (naive Bayesian) models appear in Smith and Medin (1981) and in Fisher and Langley (1990).

However, work in this framework has entered the machine learning literature only in recent years, starting in the late 1980s. Nor are the simple instance-averaging and attribute-weighting methods in Sections 4.1.2 and 4.1.3 representative of work in this area. We used them only to introduce the ideas of storing prototypes and giving their features different weights. We discuss more realistic techniques for instance-based learning, such as nearest neighbor algorithms, in the next chapter.

One might expect the same comment to hold for the naive Bayesian classifier, given its simplicity. Indeed, although first introduced by Good in 1950, this method originally appeared in the literature on machine learning as a straw man against which to compare much more sophisticated induction methods (e.g., Clark & Niblett, 1989). However, its impressive performance in many domains has led some researchers to study the Bayesian classifier in its own right (Langley, Iba, & Thompson, 1992) and others to explore extensions of the method (Kononenko, 1991; Langley & Sage, 1994a; Pazzani, 1995).

CHAPTER 5

The Construction of Decision Lists

The previous chapters dealt with the induction of concepts that one could describe using a single decision region. This focus was useful for historical reasons, and it let us introduce some basic methods for induction, but such simple learning methods seem unlikely to be useful for practical applications. In this chapter we turn to the induction of *disjunctive* descriptions, which provides one approach to creating multiple decision boundaries, and we will examine alternative schemes in the following chapters. However, we will also find that the more sophisticated methods build on the simpler ones we have already seen.

We start the chapter by considering generic issues in the representation, use, and induction of disjunctive descriptions. After this we present a number of algorithms for disjunctive induction that vary in their techniques for partitioning the training data and organizing terms in the concept description. In general, we focus on heuristic approaches rather than exhaustive ones, and we discuss incremental methods only after describing the more basic nonincremental ones.

5.1 General issues in disjunctive concept induction

As before, we initiate our discussion with some issues that go beyond particular algorithms for the induction of disjunctive concept descriptions. Below we consider data structures and interpretation schemes for representing and using such induced knowledge. After this, we attempt a more formal statement of the task of disjunctive induction.

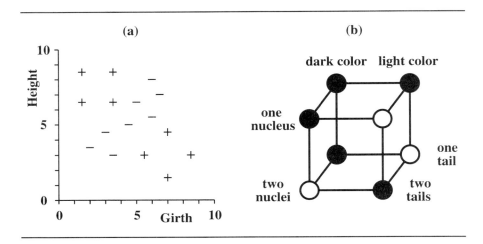

Figure 5-1. Positive and negative instances from (a) the numeric height/girth domain and (b) the three-attribute cell domain that one cannot distinguish using a single decision region. Such training sets suggest the use of representations that involve disjunctive descriptions.

5.1.1 The representation and use of disjunctive descriptions

Consider the data in Figure 5-1, which presents positive and negative instances from (a) the height/girth domain and (b) the three-attribute cell domain. Although the attributes are familiar, the distributions of the instances are quite different from those we have seen before. In neither case can one draw a single decision region that partitions the positive instances from the negatives. This characteristic is completely separate from the representational formalism one uses to express the decision boundaries, whether the logical conjunctions we encountered in Chapter 2, the threshold units we saw in Chapter 3, or the competitive descriptions we discussed in Chapter 4.

Clearly, these induction problems require some more powerful language that lets one express more than one decision region. In this chapter we will explore three alternative ways to achieve this effect. The first, which can be used to combine either logical or threshold concepts, is known as *disjunctive normal form* (DNF). This scheme combines a set of simple descriptions, D_1, D_2, ..., D_n, into the logical disjunction $\{D_1 \vee D_2 \vee \ldots D_n\}$. If any of the simple descriptions matches an instance, then one classifies the instance as a member of the concept. We will refer to each simple description within a DNF expression as a *term*.

A drawback of DNF notation is that, when extended to multi-class prediction, the expressions for more than one class can match an instance. One solution, which we will not consider in detail, is to ensure that expressions for each class are mutually exclusive. Another response is to place an ordering on the terms, so that if two or more simple descriptions match an instance, the one with precedence wins the conflict. Such an organization of knowledge, known as a *decision list*, has rather different characteristics than disjunctive normal form. A decision list typically includes a default term that occurs last but always matches, leading its associated class to be predicted if no other term applies to an instance.

Using disjunctions of rectangles and spheres, one can approximate any possible target concept, whether it involves Boolean, nominal, or numeric attributes. Disjunctions of linear threshold units can also represent any Boolean concept, but in numeric domains, the one-sided nature of linear threshold units limits the concepts they can represent. For this reason, our examples of threshold concepts in numeric domains will emphasize spherical units rather than linear ones.

Both the DNF and decision-list schemes make sense for logical and threshold descriptions, but not for competitive concepts, since the latter cannot be understood in isolation. However, there also exists a natural extension of competitive concepts to multiple decision boundaries. One simply allows two or more descriptions for each class, then selects the best of these during the match process. As before, the decision boundaries emerge from the entire set of descriptions, but some of these descriptions (and their associated regions) happen to predict the same class. We will refer to this representational scheme as a *competitive disjunction*.

The storage of multiple descriptions for each class suggests the idea of taking them all into account during the classification process. This scheme makes special sense within a competitive framework, and a variety of methods for voting and otherwise combining evidence have been developed within both the instance-based and probabilistic frameworks. We will not focus on such performance methods here, but we will return to them in Chapter 9, when we examine their use in handling noise.

5.1.2 The task of disjunctive induction

Now that we have described the basic representation and performance assumptions of disjunctive concepts, we can clearly state the task of inducing them from experience:

- *Given*: A set of training instances, each with associated class labels;
- *Find*: A disjunctive description that, to the extent possible, correctly classifies novel test instances.

Thus, methods that address this induction task must accept as input a set of classified instances, and they must generate a DNF expression, decision list, or competitive disjunction for use in classifying future instances. This task statement is very similar in form to the statements for simple induction that we presented in previous chapters. The only difference lies in the 'find' clause, which lets each class be associated with more than one simple description.

As a result, algorithms that address this task must search a space of disjunctive descriptions, rather than the smaller space of simple conjunctive, threshold, or competitive descriptions. Not surprisingly, this task is more difficult than the ones we considered in Chapters 2, 3, and 4. At least for some representations, the space of disjunctive descriptions is partially ordered according to generality, but the branching factor is so large that in practice no researchers have attempted to use this structure in any systematic way. Instead, we will see shortly that many approaches to disjunctive induction deal with this issue by partitioning the task into a set of more tractable component induction tasks.

Our discussion of disjunctive induction will focus on nonincremental methods, although we will see some incremental variants. We will also emphasize the two-class case, although we discuss some extensions to multi-class prediction. The techniques we will examine draw on the algorithms from earlier chapters, calling on them as subroutines to generate the descriptions of which the disjuncts are composed. Our examples will typically ignore the details of these subroutines' behavior and examine only the state of knowledge before and after their application. We will also emphasize heuristic subroutines, since methods that insist on perfect accuracy over the training set will fail when their assumptions are violated, as in disjunctive domains.

Table 5-1. The NSC algorithm: Nonincremental induction of DNF expressions using a separate-and-conquer approach.

```
Inputs: PSET is the set of positive training instances.
        NSET is the set of negative training instances.
        DNF is a disjunction of single-region descriptions.
Output: A disjunction of single-region descriptions.

Top-level call: NSC(PSET, NSET, { })

Procedure NSC(PSET, NSET, DNF)

If PSET is empty,
Then return DNF.
Else find a single-region description D that covers some
        instances in PSET but covers no instances in NSET.
    Add the description D to DNF.
    Remove the instances covered by D from PSET.
    Return NSC(PSET, NSET, DNF).
```

5.2 Nonincremental learning using separate and conquer

Let us start by examining the induction of descriptions stated in disjunctive normal form, for use in discriminating between two classes. One can reduce this task to the construction of a DNF expression for one of the classes and use the other class as a default when the expression fails to match. Technically, this makes the result a decision list, but only a degenerate one.

Table 5-1 presents pseudocode for a nonincremental separate-and-conquer (NSC) algorithm that addresses this learning task. The method accepts a set of positive training instances (for the preferred class), a set of negative instances (for the default class), and a DNF expression composed of disjuncts of terms, which is initially empty. NSC invokes an inductive routine to construct a description that covers some of the positive instances but none of the negative instances. Many of the logical or threshold methods from previous chapters can serve in this step, although some must be modified to favor exclusion of negative instances over coverage of positive ones.

NSC adds the resulting description to its DNF expression, puts aside the instances covered by this term, and calls on itself recursively with

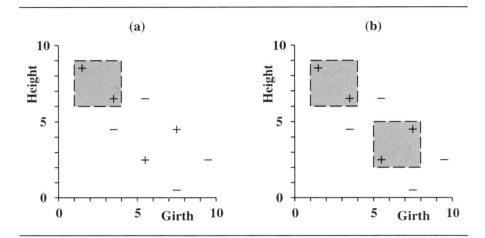

Figure 5-2. Behavior of the NSC method on training instances in the height/girth domain (a) after one call to the HSG subroutine, and (b) after a second call to the same algorithm.

this reduced training set and extended expression. If no more positive instances remain, the algorithm returns the current DNF expression and halts. Otherwise it repeats the above process until it finds an expression that covers all positive training cases but none of the negatives.

Some examples of NSC's operation should clarify its interaction with the methods from earlier chapters. Let us first consider the effects when NSC uses the HSG algorithm from Chapter 2 to determine each term in the DNF expression. Recall that HSG carries out a beam search from specific to general descriptions, using an evaluation function to direct the search and returning a set of descriptions with acceptable scores. Here we assume that HSG continues to generate more general descriptions until their evaluation scores cease to improve, then selects the best description and halts.

Figure 5-2 depicts four positive and four negative instances from the numeric domain involving **height** and **girth**. The layout makes it clear that one cannot draw any rectangle around the positive cases that does not also include some negatives. Thus, the simple conjunctive descriptions that we assumed in Chapter 2 will not suffice in this situation, and we must turn to a more powerful description language. Given these training instances, NSC's first action is to call the subroutine HSG, which immediately selects one of the positive cases as a seed, say the instance `height 8.5, girth 1.5`. Its beam search then considers progressively more general versions of this initial conjunction, eventually producing the rectangular decision region shown in Figure 5-2 (a).

No further generalizations are possible without covering negative cases, so NSC removes the two covered instances and calls HSG again on the remaining training data. The subroutine selects another seed, let us say the instance `height 2.5, girth 5.5`. After carrying out a second beam search, the algorithm finds a second conjunction that covers an additional two positive instances but no negatives. NSC adds this description to its DNF expression, giving the extensional definition shown in Figure 5-2 (b). Since this covers all the positive but none of the negative instances, the algorithm halts, returning the expression ((< `height 9`) ∧ (< `girth 4`) ∧ (> `height 6`) ∧ (> `girth 1`)) ∨ ((< `height 5`) ∧ (< `girth 8`) ∧ (> `height 2`) ∧ (> `girth 5`)) as its result.

Clearly, the NSC algorithm is not wedded to any particular routine for inducing the terms of its DNF expression. For example, one can easily replace the call to HSG with one to HGS, the method for general-to-specific beam search described in Chapter 2. This scheme also produces a disjunction of conjunctive terms, but the details will differ because of the two routines' different inductive biases. Figure 5-3 (a) clarifies this point by showing the decision boundaries that result when NSC uses the HGS routine to identify terms. Because this method prefers general descriptions to specific ones, the final DNF expression covers a larger fraction of the instance space than when HSG is used, and thus would classify more test cases as positive.

One can also use techniques for inducing threshold concepts to construct the terms in the DNF expression. The basic methods tend to give equal emphasis (and thus equal weight changes) to misclassifications of positive and negative training instances. In disjunctive domains, this leads them to produce decision boundaries that cover some positive and some negative cases. However, a simple alteration of the update functions can bias search toward threshold units that exclude negative instances while covering some but not all positives. Of course, one need not insist that each term in the DNF expression rule out all of the negative instances, and covering some negatives may even be desirable in noisy domains, but clearly the expression should cover primarily positive instances. Figure 5-3 (b) shows the result when NSC uses a modified technique for inducing spherical threshold units.

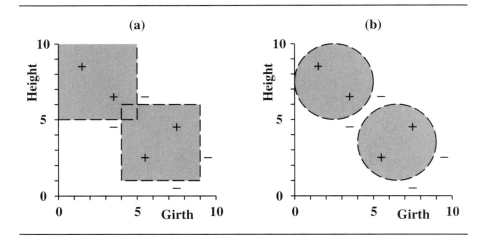

Figure 5-3. Decision boundaries produced by the NSC algorithm (a) when using the HGS routine to produce terms in the DNF expression, and (b) when invoking a modified technique for spherical threshold units.

Now let us consider a second data set from the four-attribute cell domain. Figure 5-4 (a) presents six positive instances and (b) shows four negative instances from this domain that one cannot separate with a single decision boundary. Suppose we run NSC on these data, using the HSG algorithm to generate terms in the disjunction, combined with the metric $(P_c + N_{\bar{c}})/(P + N)$ to evaluate individual conjunctions.

In this situation, the first call to HSG produces the logical conjunction `two tails` $\wedge$ `two nuclei`, which covers the first four positive instances in the figure but none of the negatives. When NSC removes these four cases from the data set and calls HSG again, the latter finds the conjunction `one tail` $\wedge$ `dark color` $\wedge$ `thick wall`, which covers the last two positives but without covering negative instances. Since no positive cases remain, NSC halts and returns the disjunction of the two terms, which Figure 5-4 (c) depicts graphically.

Similar results occur when NSC uses the HGS algorithm, combined with the same evaluation metric, to find the component terms. Although this subroutine searches from general to specific descriptions, it finds the same two-attribute conjunction to cover the first four positive instances as does HSG. However, when called on the remaining two positive cases, its different search bias leads to the more general conjunction `dark color` $\wedge$ `thick wall`. Again, NSC halts at this point,

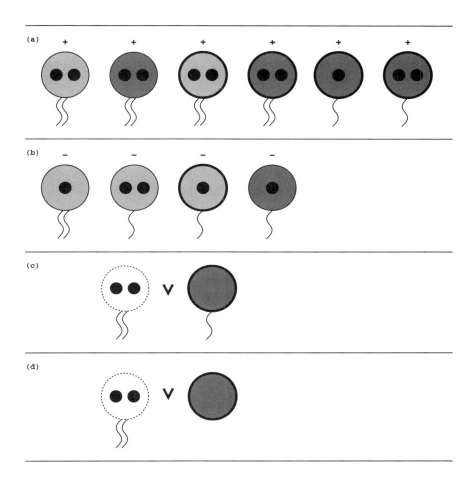

Figure 5-4. Behavior of the NSC algorithm on data from the four-attribute cell domain, given (a) six positive instances that fall into two separate decision regions and (b) four negative instances. When using HSG as a subroutine, NSC produces logical disjunction (c), whereas HGS leads to disjunction (d).

having completely separated the two classes with the disjunction shown in Figure 5-4 (d). Although the descriptions in (c) and (d) both handle the training set, they make different predictions about unseen instances, as would the DNF expressions that NSC would produce if instead it used subroutines for inducing threshold units.

Like the algorithms from previous chapters, the NSC method is designed to induce DNF expressions for a single class. However, one can use NSC as the building block for a more sophisticated scheme that

Table 5-2. The MSC algorithm: Nonincremental induction of multi-class decision lists using separate and conquer.

```
Inputs: CSET is a set of two or more class names.
        ISET is a set of classified training instances.
Output: A decision list composed of single-region descriptions.

Procedure MSC(CSET, ISET)

Let RULE-SET be the empty set.
For each CLASS in CSET,
    Let PSET be instances in ISET labeled with CLASS.
    Let NSET be instances in ISET not labeled with CLASS.
    Let DNF be NSC(PSET, NSET, { }).
    For each term D in DNF,
        Add the rule 'If D, then CLASS' to RULE-SET.
Eliminate possible conflicts among descriptions
    in RULE-SET that predict different classes.
Return RULE-SET.
```

---

handles domains involving more than two classes. Table 5-2 presents pseudocode for MSC, a separate-and-conquer algorithm designed for the task of inducing multi-class decision lists.

The input to MSC is a set of class names and a set of classified training instances. For each class, the method collects the set of training cases with that class name, as well as a set of those with other associated classes. The former become positive instances and the latter negative instances, which MSC passes on to the NSC subroutine. This returns a DNF expression, which MSC converts into an ordered set of decision rules that predict the class name. The algorithm repeats this entire process for each of the classes.

However, two problems arise with the generation of separate DNF expressions for each class. First, some regions of the instance space may remain uncovered by any expression, but one can easily correct this matter by adding a default rule. Second, some regions may be covered by more than one expression, leading to conflicts on certain test cases. Insistence on a pure DNF notation requires that one somehow ensure that the expressions for different classes have no overlap. In some cases, this can be accomplished by making some terms in the DNF expression more specific, but in other cases it requires that one decompose the expression into more terms. Since few induction methods go to such lengths, we will not consider them further.

A more elegant response simply places an ordering on the classes based on their relative frequencies. This approach transforms the DNF expression into a decision list, though one in which all terms for a given class occur together. Alternatively, one can place an ordering on each term separately, based on the number of training instances covered by each one. This scheme (combined with a default rule) produces a fully general decision list.

A related approach interleaves the term-finding process among the classes. First one uses a simple induction algorithm to find a logical or threshold expression for the most frequent class. The resulting description becomes the first term in the decision list, and one removes the instances that it covers. One then repeats the process for the class that occurs most often among the remaining instances, generating the second term in the decision list. This process continues until the remaining instances reside in a single class, which becomes the default. The interleaved decision list produced by this method may make different predictions than those generated by other techniques, but their relative performance on a given domain remains an open question.

5.3 Incremental induction using separate and conquer

In earlier chapters we argued that incremental hill climbing constitutes an important approach to learning, and we saw some uses of this idea in the induction of simple concepts. Table 5-3 presents pseudocode for ISC, an incremental separate-and-conquer version of the NSC algorithm that uses the same basic search control as the IHC scheme from Chapter 2. Like its relative, ISC retains a single hypothesis in memory, but in this case the concept description is not a simple conjunction but a disjunctive set of logical or threshold terms, which it initializes to a single term at the outset. The algorithm also retains up to the most recent k training instances for use in evaluating alternative hypotheses and, like IHC, it revises its hypothesis only when it makes an error in classification.

If ISC mistakenly classifies a positive instance as negative, it takes immediate steps to produce a more general hypothesis. There are two natural ways to accomplish this goal. The algorithm can modify a term

Table 5-3. The ISC algorithm: Incremental hill-climbing search for a DNF expression using separate and conquer.

```
Inputs: ISET is a set of classified training instances.
Output: A disjunction of single-region descriptions.
Parameters: K is the number of instances retained in memory.

Procedure ISC(ISET)

Let H be a set containing a maximally specific single-region
    description based on the first positive instance in ISET.
For each misclassified instance I in ISET,
    Let KSET be the previous K (or fewer) instances.
    If the training instance I is positive,
    Then for each term C in hypothesis H,
            Let S be the minimal revision of C that matches I.
            Generate a revision of H in which S replaces C.
        Let BEST be the best-scoring of these revisions.
        Let NEW be Add-Term(H, I).
    Else if the training instance I is negative,
        Then let BEST be a copy of H.
            For each term C in BEST that matches I,
                Let G be a minimal revision of C that
                    does not match the instance I.
                Replace C with G in the hypothesis BEST.
            Let NEW be Remove-Term(H, C).
    If Score(NEW, KSET) > Score(BEST, KSET),
    Then let BEST be NEW.
    If Score(BEST, KSET) > Score(H, KSET),
    Then let H be BEST.
Return the hypothesis H.

Note: Add-Term adds a new single-region description to the
    hypothesis H based on the positive instance I.
```

---

in its DNF expression just enough to let it match the training case. This can involve removing a test for Boolean, nominal, or numeric features, increasing the size of a rectangle, or changing the weights on a threshold unit. Because the disjunctive hypothesis may contain multiple terms, ISC must apply this generalization process to each one. At a minimum, this produces one modified description for each term.

Another alternative, not available in simpler tasks, involves adding an entirely new term, using the subroutine **Add-Term** in the table. For the resulting hypothesis to match the training instance, only one of the DNF terms must match it. The simplest way to ensure this is to add a term that matches only the positive instance itself. Another scheme would generate the most general clause that matches none of the stored negative instances; this would produce a more general hypothesis, but it also has a less incremental flavor than the other approach.

The ISC algorithm responds differently when it mistakenly classifies a negative instance as positive. Again, there are two obvious approaches to correcting the overly general hypothesis. One can modify each term matching the instance just enough to prevent the match. Depending on the representation for terms, this can involve adding a Boolean, nominal, or numeric feature, shrinking a rectangle, or modifying weights in a threshold unit. The second alternative is to eliminate an overly general term from the hypothesis entirely.

Once it has constructed the various generalizations (or specializations) of its current hypothesis, ISC uses an evaluation function to select one over the others. If the disjunctive description with a new (or removed) term has the best score, it replaces the existing description. Similarly, if one of the descriptions containing a generalized (or specialized) term appears best, it becomes the new hypothesis. For some evaluation functions, the existing description may score better than the proposed successors despite its error on the latest training instance, in which case it is retained unaltered.

However, the incremental nature of the ISC algorithm makes greater demands on the evaluation metric than does the NSC method. The latter has an implicit bias toward expressions with fewer terms, since its considers adding new terms only if the existing disjunction fails to cover some positive instances. ISC only considers adding a new term when it makes a similar error, but its incremental character can let this occur before the algorithm sufficiently masters other terms.

As a result, ISC must decide between modifying its existing terms in the disjunction and adding or deleting terms. In principle, the algorithm could simply create a disjunction composed of each positive instance it encounters, but this is not what we typically desire from an induction method. We need some way of introducing search bias into ISC's learning behavior. The most natural approach is to include some measure of an expression's simplicity in the evaluation function used to direct search. For instance, one might measure simplicity as $\frac{1}{t}$, where t is the number of terms in a disjunct. However, we must still combine this with some measure of the expression's accuracy a on the last k training cases, such as $a = (P_c + N_{\bar{c}})/k$, where P_c is the number of positive instances covered and $N_{\bar{c}}$ is the number of negatives not covered.

One obvious evaluation metric is simply to take the sum of these two quantities, $a + \frac{1}{t}$, which will range from 0 to 2. A more sophisticated scheme introduces a tradeoff parameter ω that specifies the relative importance of these two factors, giving the metric $(1-\omega) \cdot a + \omega \cdot \frac{1}{t}$, which ranges between 0 and 1. A more principled approach would use the notion of *minimum description length*, an information theoretic measure that reports the total amount of information needed to describe all the training data. Briefly, this encodes both the summary description and the incorrectly classified instances in terms of the bits it would take to communicate them, providing a uniform way to measure the tradeoff in complexity and coverage.

Figure 5-5 traces ISC's behavior on a training set from the four-attribute cell domain, assuming a logical representation for component terms, use of the evaluation function $a + \frac{1}{t}$ as described above, and retention of the last four training instances in memory. Training instances appear on the left in the order processed, and the resulting DNF expression appears on the right, along with the scores for the two components of the evaluation metric and their sum.

Item (a) shows the initial training case and the one-term disjunction that ISC produces in response: `one nucleus`, `two tails`, `thin wall`, and `light color`. Items (b), (d), and (f) illustrate positive instances that lead to more general terms in the DNF expression, whereas (c) shows a negative instance that produces a more specific term. Item (e) involves a positive instance that causes the algorithm to introduce a second term into the disjunctive hypothesis. The figure shows only the best-scoring DNF expression in each case, not the alternatives that ISC generates during its search.

As we noted in Chapter 2, induction methods that employ incremental hill climbing have low requirements for both memory and processing. They consider only one hypothesis, and they store and reexamine a constant number of training instances at each step during learning. As before, the price is a sensitivity to the order of training instances and,

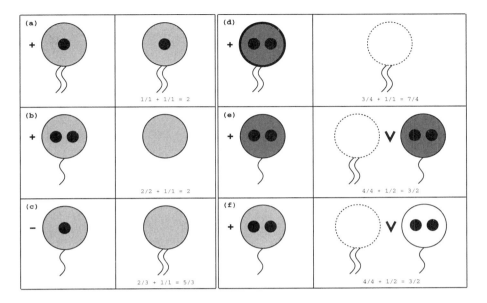

Figure 5-5. Behavioral trace of the ISC algorithm in the four-attribute cell domain, with (a) representing the first instance and DNF hypothesis and (f) indicating the sixth instance and hypothesis. Instances appear on the left, the resulting hypotheses appear on the right, and the score of the evaluation function occurs beneath the latter.

typically, a reliance on more training data to arrive at the target concept than for nonincremental heuristic methods. Moreover, algorithms like ISC are not guaranteed to converge, and in noisy domains they may change their hypothesis even if they have already reached the target concept. However, these characteristics also hold for another class of incremental learners, human beings. Both also tend to favor concept descriptions with small numbers of terms, although they can entertain more complex ones when necessary.

5.4 Induction of decision lists through exceptions

The separate-and-conquer method described above constructs a decision list in top-down order, adding the first term in the list in its first step, then the second, and so forth. But clearly one can operate in the opposite direction as well, and Table 5-4 summarizes NEX (nonincremental induction using exceptions), an algorithm that induces a decision list in this way. The resulting descriptions, sometimes called *counterfactuals*, have a very different flavor from those we saw in the previous section.

Table 5-4. The NEX algorithm: Nonincremental induction of decision lists using exceptions.

```
Inputs: CSET is a set of two or more class names.
        ISET is a set of preclassified instances.
Output: A decision list composed of single-region descriptions.

Procedure NEX(CSET, ISET)

Let C be the most common class in ISET.
Initialize DLIST with C as the default class.
NEX-AUX(CSET, ISET, DLIST).
Return the decision list DLIST.

Procedure NEX-AUX(CSET, ISET, DLIST)

Let MISSED be the instances in ISET that DLIST misclassifies.
If MISSED is the empty set,
Then return DLIST.
Else let C be the most common class in MISSED.
    Induce a maximally specific description D that
        covers the instances of class C in MISSED.
    If D differs from the first term in DLIST,
    Then add 'If D, then C' to the beginning of DLIST.
        NEX-AUX(CSET, MISSED, DLIST).
    Else select a random attribute A with range [A1, A2].
        Let M1 be instances from MISSED with A < (A1-A2)/2.
        Let M2 be instances from MISSED with A ≥ (A1-A2)/2.
        NEX-AUX(CSET, M1, DLIST).
        NEX-AUX(CSET, M2, DLIST).
```

The NEX algorithm initializes its decision list by creating a default rule based on the most frequent class. On each iteration, the method applies its current decision list to the remaining training cases, to determine ones it misclassifies. NEX selects the most common class in this set, calls on a subroutine to induce the most specific description that covers the misclassified members of that class, and adds the resulting rule to the *front* of the decision list. The algorithm continues in this manner until the decision list correctly classifies all of the training instances.

For some unusual training sets, the algorithm may find the same description twice in succession, which would lead to an infinite recursion if allowed to continue. In such cases, NEX arbitrarily selects an attribute, computes the midpoint of its range, and divides the current set of training instances into two subsets, one having values less than the midpoint and another having values above it. The algorithm continues with this strategy until it breaks out of the problem and can return to its normal mode of operation.

Let us examine NEX's behavior on the numeric height/girth domain when only two classes are present. Figure 5-6 (a) shows the results when the algorithm operates using a conjunctive subroutine with a rectangular bias, such as the specific-to-general HSG method, which ignores negative instances. Since class + is most common, NEX has selected it as the default class. As an exception to this, the method has generated a rectangular region that just surrounds all instances of class −. However, since this area includes some + members, NEX has produced an exception to the exception, shown by the inner rectangle that just contains these + cases. Figure 5-6 (b) shows the analogous but somewhat different decision boundaries that emerge when NEX uses spherical threshold units to describe each region.

Clearly, given the same training instances and the same method for creating component terms, the NEX and NSC algorithms can induce very different decision lists. For some target concepts, one method will produce more accurate descriptions than the other and vice versa. Although variants on the NSC algorithm are much more widely reported in the literature, the field has yet to identify the conditions under which each method is desirable.

Typically, the decision region for each term in a decision list is determined by the description of that term. However, the terms generated by the NEX algorithm have just enough extent to cover the instances on which they are based. For a small training set, it seems likely that an enclosed term underestimates the extent of the true region. An alternative classification scheme assigns an instance to an enclosed term whenever the instance is closer to the surface of that term's region than to the surface of the enclosing term. This approach has a competitive flavor, with the overall decision boundaries being determined by pairs of terms.

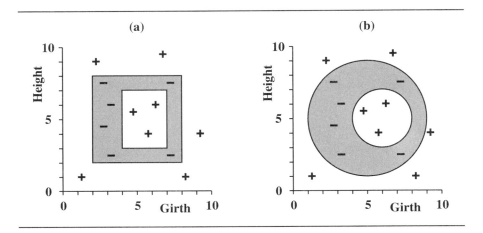

Figure 5-6. Decision boundaries produced by the NEX algorithm (a) when using the HSG routine to produce terms in the decision list and (b) when using a modified technique for spherical threshold units on the same data.

Incremental versions of the NEX algorithm are also possible. One variant, which we will call IEX (incremental induction using exceptions), stores no training cases. When the current decision list misclassifies an instance, this method checks the class associated with the term occurring just before the one that made the faulty prediction. If this has the desired class, then IEX generalizes the term just enough to let it cover the instance. If not, the algorithm adds a new term with the correct class, based on the training case, to the beginning of the decision list. The default rule uses the class of the initial training instance. Naturally, IEX loses information if it correctly classifies an instance for the wrong reason; storing the last k training cases reduces this effect, but any incremental hill-climbing scheme must pay some price of this sort.

5.5 Induction of competitive disjunctions

One can use an idea similar to those behind NSC and NEX to induce a disjunction of competitive descriptions. Table 5-5 presents an algorithm of this type, which we will call NCD (nonincremental induction of competitive disjunctions). This method invokes a simple competitive technique, like those we saw in Chapter 4, to create an initial set of descriptions. NCD then uses these summaries to classify the training set, noting which ones they assign correctly and which ones they misclassify.

Table 5-5. The NCD algorithm: Nonincremental induction of competitive disjunctions based on misclassified instances.

```
Inputs:   ISET is a set of classified training instances.
          CSET is a set of two or more class names.
Output:   A competitive disjunction (DISJUNCTS).

Procedure NCD(CSET, ISET)

For each class C in CSET,
    Average the instances of C to form a description.
    Add the resulting description to DISJUNCTS.
If DISJUNCTS correctly classifies all instances in ISET,
Then return DISJUNCTS.
Else let OLDSET be ISET.
    For each class C in CSET,
        For each class D other than C in CSET,
            Let MISSED be those instances of D in ISET that
                DISJUNCTS classifies as members of C.
            Add class D' (which predicts D) to CSET.
            For each instance I in MISSED,
                Relabel I as a member of class D'.
    If ISET equals OLDSET,
    Then return DISJUNCTS.
    Else return NCD(CSET, ISET).
```

At this point, the algorithm removes the problematic training cases from the original summaries and places them in separate 'pseudoclasses', which have a different internal name but predict the same class. NCD produces a new set of descriptions based on the new partition of the instances, again checks for misclassifications, and repeats the process until it arrives at a disjunction that correctly assigns all training cases to their classes or until it can make no further progress.[1]

The NCD algorithm relies on some method for competitive induction to construct its component terms. Let us examine the method's behavior when combined with a simple routine that averages training instances to form prototypes. Given the training data in Figure 5-7 (a),

---
1. This can occur when a small set of instances has such little effect on the decision boundaries that they remain misclassified by the new descriptions.

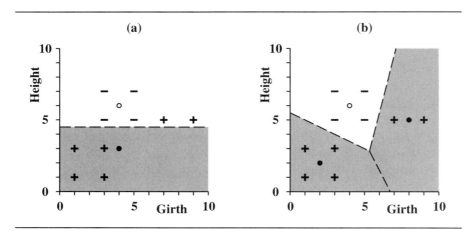

Figure 5-7. Prototypes (circles) and decision boundaries (dashed lines) produced (a) by a simple instance-averaging method and (b) by the NCD algorithm using an instance-averaging subroutine. The new decision regions cover the instances misclassified by the initial prototypes.

the algorithm computes a single prototype for each class, which gives the prototypes and decision boundaries shown. Because the resulting descriptions misclassify two of the class + instances, NCD assigns them to a new pseudoclass +', and averages them to produce a +' prototype. In addition, it removes these instances from the + average, giving the revised + prototype and decision boundaries in Figure 5-7 (b). This set of descriptions correctly classifies all training cases, so the process halts.

Clearly, one can combine the NCD algorithm with other competitive methods, such as a technique for constructing simple Bayesian classifiers, to obtain similar effects. But despite its elegance, one can easily design training sets that present difficulties for the NCD technique. Briefly, problems arise for the instance-averaging variant when the prototypes for two different classes lie near each other, and similar difficulties occur for the Bayesian version. This can produce misleading initial decision boundaries, which cause trouble on later iterations.

An alternative approach, which alleviates this problem, attempts to identify regions in another manner. One first groups instances into clusters that occur near each other (drawing on methods like those we discuss in Chapter 9), uses a competitive method like instance-averaging to generate descriptions for each class within a cluster, and then combines the results for each cluster into a single disjunction. The simplest

Table 5-6. The ICD algorithm: An incremental instance-averaging method.

```
Inputs: ISET is a set of classified training instances.
Output: A disjunction of single-region descriptions.

Procedure ICD(ISET).

Let the competitive description D be the empty set.
For each training instance I in ISET,
    Let C be the class name associated with I.
    If there are no terms that predict class C,
    Then add a new term to D based on I that predicts C.
    Else let T be the term in D that best matches I.
        If the term T predicts class C and if the
            match between I and T is good enough,
        Then update the term T by incorporating I.
        Else add a new term to D based on instance I.
Return the competitive description D.
```

---

method of this sort averages instances only if they are sufficiently close to each other, although this requires the user to specify a minimum distance. Because this scheme does not average instances from distant regions, it does not produce prototypes that fall in areas where no instances of the class occur.

One can embody similar ideas in incremental methods for inducing competitive disjunctions. Table 5-6 presents pseudocode for an algorithm of this sort, which we will call ICD (incremental induction of competitive disjunctions). Given a training instance, the technique finds the best matching of its disjunctive terms. If this description predicts the class of the instance, and if the match is good enough, then ICD averages the instance into the description for the term. Thus, it incorporates both the error-driven and clustering ideas we described above for nonincremental approaches. If these conditions are not met, then ICD adds a new term to its disjunction, basing the description on the attribute values and class of the training instance.

Figure 5-8 traces the behavior of an instance-averaging version of the ICD algorithm in the height/girth domain that involves two classes (+ and -). Here the test for a 'good enough' match means that the instance is no greater than a Euclidean distance of 5 from a prototype.

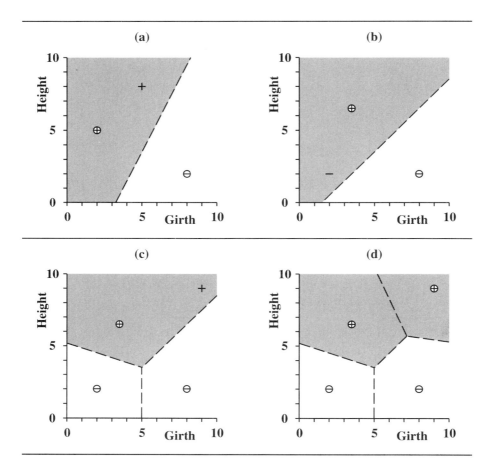

Figure 5-8. Behavioral trace of the ICD algorithm in response to three training instances, starting with one prototype for each class based on one instance each. The first instance is correctly classified (a), producing a revised prototype for +; the second instance is misclassified (b), giving a second − prototype; and the third instance is correctly labeled (c), but far enough away to produce a second + prototype (d).

After seeing one instance of class + and one of class −, the algorithm has one prototype for each class, as shown in Figure 5-8 (a). Given a new training instance of class + that falls within the decision region and the distance limit for this class's prototype, the learning method averages them, producing the revised prototype and decision boundaries in Figure 5-8 (b). Given a fourth instance, this time a member of the − class that falls within +'s decision region and thus is misclassified, the

ICD algorithm uses the instance to initialize a second prototype for class −, generating the revised decision boundaries in Figure 5-8 (c). Finally, given an instance that the + prototype correctly classifies but that is more than 5 units away, ICD creates a second prototype for this class.

Bayesian versions of the ICD algorithm are also possible, which incrementally produce disjunctions of probabilistic summaries, each with an associated base rate and a probability distribution for the attributes. If the class of training instance I agrees with the class predicted by the most probable description, and if this probability is high enough, then ICD incorporates the instance into the description, using it to update the base rate and probability distributions. However, if the instance differs sufficiently from all stored descriptions of the specified class, then the algorithm introduces a new description for that class based on the training instance.

One way to implement the 'good enough' parameter in a Bayesian framework is to use a *coupling probability*, c, which specifies the prior probability that any two instances in a class come from the same decision region. In this case, the prior probability that an instance belongs to a known region k is

$$\frac{cn_k}{(1 - c) + cn} \, ,$$

where n_k is the number of instances one has assigned to k and n is the total number of instances. On the other hand, the prior probability that an instance belongs to a new region is

$$\frac{(1 - c)}{(1 - c) + cn} \, .$$

Inserting these terms into Bayes' rule (see Chapter 4) lets one determine the overall probability that a new instance belongs to a known region and to a novel one. In the former case, the 'good enough' condition is met and ICD averages the instance into the most probable description; in the latter, the instance leads to a new term in the competitive disjunction.

One drawback of the ICD method is its sensitivity to the 'good enough match' parameter. If the user sets this parameter too low, then the algorithm will store more prototypes than necessary and learning will be slow. On the other hand, if the user sets the parameter too high, then effects of training order come into play. For example, suppose ICD first encounters two instances of class A that belong in different regions which are separated by a region of class B that it has not yet seen. In this case, the algorithm would decide that the two A instances belong to the same prototype and thus would average them. The resulting prototype could fall in the midst of the B area, and the technique would have no simple way to recover, other than eventually adding enough B prototypes near the offender to effectively guard against its retrieval, but this could take many training instances.

5.6 Instance-storing algorithms

Extending the clustering approach to its natural limit leads to the idea of storing a single prototype for each training instance. As with instance-averaging methods, one can use such knowledge to find the stored prototype that is closest to the new instance, retrieve its class, and predict this as the class of the new instance. This method, known as the *simple nearest neighbor* algorithm, produces the same results whether it operates incrementally, storing one case at a time, or nonincrementally, adding all training instances to memory en masse. Moreover, it makes no distinction between the class name and other attributes, and thus can be viewed as unsupervised.

Figure 5-9 (a) shows the decision boundaries generated by the simple nearest neighbor method on the training data from our previous example. Clearly, this approach partitions the instance space into more regions than the NCD algorithm or the clustering method. In fact, given n training instances, the simple instance-storing scheme can produce up to $n(n-1)/2$ decision boundaries. However, since some of these may be redundant, the effective number may be smaller; in the figure, only seven of the possible ten boundaries actually come into play. In any case, this approach produces different predictions on some test cases than does the instance-averaging approach.

As we noted in Section 5.1, allowing more than one description per class opens the door to combining evidence from them all when making a prediction. Given an instance-based representation, one can use a k *nearest neighbor* algorithm, which bases its decisions on a vote taken by the k nearest instances to the test case. Such voting techniques may reduce the sensitivity of instance-based techniques to irrelevant attributes, although one can also combine them with attribute-weighting methods like the one we saw in Chapter 4. Similar approaches are possible with

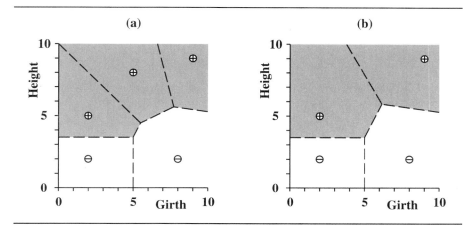

Figure 5-9. Decision boundaries produced for the training data from Figure 5-8 using (a) the simple nearest neighbor method, which stores all instances, and (b) the ECD algorithm, which stores instances only when it makes an error.

disjunctions of probabilistic summaries. These techniques produce a greater variety of decision boundaries than do simple nearest neighbor, with the details depending on the voting and matching schemes.

Simple instance-averaging and instance-storing methods fall at opposite ends of a spectrum, with the first storing one prototype per class and the latter storing every training case. The ICD algorithm provides a compromise position, storing more descriptions than the number of classes when necessary but fewer than the number of training cases. However, this solution approaches the problem from the instance-averaging perspective, and another compromise involves the selective storage of individual instances. Techniques of this sort are sometimes called *edited nearest neighbor* methods.

One such incremental method requires only two minor modifications of the ICD algorithm – removal of the averaging step and removal of the sufficient match condition. The resulting technique, which we will call ECD (error-driven induction of competitive disjunctions), learns only when it makes an error, storing a new prototype based on the misclassified training instance. In some cases, this scheme produces quite different behavior than selective instance averaging.[2]

---

2. No Bayesian versions of ECD exist, since some form of averaging is central to probabilistic methods.

For example, Figure 5-9 (b) shows the prototypes and decision boundaries that result when ECD is given the same training data, in the same order, as ICD in Figure 5-8. In this case, the second + prototype (in the upper right) has resulted not from exceeding a distance limit but from a classification error. Moreover, ECD has not modified the initial + prototype to incorporate the second + instance; since the former correctly classified the latter, it is simply forgotten. If the algorithm had observed the second + instance first, it would have stored this in memory and correctly classified both other + instances without needing to create another prototype. Thus, this method is also subject to order effects, although they seem relatively benign.

The ECD scheme tends to store prototypes that lie along the boundary of the target concept, as prediction errors tend to occur there. This observation has led to an interesting theoretical result for two-class domains. Let the target concept be a set of convex polygons having B as their total boundary length and A as their total area. Then the number of instances stored by the ECD method (and thus the number it must observe to reach a specified accuracy) is directly proportional to B/A. For a given area, more disjoint polygons mean greater boundary length, but the controlling factor is B/A, not the number of regions. In higher-dimensional spaces, this term generalizes to the ratio of the surface area and the volume, which grows rapidly with increasing dimensions.

5.7 Complementary beam search for disjunctive concepts

In Chapter 2 we encountered an interesting class of methods – genetic algorithms – that embodied a form of search that was quite distinct from others we considered. The basic method carried out a beam search that relied on genetic operators like mutation and crossover, rather than ones based on a generality ordering. Although we presented genetic algorithms initially as a technique for inducing logical conjunctions, they require only minor alterations to handle disjunctive domains, and they have interesting characteristics in this context as well.

5.7.1 Competitive and complementary descriptions

In Chapter 2 we saw that GA maintains a population of rules, each with an associated score on some evaluation metric. We viewed these rules as competitors, with each vying for precedence during classification, and this made excellent sense when the target concept was conjunctive in nature. However, in disjunctive domains one can view the same population as a decision list, with scores indicating rules' position in the ordering. In this framework, different rules for the same class handle different (possibly disjoint) regions of the instance space. In terms of the evolutionary metaphor, they occupy different *niches* in the environment.

The only difficulty lies in the genetic algorithm itself, which tends to converge on a population that contains many copies of a single high-scoring description. For a disjunctive domain, we would like a modified method that converges toward a number of distinct descriptions or 'species', one for each region or 'niche' in the instance space. If the best description for one region has a higher score than that for another region, we would like the number of candidates in the population to vary in direct proportion to that score.

One way to obtain this effect is to use a *sharing function* in determining the probability of parenthood. The basic idea is that similar descriptions must share 'resources' in the environment, thus giving a bias toward diversity in the population. For example, suppose we let the similarity $B(x_i, x_j)$ between two descriptions x_i and x_j be the number of bits they share, and let $S(x_i)$ be the unmodified score for x_i. Then one can formulate a modified score as

$$S'(x_i) = \frac{S(x_i)}{\sum_{j=1}^{k} B(x_i, x_j)} \quad ,$$

where k is the number of features in each description. The expression produces lower scores for descriptions that are similar to many others, but has little effect on descriptions that are nearly unique. This scheme encourages niche formation, with the number of competitors within each niche gradually becoming proportional to the unmodified scores.

5.7.2 An example of GA inducing a decision list

To clarify the idea of niche formation, reconsider the training data from Figure 5-4, which we examined earlier in the context of the NSC method. Let us assume that the evaluation metric used to produce the unmodified score is $(P_c + N_{\bar{c}})/(P + N)$, which ranges from 0 to 1, and a `Beam-Size` or 'population size' of 8. Given an initial population of randomly generated logical conjunctions, and using the above sharing scheme to determine

Table 5-7. An eight-rule population that might be generated by the GA algorithm after a number of generations, given the training data in Figure 5-4, and fitness scores based on a simple accuracy measure and on a sharing function.

Vector	Logical conjunction	Initial	Shared
1 1 * *	two nuclei ∧ two tails	0.8	0.050
1 1 * *	two nuclei ∧ two tails	0.8	0.050
1 1 * *	two nuclei ∧ two tails	0.8	0.050
1 1 * *	two nuclei ∧ two tails	0.8	0.050
* * 1 1	thick wall ∧ dark color	0.7	0.050
* * 1 1	thick wall ∧ dark color	0.7	0.050
* 0 1 1	one tail ∧ thick wall ∧ dark color	0.6	0.043
* 0 1 1	one tail ∧ thick wall ∧ dark color	0.6	0.043

the probability of parenthood, the GA algorithm could, after sufficient iterations, produce a population like the one shown in Table 5-7.

There are a number of aspects of the table worth noting. First, only three descriptions exist in the population, one occurring four times and the others appearing twice each. Second, the unmodified score for the first description is 0.8, higher than the 0.7 and 0.6 results for the other two terms. This is because it covers four of the positive instances, whereas the others cover only three and two, respectively.

However, the modified score based on sharing is $\frac{0.8}{4 \times 4} = 0.05$ for the first conjunction, since it shares four bits with four members of the population (including itself) and none with the others. Similarly, the modified score for the second and third conjunctions is $\frac{0.7}{2 \times 4 + 2 \times 3} = 0.05$, since they share four bits with two descriptions, three with two others, and zero with the remaining five. The analogous computation for the third description is $\frac{0.6}{2 \times 4 + 2 \times 3} = 0.043$, based on the same demoninator as for the second.

The sharing scheme reduces the score for the first description because there are many similar candidates in competition. The same effect occurs for the second and third description, which compete with each other and with copies of themselves. However, in their case the reduction is less because there are fewer descriptions in the same niche. In this light, one can view the first description as being complementary to the other two, since it competes with them for 'resources' in only minor ways.

The long-term result of this 'evolutionary pressure' is a set of descriptions that appear in the population with a frequency proportional to their unmodified scores. In this case, the first description occurs $\frac{4}{8}$ of the time, whereas the other two, taken together, appear with the same probability. Each class of description has filled its 'niche' to capacity, producing a decision list that covers the positive instances but not the negatives.

5.7.3 Variations on complementary beam search

The above scenario presents only one use of genetic algorithms in the induction of logical disjunctions. One could use an alternative evaluation function to measure fitness (e.g., that takes simplicity into account), one could use a different similarity metric, and one could use a different population size. Nor are genetic methods necessarily limited to logical descriptions; the same basic scheme should work with simple threshold concepts or even competitive descriptions as members of the population. The extension to multi-class settings is straightforward; one simply includes additional features in the description language to represent the class attribute.

We should also note that the idea of complementary beam search is not limited to genetic algorithms. For example, one can use the same control regimen with induction operators that take advantage of the generality ordering on logical conjunctions. Nonincremental versions of this strategy always move from general to specific or vice versa, evaluating terms over the entire training set rather than over subsets, as in the NSC and NEX techniques. Incremental variants retain a set of weighted terms or rules in memory and employ bidirectional operators like those in ISC, creating more general candidates when they fail to match positive instances and producing more specific ones when they match incorrectly. Candidates that fare poorly are either dropped from memory or eventually transformed into useful descriptions, which complement one another by covering different decision regions, rather than competing to cover the same instances.

Naturally, both this approach and the genetic scheme are limited by the total number of descriptions retained in memory, so that if the target concept involves more decision regions than memory can hold, the learning algorithm will only find a partially correct description, even in a noise-free environment. Thus, the user must make some assumption about the maximum number of regions in the domain before setting out, although this should not pose a problem for target concepts of moderate complexity.

5.8 Summary of the chapter

In this chapter we examined the induction of disjunctive descriptions. We found that such disjunctions organize their terms – simple logical, threshold, or competitive descriptions – into combinations that generate multiple decision regions; thus, they can represent a much wider range of concepts than the formalisms we encountered in previous chapters. However, the resulting space of disjunctive descriptions is accordingly more complex and requires new algorithms to search it, most of which use methods for inducing single-region logical, threshold, or competitive concepts as subroutines.

We saw that algorithms for disjunctive induction differ mainly in the conditions under which they invoke the simpler methods, and in these conditions' effect on the resulting organization of memory. For example, the nonincremental NSC uses a separate-and-conquer technique, finding a simple description D that covers some positive instances, adding D to its disjunctive hypothesis, removing the covered cases from consideration, and repeating the process until it has covered all positive instances. The NEX method uses a similar control structure, but it is driven by exceptions rather than uncovered instances, and adds new terms to the front of its decision list rather than to the end.

Both schemes can operate with either logical or threshold terms, but competitive representations require slightly different methods. Like NSC and NEX, the NCD algorithm is driven by classification errors and generates only enough decision regions to eliminate them, but it produces a competitive disjunction rather than an ordered decision list. In contrast, the nearest neighbor technique simply stores all training cases, creating one decision region for each observed instance.

Incremental versions exist for most of these methods. For example, ISC employs a strategy similar to NSC but invokes bidirectional operators that are driven by individual training cases. Similar relations hold between the NEX and NCD algorithms and their incremental variants, which can be sensitive to the order of training instances. The latter does not hold for the nearest neighbor scheme, which produces the same results when run incrementally or nonincrementally.

The above techniques carry out greedy or hill-climbing search through the space of disjunctive descriptions. Thus, their computational cost is tractable, provided this also holds for the routines they call to construct individual terms in the disjunction. Exhaustive search schemes might produce better results, but only at an exponential cost. Practical methods of the sort we have described exchange guarantees of optimality for efficiency during the learning process.

Most disjunctive methods place no restriction on the number of terms in each disjunction.[3] The NSC, NEX, and NCD algorithms introduce new terms only when they find training instances that are misclassified by existing ones, as do their incremental counterparts. Two exceptions to the above rule are the simple instance-storing algorithm, which stores exactly as many terms as training instances, and the genetic algorithm GA, which retains as many terms as allowed by its population size (although this specifies the maximum and not the effective number, since a term may occur multiple times).

Many variations exist on disjunctive induction, but the methods we have examined in this chapter constitute the main approaches found in the literature. Despite their simplicity, algorithms of this sort have found wide use and they have produced encouraging results in experimental studies of both natural and artificial induction tasks.

Exercises

1. Interchange the labels on positive and negative instances in Figure 5-2, then show the decision regions generated by the NSC algorithm (Section 5.2) when using the HSG subroutine on each pass. Do the same for variants of NSC that use HGS and a technique for learning spherical units, as in Figure 5-3.

2. Interchange the labels on positive and negative instances in Figure 5-4, then show the logical disjunction (using the cell notation) that NSC produces with the HGS subroutine to find individual rules. Show the same result when using the HSG algorithm instead.

---

3. Some theoretical results focus on k-DNF expressions, where each term contains at most k Boolean features. However, there are fewer results on k-term DNF expressions, in which each disjunction contains at most k terms.

3. Trace the hypotheses generated by the ISC algorithm (Section 5.3) on the training cases in Figure 5-4. Assume that the method initially sees the first two positive instances, followed by the first negative case, after which instances of the two classes alternate. Use the same evaluation metric $(a + \frac{1}{t})$ as in the text.

4. Draw the decision regions generated by the NEX algorithm (Section 5.4) given the training cases in Figure 5-2, using HSG as a subroutine. Do the same using a technique for inducing spherical units. In both cases, treat + as the majority (default) class. Repeat the process with both subroutines using – as the majority class.

5. Remove the five outermost positive cases from Figure 5-6, leaving three positive instances and six negatives. Show the decision regions produced by a simple instance-averaging method and by a version of the NCD algorithm (Section 5.5) that invokes instance-averaging as a subroutine.

6. Assume that the positive instance in Figure 5-8 (a) is negative, but that the other cases retain the same labels. Trace the decision boundaries produced by the ICD algorithm after it has processed each of these training cases.

7. Show the decision regions produced by simple nearest neighbor and by the ECD algorithm (Section 5.6) on the data from Exercise 6.

8. Compute the fitness scores for the rules in Table 5-7 on the modified data from Exercise 2, using both the initial and sharing functions from Section 5.7. Select two of the highest-scoring rules on the latter metric and show two offspring that could result from a single application of the crossover operator (Chapter 2).

Historical and bibliographical remarks

Most work on the induction of DNF descriptions and decision lists has occurred within the framework of logical induction and has built on variants of the HSG and HGS algorithms (Chapter 2). Rivest (1987) defines the notion of decision lists and presents a formal analysis of their induction. Michalski and Chilausky's (1980) AQ system was one of the earliest examples of the nonincremental separate-and-conquer (NSC and MSC) methods. Clark and Niblett's (1989) CN2 and Michalski, Mozetic, Hong, and Lavrac's (1986) AQ15 constitute more recent instances of this approach, and Quinlan's (1990) FOIL and Muggleton and Feng's (1992) GOLEM extend the same scheme to relational domains.

A few researchers have adapted the separate-and-conquer technique to nonlogical frameworks, as in Marchand and Golea's (1993) construction of decision lists composed of linear threshold terms rather than conjunctive ones.

Papers on inducing decision lists through exceptions have been less frequent than those on separate-and-conquer methods, but Vere (1980) and Helmbold, Sloan, and Warmuth (1990) describe systems that use variants of the NEX algorithm. Work on incremental hill-climbing methods for decision-list induction have been even less common, although Iba et al.'s (1988) HILLARY incorporates a strategy identical to the ISC algorithm. Bradshaw (1987), Anderson and Matessa (1992), and a few others provide examples of the ICD approach to learning competitive disjunctions, but nonincremental variants like NCD are difficult to find in the literature.

Research on instance-storing methods like nearest neighbor has a long history in pattern recognition. Nilsson (1965) describes some early work along these lines, Dasarathy (1990) contains a broad sample of work from this perspective, and Cover and Hart (1967) report theoretical results about the asymptotic accuracy of such techniques. This approach to induction, first proposed by Fix and Hodges (1951), gained attention within machine learning only in the late 1980s, when Kibler and Aha (1987), Moore (1990), and others introduced them to the literature. More recent work along these lines has been reported by Aha, Kibler, and Albert (1991), Cardie (1993), and Moore and Lee (1994). Proceedings of annual workshops on case-based reasoning contain numerous papers on nearest neighbor and related techniques. Our brief treatment reflects not the large number of published papers on this topic, but rather the simple nature of most methods.

There also exists a large literature on genetic algorithms and their use in machine learning. Holland (1986) introduces one broad class of such methods, *classifier systems*, that use the complementary beam search approach in Section 5.7, while Booker, Goldberg, and Holland (1989) review early work in this area. Wilson (1987) and Booker (1988) present examples of the genetic induction of decision lists, and many more appear in proceedings of meetings on genetic algorithms published annually since 1985. Some work in adaptive production systems (Anderson & Kline, 1979; Langley, 1987) takes a similar approach but uses specialization or generalization operators rather than crossover or mutation.

CHAPTER 6

Revision and Extension of Inference Networks

In Chapter 5, we considered methods for learning disjunctions of logical, threshold, and competitive concept descriptions, which considerably expanded the representational power of these formalisms. In particular, the resulting decision lists were able to represent concepts that involve complex decision boundaries among different classes. However, the concept descriptions we examined there remained simple in structure, and they had few implications for the *organization* of conceptual knowledge in memory.

The current chapter focuses on learning in *inference networks*, a widely used organizational framework that occurs throughout artificial intelligence.[1] Most work on this topic has emphasized the role of background knowledge in learning, and has cast induction as a problem of refining or extending an existing inference network.

We will examine three variations of this idea – extending an incomplete network, specializing a complete network, and revising an incorrect network. Finally, we will examine approaches to the more challenging problem of constructing entire inference networks from training data in the absence of background knowledge. However, we should first examine some more basic issues raised by this framework.

---

1. The literature often refers to such inference networks as *domain theories*. However, one can store domain knowledge in other organizational frameworks, so we will usually rely on the more specific term.

Table 6-1. A simple inference network, stated as propositional Horn clauses, for recognizing instances of the disease `lethargia` from characteristics of cells. Note the use of the two nonterminal symbols `simploid` and `neoplasm`.

```
lethargia  :- simploid, neoplasm.
simploid   :- one-tail, thin-wall.
simploid   :- two-tails.
neoplasm   :- one-nucleus, thick-wall.
neoplasm   :- two-nuclei.
```

6.1 General issues surrounding inference networks

As we suggested above, an inference network provides an organization for a set of concept descriptions, and this organization has implications for representational ability, performance, and learning. In this section we consider some basic issues that arise in this framework, focusing first on the structure of inference networks, then on their use, and finally on their acquisition.

6.1.1 The structure of inference networks

An inference network consists of nodes and directional links. Each node denotes either a primitive feature or some defined concept, and each link connects a lower-term feature or concept to some higher-order concept. Taken together, the set of nodes A with links pointing to concept C can be viewed as the antecedents of a 'rule', and C can be viewed as the rule's consequent. In general, the presence of nodes in A constitute evidence for the presence of C, although the nature of evidence combination varies widely. The notion of directional links is central to inference networks, and contrasts with the organizational framework we will consider in Chapter 7. Although one can view the nodes in an inference network as partially ordered, this ordering does *not* correspond to the one involving the extension of concepts discussed in previous chapters.

Table 6-1 presents a simple inference network composed of logical concepts for the disease `lethargia`. We have stated this network as a set of Horn clauses, but Figure 6-1 (a) shows an alternative depiction in terms of nodes and links. In this representation, each AND node (with an arc connecting incoming links) corresponds to the antecedent of a

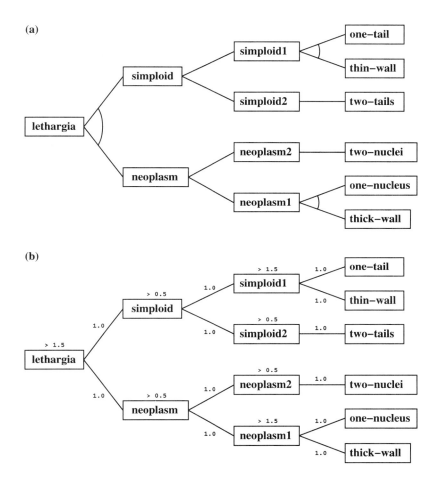

Figure 6-1. Two inference networks for the concept `lethargia` with the same extensional definition. Network (a), which maps directly onto the rules in Table 6-1, contains logical units that alternate between AND nodes (with arcs) and OR nodes. Network (b) contains threshold units with link weights and thresholds that mimic the logical network, although other numbers produce different behavior. The figure only shows links with nonzero weights.

rule in the table, whereas each OR node (with no arc on incoming links) corresponds to the head of one or more rules. The only exception is the AND node for `lethargia`, which occurs as the head of only one rule.

In general, a logical inference network alternates between AND nodes and OR nodes. In this example, the network defines a `lethargia` cell as the conjunction of a `simploid` cell and a `neoplasm` cell. It defines the concept `simploid` in turn as either a cell that has `one-tail` and a `thin-wall` or as one that has `two-tails`. Similarly, the network defines `neoplasm` as occurring in cells that either have `one-nucleus` and a `thick-wall` or that have `two-nuclei`.[2]

Figure 6-1 (b) shows a network of threshold units, often called a *multilayer neural network*, with the same structure as the logical one. Here each link has an associated weight, and each non-input node has an associated threshold. As we saw in Chapter 3, the extension of such a concept definition is a function of the weighted sum of its antecedent links and its threshold. One can use these numbers to mimic the behavior of OR nodes and AND nodes, as shown in the figure, but threshold units are not limited to such semantics. Also, in some cases they allow a simpler network structure. In this example, we could remove the nodes `simploid1`, `simploid2`, `neoplasm1`, and `neoplasm2`, connecting `thin-wall` and `two-tails` directly to `simploid`, and linking `thick-wall` and `two-nuclei` directly to `neoplasm`. The appropriate weights and thresholds give the same extension as the network shown.

One can achieve similar effects with networks of *m*-of-*n* concepts, although they provide less flexibility than arbitrary threshold units. Networks of spherical units can also produce useful decision boundaries, especially when numeric attributes are involved. Mixtures of different types of threshold units are also possible. One combination, with spherical units at the internal layer and linear units at the output level, is commonly known as a *radial basis function*. However, this organizational scheme is typically used not for classification but for numeric prediction, which we discuss in Chapter 8.

Another instantiation of inference networks involves probabilistic concept descriptions. This approach, often referred to as *Bayesian networks*, specifies one node for each attribute and one link for each dependency between one attribute and another. Stored with each node is a table of conditional probabilities that, for each value V of the dependent attribute and for each combination of values C for its parent attributes, specifies the probability that V will occur given C. For a Boolean feature X with two parents Y and Z, this means storing entries

---

2. Given only the possibility of one or two nuclei, we could remove the `one-nucleus` condition from the first `neoplasm` rule; similarly, we might remove the `one-tail` literal from the first `simploid` conjunction. However, their presence serves a function in later examples, and they would be necessary if other values were possible for the `tail` and `nucleus` attributes.

Table 6-2. A partial set of conditional probabilities for a probabilistic inference network with the same structure as in Figure 6-1, and with causal dependencies going from right to left. Each value corresponds to a prior probability or to an entry in a conditional probability table.

```
P(one-tail)   = 0.5,  P(simploid1 | one-tail) = 0
P(thick-wall) = 0.5,  P(simploid1 | one-tail) = 1
P(simploid1 | one-tail, thick-wall) = 0
P(simploid1 | one-tail, thick-wall) = 0
P(simploid1 | one-tail, thick-wall) = 1
P(simploid1 | one-tail, thick-wall) = 0
P(simploid  | simploid1, simploid2) = 1
P(simploid  | simploid1, simploid2) = 1
P(simploid  | simploid1, simploid2) = 1
P(simploid  | simploid1, simploid2) = 0
P(lethargia | simploid, neoplasm)   = 1
P(lethargia | simploid, neoplasm)   = 0
P(lethargia | simploid, neoplasm)   = 0
P(lethargia | simploid, neoplasm)   = 0
```

for $P(X|Y, Z)$, $P(X|\bar{Y}, Z)$, $P(X|Y, \bar{Z})$, and $P(X|\bar{Y}, \bar{Z})$, with analogous entries for $\bar{X}$ (though these are redundant for Boolean features).

Table 6-2 shows a partial set of table entries for a Bayesian network that is equivalent to our logical inference network, assuming the structure in Figure 6-1 (a) and assuming that causal dependencies point from right to left. In this example, all probabilities are either 1 or 0 to mimic AND nodes and OR nodes. However, probabilistic inference networks are like threshold networks in that they support a continuum of relations between the AND/OR extremes, which they represent with conditional probabilities between 1 and 0.

Although our examples have assumed Boolean features, one can extend the three formalisms to handle other types of domains. We will see an example involving numeric attributes in a logical network in Section 6.2, and the threshold and probabilistic schemes handle such tasks as well. As normally formulated, Horn clauses support predicates with arguments, and much of the recent work on learning with logical networks has dealt with such formalisms. However, we delay treatment of this topic until Chapter 8 and focus on Boolean tasks in this chapter, both for the sake of simplicity and because there has been little work on threshold and probabilistic methods for relational domains.

6.1.2 The use of inference networks

The term 'inference network' suggests the use of such knowledge structures – to make inferences about some unobserved concepts. Typically, the performance system is presented with features or literals that describe some situation in the world, and the inference network must conclude whether this constitutes an instance of some concept specified in the network. In other words, it must chain through the network, concluding consequents from antecedents, until inferring (or failing to infer) the concept in question. This is simply another form of the classification task we have encountered in previous chapters.

The details of the inference process can vary considerably. For example, the performance component associated with many logical inference networks (such as PROLOG) chains backward from the concept C it is attempting to infer. If the algorithm can construct an AND tree that proves the observed literals satisfy C's definition, it concludes that C is present; otherwise it infers by default that C is absent.[3] However, a forward-chaining control structure is also possible, with rules matching against terms that have been observed or inferred, which lead to new inferences that let other rules match. Provided one is concerned only with accuracy and not efficiency, the inference mechanism does not matter as long as it considers all possible paths before concluding it has failed.

The performance techniques used for threshold inference networks typically apply in the forward direction, computing a weighted sum of the evidence from each node at level N to determine the 'activation' of each node at level $N+1$. Some methods simply infer an activation of 1 if the sum S exceeds the threshold θ and 0 (or in some versions -1) if it does not. Other approaches employ a sigmoid function to compute the consequent activation from the antecedent activations, giving a smooth transition rather than a step function. One commonly used scheme calculates the weighted sum $S = \sum_k w_k x_k$ of the inputs, then uses the logistic function

$$\frac{1}{1 + e^{-(S-\theta)}}$$

to determine the activation of the consequent. In this approach, nodes in the network receive an activation anywhere from 0 to 1, but the overall

---

3. When applied to Horn clauses that include predicates with multiple variables, this approach can accomplish much more than classify instances. We will see examples of this power in Chapters 10 and 11.

classification task still requires an all-or-none decision. Typically, such methods conclude that the instance satisfies a concept C if the activation of C is 0.5 or greater.

One can use a very similar method for some probabilistic inference networks, provided the dependency links point from the concept C being inferred toward the observable terms. Starting from the observable terms O, one uses Bayes' rule to compute the probabilities of nodes N that only have links directly from O nodes. One then uses the results to compute the probabilities of nodes that only have dependency links directly from nodes in $O \cup N$, and so on, until reaching the target node C. However, in some domains it is reasonable to assume that the observed features cause the unobserved concept C. In this case, one can compute the probability of C from the observed terms O using more sophisticated methods, which we do not have the space to discuss here. Because probabilistic networks produce a probability for a concept rather than a decision, the same issue arises as with threshold networks. One natural response is to conclude that an instance I satisfies concept C if $P(C|I) > 0.5 > P(\bar{C}|I)$.

Earlier we emphasized the directional nature of inference networks, but the above use of probabilistic structures shows that their use is not limited to propagating beliefs in the direction of the links. A similar flexibility exists with logical networks, which one can use to make default assumptions that, if present, would let one explain the presence of some observed literal. This approach, which is often termed *abduction*, considerably extends the uses of inference networks. Nevertheless, in this chapter we will limit our attention to simpler uses of this framework.

6.1.3 The task of revising inference networks

Now that we have clarified the organization and use of inference networks, we can specify the learning task associated with them:

- *Given*: A set of training instances and their associated classes;
- *Given* (optional): An initial inference network that incorporates some knowledge about the domain;
- *Find*: An inference network that, to the extent possible, makes accurate predictions about novel test instances.

As we mentioned earlier, much of the work on inference networks has examined the role of background knowledge. In this view, learning involves adding or removing nodes or links to an existing network or modifying the weights on existing nodes or links. However, such background knowledge is not essential, and one can also construct an entire inference network entirely from the training data, although such methods can usually be characterized as starting with a degenerate network.

In either case, one can view learning as carrying out search through the space of inference networks. The operators used in this search can include actions for adding or removing nodes, adding or removing links, and altering the weights on links, and we will see examples of each in the sections that follow. Because they include nonterminal symbols, the space of inference networks (even logical ones, which include no weights) is much larger than the space of simple concept descriptions we considered in previous chapters. However, much of the work in this area assumes that the background knowledge is nearly correct and complete, so that relatively few steps are required to reach the target network.

Even when this assumption holds, learning still requires some search through the space of inference networks. Most work on the topic relies on a greedy or gradient-descent control structure that uses the entire training set to evaluate alternative changes to the network, although some incremental methods exist. Many approaches employ operators that can make the network either more specific or more general, but this is separate from whether they include operators for adding and removing structure from the network. The latter combination is associated primarily with algorithms for network revision, whereas methods for extending and constructing networks typically only add structure.

6.2 Extending an incomplete inference network

Perhaps the simplest approach to learning in the current framework is to extend an inference network that includes correct knowledge but remains *incomplete*. In particular, work in this framework typically assumes the network lacks the top-level links that connect the rest of the organization to the target concept. Thus, learning involves the induction of one or more 'rules' that specify the connections necessary for accurate classification.

Table 6-3. Disjunctive rules needed to accurately classify instances of `lethargia` without the nonterminal symbols `simploid` and `neoplasm` from Table 6-1.

```
lethargia :- one-tail, thin-wall, two-nuclei.
lethargia :- two-tails, one-nucleus, thick-wall.
lethargia :- two-tails, two-nuclei.
```

6.2.1 Extending a logical network

Most work on extending inference networks emphasizes the role of background knowledge, even when incomplete, in simplifying the induction task. In previous chapters we saw that the easiest induction tasks involve limited languages for representing concepts, such as logical conjunctions, linear threshold units, and simple probabilistic summaries. Unfortunately, many learning problems require more sophisticated representations and more complex induction algorithms.

The use of background knowledge stated as inference networks can alter this situation. For instance, reconsider the Horn clauses in Table 6-1, which characterize the concept `lethargia`. We can rewrite this description as the three rules in Table 6-3, which directly relate the top-level concept to observable features.[4] Clearly, one needs a reasonably powerful induction algorithm, such as NSC or NEX from Chapter 5, to acquire this description. A technique like HGS or HSG from Chapter 2 cannot handle disjunctive target concepts of this sort.

However, suppose we provide the learning system with background knowledge in the form of an incomplete inference network, in this case the last four rules in Table 6-1. Given training instances of the concept `lethargia`, the system can apply these rules to each case, generating an augmented instance description that may include the nonterminal symbols `simploid` and `neoplasm`. In this example, both of these higher-level features would be present in all positive instances of `lethargia`, but their combination would be absent in all negative instances. Thus, an algorithm like HGS or HSG could easily acquire the conjunctive description `lethargia :- simploid, neoplasm`. The presence of an ap-

---

4. We have omitted the fourth possible rule, `lethargia :- one-tail, thin-wall, one-nucleus, thick-wall`, because it contains two contradictory literals.

Table 6-4. A partial inference network, defining the intermediate concepts
`odd-girth` and `odd-height`, which can be used as background knowledge to
aid induction of the target concept `odd-size`.

```
odd-girth  :- girth(G), 2 < G, G < 4.
odd-girth  :- girth(G), 6 < G, G < 8.
odd-height :- height(H), 2 < H, H < 4.
odd-height :- height(H), 6 < H, H < 8.
```

---

propriate partial network has transformed a disjunctive induction task
into a simpler conjunctive one.

This approach provides some additional benefits as well. Let us consider another example involving the height/girth domain. Table 6-4
presents a partial inference network that recognizes examples of two intermediate concepts. The first two inference rules state that a person
has **odd-girth** if her **girth** falls either between 2 and 4 or between 6
and 8. (We assume that no person ever has **girth** less than 2 or more
than 8.) The last two rules classify a person as having **odd-height** if her
height has the same ranges. Figure 6-2 shows the extensions of these
two concepts, along with training instances for the higher-level concept
odd-size, which we will define as the conjunction of **odd-girth** and
odd-height. Thus, the extension of **odd-size** corresponds to the area
within the four shaded squares that occur at the intersections of the two
intermediate concepts.

Suppose a logical induction algorithm observes the positive and negative training instances the figure shows in black. As before, one can
augment the instance descriptions to include the features **odd-girth**
and **odd-height** when their definitions are satisfied. Again, a simple
conjunction of these two features suffices to discriminate the positive
training cases (black circles) from the negative ones (black squares).
Now suppose we present the performance component with the positive
test cases shown in white. These correspond to regions of the extensional definition that the induction algorithm has never seen, yet the
acquired concept correctly classifies them as positive instances of the
odd-size concept. The presence of a partial inference network can increase accuracy on unseen parts of the instance space, thus improving

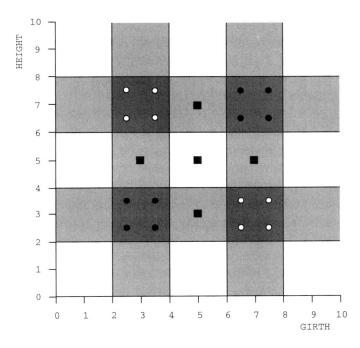

Figure 6-2. The presence of a partial inference network can increase learning rate. The two horizontal rectangles depict the extension of the **odd-height** concept defined in Table 6-4, the two vertical ones show the extension of **odd-girth**, and the four rectangles at their intersections give the extension of the target concept, **odd-size**. Small rectangles correspond to negative training cases and circles to positive ones. Training on the black instances, combined with the inference rules in Table 6-4, lets a simple conjunctive method induce a description that correctly classifies the unseen white instances.

the learning rate. This holds even for domains in which the partial network fails to eliminate the need for disjoint decision regions, and which thus require more powerful induction methods.

The above discussion assumes that the background knowledge is relevant to the current target concept. Naturally, inappropriate background knowledge will simply introduce irrelevant features, which will decrease the learning rate for any induction algorithm. Similar comments about incorrect or irrelevant structures hold for each of the methods we consider in this chapter, but we will typically assume that such structures are generally relevant and correct.

6.2.2 Extending a network of threshold units

Although the above approach is often associated with algorithms for inducing logical descriptions, it is certainly not limited to them. The same basic techniques apply equally well to other concept representations and to the methods for acquiring them. For example, in Chapter 3 we saw that methods for inducing linear threshold concepts can only master domains in which the classes are linearly separable. However, just as an incomplete set of Horn clauses can increase the power of conjunctive learning methods, so a partial network of threshold units can extend the range of threshold learning algorithms.

Let us return to the `lethargia` example. Figure 6-3 (c) shows the extension of this concept in dimensions corresponding to the three relevant attributes, which we treat here as the Booleans `one-tail`, `one-nucleus`, and `thick-wall`. One cannot separate the positive instances of this concept from the negatives by a single hyperplane, making the perceptron and LMS algorithms insufficient to induce it. But Figure 6-3 (a) and (b) show the extensions of the concepts `simploid` and `neoplasm`, which one *can* represent with single threshold units. Moreover, Figure 6-3 (d) gives the extension of `lethargia` in the instance space defined by the higher-level features `simploid` and `neoplasm`. In this context, the positive and negative instances of the concept are linearly separable.

The implication is that, given linear threshold units that correctly classify instances of `simploid` and `neoplasm`, one can use simple methods like the PCP and LMS algorithms to induce the `lethargia` concept. For instance, given background knowledge of the form

If $-1.0 \cdot$ `one-tail` $+ -1.0 \cdot$ `thin-wall` > 0.5, then `simploid`

If $-1.0 \cdot$ `one-nucleus` $+ 1.0 \cdot$ `thick-wall` > 0.5, then `neoplasm`

and training cases for the `lethargia` concept, these methods would induce a threshold unit along the lines of

If $1.0 \cdot$ `simploid` $+ 1.0 \cdot$ `neoplasm` > 1.5, then `lethargia` .

We have omitted the irrelevant features in each rule, which would be given zero weights in the first two cases and presumably would acquire small weights for the target concept.

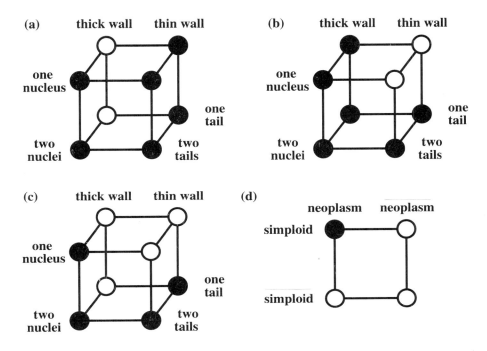

Figure 6-3. Extensional definitions of the concepts (a) `simploid`, (b) `neoplasm`, and (c) `lethargia` in the original instance space, ignoring the irrelevant feature involving cell color. Solid spheres represent positive instances of each concept, whereas open spheres indicate negative instances. Both (a) and (b) are linearly separable; this property does not hold for `lethargia` in the basic space, but (d) indicates that the concept is linearly separable in the augmented space that includes the `simploid` and `neoplasm` features.

Similar benefits occur even when the target concept is not linearly separable in the augmented instance space that includes the higher-level features. For example, suppose the extension of `lethargia` in Figure 6-3 (d) included two classes of instances – the conjunction of `simploid` and `neoplasm` and the conjunction of $\overline{\text{simploid}}$ and $\overline{\text{neoplasm}}$. Here one must invoke a more sophisticated algorithm for inducing threshold concepts, like NSC from Chapter 5, but this method should converge on the target considerably faster in the higher-order space than in the primitive one, just as should methods for inducing logical disjunctions.

6.2.3 Extending a probabilistic network

In Chapter 4 we encountered simple Bayesian classifiers, another induction algorithm that can acquire only a limited class of concepts. In this case, the learning method assumes the independence of attributes or features for instances within each class. As in the logical and threshold frameworks, one can use a partial probabilistic network to extend the power of this simple algorithm. Note that a probabilistic inference network represents exactly the correlations (stated as probabilistic causal links) that a Bayesian classifier assumes are absent. The probabilities on a link from attribute A to attribute B are *conditionally* independent of any attributes that affect A, and one can use connections in the network to factor out dependencies in a training set.

In particular, suppose one is given a probabilistic inference network that relates attributes A_1 through A_n, along with training cases of concept C that uses these attributes. Before using the training set to compute $P(A_k|C)$, one first runs the training instances through the network, producing a revised set that factors out nonindependence due to links that connect attributes. One then runs a simple Bayesian classifier on the modified data to calculate $P(A_k|C)$ for each attribute k, which together specify the probabilities on links from the concept node C to each attribute. If the initial network accurately represents the correlations among attributes, the revised training set will satisfy the independence assumption and the algorithm will have no difficulty.

If the probabilistic network specifies only some of the actual connections among the attributes, this approach should still aid a more sophisticated algorithm. By factoring out correlations between some attributes, it should let a method for inducing competitive disjunctions, like NCD from Chapter 5, acquire the target concept in fewer training instances than if this knowledge were not available.

6.3 Inducing specialized concepts with inference networks

An alternative approach to learning with inference networks assumes that one's knowledge base includes a complete and correct network for some concept C, but that the target concept T is a specialization of C. Moreover, it assumes that the intensional definition of T uses only those primitive features that occur in the definition of C, so the inference network for the latter (C) can be used to bias learning of the former (T).

Table 6-5. A revised version of the inference network from Table 6-1 that includes a rule for recognizing instances of the disease doldroma. This concept is a specialization of lethargia that makes use of the nonterminal symbol neoplasm but not simploid.

```
lethargia :- simploid, neoplasm.
simploid  :- one-tail, thin-wall.
simploid  :- two-tails.
neoplasm  :- one-nucleus, thick-wall.
neoplasm  :- two-nuclei.
doldroma  :- two-tails, neoplasm.
```

This approach is often referred to as *explanation-based generalization*, but this term covers a variety of methods, some concerned with improving the efficiency of problem solving, which we discuss in Chapters 10 and 11. Here we are concerned with the improvement of classification accuracy, and in this context the term *theory-guided specialization* seems more appropriate.

6.3.1 Induction by adding compiled explanations

Consider the intensional definition of the concept doldroma given in Table 6-5, which is a specialization of the lethargia concept we studied in the previous section. The new concept makes use of the nonprimitive feature neoplasm but not simploid, replacing this latter term with the primitive feature two-tails. The result is that the instance space contains only six cases of doldroma, a subset of the eight lethargia instances.

However, there exists a simple mechanism for using the inference network to acquire the target concept doldroma, provided one is willing to assume its special case relation to lethargia. We will call this algorithm ICE, as it involves induction through the compilation of explanations. Briefly, given a positive training instance I of the target concept T, ICE uses the inference network to prove that I is a positive instance of the more general concept C. The method then takes the features that occur as terminal nodes in the proof tree and makes them the antecedents of a rule for which the target concept T is the

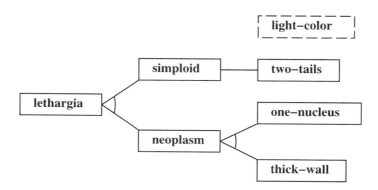

Figure 6-4. A proof tree showing that a training case described by the literals on the far right is a positive instance of the concept `lethargia`, using the inference network from Table 6-5. Literals that occur as terminal nodes in the AND tree become the antecedents of a new inference rule for the target concept, a specialization of `lethargia`.

consequent. The ICE algorithm repeats this process for each positive training instance, creating another rule in each case unless an equivalent one already exists.

Figure 6-4 illustrates the proof (shown as an AND tree) that a particular instance constitutes an example of the concept `lethargia`. In this case, the basic features include `two-tails`, `one-nucleus`, `thick-wall`, and `light-color`. The AND tree decomposes `lethargia` into `simploid` and `neoplasm` using the first rule in Table 6-5. It then uses the third rule to rewrite `simploid` as `two-tails`, which matches a literal in the instance description, and uses the fourth one to decompose `neoplasm` into `one-nucleus` and `thick-wall`, which also hold for the instance.

After generating this proof, ICE collects the literals that occur as terminal nodes[5] and uses them to construct a new inference rule. In this case, the result is

```
doldroma :- two-tails, one-nucleus, thick-wall.
```

in which the consequent refers to the target concept, `doldroma`, rather than to the more general concept `lethargia` used in the proof. Note that this rule makes no mention of the feature `light-color`, since it

---

5. In this chapter we focus on domains that one can describe using propositional clauses, which require no arguments. In Chapter 8 we consider the issues of variable binding and unification that arise with more powerful representations.

did not occur as a terminal node in the AND tree (due to its absence in the rules that define `lethargia`). As a result, the rule covers two cases in the instance space, giving some transfer beyond the training case on which it is based.

Of course, the above trace constitutes only the first step in the overall process; ICE must repeat the process for each new training instance encountered.[6] Thus, given another positive case of `doldroma` in which the literal `two-nuclei` was present, the algorithm would produce a different proof tree and the associated inference rule

```
doldroma :- two-tails, two-nuclei.
```

Note that this structure omits information about both the color and wall of the cell, letting it cover four cases in the instance space.

Taken together, these two inference rules have the same extension as the definition for `doldroma` given in Table 6-5. Thus, in a noise-free environment, we would not expect to observe any positive instances that would produce additional rules for this concept. Nor does this scheme require any negative instances to detect problems with the existing hypothesis, provided the specialization assumption is correct. The presence of noise complicates matters, in that some negative cases that have been falsely labeled as positive may be examples of the general concept but not the target. To handle this possibility, one can modify ICE to collect statistical evidence for each learned inference rule and require sufficient confidence before adding each to the network.

6.3.2 Induction over explanation structures

The above algorithm is only one among many that take advantage of a complete domain theory for one concept to bias learning about another. Returning to the terminology of Chapter 2, the approach begins with a very specific extension for the target concept (the empty set) and gradually broadens it, making the definition more general by adding new disjunctive rules. However, the existence of an inference network also suggests another method for moving toward a more general description of the target concept – replacing some of the terminal literals in learned rules with nonterminal symbols that appear in the rules' proofs.

---

6. The common claim that explanation-based methods "learn from a single instance" is misleading at best. Each instance does produce an inference rule with some generality, but this will seldom cover the entire target concept. More precisely, such methods learn one disjunctive rule from each positive training case.

For instance, given the two acquired `doldroma` rules we saw earlier, one might naturally collapse these into the single rule

        doldroma :- two-tails, neoplasm.

since the term **neoplasm** occurred as parent of the literals **one-nucleus** and **thick-wall** in one proof and as the parent of **two-nuclei** in the other. In this case, the new rule has the same extension as the two original ones, but in situations where the nonterminal literal can be decomposed in ways not yet observed in the training data, the same operation can alter predictions on novel test instances.

This algorithm, which we will call IOE (induction over explanations), will gradually move up the inference network in some areas and retain terminal literals in others, depending on the training data it encounters. In some domains, it will even decide that the target concept is equivalent to the original concept defined by the inference network. For the current network, this might occur if IOE observed an instance of `doldroma` with one tail and a thin wall in addition to those given earlier. In this case, the method might replace the more specific rules with

        doldroma :- simploid, neoplasm.

since all three possible explanation structures for the `lethargia` concept also appear to be valid for the target concept.

We have outlined a method that gradually adds compiled rules and then replaces them with more general rules as it gains experience. However, such an incremental hill-climbing strategy can lead to overly general hypotheses. A more robust algorithm would also include an operator for replacing nonterminal symbols with their decompositions if a negative instance gives evidence of overgeneralization. Such a technique would be equivalent to the ISC algorithm from Chapter 5, except that its search would be biased by the inference network that it uses as background knowledge.

Of course, one need not rely on incremental hill climbing to use an inference network to bias induction, nor need one first construct rules that contain only ground literals and then replace them with nonterminal symbols.[7] One can collect all observations at the outset and invoke a

---

7. Work in this framework is often called *multiple explanation-based generalization* to distinguish it from the simpler variety in which each disjunct is based on a single training case.

nonincremental algorithm instead, using the entire training set to compute evaluation metrics for deciding whether to collapse rules and move through the network. One can also start with the most general possible hypothesis (the definition of `lethargia` in our example), and invoke operators that replace nonterminal symbols with their decompositions as negative training cases reveal the need for such actions. Methods for the induction of specialized concepts using an inference network run the same gamut of variations that we saw in Chapter 2.

Historically, the above approach to induction has been almost exclusively associated with logical representations of knowledge. In principle, one might use an inference network composed of threshold units or competitive descriptions to bias learning of a specialized target concept, but few examples of such approaches exist in the literature.

6.4 Revising an incorrect inference network

A third approach to learning with inference networks assumes that one has some initial knowledge about the target concept C, but that the network for C is only partially correct. The knowledge may be overly specific, in that it classifies some positive instances as negative, or it may be overly general, in that it classifies some negative cases as positive. The task confronting the learner involves modifying the inference network so that it will accurately classify test cases. Work in this framework assumes that one already knows the *nodes* appropriate for the network, and that learning only involves modifying the *links*. This problem is often referred to as *theory revision*, especially when applied to logical formalisms.

6.4.1 Revision of logical theories

Table 6-6 shows a mutilated version of the inference network for `lethargia` from Table 6-1. Inspection reveals three differences from the correct network. First, the second `simploid` rule contains an extra literal, `thick-wall`, which makes the inference network overly specific so that it misclassifies some positive instances. Second, one of the `neoplasm` rules is absent, which also causes the network to label some positive cases as negative. Finally, the remaining `neoplasm` rule lacks the literal `thick-wall`, which causes the network to classify some negative cases

Table 6-6. An incorrect inference network for the concept `lethargia`. This version differs from the one in Table 6-1 by an omitted `neoplasm` rule, an omitted literal in the remaining `neoplasm` rule, and an unnecessary literal in one of the `simploid` rules.

```
lethargia :- simploid, neoplasm.
simploid :- one-tail, thin-wall.
simploid :- two-tails, thick-wall.
neoplasm :- one-nucleus.
```

---

as positive. An extra rule would also produce an overly general network, although none are present in this example.

These four sources of error in inference networks suggest four natural learning operators for correcting them. Clearly, the learner can broaden the extension of a network either by removing a literal from an existing rule or by creating an entirely new rule. Similarly, it can reduce an inference network's extension either by adding a literal to an existing rule or by completely removing a rule. Taken together, these operators can transform any inference network into any other inference network involving the same nodes, moving through a space that is larger than that for DNF expressions. If one is willing to assume that the initial theory is *nearly* correct, the problem is not so daunting, but it still requires search through the space of networks, and effective search requires some constraints or heuristics to direct the process.

An obvious constraint involves the terms used in the network. In addition to limiting attention to known terms, one can provide the learner with a partial ordering, with the class name at the top and literals from the instance language on the bottom. In the current example, one might inform the learner that `lethargia` can be decomposed into any other terms, `simploid` and `neoplasm` can be decomposed into any terms except each other and `lethargia`, and none of the instance features can be further decomposed. This knowledge limits the literals the learner can add to an existing rule. For instance, given the network in Table 6-6, it ensures that this operator does not consider adding `lethargia`, `simploid`, and `neoplasm` to any rules. In other situations, the constraint will forbid adding a literal to some rules but not to others.

Table 6-7. Behavior of different inference networks on training data for the `lethargia` concept, ignoring the color of the cell. Column (a) indicates whether each instance is actually positive (+) or negative (−), with column (b) showing the predictions made by the faulty network in Table 6-6. The remaining columns depict predictions (c) after the RLT algorithm has added the rule `neoplasm :- two-nuclei`, (d) after it has removed `thick-wall` from the second `simploid` rule, and (e) after it has added `thick-wall` to the first `neoplasm` rule.

Instance description	(a)	(b)	(c)	(d)	(e)
one-tail, one-nucleus, thick-wall	−	−	−	−	−
one-tail, one-nucleus, thin-wall	−	+	+	+	−
one-tail, two-nuclei, thick-wall	−	−	−	−	−
one-tail, two-nuclei, thin-wall	+	−	+	+	+
two-tails, one-nucleus, thick-wall	+	+	+	+	+
two-tails, one-nucleus, thin-wall	−	−	−	+	−
two-tails, two-nuclei, thick-wall	+	−	+	+	+
two-tails, two-nuclei, thin-wall	+	−	−	+	+

One algorithm for revision of logical theories (RLT) relies on greedy search directed by an evaluation function. At each step in the iterative process, the method considers all possible ways (within the allowed constraints) of modifying the theory. RLT then evaluates each network in terms of its ability to correctly classify the training data, possibly taking other factors like simplicity into account. Removing literals from existing rules and deleting entire rules are straightforward operations, and we have outlined a scheme that limits the addition of literals. The simplest approach to creating an entirely new rule is to generate all allowed rules that contain only one literal per antecedent, then to rely on other operators for adding more literals if needed. After selecting the revision that leads to the greatest improvement, RLT cycles, continuing the process until no alternative scores as well as the current theory.

Consider the sample data presented in Table 6-7, which shows the actual classes (a) of eight instances[8] from the `lethargia` domain and the classes predicted (b) by the inference network in Table 6-6. Suppose that the evaluation function used to direct the theory revision process

---

8. For the sake of clarity, we will ignore the existence of features involving the cell color, giving only eight instances in the domain. A more realistic training set would include only some of the possible instances from the domain.

simply measures accuracy on the training set, giving $\frac{4}{8}$ as the score for the initial network. Given this theory, the RLT algorithm would consider all possible ways of adding rules, removing rules, adding literals, and removing literals.

In this case, the best choice involves adding the rule `neoplasm :- two-nuclei`, which gives the score $\frac{6}{8}$ and the predictions in (c). After making this alteration to the network, RLT repeats the process. This time the best action involves removing the literal `thick-wall` from the third rule in Table 6-6, which gives the score $\frac{6}{8}$ (no better than the current theory) and a strictly overgeneral network. Finally, the best change to this structure involves adding `thick-wall` to the fourth rule in Table 6-6, which gives an accuracy of $\frac{8}{8}$ and produces the target theory from Table 6-1.

Clearly, this example sidesteps some important issues. One can design training sets that lead the RLT scheme into local optima from which it cannot recover. However, this problem is common to all greedy methods, and one can reduce its likelihood in exchange for additional search. We have also ignored the possibility that the training data contain noise, which can suggest the addition or removal of inappropriate rules or literals. Earlier chapters considered some techniques for minimizing the effect of noise, and one can adapt these methods to the revision of inference networks. In addition, one can incorporate a bias toward simplicity into the evaluation function to reduce the chances of generating a complex theory that overfits the data.

Incremental approaches to logical theory revision are also possible. In this scheme, incorrect classification of a new training case invokes the modification process. If the network labels a positive instance as negative, one attempts to generalize the theory by creating a new rule, typically encoding the entire training case, or by removing those literals that kept a rule from matching the instance. Identifying such literals is closely related to the problem of abduction we mentioned in Section 6.1.2. If the network classifies a negative case as positive, one tries to specialize the theory by removing the responsible rule or by adding literals that will keep it from matching. This approach assumes an incremental hill-climbing process, in which decisions made early in learning may be overturned later as new evidence becomes available. Obviously, a useful evaluation metric or some other constraint on search is as important here as for a nonincremental method.

Table 6-8. A multilayer threshold network for the `lethargia` concept that makes the same predictions as the logical network in Table 6-6. Each rule only shows the features with nonzero weights, but features with zero weights are also present. In this framework, theory revision involves altering weights rather than adding and deleting rules and literals.

```
If  1.0 · simploid + 1.0 · neoplasm > 1.5, then lethargia .
If  1.0 · simploid1 + 1.0 · simploid2 > 0.5, then simploid .
If  1.0 · neoplasm1 + 1.0 · neoplasm2 > 0.5, then neoplasm .
If  1.0 · one-tail + 1.0 · thin-wall > 1.5, then simploid1 .
If -1.0 · one-tail + -1.0 · thin-wall > 1.5, then simploid2 .
If  1.0 · one-nucleus > 0.5, then neoplasm1 .
If  > 0.5, then neoplasm2 .
```

6.4.2 Revision of threshold networks

Naturally, one can also revise inference networks that are composed of threshold units. In this framework, a network can have the desired structure but still make faulty predictions because its weights are incorrect. For example, consider the threshold network in Table 6-8, which is equivalent to the logical network in Table 6-6. This includes three levels or layers (not counting the primitive features), with the top layer responsible for recognizing instances of `lethargia`, the middle layer handling `simploid` and `neoplasm`, and the lowest layer noting `simploid1` and `simploid2` (the two types of `simploid` cells), as well as `neoplasm1` and `neoplasm2` (the two forms of `neoplasm` cells). One could easily add another layer on top to handle multiple forms of `lethargia`. Note that the `neoplasm2` rule lacks inputs, yet it is necessary for the revision process to approximate the `lethargia` network in Figure 6-1 (b).

Each rule in this network includes every possible feature at the next lower level, although the table omits features with 0 weights. Thus, the structure of the network subsumes the structure necessary to correctly describe the `lethargia` concept; the only problem resides in the assigned weights. As a result, the natural theory revision operators for the threshold networks involve altering the weights on links. In some cases, such modifications have the same effect as adding or removing rules or literals. However, because any given threshold unit can represent a continuum from AND to OR, weight changes often have much more complex effects.

The most commonly used algorithm for modifying weights in a network of threshold units is known as *backpropagation*, which generalizes the LMS technique that we encountered in Chapter 3. Backpropagation carries out an incremental gradient descent, revising the weights in the network in response to each training instance.[9] For each node in the network, it first computes the level of activation for the given training case. Next, for each of the top-level nodes, it compares the desired activation (usually 1 or 0) with that predicted for the instance.

Using the LMS algorithm, backpropagation modifies the weights leading into the top-level node j to reduce the difference between the desired and the predicted value. In particular, it computes

$$\Delta w_{ij} = \eta \delta_j x_i'$$

as the change in the weight from node i to node j, where x_i' is the activation of node i, $0 < \eta < 1$ is a constant gain factor, and the error term for node j is

$$\delta_j = p_j(1 - p_j)(d_j - p_j) \quad ,$$

where d_j is the desired output for top-level node j and p_j represents its prediction on the training case.

After calculating the weight changes for the top level of the network, backpropagation proceeds to the next layer, using the δ values computed at the previous level to alter the weights leading into it. In particular, it uses

$$\delta_j = x_j'(1 - x_j') \sum_k \delta_k w_{jk} \quad ,$$

where x_j' is again the prediction of internal node j, w_{ij} is the weight from node j to i, and the summation occurs over all k nodes immediately above node j in the network. Backpropagation uses this scheme to modify weights at each level in turn, until it reaches the input nodes associated with primitive features. As usual, the values for these units are either 1 (if present in the instance) or 0 (if absent), and thresholds

---

9. Like many other methods for modifying weights in threshold units, backpropagation is often run through the same training set multiple times until it converges on some global or local optimum, giving the effect of a nonincremental scheme.

are simulated by special nodes with the constant value 1. Most work on the backpropagation algorithm assumes the use of a logistic function, which we discussed in Section 6.1, to compute node outputs, but similar algorithms are possible for use with other performance methods.

Although backpropagation is the most commonly used algorithm for weight modification in threshold networks, many other techniques also exist. Most such methods also carry out gradient descent through the weight space, trying to minimize some error metric on the training set. Some work has explored more sophisticated search techniques designed to avoid problems with local optima, but a more common response is to run the learning algorithm multiple times with different starting conditions, then select the resulting network with the smallest error.

This raises another issue about work with multilayer threshold networks. Although most research on this topic requires the programmer to specify the nodes and links that constitute network structure, the initial weights on links are typically assigned in a random fashion. We have ignored this trend in order to emphasize the similarity between work on revising networks of threshold units and on theory revision in logical networks. Moreover, some recent work in the former framework does let one specify initial weights based on knowledge of the domain. But most approaches to learning with threshold units adopt the random assignment scheme to initialize the weights and thus the extension of the initial network.

6.4.3 Revision of probabilistic networks

Research on the revision of probabilistic networks has been less common than for logical and threshold networks, but many of the same issues arise. Given the assumptions of conditional independence we discussed in Section 6.1, one can use methods based on probability theory to estimate the conditional probabilities on links for a specific network structure on a giving training set. Thus, the main problem involves determining which of the possible links between pairs of attributes should be included in the network and which should be omitted.

Fortunately, well-defined methods also exist for computing the probability of a particular network structure, given that one has observed a particular set of training cases. An induction algorithm can use the resulting probability as an evaluation function to direct search through the space of probabilistic network structures. However, the size of this space encourages the introduction of constraints. One approach is to place a complete ordering on the attributes, such that there can be a link from an attribute high in the ordering to a lower one, but not vice versa. This constraint also ensures a clear causal semantics for the resulting networks.

Two natural operators arise in modifying a probabilistic network – removing an existing link or adding a new link. Since one can compute the best weights for a given structure, the only issue involves which links to eliminate and which to create. Perhaps the simplest approach uses a greedy technique that considers each possible addition and deletion, computes the probability of each alternative network given the training data, selects the most probable network, and repeats this process until no further improvement occurs. This scheme assumes one starts with an initial network that must be revised. However, one can use a similar method when no such probabilistic network is available. In this case, one can either start with the empty network, considering only the addition of links on each cycle, or start with the complete network, considering only the removal of links on each pass. As with the other frameworks, alternative search schemes are possible that reduce the chances of converging on a local optimum.

6.5 Network construction and term generation

In Sections 6.2 and 6.3, we assumed that the learner began its career with background knowledge stated in the form of an inference network. We relaxed this assumption in Section 6.4 by letting the learning process determine the links connecting the terms in such a network. Now we are ready to examine the more difficult problem of creating these terms.

The simplest approach to introducing new terms also makes the greatest demands on the developer. Briefly, if one wants the learner to acquire a network for concept C that includes intermediate terms for concepts $T_1, T_2, \ldots, T_k$, one first trains the learner on these intermediate concepts, specifying their names in each case. Thus, one would give the learner positive and negative instances of T_1 until it masters this concept, then provide it with instances of T_2, and so forth. If some terms are situated lower in the network than others, the learner must acquire the lower ones first.

One can use this strategy in conjunction with any of the representational formalisms we have examined, and it provides a practical interactive approach to building complex inference networks. However, from a theoretical perspective, it is much more interesting to require the learner to create new terms on its own initiative. This task goes by a variety of names, including *term generation*, *representation change*, and *constructive induction*. Much of the work on this problem attempts to construct an inference network from scratch, but it can also extend a partial network. As usual, we will consider induction methods that arise within a number of representational frameworks.

6.5.1 Generation of logical terms

The reader may have noted that Horn clauses have many similarities to grammars, with nonterminal symbols corresponding to parts of speech and phrasal classes, and with clauses corresponding to phrase definitions. Thus, one can view the task of term generation for a logical inference network as equivalent to the task of grammar induction from sample sentences. One difference between the two is that ground literals in the training instances are typically unordered sets rather than lists of words. Another is that negative training cases may be present to rule out overly general networks, whereas grammar induction typically assumes only legal sentences.

According to this view, there are two natural learning operators. The first creates a nonterminal symbol along with an associated rewrite rule that decomposes it into its constituents. This should be useful when certain combinations of literals tend to co-occur in positive instances of the training set. The second operator involves merging symbols, either terminal or nonterminal, into disjunctive classes. This should be useful when a set of symbols tends to occur in similar contexts. For domains in which one knows that literals fall into mutually exclusive sets (i.e., attributes), one can constrain new phrases to combine only terms of different types and new classes to include only terms of the same type.

Let us consider GLT (generation of logical theories), a nonincremental algorithm for inducing a logical inference network from positive and negative training cases. The method starts with a 'flat' network that contains only the class name and terminal symbols, with one inference rule for each positive case. Naturally, this network covers all positive and no negative training instances. The algorithm operates in a greedy fashion. GLT starts in 'term creation' mode, in which it considers all legal ways of pairing existing symbols (except the class name) to define a new term.

After eliminating redundant rules in each inference network and removing unacceptable candidates, including networks that cover negative training cases, the algorithm uses an evaluation function to select the best alternative. If the score of the resulting network is good enough, GLT revises the network and repeats the process. If not, it changes to 'term merging' mode and considers all legal ways of merging pairs of existing terms, using the same evaluation metric to select the best candidate. If the result is good enough, GLT revises the network and iterates; otherwise it switches back to term generation. This alternation between term creation and merging continues until neither mode meets the criteria for continuation.

Table 6-9 shows the behavior of GLT on a variant of the cell domain that allows three values for each attribute, using the complexity of a network (its total number of symbols) as the evaluation metric.[10] The initial inference network includes nine instances of the class somnogenic, each described as a conjunction of four literals, giving 45 as the evaluation score. The algorithm begins by considering all new terms that it can construct from legal pairs of the primitive terms. The second part of the table shows the result after six iterations, a network in which there are six new rules defining nonterminal symbols (A through F) and in which these terms have replaced the combinations of primitive terms in the original rules. The complexity of this network is 45, the same as the original one.

Beyond this stage, additional terms only increase grammatical complexity, worsening the score, so GLT turns its attention to merging terms. The third part of Table 6-9 shows the network after two more iterations, during which the algorithm merges the terms D and E into the class deprivitic, and then adds F to this class. These actions lead to a reduced complexity of 27, since after substituting class names back into the somnogenic rules, only three unique ones remain. The final part of the table shows the network that results from two additional merges, creating the class hypnagogic from A and B, to which GLT then adds the phrasal term C. The new complexity is only 21, since substitutions have

---

10. Here we assume that an evaluation score S is 'good enough' to let GLT continue in the current mode if S is equal to or less than the current score.

Table 6-9. The GLT algorithm's transformation of a grounded inference network (initial group) into one involving nonterminal symbols. The second network introduces the symbols A, B, C, D, E, and F to represent different recurring pairs of ground literals; the third network eliminates some rewrite rules by replacing D, E, and F with `deprivitic`, and the final group eliminates more rules by replacing A, B, and C with `hypnagogic`.

```
somnogenic :- one-tail, thick-wall, one-nucleus, light-color.
somnogenic :- one-tail, medium-wall, one-nucleus, medium-color.
somnogenic :- one-tail, thin-wall, one-nucleus, dark-color.
somnogenic :- two-tails, thick-wall, two-nuclei, light-color.
somnogenic :- two-tails, medium-wall, two-nuclei, medium-color.
somnogenic :- two-tails, thin-wall, two-nuclei, dark-color.
somnogenic :- three-tails, thick-wall, three-nuclei, light-color.
somnogenic :- three-tails, medium-wall, three-nuclei, medium-color.
somnogenic :- three-tails, thin-wall, three-nuclei, dark-color.
```

```
somnogenic :- A, D.        A :- one-tail, one-nucleus.
somnogenic :- A, E.        B :- two-tails, two-nuclei.
somnogenic :- A, F.        C :- three-tails, three-nuclei.
somnogenic :- B, D.        D :- thick-wall, light-color.
somnogenic :- B, E.        E :- medium-wall, medium-color.
somnogenic :- B, F.        F :- thin-wall, dark-color.
somnogenic :- C, D.
somnogenic :- C, E.
somnogenic :- C, F.
```

```
somnogenic :- A, deprivitic.
somnogenic :- B, deprivitic.
somnogenic :- C, deprivitic.
A :- one-tail, one-nucleus.
B :- two-tails, two-nuclei.
C :- three-tails, three-nuclei.
deprivitic :- thick-wall, light-color.
deprivitic :- medium-wall, medium-color.
deprivitic :- thin-wall, dark-color.
```

```
somnogenic :- hypnagogic, deprivitic.
hypnagogic :- one-tail, one-nucleus.
hypnagogic :- two-tails, two-nuclei.
hypnagogic :- three-tails, three-nuclei.
deprivitic :- thick-wall, light-color.
deprivitic :- medium-wall, medium-color.
deprivitic :- thin-wall, dark-color.
```

left only one unique **somnogenic** rule. After this, neither term merging
nor term creation leads to networks of equivalent or lower complexity,
causing the algorithm to halt.

This example ignores a number of important issues. First, the final
inference network does not move beyond the initial training data, in that
it classifies the initial nine cases as positive and no others. However,
the algorithm can produce such networks from alternative training sets,
provided that they contain enough co-occurrences of terms to reduce the
complexity score. The example also ignores the role of negative cases
in pruning the space of alternative networks, which becomes important
precisely when the learning operators produce hypotheses that move
beyond the training data.

Incremental approaches to term generation are also possible. For example, upon observing the two positive instances S :- A B D E and S
:- A C D F, one natural response would be to replace them with three
rules, involving two nonterminal symbols (S :- X Y, X :- A D, Y :-
B E, and Y :- C F) that reflect the terms held in common by the two
instances (X) and those in which they differ (Y). Work on this topic is
sometimes referred to as *inverse resolution*, because it involves generating clauses that would resolve with the original instances if only they
were present.[11] The problem with this approach, as with most incremental methods, lies in directing search through the space of hypotheses with only a small subset of the training data. As we have seen,
one solution is to include additional learning operators that support
bidirectional search and a hill-climbing strategy. In the current framework, this means adding operators for removing and splitting terms,
thus producing structures with fewer nonterminal symbols.

6.5.2 Generation of threshold units

The possibility of term generation also exists with networks of threshold
units. Most methods of this sort carry out a nonincremental greedy
search that starts with a simple network and introduces one node at
a time into the network. However, they differ in the structure of the
resulting network, in the order of node creation, and in whether training
occurs at only one level or all of them.

---

11. Most work on inverse resolution deals with more powerful representations that
    support predicates with variables, typically using true Horn clauses.

One algorithm, which we call TSC (threshold separate-and-conquer), embodies a strategy similar to that of NSC in Chapter 5. The method begins with a single-layer threshold network with one output node, $N1$, for concept C. If training reveals the data are linearly separable, no further action is taken, but failure to correctly classify all training cases suggests a need for additional units in the threshold network. If the initial network misclassifies some negative instances as positive, TSC adds two new nodes. One of these, $N2$, occurs at the same level as $N1$, and is trained only on those training cases that $N1$ classified as positive. Both $N1$ and $N2$ are connected to a second new node, $A1$, with link weights of 1 and threshold 1.5 that effectively specify the conjunction $N1 \wedge N2$. No training occurs for this AND node, only for those at the first level. If node $A1$ still misclassifies some negative cases, TSC repeats the process, creating another node, $N3$, at the first level, connecting it to $A1$ with weight 1 and increasing $A1$'s threshold by 1 to keep it conjunctive. This process continues until $A1$ covers no negative cases.

However, the addition of a first-level node Nk may also have excluded some positive training cases. When this occurs, TSC creates another second-level node, $A2$, with $N1$ through Nk as its initial inputs. As with the first AND node, the threshold on $A2$ is $k-0.5$, but the weights are all -1. This effectively computes the conjunction $\neg N1 \wedge \ldots \wedge \neg Nk$, making the node active only when none of its inputs are present. The algorithm then takes all training instances covered by this node and repeats the process above, creating and training additional first-layer nodes and adding them as inputs to $A2$, this time with weights of 1, until $A2$ covers only positive cases. If more positive instances remain uncovered, TSC repeats the initial strategy, and so forth. When this process is complete, there exists a two-layer threshold network, with AND nodes at the second level, that correctly classifies the entire training set.[12] Figure 6-5 depicts a network constructed in this manner, with four units in the first level and two in the second layer.

Other methods for constructing multi-layer networks are also possible. For instance, another algorithm begins with a two-layer network having only one node in the first (hidden) level. However, rather than storing only weights, each link also has a variance that reflects the amount of change it has undergone during training with a method like backpropa-

12. Some versions of this method include a single OR node in a third layer with threshold 0.5 and weights of 1 on links from the AND nodes. However, this is not necessary if one simply lets each AND node predict the class C.

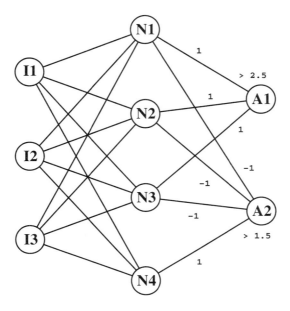

Figure 6-5. A multilayer network constructed by the TSC algorithm, with the second layer ($A1$, $A2$) defining conjunctions of the threshold units in the first layer ($N1, \ldots, N4$).

gation. If the total variance on a hidden node's links is high enough, the algorithm splits the node into two siblings with the same weights but half the variance. Continued training may reduce the variance on their links, but if this increases again, the splitting process continues, gradually increasing the number of hidden nodes until the network achieves a good fit to the training data and the weight changes stabilize.

Yet another method constructs a 'cascade' network, which may contain an arbitrary number of layers, but allows only one node at any layer but the inputs. This *cascade correlation* technique starts with a single-layer network with output node $N1$, but if training on this structure does not reduce errors to an acceptable level, the algorithm creates another node, $N2$, with incoming links from the input nodes and with an outgoing link to $N1$. The aim is to use the new node to predict the *errors* in the original network, and then to subtract them out.

To this end, cascade correlation sets the weight on the link connecting $N2$ and $N1$ to -1, fixes the weights on the original links to $N1$, and trains the new portion of the network (the weights into $N2$) on the difference between the desired outputs and the original network's predictions.

Training continues until these weights appear to have converged and, if sufficient errors remain, the algorithm introduces another node, *N3*, with incoming links from *N2* and the input units, and with an output link (weighted -1) into *N1*. Again, the method fixes all but the new weights, which it trains on the remaining errors. This process continues until the scheme generates a network structure, and associated weights, that are sufficiently accurate on the training data.

6.5.3 Generation of probabilistic terms

Term generation for a probabilistic inference network raises the same basic issues as in the threshold and logical frameworks. Here the aim is to determine the number and location of 'latent' variables or attributes that mediate effects among observable attributes. Given two correlated attributes x and y, the methods outlined in Section 6.4.3 would consider the hypotheses that x directly influences y and that y influences x. However, they would not entertain the possibility that neither directly influences the other, and that an unobserved attribute, z, influences both and thus explains their correlation.

No great effort is required to modify algorithms for revising a probabilistic network to include an operator for introducing new latent attributes. As in the other frameworks, the problem is that there exist many such terms. Thus, one needs some evaluation metric to select the best term, to determine whether creating this term is more desirable than modifying the links among existing terms, and to decide when no additional terms are required. One also needs some means for estimating the value of a latent term for each training instance from the values of known attributes.

Research on this topic remains in the early stages. Methods for identifying latent variables in quantitative data exist, but they rely on an assumption of linear relations between variables in the network. Alternative techniques have been developed for nominal domains, but these methods typically assume the probabilistic network has a tree structure and they appear to be sensitive to noise. The development of robust methods for term generation in probabilistic, threshold, and logical networks remains an open and important problem for future research.

6.6 Summary of the chapter

In this chapter, we examined a variety of methods for refining and extending inference networks. We saw that this formalism can organize logical, threshold, and competitive concepts into knowledge structures that, when combined with particular inference methods, can produce complex decision regions. We also found that much of the learning work on this topic starts with some initial inference network and uses training data to modify the structure, rather than creating it from scratch.

The simplest task of this sort involves extending an *incomplete* network, in which the existing portions are correct but which are not connected to the node for the class attribute. In this case, one can use the existing network to redescribe the training instances at a higher level of description, then use an induction algorithm to formulate some connection between existing nodes and the node for the target concept. We noted that the presence of such background knowledge can transform a difficult induction task involving multiple decision regions into a easier one involving only one region per class. As a result, one can use simple induction methods like HSG, PCP, and the simple Bayesian classifier to good effect.

Another task involves learning a *specialization* of some concept for which a complete network is available. We considered one such method, ICE, that uses the inference network to construct a proof for each positive instance, then compiles the proof into a single rule that includes only observable features. A more sophisticated algorithm, IOE, generalizes over a number of such proof trees, producing rules that may incorporate nonterminals from the original network. If one knows that the target is a specialization of a known concept, these methods can focus attention on relevant features and speed the learning process.

A more challenging problem requires the *revision* of a complete but incorrect inference network. We examined RLT, an algorithm that carries out a hill-climbing search through the space of logical networks, using operators that add and delete rules and conditions. We also saw that backpropagation, a well-known method for connectionist learning, can be viewed as revising multilayer networks of threshold units, using gradient descent in its efforts to minimize error on the training data. In addition, we noted that one can apply similar ideas to the revision of Bayesian networks of probabilistic units.

Finally, we considered methods for *constructing* inference networks in the absence of significant background knowledge. We described one such algorithm for logical networks, GLT, which uses a simplicity metric to decide between creating new terms and merging existing ones. We also presented three related schemes for networks of threshold units, though in less detail, and we noted that similar methods apply to the generation of Bayesian networks with latent variables.

Exercises

1. Add the literal `thick-wall` to the right-hand side of the second `simploid` rule in Table 6-1, and similarly add the literal `thin-wall` to the second `neoplasm` rule. Draw the extensional definitions of `simploid` and `neoplasm` that result, using the cube notation from Figure 6-3. Also, show the extension of some target concept `lethargia'` that can be learned using these higher-level features using the HGS algorithm (Chapter 2) but not without them.

2. Assume a target concept `doldroma'` with the same definition as in Table 6-5, but in which the definitions for `simploid` and `neoplasm` have been altered as in Exercise 1. Show the proof tree generated by the ICE algorithm (Section 6.3.1) for some positive instance of `doldroma'`, along with the compiled rule that results. Show the compiled rules that result from all other instances of this concept.

3. Show the result of applying the IOE algorithm (Section 6.3.2) to the set of compiled rules for `doldroma'` from Exercise 2.

4. Remove the literal `one-tail` from the first `simploid` rule in Table 6-1 and add the literal `thin-wall` to the second `neoplasm` rule. Show the succession of inference networks generated by the RLT algorithm (Section 6.4.1) for the eight training cases in Table 6-7 (a), along with each network's prediction for these instances and their overall accuracies on the training set.

5. Transform the logical inference network from Exercise 4 into a multilayer threshold network that produces the same behavior, as in Figure 6-1. Assume a desired output of 1 for positive instances of `lethargia` and 0 for negative instances. Select a training case from Exercise 4 that this network misclassifies and use the backpropagation algorithm (Section 6.4.2), with 0.1 as the gain factor, to revise the network's weights to reduce its error on the instance. Show your calculations for each weight.

6. In Table 6-9, replace all occurrences of the literal `three-nuclei` in the training cases with `two-nuclei`, and replace all occurrences of `medium-color` with `dark-color`. Summarize the major steps taken by the GLT algorithm (Section 6.5.1) on these data, reporting the rules at each stage and each theory's overall simplicity score.

Historical and bibliographical remarks

Research on learning in inference networks has occurred within a number of distinct paradigms that seldom interact with each other. As we have seen, the simplest involves extending an incomplete inference network by inducing new conceptual structures that are described in terms of existing ones. Such constructive induction (coined by Michalski, 1983) has been explored with inference networks composed of logical, threshold, and competitive units. Sammut and Banerji's (1986) MAR-VIN, Elio and Watanabe's (1991) LAIR, and Drastal, Raatz, and Czako's (1989) MIRO extend logical networks, Gluck and Bower's (1988) configural cue model learns higher-order threshold concepts, and Kononenko (1991) and Pazzani (1995) use a naive Bayesian classifier in a similar manner. Some work on constructive induction (e.g., Matheus & Rendell, 1989; Pagallo, 1989) has also occurred with organizations other than inference networks.

The late 1980s saw considerable work on 'explanation-based' learning, following influential papers by Mitchell, Keller, and Kedar-Cabelli (1986), DeJong and Mooney (1986), and Laird, Rosenbloom, and Newell (1986). Early work in this area distinguished itself from other approaches to learning, especially earlier methods for logical induction, with some initial confusion about the performance task. Two paths subsequently emerged, one emphasizing the speeding up of problem solvers, which we discuss in Chapters 10 and 11, and the other focusing on supervised concept learning. Mitchell et al.'s (1986) EBG method (see the ICE algorithm in Section 6.3.1) formed the basis for much of the work in this latter area (e.g., Pazzani, 1988). Considerable attention also focused on clearly defining the notion of an operational term (e.g., Keller, 1988), while other work explored methods for combining evidence from multiple training cases (e.g., Cohen, 1988). Our formulation of explanation-based learning as theory-guided specialization comes directly from Flann and Dietterich (1989), and their IOE system is the source for our algorithm of the same name (Section 6.3.2).

Although the attention devoted to explanation-based learning has decreased in recent years, the idea of using background knowledge to aid learning has remained. Much of the work in theory revision, such as that by Hall (1989), Ourston and Mooney (1990), and Towell, Shavlik, and Noordeweier (1990), grew directly out of this tradition. Another source of interest in this topic was expert systems, which often require refinement when constructed manually. Ginsberg, Weiss, and Politakis (1988), Craw and Sleeman (1990), and Langley, Drastal, Rao, and Greiner (1994) present theory revision work with this motivation. The two approaches have produced quite similar methods, most using variations of the RLT algorithm (Section 6.4.1). Shapiro (1981) presents early work in this area, but took a more interactive approach than later methods.

By far the most active area covered in this chapter concerns weight revision in multilayer neural networks. This approach became popular in the mid-1980s, after an extended lapse of research on threshold units, as described in Chapter 3. An important cause for the new activity was the introduction of backpropagation (Section 6.4.2), by Rumelhart, Hinton, and Williams (1986), and related methods (e.g., Fahlman, 1988), which extended techniques like LMS, for gradient-descent search through a weight space, to networks with many levels. The literature reports many extensions to this basic approach, which can be found in proceedings of annual conferences like NIPS and IJCNN, and in journals such as *Neural Computation* and *International Journal of Neural Systems*. Lippman (1987), Hinton (1989), and Widrow, Rumelhart, and Lehr (1994) present overviews of work in this active area. Most research in this framework initializes weights randomly, but Towell et al. (1990) use backpropagation to revise an incorrect domain theory, and Thrun and Mitchell (1993) take a similar approach.

In general, research on determining the structure of inference networks from scratch has been much less common than work on modifying existing structure or altering weights. The GLT algorithm from Section 6.5.1 actually borrows from work on grammar induction (e.g., Langley, 1994b; Stolcke & Omohundro, 1994), which we discuss in Chapter 9. Muggleton's (1987) DUCE and its successor CIGOL (Muggleton & Buntine, 1988) introduced methods for inverse resolution, an approach to forming new terms in logical networks. There has been some research on determining the structure of threshold networks, but this constitutes only a small fraction of work in the area. The TSC algorithm (Section 6.5.2) comes directly from Knerr, Personnaz, and Dreyfus (1990); the method for splitting nodes comes from Hanson (1990), while the cascade correlation algorithm is due to Fahlman and Lebiere (1990). Platt (1991) describes one method for constructing networks of spherical threshold units.

Research on learning in Bayesian networks has been a relatively new development. Cooper and Herskovits (1992) and Heckerman (1995) review techniques for determining the probabilities in such networks from training data, but recent work has focused on inducing the structure of Bayesian networks. Cooper and Herskovits' (1992) K2 uses a greedy algorithm to determine network structure, and others report extensions to this approach (Heckerman, Geiger, & Chickering, 1994; Provan & Singh, 1995). Glymour, Scheines, Spirtes, and Kelly (1987) describe a different approach that includes the ability to posit latent or unobserved variables, whereas Connolly (1993) employs a clustering scheme to infer new latent terms.

CHAPTER 7

The Formation of Concept Hierarchies

In the previous chapter we examined inference networks as an organization of learned knowledge. However, we noted in Chapter 1 that *concept hierarchies* provide an alternative framework for memory organization, and a considerable amount of machine learning research has taken this approach. As we will see, concept hierarchies differ from inference networks not only in their structure, but also in the algorithms that use and construct them.

Much of the work in this area has assumed logical concept descriptions, so our examples will focus on such representations. However, we will also examine some less common methods for organizing threshold and competitive concepts into concept hierarchies. In addition, most research has dealt with nonincremental approaches that construct hierarchies in a 'divisive' manner, from the top down, but we will also consider some incremental variants and some techniques that operate in an 'agglomerative' fashion, constructing hierarchies from the bottom up. As usual, we start by discussing the data structures and performance methods associated with the approach.

7.1 General issues concerning concept hierarchies

Most concept hierarchies assume that instances are described as a conjunction of attribute-value pairs; as in previous chapters, we will emphasize such representations in our examples, even though we will see in Chapter 8 that one can extend the framework to handle relational structures. There is greater variety in the nature of the concept descriptions that hierarchies organize; we will find that one can embed any of the knowledge representations presented in Chapters 2 through 4 within these larger structures. Here we focus on the organization that concept hierarchies impose on memory, on the manner in which a performance element uses these structures, and on the task of acquiring them.

7.1.1 The structure of concept hierarchies

Like an inference network, a concept hierarchy is composed of nodes and links, but with quite different semantics. Each node represents a separate concept, typically with its own associated intensional definition. The links connecting a node to its children specify an 'IS-A' or 'subset' relation, indicating that the parent's extension is a superset of each child's extension. Typically, a node covers all of the instances covered by the union of its descendents, making the concept hierarchy a subgraph of the partial ordering by generality that we discussed in Chapter 2.

We will sometimes distinguish between two types of intensional descriptions stored at nodes. A concept hierarchy uses *predictive* features or descriptions to sort new instances downward through memory. One can view these as 'tests' that discriminate among the concepts stored at each level, although such tests need not be logical in nature. In contrast, a concept hierarchy uses *predictable* features or descriptions to make inferences about aspects of new instances. Some frameworks combine these two aspects of intensional descriptions into a single structure, whereas others make a clear distinction.

For example, consider the simplest and most widely used form of concept hierarchy – the *univariate decision tree*. This organization divides instances into mutually exclusive sets at each level, splitting on the values of a single predictive feature (thus the term *univariate*). As a result, each internal node contains a very simple description for use in sorting. Only terminal nodes include a predictive feature, which specifies the class to predict upon reaching that node. A closely related organizational structure, the *discrimination network*, differs by including multiple predictable features at each terminal node, but the predictive descriptions at internal nodes are typically univariate.

In contrast, other types of concept hierarchies incorporate many predictive features into their internal nodes, in some cases including all available attributes. Decision trees of this sort are termed *multivariate*, in that each 'test' takes many variables into account.[1] Some memory structures contain a single summary description at each node and treat each feature as both predictive and predictable. For example, one such scheme stores a probabilistic description at each node, which summarizes all instances below it in the hierarchy. In any case, there exist many variations on the hierarchical organization of conceptual knowledge.

7.1.2 The use of concept hierarchies

We have hinted that the classification process involves sorting an instance downward through the hierarchy. At each level, it uses the predictive features on the alternative nodes to select one to expand, then recurses to the next level. This continues until reaching a terminal node or otherwise deciding the sorting process has gone deep enough. At this point, the process uses the predictable features associated with the current node to infer attributes missing from the instance, such as the class name. We have described a greedy sorting scheme, but one can use other techniques as well, including best-first search and even parallel methods that pass the instance down multiple branches at a time.

The details of sorting and prediction depend on the nature of the intensional descriptions stored with the nodes. As we will emphasize repeatedly, concept hierarchies can use any of the description languages we have considered in previous chapters. Thus, they use the interpreters associated with a given concept representation to make sorting decisions. For example, many hierarchies employ logical descriptions and thus use an all-or-none match at each level. Others incorporate threshold units for each node and thus use partial-match schemes. Yet others have instance-based or probabilistic representations of concepts, and so use a best-match procedure to sort instances through memory.

7.1.3 The task of forming concept hierarchies

With issues of representation and performance clearly specified, we can now state the task of constructing concept hierarchies:

- *Given*: A set of training instances and (possibly) associated classes;
- *Find*: A concept hierarchy that, to the extent possible, makes accurate predictions about novel test instances.

---

1. The numerical taxonomy literature refers to *monothetic* and *polythetic* trees, rather than univariate and multivariate ones.

As with other induction tasks, this one assumes that the acquired knowledge structure will perform well on unseen instances, even at the expense of imperfect performance on the training set. Like most of the induction problems we have examined in previous chapters, the above task allows for disjunctive or noncontiguous concepts. However, the aim is to move beyond the induction of concept descriptions to the generation of an organization of such concepts in memory.

One can view this task as involving search through the space of concept hierarchies. For example, one might cast the induction of a univariate decision tree as search through an AND/OR space, with the AND branches corresponding to attributes and the OR branches corresponding to values. This space is quite large: given a attributes with v values each, it contains some

$$\prod_{i=0}^{a-1} (a - i + 1)^{v^i}$$

possible decision trees, which is much larger than the space of possible concepts. This does not take into account the labels on terminal nodes, but the data determine these for any given tree structure. Even so, for a domain with only five attributes having two values each, we have $6^1 \cdot 5^2 \cdot 4^4 \cdot 3^8 \cdot 2^{16} > 1.65 \cdot 10^{13}$ possible trees.

Clearly, one cannot search this space exhaustively when there are more than a few attributes. For this reason, most work on decision-tree induction employs a greedy method that directs search with an evaluation function. Note that, given a consistent set of training data, there exist many alternative decision trees that completely summarize those data. However, one would also like a tree that makes useful predictions about novel instances, and both the search scheme and the evaluation function can influence the predictive ability of the resulting trees. Similar observations hold for other types of conceptual hierarchies.

Given that hierarchy formation involves search, one must organize the search in some fashion, and there are two obvious approaches. One can construct the hierarchy from the root node downward, in a *divisive* manner, or one can build it from the terminal nodes upward, in an *agglomerative* style. Although these may appear similar to the general-to-specific and the specific-to-general methods we examined in Chapter 2, they are actually quite distinct. Divisive and agglomerative methods differ in the order in which they construct their hierarchies, not in the ways they search for concept descriptions embedded in those hierarchies.

Table 7-1. The DCH algorithm: Nonincremental divisive formation of concept hierarchies.

```
Inputs: The current node N of the concept hierarchy.
        A set of training instances ISET.
Output: A concept hierarchy.
Top-level call: DCH(root, ISET).

Procedure DCH(N, ISET)

If the training set ISET is not empty,
Then generate a set of partitions for ISET.
    For each partition P,
        Evaluate P using some metric.
    Select the best partition Best.
    For each cluster JSET in Best,
        Form a node C with JSET as its members.
        Form an intensional description DESC for JSET.
        Associate the description DESC with node C.
        Let KSET be the instances in ISET matched by DESC.
        Make node C a child of node N.
        DCH(C, KSET).
```

One can use any form of concept representation in such a memory organization, and one can invoke any of the induction algorithms from earlier chapters, regardless of the order in which one constructs the hierarchy.

Another central issue in hierarchy formation involves the division of instances into subsets or *clusters*. We will encounter a variety of methods for handling this problem, but we will also find that these techniques are relatively independent of the direction of hierarchy construction and the induction algorithms used to characterize the resulting clusters.

7.2 Nonincremental divisive formation of hierarchies

The first set of methods we will examine for inducing concept hierarchies vary along a number of dimensions, but they have important features in common as well. In addition to the shared representational and performance assumptions already mentioned, all of these methods are nonincremental in nature, and they are divisive in that they construct hierarchies from the top down.

Table 7-1 presents pseudocode for DCH, a basic algorithm for the divisive formation of concept hierarchies that requires all training instances to be available at the outset. The method begins by creating the top node and grows a hierarchy downward from there. At each level, DCH divides the current training instances into alternative disjoint sets or partitions. It then uses an evaluation function to measure the desirability of each partition, and selects the one with the best score.

The algorithm creates one successor node for each cluster of instances in the selected partition, connecting this node to its parent by an IS-A link. DCH can also invoke an induction algorithm to generate an intensional description for each cluster, which it associates with the corresponding node. The method then calls on itself recursively – passing on the new node, the subset of instances in the cluster, and possibly those attributes that have not been used higher in the hierarchy. DCH does this for each successor node, constructing subtrees that summarize each subset of instances in a given cluster. This process continues ever deeper until the algorithm reaches some termination criterion, at which point it pops back to the previous level to handle other clusters in the partition.

7.2.1 Induction of decision trees

As we have mentioned, univariate decision trees constitute an important special case of concept hierarchies. Each node in such a structure specifies a single predictive feature, which it uses as a logical test to direct the sorting of instances. Typically, only terminal nodes specify any predictable features, usually the name of the most likely class. Note that most presentations of decision trees place the values of the discriminating attribute on the branches leading into nodes, and the attribute itself on the node from which they emanate. Our formulation is equivalent but clarifies connections to other work on hierarchy formation.

This organizational scheme supports a straightforward algorithm for the divisive induction of decision trees (DDT) that instantiates the abstract method from Table 7-1. As in the more general algorithm, the initial action is to create a root node for the decision tree (see Table 7-2). The method then generates one partition for each attribute, which for now we assume to be nominal, basing the clusters in each partition on those instances having the same value for that attribute. DDT then evaluates each partition in terms of its ability to discriminate among

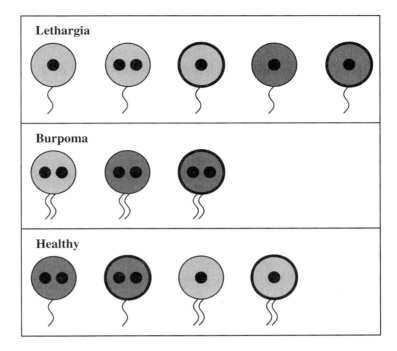

Figure 7-1. Training instances from a cell domain involving four attributes and three distinct classes.

the various classes, generating a class-by-partition contingency table for each alternative. Researchers have used many different evaluation metrics to this end, but all have the similar effect of preferring attributes with values correlated with the class.

The algorithm selects the best such partition, creates a child of the root for each cluster in the partition, and associates the appropriate attribute-value pair as its predictive summary description. If all instances in a cluster belong to the same class, then DDT stores the most likely class as the predictable feature for its associated node. Otherwise, the algorithm calls on itself recursively, passing on the instances in the cluster to use in building a subtree with the current node as its root.

Let us examine this algorithm's behavior on a variation of the cell domain from previous chapters. Figure 7-1 presents a set of training instances for three classes of patients – those who have the disease `lethargia`, those with `burpoma`, and those who are `healthy`. Each instance describes a cell from the patient in terms of four attributes –

Table 7-2. The DDT algorithm: Divisive induction of univariate decision trees.

```
Inputs: The current node N of the decision tree.
        A set of classified training instances ISET.
        A set of attributes and their values ASET.
Output: A univariate decision tree.
Top-level call: DDT(root, ASET, ISET).

Procedure DDT(N, ASET, ISET)

If the training set ISET is empty,
Then label terminal node N as UNKNOWN.
Else if all instances ISET are in the same class or
    If the attribute set ASET is empty,
    Then label terminal node N with the class name.
    Else for each attribute A in the attribute list ASET,
            Evaluate A according to its ability to
                discriminate the classes in ISET.
        Select attribute B with the best evaluation score.
        For each value V of the best attribute B,
            Create a new child C of node N.
            Place the attribute-value pair (B, V) on C.
            Let JSET be the ISET instances with value V on B.
            Let KSET be the ASET attributes with B removed.
            DDT(C, KSET, JSET).
```

---

the number of **nuclei**, the number of **tails**, the **color**, and the cell **wall**. Since each attribute takes on two possible values, there exist 16 possible instances, only 12 of which occur in the training set.

Figure 7-2 shows two versions of the decision tree that DDT generates from these training instances, with (a) depicting the standard notation with attributes on parent nodes and values on links, and (b) graphically showing the type of instances matched by each node. The algorithm's first step in constructing this tree involves examining the data and comparing the four attributes in terms of their ability to discriminate the classes. This requires some evaluation function; here we will assume the metric

$$\frac{1}{n} \sum_v C_v \quad ,$$

where n is the number of training cases sorted to the current node, the summation occurs over all values of the candidate attribute, and C_v is the number of instances with value v that are correctly classified by the most frequent class for that value. This metric has a maximum score of 1 (for a perfectly discriminating attribute) and a minimum of 0 (for one with no discriminating ability).

For the data in Figure 7-1, the number of **tails** receives the best score, in this case $\frac{5+3}{12} = 0.667$. As a result, DDT partitions the instances along this dimension and creates two children of the root node, each with a different value of this attribute. The algorithm sorts all instances of the **lethargia** class down the **one tail** branch, along with some cases of the **healthy** class. Similarly, it sends all instances of **burpoma** down the **two tail** branch, along with the remaining **healthy** patients.

The algorithm calls on itself recursively to handle each of these instance clusters. Of the remaining three attributes, it finds the cell **color** to be most discriminating for the first set, with the score $\frac{3+2}{7} = 0.714$. Thus, it creates one node for each value of this attribute, storing these values as their predictive features. All instances in the cluster with **light color** are members of the **lethargia** class; thus, DDT does not extend the decision tree further than the node for this set. In contrast, instances in the cluster with **dark color** contain some patients with **lethargia** and some **healthy** ones, so another split is needed. In this case, the most useful attribute is the number of **nuclei**, with the score $\frac{2+2}{4} = 1$. Thus, DDT creates two children that test on this feature, which also lead to pure nodes.

At this point, the algorithm returns to the second cluster of instances generated by its initial decision, which share the attribute-value pair **two tails**. Since this set contains members of two classes, DDT selects another attribute to distinguish between them. In this case it also decides on the number of **nuclei**, although this occurs at an entirely different level of the tree than the other use of the attribute. Upon creating nodes for each value of this attribute, the algorithm finds that all instances in the cluster with **one nucleus** are **healthy**, whereas all those with **two nuclei** have **burpoma**. Thus, there is no need to extend the tree further downward, and the algorithm halts. The figure shows the order in which DDT generates each node, along with the class and number of training instances associated with each terminal node.

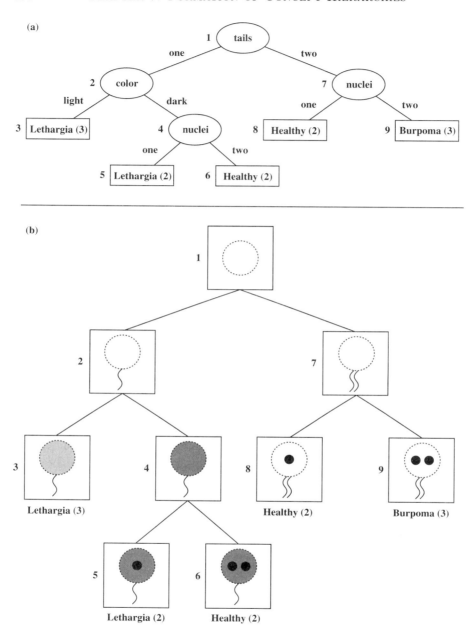

Figure 7-2. A decision tree generated by the DDT algorithm for the training instances from Figure 7-1. Each terminal node specifies an associated class name and the number of training cases covered. Numbers next to the nodes indicate the order in which the algorithm generated them. The notation in (a), which associates attributes with nodes and values with links, is equivalent to (b), which shows the instances that each node covers.

7.2.2 Variations on decision-tree induction

Upon selecting a nominal attribute, the DDT algorithm creates one branch for each value of that attribute. However, when attributes take on many possible values, one can imagine domains in which trees that incorporate *sets* of values would give simpler output and greater classification accuracy. Naturally, the basic technique can be extended to construct trees of this sort. The simplest scheme involves creating a binary decision tree in which two branches emerge from each internal node, one specifying a particular value for an attribute and the other specifying its negation.

Modifying the DDT algorithm to construct such a binary tree is not difficult, but it does introduce additional search. The cost of the basic method is linear in the number of attributes, since at each decision point, it must iterate through all unused attributes. In order to construct a binary tree of this sort, DDT must also iterate through each *value* of each attribute, giving a cost that is linear in both the number of attributes and the number of values. In addition, if an attribute has more than two values, it must reconsider splitting on its remaining values when recursing down the negated branch. We cannot illustrate this method with the cell domain, since its attributes take on only two values each.

One can extend this scheme further by constructing binary trees in which each branch contains an arbitrary subset of an attribute's values. Again, there is no problem in modifying the DDT algorithm to induce such trees, and some variants take precisely this approach. However, this extension is even more expensive, since it must consider all two-set partitions of values for an attribute. An even more extreme variant allows decision trees with an arbitrary number of branches, in which each branch specifies an arbitrary set of an attribute's values; this method introduces additional costs into the induction process but may produce simpler or more accurate hierarchies.

Although decision trees were originally designed to handle nominal (symbolic) data, they can easily be extended to deal with integer-valued or real-valued attributes. Given N instances, one first sorts those instances in terms of increasing values on the numeric attribute A. Each successive pair of values V_k and V_{k+1} defines a possible threshold test, $A > (V_k + V_{k+1})/2$, that partitions the instances into two sets. Thus, one computes an evaluation score for each of the $N - 1$ tests, retaining the best such test and its score. Finally, one compares this test's score to those obtained for other attributes, whether nominal or numeric, and selects the best-scoring test for the current level in the decision tree.

One can view this approach to building decision trees as partitioning an N-dimensional space, with each terminal node representing one hyper-rectangle and each test specifying one of its faces.[2] The technique noticeably increases the complexity of the decision-tree building process, but not outrageously so. Given M numeric attributes and I instances, the cost at each level of the tree is $M(I-1)$ times an equivalent task involving the same number of nominal attributes. The cost of constructing the overall tree is more difficult to compute, since a numeric attribute must be reconsidered for additional tests lower in the tree, unlike nominal ones. Many of the tests reported in the literature on natural domains have relied on this extension.

One can even adapt the basic DDT algorithm to construct decision trees from unsupervised training data. In this scheme, the modified algorithm still generates a set of alternative partitions based on the various attributes. However, it cannot evaluate them on their ability to discriminate among the classes, since there is no class information. Instead, the method measures a partition's ability to discriminate among the values of those attributes not used to form the partition.

Thus, given a domain with A attributes, one of which has been used to create partition P, the unsupervised algorithm treats each of the remaining $A-1$ attributes as 'class names' in turn, measuring the partition P's ability to discriminate among the values of the first attribute, then the second, and so forth. The method then selects the partition with the best *average* discriminating ability across all the attributes, creates nodes for each cluster in this partition, and recurses as in the standard algorithm.

This approach to evaluating partitions has clear links to the natural performance task for unsupervised induction, which involves predicting any attribute that is missing from a test instance. The univariate nature of decision trees introduces difficulties for instances that omit attributes used as tests but, as we discuss in Chapter 8, there are a number of remedies for this problem.

---

2. Thus, decision-tree methods form decision boundaries that are parallel to the axes of the instance space, like the conjunctive methods in Chapter 2.

7.2.3 Formation of multivariate concept hierarchies

Other variations on the DCH framework construct hierarchies that are *multivariate* in nature, in that each node or concept incorporates multiple predictive features. One such scheme still generates partitions on the basis of a single attribute, but does not necessarily include it as one of the predictors stored on children. Instead, it invokes one of the algorithms for inducing logical descriptions that we described in Chapter 2, such as HGS or HSG. These routines generate a conjunctive summary for each cluster of instances, using members of other clusters as negative training cases. The resulting descriptions are likely to include the attribute used to formulate the partition, but this is not guaranteed. They are also likely to be more specific, and thus more conservative in making predictions, than the single-attribute approach. For example, a new instance might not match the description associated with any child, forcing the performance module to reply 'unknown' or to predict the most likely class at the current level.[3]

Actually, one can combine this partitioning scheme with any conceptual representation and with any algorithm for inducing simple concept descriptions. After generating a partition, the DCH algorithm could instead use the LMS or IWP technique (Chapter 3) to generate a threshold concept for each cluster, using members of that cluster as positive instances and members of others as negatives. Another alternative is to use an instance-averaging method or a naive Bayesian classifier (Chapter 4) to generate one competitive concept description for each cluster of training cases.

Recall that, when used in isolation, techniques like HSG, LMS, IWP, Bayesian classifiers, and simple instance averaging are severely limited in their representational ability, and thus in their ability to learn. However, the current approach should not suffer from such limitations because the hierarchy stores knowledge at multiple levels of abstraction. Subdivisions at lower levels overcome the representational drawbacks at a given level, letting the hierarchy as a whole represent complex extensional definitions even though each level only describes simple ones. For the same reason, there seems no reason to invoke more powerful

---

3. One can even delay evaluation of partitions until after finding summary descriptions for each set of clusters, then use evaluation criteria that measure characteristics of these descriptions, like 'simplicity', to select among the partitions. This idea is common in techniques for *conceptual clustering*.

Table 7-3. The DMT algorithm: Divisive induction of multivariate trees.

```
Inputs: The current node N of the concept hierarchy.
        A set of classified training instances ISET.
Output: A multivariate concept hierarchy.
Top-level call: DMT(root, ISET).

Procedure DMT(N, ISET)

If all instances ISET are in the same class,
Then label terminal node N with the class name.
Else for each class C occurring in ISET,
        Let JSET be the members of ISET having class C.
        Form a node S with JSET as its members.
        Form an intensional description DESC for JSET.
    For each cluster JSET and associated S and DESC,
        Let KSET be the instances in ISET matched by DESC.
        Form a revised description DESC based on KSET.
        Associate the description DESC with node S.
        Make the node S a child of node N.
        DMT(S, KSET).
```

---

induction methods in this context, since they would add little to the overall effectiveness.

Another approach to forming multivariate concept hierarchies, less common in the literature, uses an even simpler partitioning scheme. Table 7-3 presents pseudocode for DMT (divisive induction of multivariate trees), another specialization of the DCH algorithm. At each level, this method simply groups instances by class names, then uses one of the above induction methods to generate intensional descriptions for each cluster. Next, DMT uses these descriptions to reassign instances, which leads to a revised partition and new summaries. In most situations, the second set of descriptions will not completely discriminate among the classes, so the revised partition will differ from the original one, as will the two sets of descriptions.

As usual, if a cluster contains instances from more than one class, DMT calls on itself recursively to further subdivide the data and to form more specific concept descriptions for each subclass. This approach makes less sense if one's goal is a univariate hierarchy, since the

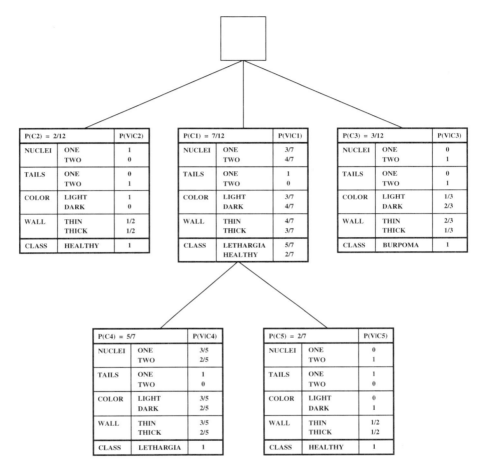

Figure 7-3. A multivariate concept hierarchy generated by the DMT algorithm for the training instances from Figure 7-1. Each node contains a probabilistic summary, which a Bayesian classifier uses to sort instances and to make predictions.

DDT algorithm generates one more directly. Nor can one easily adapt this scheme to handle unsupervised training data, since it relies on class information to form partitions. On the other hand, it provides an interesting approach to generating multivariate hierarchies from supervised training data.

Figure 7-3 depicts the concept hierarchy generated by DMT for the data in Figure 7-1 when it uses a Bayesian classifier as the induction subroutine. As in most probabilistic concepts, each node includes a base rate and a conditional probability for each attribute-value pair. In generating this tree, the algorithm first partitions the training instances into three clusters, one for each class, and then uses a Bayesian classifier to produce a probabilistic summary for each set. The resulting descriptions predict the correct class names for all instances of `lethargia` and `burpoma`, as well as for the second two `healthy` cases. However, it assigns the first two `healthy` cells to the `lethargia` class.

In response, DMT generates a revised partition based on these three groups of instances, then computes a revised probabilistic summary for each one. Because one of the clusters contains instances from two classes, it calls itself recursively on this subset of instances. Thus, the algorithm creates one partition for the five `lethargia` cases and another for the two `healthy` instances, after which it invokes the Bayesian classifier a second time to produce descriptions for each such cluster. This time the probabilistic summaries correctly predict the class associated with each instance, so DMT halts its construction of the probabilistic concept hierarchy.

7.2.4 Iterative optimization

A third approach to clustering, more common for unsupervised tasks, is known as *iterative optimization*. The basic method requires the user to specify the number of clusters at each level, although some variants iterate through different numbers on their own. The basic algorithm begins by selecting k instances to serve as seeds for each cluster. Typically the seeds are selected randomly, but more directed strategies are also possible. Next the method selects an unassigned training case and tentatively adds it to each cluster; after comparing the alternatives on some evaluation metric (e.g., distance to the cluster mean), it selects the best cluster and assigns the training case to it. The algorithm repeats this process for each nonseed instance in the current set.

At this point, the routine invokes some induction method to generate a summary description for each resulting cluster of instances. In some versions, it constructs this incrementally after each incorporation and uses the descriptions in its assignment decisions. In either case, iterative optimization then uses the summary description for each cluster to select or construct a new seed for that cluster. The algorithm then repeats the assignment process, placing each nonseed instance in one of the clusters, possibly a different one than on the previous pass. This iterative procedure continues until it reaches some halting condition, typically when it selects the same seeds twice in a row, which suggests that the partition and summaries have stabilized. Once iterative optimization has settled on a partition, one can recursively apply the method to produce lower levels of the hierarchy if desired.

As we have noted, iterative optimization is most widely used for unsupervised learning tasks, when the simpler methods do not apply. The scheme is most closely associated with nearest neighbor or instance-based methods, where the summary description for each cluster is either the set of training instances in that cluster or their average; this latter approach is often called *k-means clustering*. However, one can also combine the above technique with probabilistic induction methods, threshold learning algorithms, and even logical induction schemes. An important special case, known as the *expectation maximization* (EM) algorithm, probabilistically assigns instances to each cluster, updating the probabilistic summaries by the fractional amount assigned to each.

Unlike the simpler clustering methods we have discussed, iterative optimization involves a hill-climbing search through the space of possible partitions. A number of factors can affect the details of this search, including the initial seeds, the halting criterion, and even the order in which one assigns instances to clusters. But despite its computational cost and its sensitivity to these factors, the method has seen widespread use within algorithms for unsupervised learning.

7.3 Incremental formation of concept hierarchies

Now that we have reviewed some nonincremental algorithms, we can consider some incremental approaches to forming concept hierarchies. As we have noted earlier, incremental learning leads naturally to the integration of learning with performance. In most incremental systems, action by the performance component drives the learning element, and this also holds for the organization of memory. In Section 7.1, we noted that performance for a hierarchy-forming system involves sorting instances down through the concept hierarchy. As a result, it seems natural to acquire such hierarchies in a top-down fashion as well, and incremental methods typically construct their hierarchies in a divisive manner. One can view methods of this sort as carrying out an incremental hill-climbing search through a space of concept hierarchies.

Table 7-4. The ICH algorithm: Incremental formation of concept hierarchies.

```
Inputs: A set of training instances ISET.
Output: A concept hierarchy.

Procedure ICH(ISET)

Create a root node N based on the first instance J in ISET.
For each instance I other than J in ISET,
    ICH-Aux(N, I).
Return the concept hierarchy with the root node N.

Procedure ICH-Aux(N, I)

Let FLAG be False.
For each child C of N,
    If I matches C's predictive features well enough,
    Then let FLAG be True.
        If I mismatches C's predictable features,
        Then [expand the concept hierarchy downward]
            Create a child P of node N.
            Base the description of P on C and I.
            Create a child D of P based on I.
            Make C a child of P rather than N.
        Else modify the description of C based on I.
            ICH-Aux(C, I).
If FLAG is False,
Then [expand the concept hierarchy outward]
    Create a child E of node N based on instance I.
```

Because such methods can be sensitive to the training order, many of them include bidirectional learning operators that can reverse the effects of previous learning should new instances suggest the need.

Table 7-4 presents pseudocode for ICH, an abstract algorithm for the incremental divisive formation of concept hierarchies. The top-level algorithm uses the first training case to initialize the hierarchy (attaching initial predictive and predictable descriptions) and then iterates through the remaining instances, calling on ICH-Aux to carry out the main work. Given an existing hierarchy and an instance I, the subroutine sorts I through memory, starting at the root node. At a given node N, ICH-Aux compares I to the predictive features stored at each child C of N.

If the instance does not match any of these well enough, this suggests the need for a new category; thus, the algorithm creates a new child of N based on the instance, making the hierarchy wider at this level.

In contrast, if the instance I matches the predictable features for child C sufficiently well, the algorithm incorporates I into that node's description and recurses. If the predictive features match but the predictable ones do not, this suggests the need for making further distinctions. Accordingly, ICH-Aux extends the hierarchy downward by creating a new node P that becomes a child of N and the parent of C and a second new node, D, based on I. A special case occurs when the algorithm reaches a terminal node with predictable features that differ from the training case. The ICH algorithm calls on ICH-Aux anew for each training case, expanding the tree in breadth and depth as experience suggests.

7.3.1 Incremental induction of decision trees

Let us examine how one can adapt the above approach to the incremental induction of univariate decision trees. The specialized algorithm, which we will call IDT (incremental induction of decision trees), initializes the tree to contain a single root node with no predictive features and a single predictable feature, the class of the instance. It also stores the description of the instance with the node for use during learning. If the second instance has the same class as the first, then IDT takes no action, but if they disagree, it compares the new instance with the stored one to find their differences. The algorithm selects one difference at random and uses the attribute-value pairs as predictive tests on the two nodes it creates in expanding the tree downward. IDT stores the first instance with one child and the second instance with the other.

The algorithm repeats this process with successive training cases, sorting them through memory until they fail to match any of the nodes at a given level or until they reach a terminal node. In the former situation, IDT creates a new child with a predictive test that incorporates the same attribute as other nodes at that level; it also stores the training instance with this new node. In the latter case, the algorithm compares the class predicted by the terminal node to the class of the instance. If they disagree, IDT extends the tree downward, using some difference between the new instance and the stored one to identify a predictive attribute for the new nodes. If they agree, the algorithm makes no changes to memory.

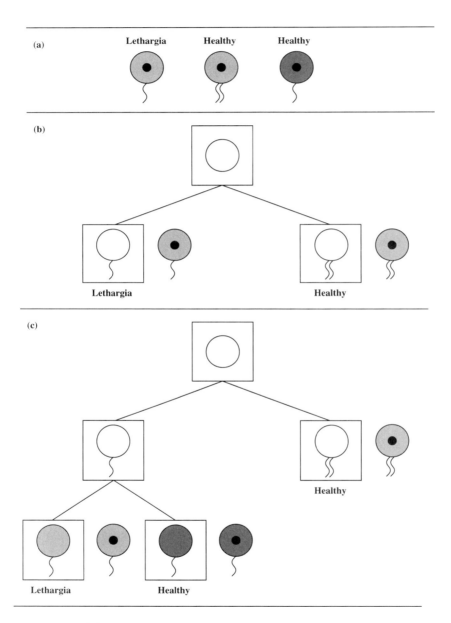

Figure 7-4. (a) Three training instances in the order presented to the IDT algorithm; (b) the decision tree generated by IDT after the first two training cases; and (c) the decision tree produced after processing the third case. Each node includes an associated instance for use in learning, shown immediately to its right.

Figure 7-4 shows a decision tree at two stages during its construction by the IDT algorithm when presented with training instances from the cell domain. The first training instance, a member of the `lethargia` class, leads to an initial one-node tree (not shown). Upon encountering the second training case, from a `healthy` patient, the algorithm finds that the predicted and observed class disagree. As a result, it compares the new and the stored instance, which reveals only one difference: the new instance has `one tail`, whereas the earlier one had `two tails`. Thus, IDT creates two new nodes, one with `one tail` as its predictive feature and `lethargia` as its predictable class, the other with `two tails` as its predictive feature and `healthy` as its associated class. Figure 7-4 (b) shows this state of the decision tree.

Upon processing a third instance, this one also from the `healthy` class, IDT finds that the case matches the predictive test for the leftmost child, causing it to sort the instance down this branch. However, the instance's class again fails to agree with the predicted one, causing a second discrimination to occur. This time the only difference between the stored and new instance is the `color`, leading to two new children with predictive tests based on this attribute. One of these predicts the `lethargia` class, whereas the other predicts `healthy` cells. This process continues, with the method extending the decision tree downward only when an instance's class differs from that stored on the node that it reaches.

Of course, we have simplified this example for the sake of clarity. In a domain with attributes having more than two possible values, the algorithm would also broaden the tree when an instance fails to match the descriptions of any children. More important, the example uses a training order in which IDT finds only one difference between instances. Given a benign training order, the algorithm will create the same decision tree as that generated by its nonincremental counterpart DDT. However, some training orders generate multiple differences, and the algorithm might well select one that it would later regret, since it has no mechanism for retracting such choices.

One can easily extend this general approach to learn discrimination networks from unsupervised training data. Rather than storing the class name as the predictable feature for a terminal node, the method instead stores one or more features of the instance itself. These may or may not include features used as predictors along the path to that node.

The modified algorithm bifurcates the tree and extends it downward whenever features of a training instance I differ from the predictable features stored at the terminal node to which I has been sorted.

7.3.2 Heuristic revision of univariate decision trees

The above schemes, whether applied to supervised or unsupervised data, will construct a decision tree or discrimination network that summarizes the instances. However, the random selection of predictive features means that the resulting hierarchies may be more complex than necessary. In addition, one can easily mislead IDT by adding noise to the training data. An obvious response to both problems is to use a more conservative method that collects statistics on the various features across a number of instances, as does the IHC method in Chapter 2.

For example, one might store with each node N the number of instances of each class that have passed through N, along with the number of times it has observed each attribute-value pair in instances sorted through N. Recall that the nonincremental DDT generates contingency tables directly from a set of instances; this scheme stores similar tables in the tree itself, opening the way for incremental updates.

Table 7-5 presents the algorithm HDT (heuristic revision of decision trees), which updates the class and attribute-value counts each time it sorts an instance through a given node. Occasionally, the algorithm sorts an instance having a value V on attribute A to a node that has never encountered this value. In this case, it creates a new branch labeled V, pointing to a new terminal node that predicts the observed class.

In addition to updating the counts at each node, HDT also recomputes the evaluation score for each predictive attribute after incorporating a new instance. For terminal nodes, this can lead the algorithm to extend the decision tree downward, adding new branches based on the values of an attribute that now appears useful. For nonterminal nodes, it can lead the system to replace an existing attribute with another one that now appears more discriminating. In this case, HDT removes the existing subtree below this node and gradually constructs a new subtree from additional training cases that incorporates the new attribute. In taking such a drastic step, the method loses information about previous instances. This effectively means trading smaller processing costs per instance for more instances during the tree-construction process.

Table 7-5. The HDT algorithm: Heuristic incremental induction of univariate decision trees.

```
Inputs: A set of classified training instances ISET.
Output: A univariate decision tree.

Procedure HDT(ISET)

Create a root node N for the decision tree.
For each training instance I in ISET,
    Let C be the class of instance I.
    HDT-Aux(N, I, C).
Return the decision tree with root node N.

Procedure HDT-Aux(N, I, C)

Use I to update the contingency table for node N.
For each attribute A in the attribute list ASET,
    Compute an evaluation score E_A for attribute A.
Select the attribute B with the best score E_B.
If B differs from the current attribute Y on N,
Then replace Y with B as the attribute associated with node N.
    Remove all existing subtrees of node N.
    If the best score E_B is sufficiently high,
    Then for each value V of B stored on N,
            Create a child S of node N.
            Place the attribute-value pair (B, V) on S.
            Initialize the counts on S to zero.
Else let A be the attribute associated with N.
    Let V be the value of instance I on attribute A.
    If N has a successor S with test (A, V),
    Then HDT-Aux(S, I, C).
    Else create a new successor S of N.
        Place the attribute-value pair (A, V) on S.
        Initialize the contingency table for S to contain
            zero entries for each attribute-value pair.
```

A more sophisticated variant of this algorithm, which we will call HDT', stores all training instances at the terminal nodes to which they were sorted, thus avoiding loss of information. Upon deciding to replace attribute A at a node with an attribute B that occurs lower in the hierarchy, the modified method moves the B test to the current node, moves A to the level immediately below, and recursively pushes attributes lower in the hierarchy one level down. If B does not occur in any subtree of the current node, HDT$'$ simply introduces it and pushes all subtrees downward by one level. This procedure is guaranteed to produce the same decision tree as DDT on any given training set, but only at the cost of reprocessing more instances than HDT.

Both approaches incorporate the notion of bidirectional operators that are central to robust methods for incremental hill climbing. Even using statistical techniques, nonrepresentative training sequences can mislead a learning algorithm; thus, it should be able to change its mind, and the operator for replacing one predictive attribute with another gives this capability.

7.3.3 Incremental formation of multivariate hierarchies

The methods we have examined let one construct univariate decision trees and discrimination networks in an incremental manner, but they do not support the formation of multivariate hierarchies. When generating structures that incorporate multiple features at each level, it makes little sense to use the values of a single attribute to partition the training instances. The central issue in such methods concerns when to create a new sibling at a given level.

Given classified training data, one can use errors in the class prediction to drive the creation of new nodes, as in many methods we have examined for incremental learning. Thus, one can employ incremental hill-climbing versions of the DMT algorithm, which partitions instances by their class name and constructs subtrees only when the descriptions induced for the current level fail to completely discriminate among the classes. One can instantiate this scheme using any of the incremental methods for inducing logical, threshold, or competitive concepts from Chapters 2 through 4.

Another approach, not driven by errors, draws on the incremental ICD algorithm from Chapter 5, which creates new disjuncts when a training instance differs enough from existing descriptions. Table 7-6 summarizes an algorithm that employs this idea to constrain the incremental formation of multivariate hierarchies (IMT). This method sorts a new training instance downward through its hierarchy, at each level deciding whether the instance is 'close enough' to the predictive de-

Table 7-6. The IMT algorithm: An incremental method for the formation of multivariate concept hierarchies.

```
Inputs: A set of training instances ISET.
Output: A concept hierarchy.

Procedure IMT(ISET)

Create a root node N based on the first instance J in ISET.
For each instance I other than J in ISET,
     IMT-Aux(N, I).
Return the concept hierarchy with the root node N.

Procedure IMT-Aux(N, I)

If N is a terminal node,
Then replace N with a node S that summarizes N and I.
     Create a node M based on instance I.
     Store N and M as children of S.
Else modify N to incorporate instance I.
     For each child C of node N,
          Compute the desirability of placing I in C.
     Let B be the child with the best score S_B.
     Let S_new be the score for creating a new node.
     Let S_merge be the score for merging B with its sibling D.
     Let S_split be the score for splitting B into its children.
     If S_new is the best score,
     Then create node R with a description based on I.
          Store node R as a child of node N.
     Else if S_B is the best score,
          Then IMT-Aux(B, I) (place I in category B).
          Else if S_merge is the best score,
               Then Merge(B, D, N).
                    IMT-Aux(B, I).
               Else Split(B, N).
                    IMT-Aux(N, I).
```

---

scription of one of the existing children. If not, IMT creates a new child at the current level, basing its description on that of the instance. In contrast, if the instance matches one of the existing children well enough, the algorithm incorporates the instance into that child's description (by changing logical constraints, weights on threshold units, or altering competitive summaries) and recurses to the next level.

Although these steps are sufficient to form a multivariate hierarchy in an incremental manner, by themselves they would be quite sensitive to the instance presentation, creating quite different hierarchies from different orders of the same data. For example, if the first instances are all dogs, the scheme would create subcategories of these at the top level. When it finally encountered instances of cats, it would create one category for them at the top level. However, it would still have all the dog instances at this same level, when one would prefer them grouped under a separate category.

IMT includes two additional operators to help it recover from such nonoptimal hierarchies. At each level of the classification process, the system considers *merging* the node that best classifies the new instance with its various siblings. If the resulting partition is better than the original according to some evaluation function, IMT combines the two nodes into a single category, although still retaining the original nodes as its children. This transforms a level with N nodes into one having $N - 1$ nodes.

The algorithm also incorporates the inverse operation of *splitting* nodes. At each level, if IMT decides to classify an instance as a member of an existing category, it also considers removing this category and elevating its children. If this action leads to an improved partition, the system changes the structure of its hierarchy accordingly. Thus, if one of N nodes at a given level has M children, splitting this node would give $N + M - 1$ nodes at this level. Taken together, these two operators can help IMT recover from early decisions that would otherwise produce undesirable hierarchies, in the same way that alternative bidirectional operators aid other incremental hill-climbing methods.

7.4 Agglomerative formation of concept hierarchies

A quite different approach to the construction of concept hierarchies operates in an *agglomerative* manner, grouping instances into successively larger clusters rather than refining them, as in the divisive scheme. Although one can run such methods on supervised training data, they are typically used on unsupervised learning tasks. Also, they are nearly always nonincremental in nature, requiring that all instances be present at the outset.

Table 7-7. The ACH algorithm: A nonincremental agglomerative method for generating concept hierarchies.

```
Inputs: A set of training instances ISET.
        A set MATRIX that gives the distances between
          each pair of training instances in ISET.
Output: A concept hierarchy.

Procedure ACH(ISET, MATRIX)

Let (A,B,DIST) be the MATRIX entry with the least distance.
Create a new node C with A and B as its children.
Generate a description D_C based on D_A and D_B.
Remove A and B from ISET.
If ISET is empty,
Then return the tree with top node C.
Else add the node C to ISET.
    Remove all entries containing A and B from MATRIX.
    For each entry I in ISET,
        Compute the distance DIST between D_I and D_C.
        Insert the triple (D_C,D_C,DIST) in MATRIX.
    ACH(ISET, MATRIX).
```

Researchers in *numerical taxonomy* have developed a variety of such algorithms, but here we will focus on a typical one, which we will call ACH (agglomerative formation of concept hierarchies). Table 7-7 presents pseudocode for this method, which accepts a set of training cases and a matrix that specifies all pairwise distances between the instances. Given this input, ACH finds the closest pair of entries A and B, which may be observed instances or, on later calls, conceptual summaries for sets of instances. The algorithm combines the two entries into a new cluster C, storing A and B as its children in the hierarchy and generating an intensional description for C. For numeric data, the simplest approach for agglomerative algorithms is to use an averaging technique that computes a single prototype for C based on the prototypes for A and B. However, one can also store the instances themselves or generate a logical, threshold, or probabilistic summary.

Next the algorithm checks to see if any entries remain to be incorporated. If not, ACH halts, returning the entire hierarchy it has generated

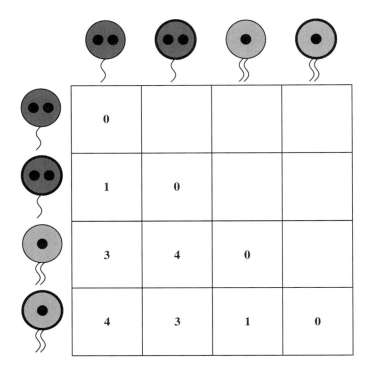

Figure 7-5. The initial distance matrix generated by the ACH algorithm from the four `healthy` instances in Figure 7-1, using the city block distance metric or Hamming distance.

along the way. If entries remain, it removes all pairs containing A and B (since they are now covered by C) and calculates all pairwise distances between C and the remaining entries, sorting them into the ordered list. ACH then calls itself recursively on the new set of pairs, combining the closest pair of entries, adding a new node to the hierarchy, and so forth, until it has combined all entries into a single taxonomic structure.

Although agglomerative methods are typically run on numeric data, we will demonstrate ACH's behavior in a nominal domain for the sake of comparison with other methods. Figure 7-5 shows the distance matrix generated for the four `healthy` cells from Figure 7-1, using a city block measure (i.e., Hamming distance) that contributes 1 for each mismatched feature and 0 for each matched attribute. The matrix shows that two pairs of cells differ on only one feature, but that others have greater distances. Thus, ACH selects one of the nearest pairs at random to form the first cluster, producing the revised matrix in Figure 7-6.

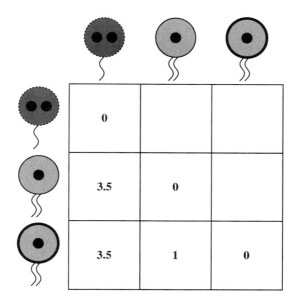

Figure 7-6. The second distance matrix generated by the ACH algorithm, after creation of the first cluster from the four `healthy` instances in Figure 7-1, using a probabilistic version of the city block distance metric.

To compute the distances in this second matrix, ACH must take some stand on the distance between instances and clusters. Here we assume a variant of the city block metric that assumes probabilistic cluster descriptions and gives credit for partial values. For example, the probabilistic average of the two merged instances can be stated as

```
tails    one    1 two    0
nuclei   one    0 two    1
color    light  0 dark   1
wall     thin   ½ thick  ½
```

Thus, the distance between this summary and the third cell, which has **two tails, one nucleus, light color,** and a **thin wall,** would be $1 + 1 + 1 + \frac{1}{2} = 3.5$, which equals the average distance between the two members of the cluster and the instance. This measure also lets the method compute the distance between pairs of cluster summaries.

In any case, the distance between the pair of remaining instances is much less than either's distance to the initial cluster, which leads ACH to combine them into a second cluster with its own probabilistic de-

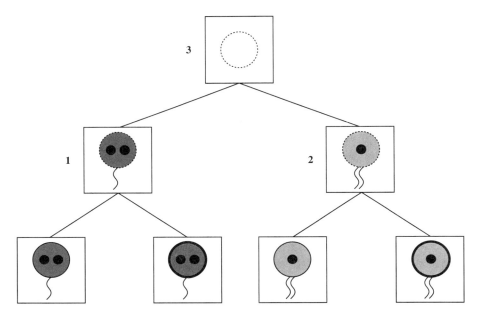

Figure 7-7. A concept hierarchy formed by the ACH algorithm from the four **healthy** instances in Figure 7-1, using a probabilistic version of the city block distance metric. Numbers next to the nodes indicate the order in which ACH generated them. The probabilistic descriptions for nodes are not shown.

scription. This in turn causes the algorithm to produce a new matrix with distances between the clusters. However, as there exist only two entries, ACH simply attaches them to a root node and returns the resulting hierarchy. Figure 7-7 shows the resulting structure, along with the order in which nodes are created.

Clearly, the ACH algorithm constructs a binary concept hierarchy with exactly two children for each nonterminal node. One can modify the algorithm to find the k nearest entries on each recursion, thus generating a branchier tree. Another alternative is to use some threshold to determine the minimum distance between entries before placing them in the same cluster. If the user is willing to specify the branching factor of the hierarchy at the outset, he can even employ iterative optimization (Section 7.2.4) to determine the clusters that are merged at each level.

There exist many dimensions of variations on the basic agglomerative approach, the most important involving the manner in which they measure distance. The version we saw above found a central tendency for each cluster and computed distances between them. However, one can describe clusters using the training cases themselves and compute the distance between the two nearest instances in each cluster. For some data sets, this strategy can generate very different hierarchies from those produced with schemes that use central tendencies. The distance measure itself can also greatly affect the resulting taxonomies, and researchers have explored a wide variety of such metrics.

Research in numerical taxonomy, where methods like ACH originated, has typically been aimed at exploratory data analysis. Thus, users have often been more concerned with forming understandable clusters than in measuring their ability on some performance task. However, experimental comparisons suggest that these methods can produce as accurate knowledge structures as the divisive algorithms we described in previous sections.

7.5 Variations on hierarchy formation

Now that we have considered some basic approaches to the formation of concept hierarchies, we can consider some refinements that cut across the methods. In this section we examine a variety of extensions, including alternative search-control schemes, extensions to more complex memory organizations, and methods for transforming concept hierarchies into other structures.

7.5.1 Alternative search algorithms

The algorithms we have presented in this chapter have an important feature in common – they carry out greedy or hill-climbing searches through the space of concept hierarchies. Our bias toward such methods reflects a strong trend in the literature, but this does not mean that more sophisticated, search-intensive methods are not possible. For instance, one might retain multiple competing hierarchies rather than only one, pursuing a beam search that uses the same learning operators and evaluation metrics.

A less obvious extension involves lookahead search in the hierarchy space. For example, in constructing a univariate decision tree, the attribute that appears most discriminating at the current level might lead to clusters that cannot easily be distinguished further. In contrast, a second attribute might look less informative in isolation, but lead to excellent distinctions when combined with a second feature. A revised version of DDT that considers all *pairs* of attributes, which equates to looking two steps ahead in the search, will detect such situations. Deeper lookaheads will be more expensive but can find more complex interactions among attributes. An extreme version of this approach carries out best-first search through the space of concept hierarchies.

Another scheme uses a greedy method to efficiently construct an initial concept hierarchy, then applies hierarchy-altering operators in the hope of producing better structures. This approach requires an evaluation metric over the entire hierarchy, which it can use to decide whether a revised structure is preferable to the current one. This method constitutes a form of 'anytime learning', in that it continues running as long as computational resources are available, with longer runs tending to produce better hierarchies, at least on the training set.

7.5.2 Forming more complex structures

Although most research on hierarchy formation has dealt with tree structures, one can imagine domains in which more complex organizations of memory would be useful. For example, a univariate decision tree requires $2^{k+1} - 1$ nodes to represent a k-bit parity concept, in which an instance is positive if an even number of the k relevant Boolean features are true and negative otherwise. In contrast, one can represent the same target concept with only $2k + 1$ nodes, provided that one uses a directed acyclic graph (DAG) rather than a tree.

The DDT algorithm requires two modifications to construct such 'decision DAGs'. First, one must include an operator for merging two nodes into a single node, which is needed to obtain nodes with multiple parents. Second, one must use an evaluation metric that, in some cases, prefers a DAG structure to the equivalent but more complex tree structure. Notions of minimum description length (Chapter 5) seem well suited for this purpose. In addition, DDT constructs decision trees in a depth-first fashion, expanding nodes on the left before expanding with ones further to the right. Formation of decision DAGs is aided by a more flexible control structure that expands whichever node best improves the quality of the hierarchy.

In unsupervised learning, the performance task can involve prediction of multiple features. In some domains, the best hierarchy for predicting one feature may differ from the best hierarchy for predicting another. For example, suppose some animals are carnivores, whereas others are herbivores; also suppose that some occur in a zoo and others in homes. One might well want to organize the instances into two interleaved trees, the first related to eating habits and the second to surroundings, with the predictable and predictive features differing in the two trees. One response to this situation is to formulate a hierarchy that interleaves OR nodes, which sort instances down one branch or another, with AND nodes, which sort instances down all branches.

One can adapt both divisive and agglomerative approaches to the construction of such hierarchies. For example, in generating a univariate concept hierarchy, one might select the k most discriminating attributes rather than only one, and thus produce a tree with k complementary AND nodes at each choice point, alternating with OR nodes. A similar approach applies to the divisive formation of multivariate concept hierarchies. The challenge here involves deciding on the appropriate number of AND children for a given OR node, just as one must decide on the number of OR children in simpler multivariate tree structures. In the agglomerative framework, one can select the k nearest neighbors at each level, creating multiple interleaved trees from the bottom up that organize instances in complementary ways.

7.6 Transforming hierarchies into other structures

As we have seen, concept hierarchies impose a particular organization on memory. This structure seems quite different from those we considered in Chapters 5 and 6, but there are special cases in which there exists a clear mapping from one type of organization to another. For example, univariate decision trees are a strict subset of decision lists with logical tests, and there is a simple method that transforms the former structures into the latter.

Table 7-8 presents pseudocode for DTL (decision tree to decision list), an algorithm that carries out this transformation. Given a univariate decision tree, the method traverses each path through the tree, collecting tests along the way. Upon reaching each terminal node, it creates a logical rule using the tests it has collected in the left-hand side and

Table 7-8. The DTL algorithm for transforming a univariate decision tree into a decision list.

```
Inputs: The current node N of the decision tree.
        The RULES collected so far.
        The conditions LHS collected for the current rule.
Output: A logical decision list.
Top-level call:  DTL(root, { }, { })

Procedure DTL(N, RULES, LHS)

  If N is a terminal node,
     Then let C be the class stored at N.
          Insert the rule 'If LHS, then C' into RULES, using the
             percentage of C instances at N to determine order.
          Return RULES.
     Else for each child S of node N,
          Let T be the attribute-value test for node S.
          Let LHS' be the union of T and LHS.
          Let RULES be DTL(S, RULES, LHS').
```

---

the class for the terminal node in the right-hand side. DTL uses the accuracy of each terminal node on the training set (the percentage of instances with the specified class) to order rules in the decision list.

One cannot turn any multivariate decision tree into a decision list, but such a tree can be transformed into a special form of inference network. Consider a binary multivariate tree in which each pair of siblings is discriminated by a linear threshold unit. We can redraw such a tree as a three-layer inference network. Each internal node from the tree becomes a node in the first layer, each *path* through the tree produces a conjunctive node in the second layer (with inputs from each internal node along the path), and each class produces a disjunctive node in the third layer (with inputs from each path that predicts that class). Similar mappings exist for multivariate trees that organize logical and competitive descriptions, although the former produces two levels of conjunctive nodes that could be combined into a single layer.

The above treatment suggests that concept hierarchies are simply special cases of decision lists and inference networks. However, our examples have focused on decision trees, in which a single predictable attribute (the class) is stored with terminal nodes. The relationship is less clear for concept hierarchies that store multiple predictable attributes (sometimes at internal nodes), and for hierarchies that alternate between AND and OR nodes or that organize concepts into directed acyclic graphs.

7.7 Summary of the chapter

In this chapter we examined concept hierarchies as an organization for memory, along with the use and acquisition of such structures. We found that, like inference networks, concept hierarchies can organize logical, threshold, or competitive concepts, but that they work in a quite different manner. In general, the performance component sorts a new instance downward through the hierarchy, at each choice point using predictive features to select a branch, and using predictable features to make inferences when the sorting process halts.

Although performance always takes place from the top down, we found that the formation of hierarchies can occur in either a divisive or agglomerative fashion. We encountered three nonincremental algorithms that operate divisively: the DDT method clusters training cases into groups based on a single attribute's values and creates univariate trees; DMT forms clusters based on instances' class and constructs multivariate hierarchies; and iterative optimization uses a more sophisticated hill-climbing process to cluster the data.

We also saw two divisive algorithms that operate incrementally, thus integrating performance with learning. The first, HDT, retains statistics for predictive attributes with each node that let it revise a univariate tree in the light of new data. The second, IMT, stores similar information for use in extending or revising multivariate concept hierarchies. Both methods rely on bidirectional learning operators to minimize the effects of training order.

Finally, we considered ACH, an agglomerative method that constructs concept hierarchies from the bottom up. This algorithm computes the distance between all pairs of training instances, selects the closest for merging, replaces the pair with their parent, and repeats the process. Because agglomerative methods reconsider many instances on each iteration, they are typically nonincremental. Research on these techniques has used a variety of distance metrics that can produce quite different hierarchies for the same data.

Most research on the formation of concept hierarchies has focused on tree construction using greedy algorithms, but similar methods can organize concepts into more complex structures such as directed acyclic graphs, and more sophisticated search schemes are also possible. Both types of extension require search through an expanded space, but in some cases they can produce hierarchies that are both simpler and more accurate on novel test cases. We also saw that one can transform decision trees into decision lists or inference networks, if one prefers such organizations, but that this does not necessarily hold for arbitrary concept hierarchies.

Exercises

1. Show a univariate decision tree that the DDT algorithm (Section 7.2.1) constructs from the training data in Figure 5-4 (from Chapter 5), along with the evaluation scores for each attribute selected. Break ties among attributes randomly. If a tie occurs at the top level, show a second decision tree based on selecting a different split.

2. Draw a univariate decision tree that DDT constructs for the numeric data in Figure 5-2 (from Chapter 5). Also show the decision regions that this tree produces, labeling each boundary with the order in which the algorithm introduces it. Repeat this process for the training data in Figure 5-7.

3. Show the multivariate decision tree that the DMT algorithm (Section 7.2.3) generates for the cases in Figure 5-2, using an instance-averaging subroutine (Chapter 4). Show the mean values for the attributes at each node in the hierarchy, along with the decision boundaries they produce. Do the same for the data in Figure 5-7.

4. Ignore the classes associated with instances in Figure 5-7 and apply k-means clustering, with $k = 2$, to divide the data into two groups. Select the bottom left and far right instances as initial seeds, and show both the clusters and their means on each iteration of the method until it converges. Repeat the process with the two leftmost instances as seeds.

5. Trace the IDT algorithm (Section 7.3.1) on the training data in Figure 5-5 (from Chapter 5), showing which instances lead to changes in the decision tree and the structure that results in each case. Do the same for a similar training set in which the fourth instance (d) is negative rather than positive.

6. Trace the behavior of the HDT algorithm (Section 7.3.2) on the training data from Figure 5-4, showing the scores of each attribute at the affected node whenever the tree structure changes. Assume that the method initially sees the first two positive instances, followed by the first negative case, after which instances of the two classes alternate. Show the tree that results if one runs the data through twice in the same order.

7. Trace the behavior of the IMT algorithm (Section 7.3.3) on the training data in Figure 5-8 (from Chapter 5). Use Euclidean distance of an instance from a node's mean as the latter's score, and assume that each instance is always sorted to a terminal node (i.e., ignore node merging, splitting, and creation at nonterminal levels). Repeat this process on the same data, but prefer node creation when the Euclidean distance is greater than 5 from the nearest node's mean.

8. Show the distance matrix for the five instances from Exercise 7, using Euclidean distance, along with the revised matrix after the ACH algorithm (Section 7.4) creates the first cluster. Draw the structure of the hierarchy that ACH generates, and specify the mean values for each node in the hierarchy.

9. Recall that the data summarized by the decision tree in Exercise 1 can also be described by the DNF formula in Figure 5-4 (d). Draw a decision DAG (Section 7.5.2) that is equivalent to this formula, without specifying the algorithm used to construct it. Compare the number of nodes in this DAG to the number in the tree from Exercise 1.

10. Use the DTL algorithm (Section 7.6) to transform the decision tree from Exercise 1 into a decision list. Can you remove any conditions from the resulting rules without altering the decision list's behavior on the training data?

Historical and bibliographical remarks

Univariate concept hierarchies (simple decision trees and discrimination networks) have played a central role in machine learning since its earliest days. Hunt (1962) describes CLS, an early version of the nonincremental DDT algorithm, which he proposed as a model of human learning; Hunt, Marin, and Stone (1966) built on this approach and presented the first extensive experimental study of concept induction. Quinlan's (1983) ID3 extended the CLS framework to incorporate a decision-theoretic evaluation metric and other features; his system has been used by many researchers in comparative studies but no longer has status as a psychological theory. Its successor, C4.5 (Quinlan, 1993b), is also widely used by induction researchers; it includes a number of improvements, including use of the DTL algorithm (due to Quinlan, 1987) to translate a decision tree into a decision list. Mingers (1989a) reviews many of the evaluation metrics used in decision-tree induction and reports an experimental comparison, as do Buntine and Niblett (1992).

Independent but related lines of research come from the social sciences and statistics. In the former community, Sonquist, Baker, and Morgan (1977) proposed AID, a method for univariate decision-tree induction that uses a statistical measure to select discriminating attributes. Biggs, de Ville, and Suen (1991) review this approach and various extensions, broadly referred to as CHAID. In statistics, Friedman (1977) described another variant of the DDT algorithm for creating decision trees, which Breiman, Friedman, Olshen, and Stone (1984) developed into CART, a software package that has been widely used in statistics and, to a lesser extent, in machine learning.

Much of the recent research has explored variations and extensions of the basic DDT algorithm. Patterson and Niblett (1982) and Breiman et al. (1984) describe approaches to creating binary splits from numeric attributes, Cestnik, Kononenko, and Bratko's (1987) ASSISTANT constructs binary trees that contain arbitrary subsets of nominal values, and Breiman et al.'s CART creates trees with n branches, each with an arbitrary subset of nominal values. CART was also the first system to induce multivariate decision trees, using the IWP algorithm from Chapter 3 as a subroutine. More recently, Utgoff and Brodley's (1990) LMDT method induces multivariate trees composed of linear machines, Murthy, Kasif, Salzberg, and Beigel's (1993) OC1 uses a variation on the CART scheme, and Langley's (1993) recursive Bayesian classifier uses the DMT algorithm (Section 7.2.3) to form a hierarchy of probabilistic descriptions.

Research on the incremental formation of concept hierarchies also has a long history. The ICH algorithm in Section 7.3 is based on Feigenbaum's (1961) EPAM, a model of human memorization and retrieval that has had a pervasive influence on both psychology and machine learning. Richman (1991) reviews some recent extensions to EPAM and the system's psychological status. Lebowitz's (1987) UNIMEM revised the EPAM approach to handle multivariate concept hierarchies, and Fisher's (1987) COBWEB (the basis of our IMT algorithm) refined this approach and provided a probabilistic semantics. Hadzikadic and Yun (1989), McKusick and Langley (1991), and Martin and Billman (1994) have also done work in this tradition. A collection by Fisher, Pazzani, and Langley (1991) contains a representative sample of work on the incremental induction of concept hierarchies. The HDT algorithm for incremental induction of decision trees, which represents a somewhat different line of research, comes from Schlimmer and Fisher's (1986) ID4, which Utgoff (1989) extends in his ID5R system.

Work on agglomerative methods like the ACH algorithm has been less common within the machine learning community, though Hanson and Bauer's (1989) WITT is one exception. Agglomerative techniques are more widely used within numerical taxonomy; Annenberg (1973) and Everitt (1980) provide broad reviews of this area, while Fisher and Langley (1986) discuss its relation to machine learning work on hierarchy formation. Techniques for iterative optimization like the k means and EM algorithms are also widely used in numerical taxonomy, but some work (e.g., Michalski & Stepp, 1983; Jordan & Jacobs, 1993) also appears in the machine learning literature on hierarchy construction.

A few researchers have explored variations on the basic methods for forming concept hierarchies, as outlined in Section 7.5. For example, Norton (1989) describes an extension of the DDT algorithm that uses multi-step lookahead. Oliver (1993) reports a version of DDT for inducing univariate decision DAGs, whereas Kohavi (1994) presents a quite different approach to the same task. Martin and Billman (1994) describe a variation of the IMT method that creates concept hierarchies with interleaved AND and OR nodes. Our DTL algorithm for translating decision trees into decision lists borrows from Quinlan's (1987, 1993b) work in this area.

CHAPTER 8

Other Issues in Concept Induction

In the previous chapters we have examined a variety of methods for inducing logical, threshold, and competitive concepts, along with techniques for organizing them into larger knowledge structures like decision lists, inference networks, and concept hierarchies. However, our treatment of these algorithms made a number of simplifying assumptions about the nature of the training and test data.

In particular, we assumed that the domains were generally free of attribute and class noise, and that most features were actually useful in the prediction process. We also supposed that the aim of learning was to improve the accuracy of predicting a given class attribute, and that this attribute took on a small set of nominal values. Finally, we assumed that instances were described as a set of attribute-value pairs rather than in some more sophisticated formalism, and that each instance was completely described in terms of these attribute values.

In this chapter we consider some extensions to the basic algorithms that go beyond these assumptions, letting them deal with noisy domains, irrelevant features, numeric prediction, unsupervised data, first-order descriptions, and missing attributes. In each case, we attempt to formulate these extensions in the most general way possible, as they often apply not to specific methods but to entire classes of them.

8.1 Overfitting and pruning

As we noted in Chapter 1, some domains contain noise in attribute or class information, yet many of the algorithms we have considered assume noise-free data. Given either form of noise, constructing concept descriptions that cover all the training cases will produce an idiosyncratic knowledge structure that performs poorly on separate test data.

Researchers have explored a number of extensions designed to prevent such *overfitting* of the training data, and here we consider the main alternatives along these lines.

8.1.1 Pruning knowledge structures

Perhaps the most straightforward approach, often called *pre-pruning*, operates in conjunction with any induction method that moves from simple structures to more complex ones. This includes techniques for the divisive construction of concept hierarchies, separate-and-conquer methods for decision lists, and many schemes for determining the structure of inference networks. Rather than continuing to extend a knowledge structure by adding branches, rules, or nodes whenever these improve accuracy on the training set, one uses some more conservative test to determine whether this addition is likely to improve behavior on separate test cases. Only if this appears to hold does the algorithm continue; otherwise it halts and returns the current structure, even though this does worse on the training data than would the extended one.

For example, in constructing a decision tree, a pre-pruning version of the DDT algorithm from Chapter 7 would check, each time it is about to extend the tree downward by adding children to an existing node, whether this extension is actually desirable. If not, then the method would not add the children and it would halt tree construction, at least in this portion of the tree.

Another approach to minimizing the effect of noise on induction algorithms, often called *post-pruning*, operates in the opposite direction. Here one uses some induction method to construct a knowledge structure that minimizes error on the training set, ideally so that it correctly classifies all observed instances.[1] Naturally, this produces an overly complex and idiosyncratic knowledge structure if the data are noisy. However, one then goes back through the structure, pruning components that do not significantly aid in classification, again using some conservative test that estimates accuracy on test data.

For instance, one can use the DDT algorithm to construct a decision tree that correctly classifies all of the training cases (or as many as possible if some are inconsistent), then prune this tree back to avoid

---

1. Some algorithms must be modified somewhat to handle inconsistent data sets that contain identical instances with different associated classes.

Table 8-1. A logical decision list from the cell domain (a) before pruning and (b) after post-pruning has removed the last `lethargia` rule and eliminated one condition in another rule.

(a) `lethargia :- one-tail, thin-wall, two-nuclei.`
    `healthy :- one-tail, thin-wall, one-nucleus.`
    `lethargia :- two-tails, thick-wall, one-nucleus.`
    `lethargia :- two-tails, two-nuclei.`
    `healthy :- true.`
(b) `lethargia :- one-tail, thin-wall, two-nuclei.`
    `healthy :- one-tail, thin-wall, one-nucleus.`
    `lethargia :- two-tails, one-nucleus.`
    `healthy :- true.`

---

overfitting. The standard scheme uses a bottom-up greedy algorithm that, on each step, considers the result of deleting one of the lowest subtrees. If the evaluation function suggests that this removal would not hurt accuracy on a test set, then it is pruned; otherwise, the subtree is retained. The process then considers another of the lowest subtrees, tries pruning it, and continues until no further deletions are justified.

Although pre-pruning and post-pruning were originally developed in the context of decision-tree induction, they can be combined with any learning technique that deals with more than the simplest structures. For example, one can use a similar greedy method to prune decision lists by deciding to remove (or not to add) individual conditions or by deciding to eliminate (or not to create) entire rules. Table 8-1 shows a logical decision list for the cell domain before and after a post-pruning scheme has been applied.[2]

One can adopt similar ideas in deciding when to stop removing nodes and links from (or when to stop adding them to) a multilayer inference network. One can even collect statistics on stored cases in a nearest neighbor framework, then remove instances that historically have made

---

2. One advantage of this technique is that it lets the learner remove conditions added early to a rule without sacrificing those added later, whereas post-pruning in decision trees typically removes tests only in the reverse order from which they were added. For this reason, some systems convert decision trees to decision lists and then prune the latter.

poor predictions or add ones that would have fared well. The idea of pruning is one of the most general within machine learning, although its incarnation naturally differs across frameworks.

8.1.2 Evaluation metrics for pruning

We have considered a number of pruning algorithms, but we have been intentionally vague in our treatment of the evaluation measures they use in making decisions. We have done so because, generally speaking, one can combine any pruning scheme with any evaluation metric. The literature contains a variety of such metrics, but they fall into three basic classes, which we now consider.

The simplest method involves some form of significance test on the training data. For example, in deciding whether to prune a subtree from a concept hierarchy, one can use a χ^2 test to determine whether the unpruned tree is significantly better at discriminating classes than the pruned version.[3] This test measures the degree to which different values of an attribute are associated with different classes. Like all statistical tests, χ^2 requires one to specify a confidence level. Thus, one might want to include the subtree if there exists a 5% chance that the observed difference is due to noise, or one might be more conservative and include it only if there is a 1% chance. In general, the latter criterion will require either greater differences or more data than the former. This general class of metrics is sometimes said to rely on *resubstitution error*, because it involves resubstituting the training data into the induced structure and using it to estimate the error rate.

Some statisticians argue that resubstitution error is a poor measure even when combined with statistical tests. Instead, they recommend holding some training data back as a separate *evaluation set*, then using relative accuracy on this set to make pruning decisions. This approach, which is closely related to techniques for *cross validation*, means that less data are available for training, but it can provide a better estimate of accuracy on novel test cases because the induction algorithm has not seen instances in the evaluation set. As with resubstitution estimates, one can combine this scheme with tests for statistical significance, but they are not strictly needed; one can simply continue to simplify or extend the concept hierarchy, decision list, or inference network until accuracy on the evaluation set decreases.

---

3. This statistic is not reliable for data sets containing four or fewer instances, but one can use Yates' correction in such circumstances.

The third broad class of metrics implement a tradeoff between accuracy on the training set and some measure of simplicity. We saw a very simple form of this idea in Chapter 2, in the context of the IHC algorithm, but more sophisticated versions are possible. The most common of these formulations, known as *minimum description length*, is based on information theory. In particular, it measures the total number of bits needed to encode the hypothesized knowledge structure H and the number of bits needed to encode exceptions to H in the training data D, then takes their sum. Mathematically, this is expressed as

$$-log\ p(H|D)\ =\ -log\ p(H)\ +\ -log\ p(D|H)\quad,$$

where one desires to minimize the left-hand term. This measure requires one to specify a coding scheme for hypotheses and data but, having done this, one can combine it with any induction algorithm to determine when to stop adding structures (pre-pruning) or when to remove them (post-pruning).

A closely related idea can be used with algorithms for revising weights in multilayer inference networks. This variation, often called *weight decay*, incorporates a bias toward simplicity into methods like backpropagation by modifying the error term to prefer weights that are very small or large, but not intermediate in size (say around 1). A way to implement this idea is to modify the error function to be minimized (and which is used in determining the updating rule) so that it includes not only the mean squared difference between predicted and observed outputs, but also a term for the sum of the squared weights in the network. A generalization of this scheme rewards the weight-revision method for using weights that are close to any of a small set. Such modified error functions operate in a similar way to minimum description length for pre-pruning, in that they cause the learner to halt not when it minimizes the normal definition of error on the training set, but rather when it minimizes the revised measure that prefers fewer distinct parameters.

8.1.3 Dynamic pruning methods

The approaches described above all attempt to handle noise by altering the knowledge structure created during learning, typically by restricting the number of effective parameters. However, another viable approach involves inducing an unrestricted knowledge structure but then using it in some way that avoids overfitting. Such *dynamic pruning* has a quite different flavor from the methods considered so far, but it can have a similar effect on performance.

One simple technique for dynamic pruning involves the selective use of the components in a learned knowledge structure. For example, given an induced concept hierarchy, one might decide to halt the sorting of a test case before it reaches a terminal node because the statistics for a particular branch suggest that it is unreliable. Similarly, one can decide not to base a prediction on a particular rule in a decision list or on a given instance stored in case memory if its behavior on the training set suggests it cannot be trusted. This approach, designed mainly for incremental algorithms that must make decisions before seeing all the training data, can be adapted to emulate the effects of most pruning techniques and can incorporate most evaluation measures.

Another version of dynamic pruning relies on the notion of *voting*. This approach seems most natural with Bayesian schemes, as one can compute the probability of each concept description given the test case, then use these scores to make a weighted prediction. The k nearest neighbor method embodies a similar idea, especially with versions that weigh the votes of distant cases less than the votes of nearer ones. Both approaches are designed to minimize reliance on individual descriptions and thus should guard against overfitting effects.

However, one can easily adapt the voting scheme to other frameworks. Most techniques for determining weights in a multilayer neural network assign initial weights randomly. As a result, different runs typically produce networks with different final weights. In making predictions, one can simply take the majority vote of these alternative knowledge structures. A more sophisticated approach assigns a weight or probability to each network proportional to its accuracy on the training set, then bases the final prediction on their weighted vote.

The adaptation of this idea to logical concept induction is less obvious, as most such methods are deterministic in nature. However, rather than carry out a greedy search through the space of logical descriptions, one can instead carry out a beam search with some small beam width, which produces a set of alternative hypotheses as output. Again, one can simply take the vote of these descriptions to classify test cases or one can estimate their predictive accuracies and use these scores to weight their votes accordingly.

8.2 Selecting useful features

One of the central issues in induction concerns the selection of useful features. Although most learning methods attempt to either select attributes or assign them degrees of importance, both theoretical analyses and experimental studies indicate that many algorithms scale poorly to domains with large numbers of irrelevant features. For example, the number of training cases needed for simple nearest neighbor (see Chapter 5) to reach a given level of accuracy appears to grow exponentially with the number of irrelevant features, independent of the target concept. Even methods for inducing univariate decision trees, which explicitly select some attributes in favor of others, exhibit this behavior for some target concepts. And some techniques, like the naive Bayesian classifier (Chapter 4), can be very sensitive to domains with correlated attributes. This suggests the need for additional methods to select a useful subset of features when many are available.

8.2.1 Feature selection as heuristic search

Following the theoretical bias we have used elsewhere in this book, we can view the task of feature selection as a search problem.[4] As Figure 8-1 depicts, each state in the search space specifies a subset of the possible features, and one can impose a partial ordering on this space, with each child having exactly one more feature than its parents. As with any such problem, techniques for feature selection must take a stance on four basic issues that arise in the heuristic search process.

First, one must determine the starting point in the space, which in turn determines the direction of search. For instance, one might start with no features and successively add attributes, or one might start with all attributes and successively remove them. The former approach is sometimes called *forward selection*, whereas the latter is known as *backward elimination*. One might also select an initial state somewhere in the middle and move outward from this point.

A second decision involves the organization of the search. Clearly, an exhaustive search of the space is impractical, as there exist 2^a possible subsets of a attributes. A more realistic approach relies on a greedy method to traverse the space. At each point in the search, one considers

---

4. One can also adapt techniques for feature selection to determine attribute weights, but we will not focus on that issue here.

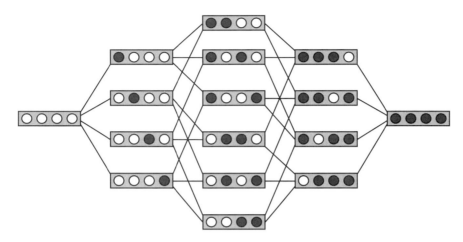

Figure 8-1. Each state in the space of feature subsets specifies the attributes that one might use during induction. Note that the states (in this case involving four features) are partially ordered, with each of a state's children (to the right) including one more attribute (dark circles) than its parents.

local changes to the current set of attributes, selects one, and then iterates, never reconsidering the choice. A related approach, known as *stepwise* selection or elimination, considers both adding and removing features at each decision point, which lets one retract an earlier decision without keeping explicit track of the search path. Within these options, one can consider all states generated by the operators and then select the best, or one can simply choose the first state that improves accuracy over the current set.

8.2.2 Filter and wrapper approaches to feature selection

A third issue concerns the evaluation strategy used to select among alternative subsets of attributes. One broad class of strategies considers attributes independently of the induction algorithm that will use them, relying on general characteristics of the training set to select some features and to exclude others. These are sometimes called *filter* methods, because they filter out irrelevant attributes before the induction process occurs. In contrast, *wrapper* methods generate a set of candidate features, run the induction algorithm with these features on the training data, and use the accuracy of the resulting description to evaluate the feature set. Within this approach, one can use accuracy on the training set or a more conservative estimate computed by cross validation.

The general argument for wrapper approaches is that the induction method planned for use with the feature subset should provide a better estimate of accuracy than a separate measure that has an entirely different inductive bias. The major disadvantage of wrapper methods over filter schemes is the former's computational cost, which results from calling the induction algorithm for each feature set considered. This cost has led some researchers to invent ingenious techniques for speeding the evaluation process that cache hypothesized structures or that reduce the number of training cases used for accuracy estimates.

Finally, one must decide on some criterion for halting search through the space of feature subsets. Within the wrapper framework, one might stop adding or removing attributes when none of the alternatives improves the estimate of classification accuracy, one might continue to revise the feature set as long as accuracy does not degrade, or one might continue generating candidate sets until reaching the other end of the search space and then select the best. Within the filter framework, one criterion for halting notes when each combination of values for the selected attributes maps onto a single class value. Another alternative simply orders the features according to some usefulness score, then determines some break point below which it rejects features.

Note that the above methods for feature selection can be combined with *any* induction algorithm to increase its learning rate in domains with irrelevant attributes. The effect on behavior may differ for different induction techniques and for different target concepts, in some cases producing little benefit and in others giving major improvement. But the basic idea of searching the space of feature sets is conceptually and practically distinct from the specific induction method that benefits from the feature-selection process.

8.3 Induction for numeric prediction

Most research in machine learning has focused on the induction of knowledge for classification purposes, and our treatment in previous pages has reflected this emphasis. However, some tasks instead involve *regression* – the prediction of numeric values – and there also exists a sizable literature on this topic. In this section we consider those methods from Chapters 5, 6, and 7 that lend themselves directly to the induction of regression knowledge, some other techniques that can be adapted to regression problems, and a new class of methods designed to find explicit functional expressions.

Naturally, overfitting can be as much an issue for regression as for classification, since noise also occurs in numeric domains. Most of the responses we considered in Section 8.1, including pre-pruning, post-pruning, and voting, also apply to learning for purposes of numeric prediction, as do evaluation schemes like significance tests, separate evaluation sets, and minimum description length, although some changes are needed in their details. The same comments hold for feature selection.

8.3.1 Direct approaches to regression

Some techniques, such as nearest neighbor methods, make no distinction between classification and regression problems. The unedited versions of this approach simply store training cases in memory during learning, and during testing they simply predict the value of the missing attribute. Whether this attribute takes on nominal values (as with class names) or numeric ones makes no difference to the induction process, and prediction requires only minor changes, such as replacing the voting process in k nearest neighbor with a weighted averaging scheme.

Yet other methods, although we introduced them in the context of classification, were actually designed with numeric prediction in mind. Two important examples are the LMS algorithm from Chapter 3 and the closely related backpropagation method from Chapter 6. Recall that the performance elements for these techniques compute a weighted sum of the observed, predictive attributes. The thresholds on these sums serve partly to transform numeric predictions into classification decisions.

The LMS and backpropagation algorithms themselves require no modification to learn from numeric data. One simply replaces the 1 or 0 that represents the class name in the training data with some real value. As before, the induction method computes the difference between the predicted and observed values, then uses this information to direct a gradient-descent search through the weight space in an effort to minimize mean-squared error or some other function.

As we noted in Chapter 6, one can use backpropagation with inference networks that are composed entirely of linear units, entirely of spherical units, or some combination of these representations. One method commonly used for numeric prediction, radial basis functions, computes a linear combination of the outputs of spherical units. These are sometimes called *mixture models* because they describe a regression function as a weighted mixture of Gaussian or similar distributions.

8.3.2 From classification to regression

One can also transform an induction algorithm designed for classification tasks into one that handles regression problems. The first step involves a simple change in representation; rather than associating a class name with each decision region, one instead associates some numeric value. Thus, one can attach real or integer values to the right-hand sides of rules in a decision list, to the terminal nodes of decision trees and concept hierarchies, or to the predicted attribute of a competitive description. The performance component typically remains unchanged, with the system determining the best rule, node, or competitor for a given test case and then simply predicting the requested value.

The induction process can also carry over nearly unchanged from classification domains. For example, one can adapt the DDT algorithm from Chapter 7 to select attributes in a univariate decision tree based not on their ability to discriminate among different classes, but on their ability to separate different numeric values that occur in the training data. The NSC method from Chapter 5 can be altered in a similar way to select conditions for rules that distinguish among different real or integer values.

Figure 8-2 (a) shows an example *regression tree* from the height/girth domain, which takes the form of a univariate decision tree but which specifies numeric values at its terminal nodes rather than class names. Figure 8-2 (b) shows the decision regions produced by this knowledge structure, each of which is a rectangle with an associated numeric score. Here the terminal nodes predict a person's health insurance premium as a function of his or her height and girth. The tree first divides people into those shorter and taller than 5.5 feet. It partitions the first group further into people with girth less than 2.5 feet (with the predicted rate 200) and those greater (with predicted rate 300). Similarly, the taller group is divided into those with girth less than 3.0 feet (with predicted rate 220) and those greater (with predicted rate 330).

The figure shows that this tree produces a step function over the dependent variable. Although this may be desirable for some domains (like predicting insurance costs), in others (like predicting a person's

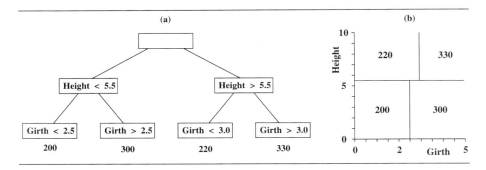

Figure 8-2. (a) The structure of a univariate regression tree that predicts insurance rates as a function of height and girth, and (b) the decision boundaries generated by this tree.

weight) a more continuous function seems desirable. One modification to this basic approach involves the use of multivariate *splines* during the prediction process. The spline interpolation process produces continuous curves with gradual transitions across the decision boundaries, which can greatly increase predictive accuracy in domains that involve continuous functions.

8.3.3 Inducing numeric functions

Many adaptations of classification learning schemes to numeric prediction assume that the target function can be divided into a set of decision regions, each with a constant value, and thus they focus on identifying the appropriate boundaries. Another line of research instead assumes that some more complex function holds over the entire instance space and attempts to discover its nature.

The simplest example of this approach is *linear regression*. Given a single predictive variable x and predicted variable y, this method assumes a function of the form $y = ax + b$ and algorithmically determines values for the slope a and intercept b that minimize squared error on the training data. The statistical literature abounds with variations on this method, some of which are designed to handle linear combinations of multiple predictive variables.

However, most work on this topic within the machine learning literature has focused on heuristic methods for finding nonlinear functions. One simple method of this sort, which we will call NLF (numeric law

Table 8-2. The NLF algorithm's rediscovery of Kepler's third law of planetary motion, relating a planet's distance D to its period P. The method defines new variables in terms of the observables until finding one with a constant value.

PLANET	D	P	D/P	D^2/P	D^3/P^2
MERCURY	0.387	0.241	1.606	0.626	0.998
VENUS	0.724	0.616	1.175	0.851	0.999
EARTH	1.000	1.000	1.000	1.000	1.000
MARS	1.524	1.882	0.810	1.234	1.000
JUPITER	5.199	11.880	0.438	2.275	0.996
SATURN	9.539	29.461	0.324	3.091	1.000

finder), induces numeric laws by searching the space of products and ratios of primitive variables, in an attempt to find some higher-order term that has a constant value. The algorithm starts by computing correlations among pairs of observable numeric attributes. NLF defines a new ratio term upon noting a positive correlation between two variables and a new product term for a negative correlation. If a new term T's values are constant, or if they are linearly related to another term, the method posits a law based on this relation. Otherwise, the algorithm considers T's correlations with other features and continues to search the space of higher-order terms.

Table 8-2 shows NLF's reconstruction of Kepler's third law of planetary motion, which relates a planet's period P to its distance D from the sun. Given observed values for these variables (in years and astronomical units), the algorithm notes that D increases with P, suggesting that their ratio *might* be constant. This relation does not actually hold, but upon computing values for the ratio D/P, NLF finds that this higher-order variable decreases as D increases, suggesting that it examine their product D^2/P. Again, this term is not constant, but its values increase as those of D/P decrease, suggesting their product D^3/P^2. Upon noting that the value of this term is always near 1, NLF postulates Kepler's law, that D^3/P^2 is constant.

One can view the discovery procedure embodied in NLF as constructing an inference network in which the nodes are arithmetic combinations of their children. In this sense, it bears some similarity to the methods described in Chapter 6 for constructing such networks, although the heuristics for directing search are quite different. Moreover, NLF attempts to find a functional description that is easily interpretable, whereas methods like cascade correlation are concerned only with predictive accuracy.

Other approaches to finding interpretable numeric laws are also possible. One such method attempts to fit predefined templates to training data, determining the best parameters as in linear regression but supporting more complex functional forms. One can also combine partitioning schemes with methods like linear regression or NLF to find numeric relations that involve different constants in different regions. One technique of this sort adapts the EM algorithm (Chapter 7) to determine a partitioned linear description of the training data. Another uses a version of the DDT algorithm (Chapter 7) to induce a decision tree in which the terminal nodes specify linear regression equations that incorporate multiple variables.

8.4 Unsupervised concept induction

Until now we have focused our attention on supervised induction tasks, in which the performance task is to predict the class of an instance. However, as we noted in Chapter 1, not all learning tasks involve a special attribute that corresponds to the class. For such *unsupervised* induction problems, we must specify some other performance problem.

One natural performance task involves the prediction of any unknown attribute values from the others, without knowledge at the outset about which attributes will be predicted or which the predictors. This task is sometimes called *flexible prediction*, because one can predict any feature from any others, and sometimes *pattern completion*, because one must complete a partial description of a pattern (i.e., an instance). An obvious performance measure for this task is simply the average predictive accuracy over all attributes. Another metric involves the ability to estimate the probability that each possible instance will be observed.

8.4.1 Simple approaches to unsupervised learning

Some induction methods require no modification at all to learn from unsupervised data and to perform flexible prediction. For example, the basic nearest neighbor method from Chapter 5 stores and retrieves training cases in the same way regardless of whether they have special class attributes, although some edited versions do need class information. Most methods for constructing probabilistic inference networks (see Chapter 6) also operate in the same manner whether or not one attribute has different status from the others. And some partitioning schemes, such as k-means clustering and the EM algorithm (Chapter 7), also make no special use of class attributes, treating them as just another feature when they are available.

For other induction algorithms, one can always adapt a supervised method to an unsupervised task through a simple transformation. Given k attributes, one runs the algorithm k times, in each case with a different feature playing the role of the class attribute one aims to predict. The result is k different classifiers, each designed to accurately predict one attribute as a function of the others.[5] For example, one might use the NSC algorithm from Chapter 5 to construct k separate decision lists or the backpropagation method from Chapter 6 to determine weights on k different inference networks. Figure 8-3 (a) depicts the structures that result when three attributes are involved and there are two nonterminal symbols (hidden units) in each network.

8.4.2 More sophisticated unsupervised methods

This divide-and-conquer scheme may work well in domains where the performance task involves prediction of isolated attributes, but it can well have difficulty when asked to predict many features for each test case. In such situations, one may instead prefer a single knowledge structure that maximizes predictive ability across all attributes. Some supervised methods are easy to adapt along these lines. As we noted in Chapter 7, one can modify the evaluation metric used in constructing concept hierarchies to reward partitions that lead to improved prediction over all attributes rather than just the class name. The result is a hierarchically organized set of clusters that describe similar instances and that can be used in flexible prediction.

Research on unsupervised learning in inference networks has often taken a different approach. One idea here is to include each feature as both an input node and an output node, but to place them in a single knowledge structure that shares nonterminal nodes or hidden units. Figure 8-3 (b) illustrates such a structure that involves three input units

---

5. One can use a variant of this idea with numeric attributes, using the techniques discussed in Section 8.3 to find k knowledge structures for numeric prediction.

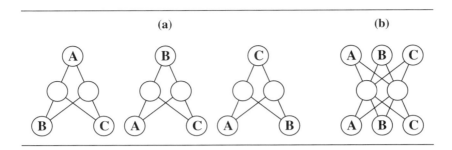

Figure 8-3. Knowledge structures for unsupervised learning that consist of (a) three separate inference networks, one for predicting each attribute from the others, and (b) a single inference network that shares hidden units for predicting various attributes.

and three output units. One then uses an induction method like back-propagation to reduce the predictive error on an output node as a function of other attributes, repeating this process for each output. This technique tends to create weights for links to nonterminal symbols that reflect clusters of instances, much as in unsupervised techniques for the induction of concept hierarchies.

Of course, these two approaches to unsupervised induction – creating separate knowledge structures and one shared structure – represent extremes along a continuum. Given an unsupervised learning task with k features, one may instead want to create more than 1 but fewer than k predictive structures. This makes sense in domains where certain subsets of attributes are correlated with each other but where the different subsets are uncorrelated. If one can identify the appropriate j sets, one can apply an induction algorithm to each in turn to produce j separate knowledge structures that, when taken together, should maximize predictive ability over all of the attributes.

8.5 Inducing relational concepts

Although our examples of induction have so far assumed attribute-value descriptions, we noted in Chapter 1 that learning can also occur over representations that involve relations among objects or entities. In other words, one can carry out induction not only over propositional descriptions but also over first-order statements. Work on relational induction dates back at least to 1970, but in recent years it has become a very active area under the name *inductive logic programming*, as most approaches represent the result of learning as Horn clause programs.

In this section we examine the adaptation of methods from previous chapters to the task of relational induction. We will focus on logical and competitive schemes, as this area contains very little work that builds on threshold units. In our examples, we will use a version of the cell domain from previous chapters, revised so that each instance describes two cells using not their actual values but rather the relations between them. Our representation will assume 6 possible predicates – `tails>(X,Y)`, `nuclei>(X,Y)`, `shade>(X,Y)`, `tails=(X,Y)`, `nuclei=(X,Y)`, and `shade=(X,Y)` – that, respectively, describe situations in which X has more tails than Y, X has more nuclei than Y, X is darker than Y, and X and Y are the same on these dimensions.[6]

8.5.1 Induction of relational conjunctions

Much of the work on relational induction has focused on logical conjunctions and has emphasized exhaustive "incremental" methods like ISG and IGS from Chapter 2. In fact, one can use these very algorithms on relational data, provided that one replaces the scheme for generating new hypotheses in response to each training case. Recall that both methods retain a set of descriptions that are consistent with the data observed so far, but that IGS starts with a very general hypothesis and generates more specific successors, whereas ISG operates in the opposite direction.

We can extend the IGS algorithm to handle relational data by letting it entertain relational conjunctions as hypotheses and, when a candidate H misclassifies a negative instance N as positive, by letting the algorithm generate all minimal ways to add literals to H that prevent it from matching N. For example, suppose H is the two-literal description `tails=(X,Y)` $\land$ `tails=(Y,X)`, and that this hypothesis incorrectly matches the negative training case

`tails=(a,b),tails=(b,a),nuclei>(a,b),shade=(a,b),shade=(b,a).`

If we assume the learning algorithm knows the literals `nuclei=(X,Y)`,

---

6. Because equality is symmetric, an instance that includes `tails=(a,b)` will also include `tails=(b,a)`. Thus, for 2 cells, there are 12 possible relations, no more than 6 of which are present in any instance, giving $3^3 = 27$ possible instances.

`nuclei>(X,Y)`, and `nuclei>(Y,X)` are mutually exclusive, that the same holds for color relations, and that equality relations are redundant, then IGS will generate four minimally more specific hypotheses:

```
tails=(X,Y) ∧ tails=(Y,X) ∧ nuclei=(X,Y)
tails=(X,Y) ∧ tails=(Y,X) ∧ nuclei>(Y,X)
tails=(X,Y) ∧ tails=(Y,X) ∧ shade>(X,Y)
tails=(X,Y) ∧ tails=(Y,X) ∧ shade>(Y,X) .
```

In more complex situations, some minimal changes will require the addition of two or more literals, but none occur in this example.[7] Of course, future negative cases may show that one or more of these revised hypotheses are still too general, leading to further specialization, or future positive instances may show them to be overly specific, leading to their removal.

We can alter the ISG algorithm in an analogous manner. Recall that this technique initializes memory to contain a single, maximally specific hypothesis based on the first positive training instance. Let us suppose that this hypothesis is

```
tails=(X,Y) ∧ tails=(Y,X) ∧ nuclei>(Y,X) ∧ shade>(X,Y) ,
```

where we have replaced the names of specific cells with the variables X and Y. Given a second positive instance

```
tails=(c,d), tails=(d,c), nuclei>(c,d), shade>(c,d) ,
```

the ISG algorithm would generate two minimally more general hypotheses that match this new case:

```
tails=(X,Y) ∧ tails=(Y,X) ∧ nuclei>(X,Y)
tails=(X,Y) ∧ tails=(Y,X) ∧ shade>(X,Y) .
```

Each revised conjunction is a generalization of the initial hypothesis that matches the new positive instance, but future positive cases may require further revisions or negative ones may lead to their elimination.

We can view the process of finding the most specific (or least general) description in terms of an exhaustive search through the space of partial matches. From this perspective, one starts with no mappings between the literals in hypothesis H and instance I, then selects the first literal

---

7. One can also compute differences between the current negative case and recent positive instances to constrain the search for more specific hypotheses.

in H and considers each way of mapping it into one of I's literals. Each successful mapping, which must involve the same predicate and produce consistent bindings, leads to a successor state that includes those bindings as additional constraints that must hold later in the search. The null mapping also generates a successor state, in which the H literal maps onto no I literal.

One then repeats this process for the second literal in H, generating successor states for each successful mapping onto the remaining literals in I, again including the null mapping. This scheme continues until all literals in H have been mapped onto those in I, at which point it removes all terminal nodes in the search tree that are strictly more specific than others, then returns this reduced set. Each such mapping specifies a subset of the literals in H that correspond to a most specific generalization with the training instance I.

Recall that, in the attribute-value version of ISG, there was always a unique way to make the current hypothesis more general, so that no search through the space of hypotheses was needed. In the relational formulation just given, this situation no longer holds, and ISG must carry out a breadth-first search in the same way as the IGS method. However, some recent approaches to inductive logic programming retain the idea of a maximally specific (or least general) generalization for relational domains by focusing on the idea of unification rather than matching.

For example, given the initial hypothesis and positive instance above, this scheme would produce the single revised hypothesis

```
tails=(U,V) ∧ tails=(V,U) ∧ tails=(W,Z) ∧
tails=(Z,W) ∧ nuclei>(U,V) ∧ shade>(Z,W) ,
```

which is the most specific description that unifies with both the previous hypothesis and the instance. This approach has the advantage that the hypothesis set does not grow as the algorithm encounters more positive instances. However, the size of the description itself can grow, whereas in the previous method, the size of the set grows but the size of hypotheses actually shrinks. Which approach does better in practice, in terms of computational cost and accuracy, is an open question, although the unification approach currently dominates the literature.

Naturally, heuristic versions of the above methods also exist. One can adapt the IHC algorithm from Chapter 2 to carry out incremental hill climbing through the space of relational conjunctions in a similar way, using operators that make the current hypothesis either more specific or more general. Nonincremental techniques like EGS and ESG are also possible, although these methods use training cases only to evaluate alternative hypotheses, not to generate them.

8.5.2 Induction of complex relational structures

Given techniques for inducing conjunctive relations, one can embed these methods in algorithms for learning decision lists, inference networks, and concept hierarchies, as we saw in Chapters 5, 6, and 7, respectively. In general, handling relational data with these more complex structures introduces no additional issues beyond those that arise in learning the conjunctions themselves. That is, once the subroutines for finding individual rules are replaced by a method for finding relational conjunctions, the algorithms will operate in relational domains.

One exception involves techniques for theory-based specialization, like the ICE algorithm described in Chapter 6. Recall that this approach assumes that the target concept is a specialization of a known inference network, and that each training case leads to a "proof" that, when compiled, produces a logical rule that covers the instance and similar ones. Although not emphasized in Chapter 6, most work on this topic assumes a relational representation for both instances and background knowledge, the latter described as a function-free Horn clause program.

In propositional domains (where predicates take no arguments), the compilation of proofs is straightforward, in that one simply takes the features that appear as terminal nodes in the proof tree and makes them the conditions of the new rule. The process is similar for relational inference networks, but here one must be concerned about how variables are shared across literals.

The standard approach uses a trace of the unifications made at each node in the proof tree to determine which arguments must be the same and which need not. Often this process leads to compiled rules with literals that share variables precisely when these arguments take on the same values in the training case, but this result does not always occur. In some cases, the method leads to the introduction of inequalities, not present in the original inference network, that must hold for the new rule to match. We will see an example of this effect in Chapter 10, in the context of learning search-control knowledge.

8.5.3 Competitive descriptions and structural analogy

Although most work on relational induction has assumed the use of logical interpreters, some efforts have dealt instead with competitive schemes, specifically variants of the nearest neighbor algorithm. Recall that this method computes the distance between a test instance and a stored training case, using some measure that rewards common features. For attribute-value representations, this computation is simple and efficient, involving the pairwise comparison of values for each attribute. However, the situation for relational descriptions is much more complex, in that it requires the computation of partial matches between the test instance and each relational case in memory.

Research on this topic, which is often called *structural analogy*, relies on techniques very similar to the relational version of the ISG algorithm described above. That is, analogical methods typically attempt to find the maximal partial match (most specific generalization) between the test instance (sometimes called the *target*) and the stored case (sometimes called the *source*). For example, suppose memory contains the source case

```
tails=(a,b), tails=(b,a), nuclei>(b,a), shade>(a,b) ,
```

and that one encounters the target instance

```
tails=(c,d), tails=(d,c), nuclei>(c,d), shade>(c,d) .
```

For this pair of instances, there are two structural analogies that constitute maximal partial matches:

```
tails=(a,b) ∧ tails=(b,a) ∧ nuclei>(a,b)
tails=(a,b) ∧ tails=(b,a) ∧ shade>(a,b) ,
```

where a maps onto d and b maps onto c in the first analogy and where these bindings are flipped in the second. Note that this example is identical to the one from Section 8.5.1 involving most specific generalizations, except that the partial match occurs between two instances, rather than between an hypothesis and an instance.

Because there can be more than one such match, the analogical system must decide which one to select for use. Work on structural analogy is often unsupervised and, to the extent that a performance task is specified, it involves the inference or prediction of literals omitted from the test instance. The task of analogical matching over relational descriptions is difficult enough that most work in the area has dealt with memories containing a small number of stored cases. Nevertheless, conceptually the approach has much in common with the simpler competitive methods, such as nearest neighbor and its relatives, that we considered in earlier chapters. Two important differences revolve around the idea of merging two separate analogies to increase predictive power and using background knowledge or higher-order relations to constrain the matching process or to bias the distance metric. These ideas are equally applicable to propositional versions of nearest neighbor, but they seldom occur in that paradigm.

8.6 Handling missing features

The algorithms we have considered in previous chapters were originally designed to accept complete training cases, in which all attribute values were present, and similarly to handle test cases that are complete except for those attributes to be predicted. However, there are many situations in which some features are absent from either training or test data, and which can require modifications of the basic algorithms. Here we discuss the issues that arise in such situations and consider some of the available responses.

8.6.1 Assumptions about missing features

Most work in machine learning assumes that, when attribute values are absent, the omission is due to some random process, such as failure to record a value during transcription. In other words, the standard view is that information regarding which features are present in the training data is not useful to the learning process. Our treatment will rely on this standard assumption, as nearly all research on missing attributes has occurred in that context.

However, this assumption is violated in some data sets, and we should discuss them briefly. In some situations, such as medical diagnosis, where the questions asked by doctors are correlated with the disease they conclude, the features that are absent can provide useful information for the learning process. In other situations, as in voting records, where a missing representative's vote may indicate intentional absence, "missing" may be treated best as a separate value during both training and testing. Researchers must use their judgement in deciding which interpretation is most appropriate for a given domain.

A different issue arises in relational domains. Here one must decide whether the absence of a literal L in some instance I means that L is false for I or simply that it was not observed for some reason. For this issue, most researchers have assumed that absence implies falsehood, as this lets them treat each training and test case as complete and thus simplifies the algorithms for learning and performance. For this reason, most work on relational induction has not dealt directly with missing features, and we will not consider such algorithms here.

8.6.2 Missing features during testing

Before we can understand how to handle missing features during learning, we must first examine their effect on testing and performance. Many competitive techniques like nearest neighbor and probabilistic methods can simply ignore attributes that are missing and use only the observed features in computing a score for each competitor. However, for logical descriptions and threshold units the situation is more complicated. The former's reliance on an all-or-none matching scheme assumes that all important features are present;[8] the latter's partial match is more flexible but its thresholds are designed with all features in mind. As a result, the most common alteration for both approaches involves inferring the values of missing attributes and using these in making predictions.

The simplest such inference method uses the overall modal (most frequent) value for nominal attributes and Boolean features and uses the overall mean for numeric attributes. But one can also apply this idea locally. For example, consider a univariate decision tree that contains a test relying on a missing attribute; in this case one can use the modal or mean value for just those training instances used to construct that portion of the tree, which makes sense given that the test on this attribute occurs only in the context of those above it.

Another approach assigns missing values probabilistically, much as in the voting scheme described in Section 8.1.3. For example, given a test case with a missing feature that occurs at a node N in a uni-

---

8. Of course, the matching process for logical concepts is unaffected by a missing feature if that feature is not included in the logical description; our concern here is with attributes that occur in such descriptions but that have missing values.

variate decision tree, one sorts the case fractionally down all branches below the node N to determine which terminal nodes it reaches, then uses the predictions of these nodes in a weighted voting scheme to select the class. One can also use this idea with logical decision lists and logical inference networks. For knowledge structures that incorporate threshold units, which typically have separate input nodes for alternative attribute values, one can activate these nodes as a function of each value's probability, then predict the output (class) node as usual.

An even more sophisticated scheme involves the induction of knowledge structures for predicting an attribute's value from the values of others, then using these structures to infer the attribute's value (using either the most likely value or its probability distribution) when it is missing. This approach is very similar to that taken by some unsupervised learning methods, which seem better suited to data sets with missing features due to their emphasis on flexible prediction.

8.6.3 Missing features during training

Similar issues arise when features are absent during the learning process, and similar responses to this problem suggest themselves. For most probabilistic methods, one simply does not update counts for omitted attributes, and for nearest neighbor methods one simply stores abstract cases that make no commitment about these features. The competitive nature of such approaches means that they require little modification.

For logical and threshold techniques, all of the methods described for the testing situation are available during training. Thus, one can simply insert the overall mean or modal values, provided that the method is nonincremental and thus has these statistics available from the training data. Techniques for inducing decision trees and concept hierarchies can instead use local estimates, at least those that construct trees in a divisive or top-down manner.[9] Again, one can also use a probabilistic approach that generates fractional instances for use in computing evaluation scores or gradients. These probabilities may be based on simple summary statistics or on the predictions of classifiers induced specifically to infer missing values.

---

9. Incremental learning methods must retain running estimates of means and modes, basing their estimates on the data seen so far.

The issue of missing features has received much less attention in the literature than the other topics we have considered in this chapter. Accordingly, there have been fewer alternatives proposed and fewer experimental or theoretical comparisons than for other variations on the task of concept induction.

8.7 Summary of the chapter

In this chapter we considered six major extensions that cut across the induction methods described earlier. Some of these techniques are designed to improve the robustness of the induction process. In particular, pruning methods can greatly improve learning algorithms' resistance to overfitting on noisy data. Techniques for selecting subsets of features for use in prediction can significantly improve the learning rate in domains with many irrelevant attributes. And methods for inferring the values of missing attributes can aid learning when training or test cases are incomplete.

Other extensions we examined instead broaden the type of induction task addressed. For example, algorithms for learning regression knowledge let the performance element predict numeric values rather than class names. Unsupervised induction methods let one learn from data in which there is no special class attribute, and thus support more flexible prediction strategies. Finally, techniques for relational learning allow induction using instances and hypotheses described not as attribute-value pairs but as first-order relations.

Although these methods considerably extend the range and robustness of the induction process, they clearly build directly on the simpler algorithms we discussed in earlier chapters. Each technique is a straightforward variation on some more basic scheme, rather than being essentially different, as the literature on machine learning often suggests.

Exercises

1. Assume a pre-pruning variant of the DDT algorithm (Chapter 7) that extends the decision tree downward only if the new children reduce the number of classification errors made by the current node by more than two. Show the decision tree produced by this strategy on the training data in Figure 7-1 from Chapter 7, and compare it to the tree in Figure 7-2.

2. Use the DTL algorithm (Chapter 7) to generate a decision list from the decision tree that the (unmodified) DDT method induces from the data in Figure 5-4. Apply greedy post-pruning (Section 8.1.1) to this decision list, using accuracy on the training set (not on a separate evaluation set) as the evaluation metric, and considering rules and conditions in the order in which they occur.

3. Consider the stored training cases in Figure 5-9 (a). Show two test instances that the k nearest neighbor method, with $k = 2$, would classify differently from simple nearest neighbor. Report the distance computations involved in each decision.

4. Assume a simple logical representation of knowledge, known as a *determination*, that takes the form of a table in which each cell corresponds to a specific combination of attribute values and contains the predicted class. Further assume that each cell is filled with the most frequent class observed for that combination or, if none have been seen, with the most frequent class. Starting with a table that incorporates all four attributes from the cell domain, use the greedy wrapper method from Section 8.2 to search the space of tables that incorporate only some attributes. Use accuracy on the training data in Figure 7-1 as the evaluation metric, but change the `color` of the last `healthy` instance to `dark`. Show the score for each candidate set of features considered during the search.

5. Generate six instances that satisfy Galileo's law of uniform acceleration, $D = 9.8T^2$. Show the terms generated by the NLF algorithm (Section 8.3.3) in rediscovering this law.

6. Ignoring the cell wall thickness and the classes for the data in Figure 5-5, show a set of logical rules that, to the extent possible, predict each of the remaining attributes in terms of the other two features. Compute percentage accuracy for each predicted attribute.

7. Suppose one has an hypothesis about the definition of a new kinship relation, `parent(X,Y)` $\wedge$ `parent(Y,Z)` $\wedge$ `male(X)`, but that this matches the negative case `parent(joe,sam)`, `parent(sam,mary)`, `male(joe)`, `male(sam)`, `female(mary)`. Show the set of minimally more specific hypotheses about the kinship relation, assuming knowledge that `male` and `female` are mutually exclusive.

8. Suppose one's hypothesis about a new kinship relation, `parent(X,Y)` $\wedge$ `parent(Y,Z)` $\wedge$ `male(X)` $\wedge$ `male(Y)` $\wedge$ `female(Z)`, fails to match the positive training case `parent(joe,mary)`, `parent(mary,sam)`,

`male(joe)`, `female(mary)`, `male(sam)`. Show the set of minimally more general hypotheses that match this case, based on the matching scheme in Section 8.5.1. Show the unique hypothesis generated by the unification approach described later in that section.

9. Assume that the `tails` attribute is unspecified for the even-numbered instances in Figure 7-1. Given the decision tree in Figure 7-2, compute the percentage accuracy on these instances if one infers the modal value when an attribute is missing from a test case. Show the decision tree that the DDT algorithm would construct if given these instances as training data and if it used the same inference strategy in this context.

Historical and bibliographical remarks

The notion of overfitting has roots in the statistical literature on higher-order regression, but Breiman, Friedman, Olshen, and Stone (1984) first raised the issue in work on decision-tree induction and used a post-pruning technique in their CART system. Quinlan (1986) popularized the idea within the machine learning community, with his ID3 algorithm for decision-tree induction initially using pre-pruning but his later C4.5 system (1993) emphasizing post-pruning. Mingers (1989b) reports an experimental evaluation of different methods for pruning decision trees, and Hassibi and Stork (1993) describe a post-pruning scheme for multilayer neural networks.

Quinlan and Rivest (1989) describe the use of minimum description length in pruning decision trees, while Iba, Wogulis, and Langley (1988) present a similar method for decision lists. Weigend, Huberman, and Rumelhart (1990) incorporate a penalty term into their error function for backpropagation in neural networks. Fisher (1989) reports a dynamic pruning scheme for use with probabilistic concept hierarchies, Aha (1992) describes a related method for handling noise in the nearest neighbor framework, and Buntine (1990) uses a weighted voting technique that combines predictions from multiple decision trees.

Research on feature selection, as separate from other aspects of induction, also has a long tradition in statistics, but mainly in the context of regression (e.g., Devijver & Kittler, 1982). Within machine learning, Kira and Rendell (1992) describe a filter approach that orders features by relevance, whereas Almuallim and Dieterich (1991) present an exhaustive method that generates minimal sets of predictive attributes.

John, Kohavi, and Pfleger (1994) provide the first general formulation of the wrapper approach, which they combine with decision-tree induction, as do Caruana and Freitag (1994). Moore and Lee (1994), Langley and Sage (1994b), and Aha and Bankert (1994) use the wrapper framework to select relevant features for nearest neighbor prediction, while Langley and Sage (1994a) use it to remove correlated attributes in naive Bayesian classifiers. Langley (1994a) reviews recent work in this area.

Work on regression also has a long history in statistics. Widrow and Hoff (1960) used the LMS algorithm to improve numeric predictions and, more recently, Weigend et al. (1990) and others have put more sophisticated neural network techniques to similar ends. Kibler, Aha, and Albert (1989) and Moore and Lee (1994) report uses of nearest neighbor in predicting real values; Jordan and Jacobs (1993) have used the EM algorithm to generate mixtures of Gaussians for regression purposes, and Moody and Darken (1991) have used backpropagation on radial basis functions with the same goal. Breiman et al. (1984) introduce the idea of a regression tree that can be induced using DDT-like methods, and Friedman's (1991) Mars system extends this approach to use splines for smoothing during prediction. Quinlan's (1993a) M5 is another variation of the DDT scheme that stores regression equations at the terminal nodes of trees, Weiss and Indurkhya (1993) describe a method that forms numeric decision lists, and Rao and Lu (1992) achieve similar effects with a variant of k-means clustering that uses regression equations rather than means. Gerwin (1974) did early work on the discovery of explicit functional expressions, but Langley, Bradshaw, and Simon's (1983) Bacon popularized this approach within the machine learning community. More recently, Falkenhainer and Michalski's (1986) Abacus, Nordhausen and Langley's (1990) IDS, and Zytkow, Zhu, and Hussam's (1990) Fahrenheit have extended this approach to broader classes of expressions and more situations.

There exists a large literature on unsupervised learning within the areas of numerical taxonomy and clustering (Everitt, 1980), aimed largely at data analysis. Michalski and Stepp (1983) were influenced by this work in their formulation of "conceptual clustering" and in development of their Cluster/2 system, which incorporated k-means clustering (Chapter 7) as a subroutine. Cheeseman et al.'s (1988) Auto-Class, which uses the EM algorithm (Chapter 7), and Hanson and Bauer's (1989) Witt, which uses agglomerative clustering, constitute other extensions of this tradition. A separate line of work, concerned with modeling the incremental nature of human learning, was initiated by Feigenbaum's (1961) EPAM model. Lebowitz's (1987) UNIMEM, Fisher's (1987) COBWEB, and McKusick and Langley's (1991) ARACHNE explore variations of this scheme that use more flexible representations, and Fisher, Pazzani, and Langley (1991) contains a number of related papers. Martin's (1989) CORA adapts a simple rule-induction method to unsupervised learning and flexible prediction, and Kohonen (1982), Rumelhart and Zipser (1985), and Grossberg (1987) have used competitive learning in neural networks to achieve similar effects.

Much of the machine learning research during the 1970s focused on the induction of relational conjunctions. Winston's (1975) heuristic method and Mitchell's (1977) exhaustive candidate elimination algorithm are perhaps the best known from this period, but Vere (1975) and Hayes-Roth and McDermott (1978) also contributed to this area. A few researchers, such as Anderson and Kline (1979) and Langley (1987), developed related methods for inducing logical decision lists. Plotkin (1970) introduced the notion of least general generalization based on unification, but Muggleton and Feng (1992) popularized the idea in the context of inductive logic programming. Quinlan's (1990) FOIL, a system for inducing logical decision lists, uses a relational variant of the HGS algorithm, whereas Muggleton and Feng's (1992) GOLEM incorporates a technique similar to the HSG algorithm. Proceedings of meetings on inductive logic programming have appeared annually since 1992, and a text (Lavrac & Dzeroski, 1993) even exists on the topic.

Research on structural analogy dates back to Evans (1968), but more recent work has been done by Greiner (1988), Falkenhainer, Forbus, and Gentner (1989), Thagard, Holyoak, Nelson, and Gochfield (1990), and Gentner and Forbus (1991), the last two having addressed not only matching but also issues of retrieval. Hall (1989) reviews work on analogy through that date, some of which deals with analogical matching and other work with problem solving, which we discuss in Chapter 11.

Concern with missing attributes has come relatively late to machine learning and thus far has received only minor attention. Quinlan (1986) reports on a variety of methods for inferring missing features in the context of decision-tree induction, while Ahmad and Tresp (1993) compare different neural network techniques for handling this problem. Rao, Greiner, and Hancock (1994) describe a method that takes advantage of missing attributes to constrain the induction task.

CHAPTER 9

The Formation of Transition Networks

As we saw in Chapters 5, 6, and 7, decision lists, inference networks, and concept hierarchies typically organize knowledge about static entities. However, many domains involve some form of *temporal* or *sequential* information. In such situations, a more appropriate organization is the *state-transition network*. This framework assumes that each instance consists of a sequence of states, and that transitions from one state to another occur under certain conditions or have certain effects.

Much of the research in this area has focused on the induction of grammars for use in natural language processing, although there has also been work on speech recognition, molecular biology, and other problem areas. As we will see, most transition networks incorporate only very simple descriptions on each node or link, rather than the complex intensional descriptions we encountered with other organizational schemes. Thus, the structure of the induced transition networks is even more central to this framework than for decision lists, inference networks, or concept hierarchies, and our primary focus will be on these structures.

9.1 General issues for state-transition networks

As usual, before we examine alternative methods for the induction of state-transition networks, we will consider some basic issues in their representation, use, and acquisition. Many of the central concepts will be familiar to readers with a background in computer science, since the representations are often used in work on compilers and programming languages.

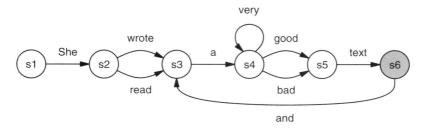

Figure 9-1. A simple transition network that specifies a finite-state grammar. In this network, **s1** is the starting state and **s6** (shaded) is the only accepting state. The presence of loops lets the network recognize sequences of arbitrary length.

9.1.1 Finite-state transition networks

State-transition networks represent sequential or temporal knowledge about the order in which events occur. Like the organizational schemes in Chapters 6 and 7, they achieve this with combinations of nodes and links, but the semantics of these structures is rather different from that for inference networks or concept hierarchies. Each node in a transition network represents a *state* of the world or memory, whereas each link represents a *transition* from one state to a successor state. Typically, each link includes some condition or intensional description that must be satisfied before the specified transition occurs or, alternatively, some effect that is generated during transition.

Figure 9-1 presents an example transition network that encodes grammatical knowledge for parsing a simple class of sentences. The left-most node corresponds to the initial state; other nodes are reached only along paths through the specified links. Each link specifies a word in the language that must occur next in the observed sequence. The network *recognizes* or *accepts* a sequence if there exists a path for the sequence that ends in an *accepting* state.

For example, the network in the figure would recognize the sentence *She wrote a good text*, because this sequence would pass through states **s1**, **s2**, **s3**, **s4**, **s5**, and **s6** in turn, and because **s6** is an accepting state (indicated by shading). Similarly, the network would accept the sentence *She read a very very bad text*, passing it through the states **s1 s2 s3 s4 s4 s4 s5 s6**, since the network allows looping on the word **very**. The sentence *She read a very good text and a bad text* is also grammatical, since the link emerging from state s6 (labeled **and**) allows looping back to s3. By using such loops, networks of this sort – often referred to as *finite-state machines* – can recognize sequences of arbitrary length, thus supporting an infinite extension of legal sentences.[1]

To use a finite-state machine to parse sentences in this manner, one requires some performance system that steps through the network, keeping track of the current state S and the current word W in the sentence. On each step, it compares W to the words on links leading out of S, selecting a link that agrees (if one exists) and moving on to the next state and word, or returning failure otherwise. For *deterministic* finite-state machines, in which each link emerging from a state has a different word, a simple greedy algorithm suffices to accept or reject strings. *Nondeterministic* machines, in which the same word can occur on multiple branches emerging from a state, require more memory-intensive search methods such as depth-first or breadth-first search. We will not focus on the details of performance components in this chapter, as most methods differ only in their parsing efficiency, not in their accuracy.

A closely related class of transition networks, known as *Markov models*, incorporates a probability on each transition link, with the probabilities on all the links that emanate from each state summing to 1. Markov models associate symbols with states rather than with links, giving them a somewhat different flavor from other sorts of finite-state networks. An important class of these grammars, *hidden Markov models*, assumes that one cannot determine the state directly but only through observable events associated with them. Moreover, there may be multiple events associated with each state, each with its own probability of occurrence within that state. Given an observed event, one cannot directly determine the state that generated it; this is the reason such Markov models are referred to as *hidden*.

Figure 9-2 shows a simple example of such a transition network that can handle a variety of sentences. Separate paths through this network reflect quite different meanings. For instance, the sentence *He saw the binoculars by the boy*, which can be parsed only by the state sequence s1 s2 s3 s4 s5 s3 s4, seems very different from *He saw the boy through the telescope*, which can be parsed only by the sequence s1 s2 s3 s4 s6 s7 s8. The ambiguous sentence *He saw the boy with the telescope*

---

1. Every finite-state machine maps directly onto a *regular grammar*, which represents the same knowledge in a different notation that we will not emphasize here.

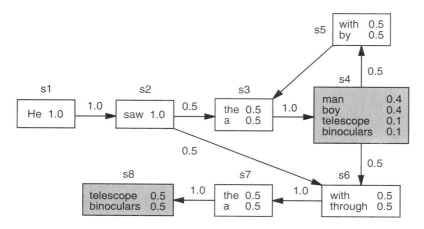

Figure 9-2. A hidden Markov model that produces two parses of the sentence *He saw the boy with the telescope* that have nonzero probability. In this network, **s1** is the starting state, whereas **s4** and **s8** (shaded) are accepting states.

can be parsed by either sequence, but the second path is more likely given the higher probability for *telescope* in state **s8**, which agrees with our intuitions.

Because the same observable event can be produced by different states in a hidden Markov model, one cannot typically determine an unambiguous path through the network for an observed sequence. However, one can calculate the *probability* of each possible path for a given sequence and network. There are a number of methods for determining the most likely path through the network, which differ in the criterion they attempt to optimize. Perhaps the best-known method is called the *Viterbi algorithm*, but we do not have the space to describe it here.

The probabilistic nature of hidden Markov models lends them to use for classification tasks in uncertain domains that involve time, such as speech recognition. In this case, one creates a separate hidden Markov model for each word, determines the most probable path through each network given an observed sequence of sounds, then selects the word associated with the most likely network. Hidden Markov models also let one associate multiple observable attributes, including numeric ones, with each state, making them even more attractive for temporal classification tasks.

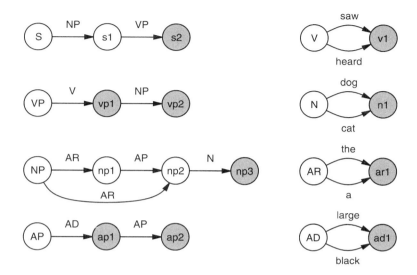

Figure 9-3. A recursive transition network that specifies a context-free grammar. In this grammar, the starting state is S in the top left network, which calls on the subnetworks NP and VP by specifying them as tests on its links. These in turn call on other subnetworks. Note the recursive nature of the AP subnetwork, which calls on itself. The networks on the right correspond to word classes and thus use only words on their links.

9.1.2 Recursive transition networks

A more powerful organizational scheme, known as *recursive transition networks*, lets tests on links refer to either terminal symbols or to entire subnetworks. In general, the structure of individual subnetworks in this framework is simpler than finite-state machines because the former can achieve iteration through recursion and because they let one replace repeated substructures with calls to subnetworks. The space of recursive transition networks constitutes a proper superset of finite-state machines and regular grammars. Recursive networks need not make recursive calls; their name derives from the potential for such structures.

Figure 9-3 shows a recursive transition network for a simple language that handles a subset of English declarative sentences. The top-level network at the top left, which begins with the start symbol S, states that a legal sentence must consist of a noun phrase (NP) followed by a verb phrase (VP); the figure also shows subnetworks for these components. A verb phrase must consist in turn of a verb (V) followed by an

Table 9-1. A context-free grammar equivalent to the recursive transition network in Figure 9-3. Nonterminal symbols correspond to the names of subnetworks in the figure, and each rewrite rule translates into a separate path through one of the subnetworks.

$S \rightarrow NP\ VP$	$V \rightarrow saw$	$AR \rightarrow the$
$VP \rightarrow V\ NP$	$V \rightarrow heard$	$AR \rightarrow a$
$NP \rightarrow AR\ N$	$N \rightarrow dog$	$AD \rightarrow large$
$NP \rightarrow AR\ AP\ N$	$N \rightarrow cat$	$AD \rightarrow black$
$AP \rightarrow AD$		
$AP \rightarrow AD\ AP$		

optional noun phrase, whereas a noun phrase must contain an article (AR) followed by an optional adjectival phrase (AP) and then a noun (N). Adjectival phrases consist of one or more adjectives (AD), which the lower left subnetwork specifies with a recursive call to itself. A more complete grammar would support relative clauses by including an optional link at the end of the NP subnetwork, defined as a relative pronoun followed by a recursive call to NP.

A recursive transition network must ultimately ground out in terminal symbols. In some work on natural language, these symbols are defined as disjunctive sets or word classes associated with names for parts of speech, such as V, N, AR, and AD. For the sake of consistency, we have chosen to represent them as separate subnetworks that contain tests for individual words on their links, as shown in the right parts of the figure.

The space of recursive transition networks is equivalent to the space of *context-free grammars*, which are represented as a set of rewrite rules similar to Horn clauses. The main difference is that the symbols in the right-hand side of rewrite rules are *ordered* and thus reflect the sequential nature of the knowledge, whereas Horn clauses are not. Table 9-1 shows a context-free grammar that specifies the same language as the recursive transition network in Figure 9-3. Each rule in this encoding corresponds to one path through a subnetwork in the network representation. We will use the network formalism in this chapter, but both occur in the literature on grammar induction.

The performance elements used to process recursive transition networks are similar in nature to those used for finite-state networks. These

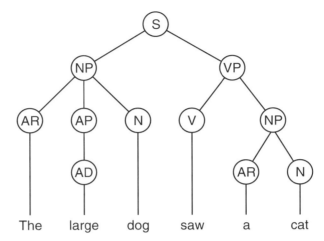

Figure 9-4. A parse tree generated by the recursive transition network in Figure 9-3. Terminal nodes correspond to words in the sentence (in the order they occur), whereas nonterminal nodes indicate the names of networks or subnetworks used to process the words beneath them.

start with the S node in the top-level network, then proceed through successive arcs, going down into a subnetwork if the symbol on an arc is not primitive. If the subnetwork succeeds in parsing a substring, the performance system returns to the point of call and traverses the arc; if the subnetwork fails, it returns to the same point and continues down an alternative branch.

A successful parse returns a *parse tree* like that shown in Figure 9-4, which reflects the structure of the path taken through the network. In particular, each nonterminal node in the tree corresponds to a specific subnetwork and each link in the tree to a link in the network, with terminal nodes corresponding to words in the grammar. The parse tree shows nothing about alternatives considered during the parsing process, only about the path that produced the successful parse.

Just as probabilistic versions of finite-state machines are possible, so are probabilistic versions of recursive transition networks. The most widespread such formalism, known as *stochastic context-free grammars*, represents knowledge as a set of rewrite rules, each with an associated fraction. These numbers indicate the probability that, given that the term in the left-hand side appears in a successful parse tree, it will be expanded to the terms in the right-hand side; thus, the numbers for all rules with the same term in the left-hand side must sum to 1. Such grammars are often cast in Chomsky normal form, in which each rewrite rule has either two nonterminals or one terminal in its right-hand side.

Stochastic context-free grammars are most useful in domains in which there tend to be many possible parses. In such cases, one can compute the probability of each successful parse and then select the most likely. One can also use partial probability calculations to direct search through the space of parse trees, increasing parsing efficiency for grammars with many rewrite rules. Again, the details of these processes need not concern us here.

9.1.3 Predictive rules and networks

Finite-state and recursive transition networks represent knowledge in large-scale structures, but one can achieve similar effects using a collection of smaller knowledge structures that predict upcoming events in terms of previous ones. This approach is especially useful in domains where states involve many observable attributes, only some of which are relevant for prediction. In such situations, abstract descriptions that ignore certain features can represent only implicit connections between states, supporting a more flexible organization of memory than other methods. Figure 9-5 depicts this situation graphically, showing that the set of states produced by two rules may overlap without being identical. Moreover, such predictive descriptions can easily incorporate historical information about previous states or previous actions. Collections of such structures are related to *context-sensitive* grammars, which define a strictly more general class of languages than context-free grammars.

One common encoding of such knowledge takes the form of logical rules that are interpreted by a *production system*, which operates in cycles. On each cycle, the condition side of each rule is matched against the contents of a dynamic working memory, which can contain a description of the current state, previous states, or yet other information. If the condition side of a rule matches against the contents of this memory, the interpreter carries out the associated actions, which modify working memory by adding or deleting elements, including predictions about the next state. On the next cycle, the condition sides of other rules may be satisfied, leading to different actions, and so forth.

Although production systems typically assume a logical representation, a closely related approach relies on a network of threshold units.

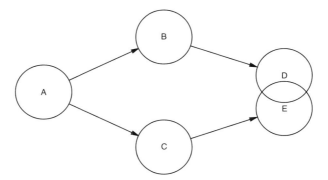

Figure 9-5. Abstract depiction of a set of condition-action rules as a generalized finite-state grammar. Each condition side specifies a class of states, whereas each action side specifies another class in terms of its differences from the state matched by the condition side. The classes of states described by a set of rules may overlap completely, as in a finite-state machine and as in A, they may be entirely distinct, as in a finite-state machine and as in B and C, or they may hold only some states in common, as in D and E.

In this scheme, known as a *recurrent* or *time-delay* network, the inference network inputs not only features describing the current state but also inferences made on one or more previous time steps. Such systems also operate in cycles, modifying a temporary memory on each pass, but they represent knowledge in a single interconnected inference network rather than as independent condition-action rules. In some versions, the output of the inference network at time t is fed back as input for time $t + 1$; in others, the settings for nonterminal symbols or 'hidden units' are used instead.

One common use of recurrent networks has involved grammatical prediction. Given a vocabulary of n words, one can represent each state in a sentence as an n-bit feature vector. One can then attempt to predict, given the current vector and historical information, the words that may follow. The recurrent network predicts another n-bit vector, with a sufficiently high score for a feature indicating that the word for that feature may occur. If not, the parse for the current sentence fails; otherwise, the network continues on to the next word, judging the sentence legal if each successive word was predicted as an option. This approach can also use more distributed encodings for each word. Most work in this framework has dealt with threshold units, but one can apply the same basic idea to other representations, including logical rules.

Our examples have focused on parsing natural language, but there exist many other tasks with temporal components. One of the most common tasks, at least within artificial intelligence, involves predicting the effect of some action in the external world. Most work on this problem assumes that one can describe each world state as a conjunction of features or literals, and that an action transforms this state into another one by removing some features and adding others. Thus, one can describe this transformation as an abstract rule (typically logical in form) that maps one class of states into another class.

Consider a rule that predicts the effect of picking up an object from a table. We might state this rule as

```
(pickup (?x)
  (on ?x ?t) (table ?t) (clear ?x) (arm-empty) =>
  (<add> (holding ?x)) (<delete> (on ?x ?t) (arm-empty)))
```

where **pickup** is the name of the action and **?x** is the object being lifted. The literals before the arrow indicate the conditions under which this action will be effective, the **add** specifies new literals in the resulting state, and the **delete** indicates literals removed from the resulting state. We will return to this example in Chapter 10.

Taken together, a set of such rules can be used to predict the effects of an entire sequence of actions. This process involves chaining through the predictions of each individual rule and matching the conditions of each action in the sequence against the state predicted by its immediate predecessor. Given accurate predictive rules, this scheme lets one project the effects of actions many steps into the future, which can be very useful for purposes of planning.

9.1.4 The task of inducing transition networks

We are now ready to state the learning task associated with the organizational framework we have been considering:

- *Given*: A set of positive and (possibly) negative training sequences;
- *Find*: A state-transition network that, to the extent possible, recognizes novel positive sequences but not negative ones.

Most work on this task has focused on constructing transition networks from scratch, rather than on revising an initial network that is provided as background knowledge. However, we will see that the initial hypothesis for some nonincremental methods is a specific but detailed network based on the positive training cases, which is then modified, and revising an existing structure is central to any incremental approach. Thus, many existing algorithms could easily be adapted to take advantage of a user-provided background network.

One can view the above induction task as a search problem, with operators that differ according to both the class of networks and the learning algorithm. Some methods for inducing finite-state networks rely entirely on operators for merging (or splitting) nodes. Others include operators for adding or removing nodes or links, altering the source or destination of links, and changing nodes from accepting to rejecting or vice versa. Techniques for constructing recursive transition networks draw on similar actions, but they also typically include operators for creating or removing subnetworks.

The space of state-transition networks is infinite in size, in that one can always introduce nodes, links, or subnetworks into any given structure. However, most such networks contain degenerate components (e.g., one-link subnetworks) that can be removed without altering their extension. Others include components that are not used in recognizing any positive training sequences and so can be safely removed. There exist only a finite set of 'simple' transition networks that include no degenerate or unnecessary components. For finite-state machines, there is also an important theoretical result that for every *nondeterministic* machine, there exists an equivalent *deterministic* machine. This means that one can limit the finite-state induction task to deterministic machines, which considerably restricts the space of hypotheses.

All of the search schemes we have considered in previous chapters are applicable to the formation of transition networks. In later sections, we will see examples of both exhaustive and heuristic methods, and both nonincremental and incremental approaches. Many techniques make use of some partial ordering on the network space. Some direct search by preferring simpler networks to more complex ones, whereas others emphasize generality as measured by the network's extension. Clearly, these introduce different inductive biases, although their exact relation to behavior on novel test sequences remains unclear.

Another central issue involves where to start the search. One natural scheme for finite-state problems begins with a very specific transition network that includes a set of disjoint paths, one for each positive training sequence, emanating from a common start node. A less common alternative starts with the most general network, which contains a single accepting node with one iterative loop for each observed word or terminal symbol in the positive training set. Some incremental methods start instead with the simplest possible network (a single accepting node), expanding it as necessary for handling new cases. Analogous alternatives exist for recursive transition networks, as we will see in Section 9.3.

The literature on grammar induction has made much about the role of negative training sequences. In particular, some theoretical results show that, without such negative instances, there exists no induction method that is guaranteed to converge on an arbitrary target grammar, given any finite training set (even a very large one). However, such negative results have little to say about heuristic methods, which do not attempt to guarantee results. On the other hand, negative training sequences, when available, are clearly very useful for eliminating overly general hypotheses, and many algorithms we will examine take advantage of them. We will also encounter some approaches that effectively extract negative instances from positive training strings by reformulating the induction task.

9.2 Constructing finite-state transition networks

Let us consider the induction of finite-state machines first, as they involve simpler structures than recursive transition networks. We will examine four basic approaches to the acquisition of finite-state knowledge from training sentences.

9.2.1 Hill-climbing search for finite-state networks

We noted above that one class of method for constructing finite-state machines begins with a specific network that has one path for each positive training sequence. An exhaustive, breadth-first version of this approach would consider all grammars that result from merging pairs of nodes, rejecting any that cover negative training sentences but retaining the rest. The method repeats this process, considering all possible merges at each level of the search, until arriving at the set of most general finite-state networks that cover the positive cases but none of the negative ones. One can then select from among the remaining grammars using other criteria like simplicity. This scheme, which is similar to the ESG method from Chapter 2, also has the same problem with combinatorial explosion. A more tractable approach, analogous to the HSG algorithm from Chapter 2, replaces breadth-first search with hill climbing or beam search.

Another method, which we will call HFS, also uses hill climbing to search the space of finite-state machines, but it starts with a randomly generated network that has a user-specified number of states and that has link labels taken from the symbols in positive training sequences. At each step in its search, HFS considers six basic operators: adding a link, removing a link, changing a link source, changing a link destination, changing a rejecting state to an accepting state, and changing an accepting state to a rejecting one. The algorithm considers all ways of applying these operators, then selects the best according to some evaluation function. One metric reported in the literature computes the network's accuracy, taking the number of correctly recognized positive training sentences minus the number of incorrectly recognized negative cases. This measure generally drives HFS toward a grammar that covers all of the positive instances but none of the negatives. Table 9-2 presents pseudocode for the HFS algorithm.

However, the resulting network may be more complex than necessary, even after removing disconnected (useless) nodes. One response is to incorporate some measure of simplicity into the evaluation function, but another approach, which we may call HFS', separates the issues of accuracy and simplicity. This variant also uses a hill-climbing search like that described above to generate an accurate network, but then it enters a second phase that uses this network as the starting point for a second hill-climbing search. This phase uses the same operators but invokes a metric that prefers networks with fewer nodes and links, provided they retain the same accuracy. Hill climbing continues until any further simplification reduces accuracy. This resulting network may not be the smallest one possible, but that is the standard price of satisficing search.

9.2.2 Order-reliant induction methods

Much of the research on the induction of finite-state grammars has dealt with nonincremental methods, but some work has explored incremental approaches. As we saw in earlier chapters, one can typically adapt nonincremental techniques to process one or a few instances at a time.

Table 9-2. The HFS algorithm: Hill-climbing for finite-state networks.

```
Inputs: A set of positive training sequences PSET.
        A set of negative training sequences NSET.
        A randomly generated network N with K states.
Output: A finite-state transition network.

Procedure HFS(PSET, NSET, N)

Let NEW be the empty set.
For each state S in network N,
    For each state T other than S in N,
        If there is no link from S to T in N,
            For each symbol W that occurs in PSET,
                Add to NEW a modified version of N
                    with W on a link from S to T.
        Else add to NEW a modified version of N
                    with no link from state S to T.
    If S is a rejecting state in network N,
    Then add to NEW a modified version of N in
            which S is an accepting state.
    Else add to NEW a modified version of N in
            which S is a rejecting state.
For each link L in network N,
    For each state S in N not the source of link L,
        Add to NEW a modified version of N in
            which S is the source of L.
    For each state S in N not the destination of link L,
        Add to NEW a modified version of N in
            which S is the destination of L.
Let BEST be the most accurate network in NEW.
If N is more accurate than the network BEST,
Then return the current network N.
Else return HFS(PSET, NSET, BEST).
```

Thus, one might attempt to retain all transition networks consistent
with the training sequences observed to date, as in the ISG algorithm
from Chapter 2. Alternatively, one might adapt the HFS scheme described above to operate on a window of recently observed sentences.
However, the space of finite-state networks is generally much larger than

the space of concept descriptions for attribute-value domains, making their incremental acquisition sufficiently difficult that work in this area typically invokes simplifying assumptions to make the task tractable.

A common response to the difficulty of finite-state induction is to provide both positive and negative training cases to the learning algorithm, since the latter can be used to rule out entire classes of overly general grammars. However, the problem remains challenging even with negative evidence, which has led some researchers to design incremental hill-climbing algorithms that rely on certain *orders* of training cases.

One such approach places a lexicographic ordering on the training cases, as used in a dictionary. This means that shorter sentences are presented before longer ones, which lets the learner start with simple grammars and increase complexity only when failure of the current hypothesis indicates that it is necessary. In particular, failure to recognize a positive sequence because no branches exist for a symbol suggests the need for a new state or link, whereas removal of a link is indicated if such a failure occurs because the positive sequence ends in a rejecting state. Failure to reject a negative sequence suggests the need for removing a link.

A related class of methods assumes that the learner can query a tutor or oracle about the legality of sample sentences. Given some ordering on finite-state networks, such as generality, such a scheme constructs an initial network at one extreme of the ordering. It then selects two successors of this network, H_1 and H_2, and generates a sentence S that H_1 will recognize but H_2 will not. If the tutor states that S is legal, then the method eliminates H_2 and all more specific networks. In contrast, if S is accepted as legal, then the algorithm eliminates H_1 and all more general networks. The process continues until only one finite-state network remains. Such methods require considerable user interaction, but they do make the task tractable.

9.2.3 Induction of k reversible grammars

Another response to the demands of incremental processing involves narrowing the space of target grammars. One interesting specialization is known as a k *reversible* grammar. The definition of such a grammar relies on the notion of a *prefix* (a substring at the beginning of a legal sentence), a *suffix* (a substring at the end of a legal sentence), and a *tail* (the suffix that follows a given prefix). Suppose a finite-state language L

Table 9-3. Algorithm KRG: Incremental induction of k reversible grammars.

```
Inputs: A set of positive training sequences PSET.
Output: A k reversible finite-state network.
Params: The number of symbols K retained for a prefix.

Procedure KRG(PSET)

Construct a linear network N from the first sequence in PSET.
For each remaining positive sequence P in PSET,
     Add a linear path L to the network based on P, starting
          at the start state used for the first sequence.
     KRG-Aux(N, L).
Return the network N.

Procedure KRG-Aux(N, L)

For each state S in the new path L,
     For each state T not in the path L,
          If the state R arcs into S and T on the same symbol,
          Then merge states S and T in network N.
          Else if there exists a path to S and a path to T
                    that have their last K symbols in common,
               and if S and T are both accepting states, or
                    if S and T arc to state U on the same symbol,
               Then merge states S and T in network N.
```

---

contains two sentences, P_1T_1 and P_2T_1, in which P_1 and P_2 are prefixes whose last k words match. We say that L is a k reversible grammar (for a nonnegative integer k) if the inclusion of the sentence P_1T_n in L implies the inclusion of P_2T_n for all tails T_n, and vice versa.

For example, suppose we have a 0 reversible language L_0 that includes the sentences *Joan writes texts* and *Mark writes texts*. If L_0 also includes *Joan reads novels*, this implies that the language also contains *Mark reads novels*, since we know that *Joan* and *Mark* have interchangeable tails. Moreover, inclusion of *Joan writes novels* implies three additional sentences: *Mark writes novels*, *Joan reads texts*, and *Mark reads texts*.

Now consider instead a 1 reversible language L_1 that includes *Joan writes texts* and *Mark writes texts*. In this case, inclusion of *Joan reads novels* implies no additional sentences in L_1, since tails are interchangeable only for prefixes whose last two words match. Thus, inclusion of *Joan writes novels* in L_1 implies *Mark writes novels*, but not the other sentences associated with L_0. As one increases k, the generalization of k reversible grammars from sample sentences becomes more conservative.

Such grammars are intriguing because there exists a simple incremental algorithm for inducing them. Table 9-3 gives pseudocode for this technique, which we will call KRG (induction of k reversible grammars). The method uses the initial training sentence to construct a completely linear finite-state machine. As KRG observes new sentences, it adds each to the network as an additional disjoint path with the same start state but with its own accepting state. However, after each such addition, the algorithm merges any pair of new and old states if they have links entering from another state with the same test; this ensures that the resulting network is deterministic. The algorithm also merges two states S and T if they share a length k link sequence entering them, provided that S and T are either both accepting states or both have links to a third state with the same test. This method can incrementally induce some parts of English grammar, including the auxiliary system and noun phrase specifiers.

9.2.4 Inducing hidden Markov models

Research on the induction of probabilistic finite-state networks has emphasized a different type of approach, based on the expectation maximization (EM) method we considered in Section 7.2.4. Suppose we have a hidden Markov model with h hidden states and j observable symbols, which we can characterize as an $h \times h$ matrix of transition probabilities and an $h \times j$ table of probabilities that one will observe a symbol given a state. Given a set of training sentences, O, each consisting of a sequence of observable symbols, we would like to find the probabilities λ for the two tables that maximize the probability of O.

The *forward-backward algorithm* constitutes the standard approach to this problem. This method starts by assigning random probabilities to each entry in the two tables, that is, for each pair of states and each combination of state and observable symbol. Next, for each training sentence O_i, the algorithm computes the most likely sequence of states q that generates the sentence. Using this information, it then estimates the fraction of times each state follows every other state and the fraction of times each state produces each symbol.

We will not recount the details of these calculations, but the first step propagates probabilities *forward* through the network, whereas the second step propagates them *backwards*, which is the source of the algorithm's name. After completing these steps, the method replaces the old probabilities with the newly computed ones and repeats the process, continuing until no significant changes occur in the two tables.

The above description assumes a hidden Markov model that is fully connected, but one can constrain the process by insisting that certain table entries be 0. For example, a common assumption in speech understanding is that states are ordered, with the only loops going from a state to itself. One can also specify local connectivity, such that each state has only a few immediate successors. Such constraints, if satisfied by the domain, can increase the learning rate by reducing the number of parameters to be fit, and thus reducing the size of the search space.

The forward-backward algorithm assumes the specification of such constraints and, more fundamentally, of the number of hidden states. However, one can embed this method within other techniques that search the space of hidden Markov structures. For example, one might carry out an iterative search, starting with one state, then two, and so forth, on each cycle using the forward-backward scheme to determine the most likely set of probabilities. One would continue to add states until cross validation or some simplicity bias suggests that accuracy on a separate test set has begun to decrease.

Like the EM algorithm and other heuristic methods we have examined, the forward-backward technique is only guaranteed to find local optima. One response to this limitation is to run the method many times from different random starting points. But even without such embellishments, this approach has been successfully used in many sequential domains that involve uncertain events.

9.3 Forming recursive transition networks

Finite-state grammars have only limited representational power, and many aspects of human language seem to require more sophisticated forms of grammatical knowledge. Thus, some researchers have focused instead on the induction of context-free grammars. As we saw in Section 9.1, one can represent such knowledge in terms of recursive transition networks, in which the tests on links can make reference to subnetworks. In this section we consider three broad approaches to acquiring such grammatical knowledge. However, we first examine an important source of information that complements training sequences.

9.3.1 The advantages of parse trees

In some sequential domains, the performance task involves mapping the input sequence onto some other structure. For example, a common goal in natural language understanding is to transform a sentence into a parse tree or into some closely related representation of the sentence's meaning. Thus, it seems fair to provide the desired structure as part of the training data. The psychological motivation for this scheme, commonly cited in computational models of first language acquisition, is that children hear sample sentences in the context of ongoing events, which provides information about the sentence's meaning and thus its likely parse structure. We will see that such information also alters the learning problem in interesting ways.

The presence of parse trees provides information about the structure of the recursive network required to generate them. The translation from a parse tree to a recursive network is straightforward. Briefly, one creates a transition network for each nonterminal node in the tree, with one link for each of its children. If a child C is also nonterminal, then the test on the link leading into C refers to the network for C; otherwise the link refers to the terminal symbol itself. Figure 9-6 shows an unlabeled parse tree for the sentence *The large dog saw a cat* and the recursive transition network that results. This contains a total of eleven subnetworks, one for each nonterminal node in the parse tree.

Providing a parse tree simplifies the induction task by indicating the componential structure of the target grammar. In the language of recursive transition networks, the parse tree specifies the relation between each network and its subnetworks; in the language of Horn clauses, it specifies the nonterminal symbols and their relation to ground literals. However, the nonbranching networks produced from parse trees do not move beyond the training sequences. Generalization over the observed sentences requires that one merge subnetworks in some manner.

For example, given the structures in Figure 9-6, one would hope (given our knowledge of English) to merge the networks for Na and Nb, for ARa and ARb, and for NPa and NPb. The first two involve a simple combination of links, leading to subnetworks like those for N and AR in

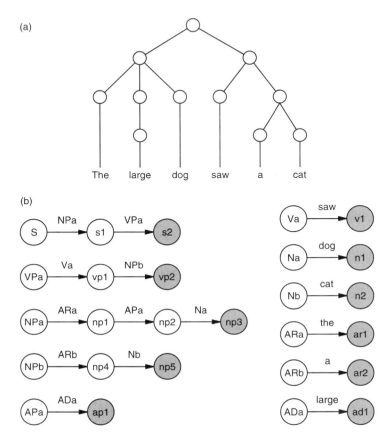

Figure 9-6. A parse tree (a) for the sentence *The large dog saw a cat* and the recursive transition network (b) that results. Each nonterminal node in the former corresponds to a subnetwork in the latter.

Figure 9-3. The third case is more complex, in that **NPa** and **NPb** have different numbers of links and thus multiple alignments are possible. In such situations, one might prefer the resulting network with the fewest number of links. For instance, if merges have already occurred for **ARa** and **ARb**, and for **Na** and **Nb**, this strategy would produce a subnetwork like **NP** in Figure 9-3.

One can also constrain the result of merging two subnetworks by providing *labels* on the branches in the parse tree. For example, one might specify that the top left branch in Figure 9-6 (a) is the **subject** of the event and that the top right branch is its **predicate**. Similarly, one might label the two branches under the latter as the **action** and the object of the predicate. Labels of this sort constitute information about the functional role of nodes in the parse tree. When such labels are present, one can use them to align nodes when combining subnetworks. Thus, when merging the networks for NPa and NPb in Figure 9-6 (b), such information might indicate that NPa aligns with NPb, np1 aligns with np4, and np3 aligns with np5.

9.3.2 Inducing recursive networks from parse trees

Even given a method for determining the subnetwork that results from a particular merge, we still require some means for searching the space of possible merges. One nonincremental approach, similar to HFS from Section 9.2.1, takes the union of the networks generated by each training sequence, then carries out a greedy search, using an evaluation function to select the best merge at each step. As usual, this process continues until the evaluation metric indicates that no further improvement is possible. Natural metrics would take into account the simplicity of the grammar and its ability to reject negative training sequences, if they are present.

However, if more than a few training sequences are available, it may be prohibitive to consider all possible merges at each stage in the search process, and heuristics may be needed to narrow the pairs examined. If the parse trees are labeled, one can use this information to constrain merging only to those subnetworks that play the same functional role. For Figure 9-6, this would limit possible merges to Na and Nb, and to ARa and ARb. A number of other heuristics are possible, some focusing on similarity comparisons between subnetworks and others constraining merges to subnetworks that occur in similar contexts within higher-level networks.

We should note one side effect of merging subnetworks that is not obvious. Consider Figure 9-7 (a), which shows two subnetworks for noun phrases constructed from different parts of sample parse trees. The first subnetwork, NP1, calls on the second, NP2, in the context of a relative clause, following a member of the word class REL (i.e., which or that). Given their similarity, one might merge the two networks into the single structure, NP, shown in Figure 9-7 (b). However, this subnetwork now calls on itself recursively, giving it the ability to parse noun phrases with embedded relative clauses; this step moves considerably beyond the training sequences.

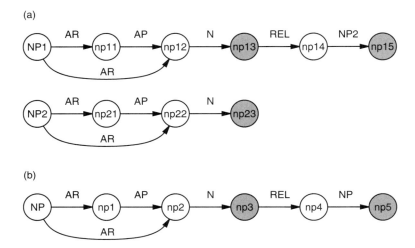

Figure 9-7. Two subnetworks (a) for noun phrases, one of which calls on the other, and the subnetwork (b) that results from merging them. This latter network calls on itself recursively, supporting parses of embedded relative clauses.

Within the framework of learning from parse trees, incremental approaches are more common than nonincremental ones, and these methods seldom assume the presence of negative training sentences. Table 9-4 presents one basic scheme, which we will call IPT (incremental learning from parse trees), that involves modifying the transition network in the minimal way required to cover each new positive instance. This method constructs a *partial parse* of the new sentence using the existing network, then adds the structure needed to complete the parse. For example, given the network in Figure 9-6 and the new sentence *A black cat heard the dog*, the minimal changes would add a cat link to the Na subnetwork, dog to the Nb network, heard to the Va network, a to the ARa network, the to the ARb network, and black to the ADa network. The IPT algorithm also merges two subnetworks if their structure is similar enough. In this example, given a liberal enough setting, it would merge Na with Nb and ARa with ARb, giving the word classes shown in Figure 9-3.

Matters are more complicated when the structure of the sample parse tree differs from the structures handled by the existing network. In such cases, more than one partial parse is possible. This problem is similar to the merging alignment issue we mentioned above, and, if available,

Table 9-4. The IPT algorithm: Incremental induction of recursive transition networks from parse trees.

```
Inputs: A set of training sequence/parse tree pairs PSET.
Output: A recursive transition network.

Procedure IPT(PSET)

Let I be the first sequence/parse tree pair in PSET.
Construct an initial network N from the parse tree in I.
For each remaining pair P in PSET,
    Let S be the sequence in P.
    Let T be the parse tree in P.
    If the network N does not produce parse tree T for S,
    Then use the network N to construct a partial parse of S.
        For each symbol in S not covered by the partial parse,
            Extend the network N in the minimal way needed
                to produce the parse tree T for sequence S.
        For each pair of subnetworks N1 and N2,
            If N1 and N2 are similar enough in structure,
            Then merge N1 and N2 in the minimal way.
Return the network N.
```

IPT can use labels on the sample parse tree to constrain the process. Moreover, some modifications provide different but equivalent networks. For example, given the network in Figure 9-6 and the new sentence *The dog saw a cat*, IPT would modify the NPa network to let the parse complete. To this end, it would bypass the ARa test either by adding a new link from NPa to np2 (with an ARa test) or from np1 to np3 (with an Na test) but, because they produce identical extensions, the choice does not matter. Yet another alternative would be to create an entirely disjoint path from the NPa start node.

Incremental algorithms of the above sort differ from each other primarily in their heuristics for selecting among partial parses and in their criteria for merging subnetworks. But they share a strong reliance on the parse tree for providing the componential structure of the transition network, which strongly restricts the possible revisions to the current hypothesis. Such constraints prove especially important when merging can produce recursive calls, as in noun phrases with relative clauses.

9.3.3 Inducing recursive networks from sample sentences

One can also approach the task of inducing recursive transition networks without the benefit of parse trees. However, in this case the learner must determine the appropriate componential structure as well as the grouping of symbols. One response involves considering the set of all possible parse trees for each positive training instance, then taking the cross product over the entire training set. This approach produces a very large but finite set of grammars, which one can winnow using negative instances. The simplest version of this scheme is clearly intractable for large training sets, but introduction of additional constraints on the space of networks improves the situation.

A more commonly used source of information about network structure involves the statistical distribution of symbols within the training sequences. Intuitively, if a given subnetwork exists in the target grammar, recurring subsequences of symbols will appear in the sample sentences. Thus, a plausible heuristic considers creating a subnetwork only upon observing such a recurring subsequence.

This idea is very similar to the one we presented in Section 6.5.1, except that here the components of new conjunctive terms (subnetworks) must occur in sequence. Thus, one can use a slightly modified version of the GLT algorithm, which we will call GLT', to construct recursive transition networks. As in attribute-value domains, the technique begins by constructing a very specific knowledge structure with one path through the network for each positive instance. However, in this context the initial structure is a degenerate one-level transition network like that shown in Figure 9-8, rather than a set of propositional Horn clauses.

From this starting point, GLT' considers all possible ways to construct new subnetworks (which correspond to phrases) from pairs of symbols that occur in the initial network. After removing redundant substructures, GLT' uses an evaluation function to select among the remaining alternatives. One natural measure involves the *simplicity* of the transition network, as measured by the number of nodes in the top-level transition network and all of its subnetworks. GLT' repeats this process until subnetwork creation ceases to produce any improvement on the metric. For the current example, using our measure of simplicity, this occurs after four steps, giving the network in Figure 9-9 (a), which contains four subnetworks for slightly different types of noun phrases.

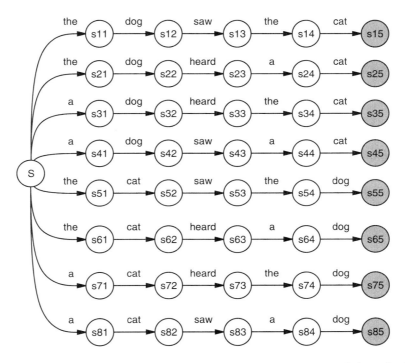

Figure 9-8. A degenerate recursive transition network, generated directly from eight positive training sequences, that serves as the initial hypothesis for the induction process summarized in Figure 9-9.

At this stage, GLT′ changes strategies and begins to consider merging existing subnetworks, again selecting the simplest competitor after eliminating ones that cover any negative training sequences (we assume none in this example). In this case, three steps of this sort generate the network in Figure 9-9 (b), which has merged the four varieties of noun phrase and removed six of the eight (now redundant) paths in the top-level network. The merging of two additional structures, in this case terminal symbols, produces the recursive transition network in Figure 9-9 (c), which includes one top-level structure, one structure for noun phrases, and one subnetwork each for nouns and verbs. Given the training sequences in this example, the algorithm does not create a subnetwork for the articles *the* and *a*, but given additional data about their occurrence in similar contexts, GLT′ would take this step as well. The algorithm will not always produce such an interpretable network, but the same basic scheme has been used in a number of studies with some success.

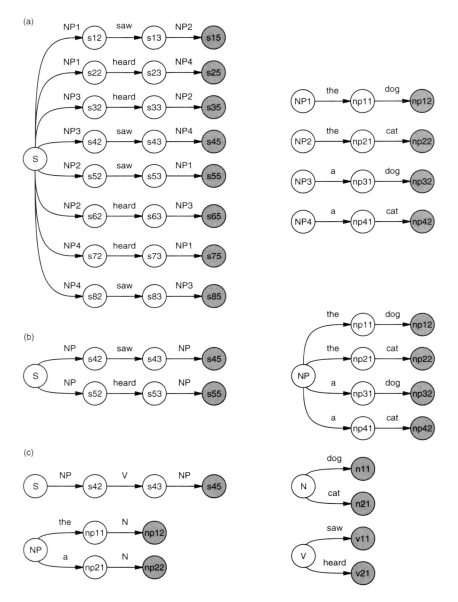

Figure 9-9. Transformation of the one-level recursive transition network in Figure 9-8 into one involving nonterminal symbols. The first network (a) introduces the subnetworks NP1, NP2, NP3, and NP4 to represent recurring subsequences; the second network (b) merges these into the single subnetwork NP, and the final group (c) introduces two classes of terminal symbols, V and N, which allow further merging of subnetworks.

9.3.4 Inducing stochastic context-free grammars

We have seen that one type of recursive network, the stochastic context-free grammar, is stated as rewrite rules with associated probabilities. These probabilities introduce an additional step into the induction process, as one must determine their appropriate settings from training data. The standard method, known as the *inside-outside algorithm*, is a variation on the forward-backward method for hidden Markov models that we saw in Section 9.2.4. This approach assumes that the grammar is stated in Chomsky normal form.

Given a set of positive training sentences and a stochastic grammar with randomly assigned initial probabilities for each rule, the inside-outside algorithm first computes the most probable parse tree for each training sentence. The method then uses these derivations to reestimate the probabilities associated with each rule, updates them accordingly, and repeats the process until no significant changes occur. The 'inside' step roughly corresponds to the 'forward' process for hidden Markov models; the 'outside' computation maps onto the 'backward' step.

Before invoking the inside-outside algorithm, one must decide on some *structure* for the stochastic context-free grammar. This structure can be initialized to include all possible rewrite rules over a user-specified set of nonterminals and the observed words. However, one can also use a method like GLT′ to infer this structure from distributional information in the training sequences, or one can even use parse trees, if available, to constrain the rewrite rules passed on to the process for estimating probabilities. Thus, the inside-outside method is best seen as complementing other techniques for the induction of recursive transition networks, rather than as replacing them.

9.4 Learning rules and networks for prediction

In Section 9.1.3, we saw that one can can mimic parsing by predicting the next word in a sequence as a function of previous words. Because the recurrent networks and predictive rules used for this purpose do not explicitly represent temporal structure, their associated induction methods are more akin to techniques for classification learning than to others we have seen in this chapter. In fact, transforming a sequential learning task into one involving classification learning requires only a simple step: each word in the sequence becomes one training instance, which is described by the k previous words in the sequence. One then attempts to induce some inference network or decision list that makes correct predictions on these training data and novel instances.

Much of the work along these lines has used recurrent neural networks, which incorporate their output as the input on the next predictive cycle. The typical approach uses a version of backpropagation (Section 6.4.2) that has been slightly modified to take this recurrence into account, although other updating methods are possible. Briefly, this scheme modifies weights in the network in response to errors in predicting each word from its predecessors. Although somewhat counterintuitive, a number of studies have shown that this approach can learn interesting grammars from sample sentences.

A similar approach applies to the induction of action models. Given a set of training cases that describe the environment before and after application of some action, one can divide these cases into positive instances (in which the action alters the world) and negative instances (in which it has no effect). One then invokes some induction algorithm to determine the conditions under which the action is effective. This scheme assumes that an action, when operative, always affects the world in the same way. If conditional effects are possible, one can decompose the task further and learn separate predictive rules for each feature or literal used to describe states.

The above scenario assumes that the learner knows which action was applied in each case. When this information is not available, one can use clustering methods (Chapter 7) to group sample transitions into sets that involve similar changes. Each cluster then represents a different class or action in a supervised induction task, which attempts to learn rules for predicting the conditions under which it produces the observed effect. The scheme is repeated for each action, producing a complementary set of action models.

9.5 Summary of the chapter

In this chapter, we examined state-transition networks, an organizational framework designed to handle domains with sequential or temporal aspects. We encountered three variations on this framework: finite-state machines, recursive transition networks, and predictive rules. The most basic versions of these formalisms assume logical descriptions, but we also found that probabilistic versions, specifically hidden Markov models and stochastic context-free grammars, can handle domains with inherent uncertainty. We viewed the induction of such transition networks in terms of heuristic search, and we saw that learning methods can exploit structure in the space of networks, as with other frameworks.

We considered four classes of methods for inducing finite-state machines from training sequences. The first approach, exemplified by the HFS algorithm, carries out a hill-climbing search through the space of finite-state networks, starting with a randomly generated network and using an evaluation metric to select among modified networks produced by operators that alter links and states. Order-reliant methods operate in an incremental manner, but they depend on receiving training sequences in a certain order (sometimes self-generated) to keep their set of hypotheses to a manageable size. Another incremental approach constrains the space of allowable networks, say to k reversible grammars, to limit or eliminate search. Finally, we examined the forward-backward algorithm, which estimates the probabilities in a hidden Markov model from training sequences, but which can also be embedded in other methods that postulate network structure.

After this, we turned to the induction of recursive transition networks. We examined the constraints introduced when parse trees are provided for each training sequence, as they indicate the componential structure of the target network. We presented an incremental algorithm, IPT, that takes advantage of such information, but we also studied another method, GLT', that instead determines network structure from distributional regularities in the training set. One can also combine these techniques with the inside-outside algorithm, a method for estimating probabilities on the rewrite rules in a stochastic context-free grammar that assumes these rules have already been provided.

Finally, we considered two broad methods for inducing predictive rules. One approach, typically associated with recurrent neural networks, learns to predict the words in a sentence as a function of previous words, transforming the problem of learning a network structure into a classification learning task, with one training case for each word in a training sequence. The other scheme focuses on learning action models, which specify the effects of external actions and the conditions under which these occur. This approach, which operates on training instances that describe the environment before and after the action occurs, can use a variety of induction methods but often relies on logical techniques.

Although most work on the induction of state-transition networks has focused on natural language, the techniques developed for this task are quite broad and also apply to many other domains. These methods remain less refined than algorithms for simple classification tasks, with most lacking the ability to handle noise and other complications, but the potential of transition networks is clear, and future work on this topic should produce improved methods and should identify the conditions under which they lead to useful results.

Exercises

1. Generate all sentences of 10 words or less that are recognized by the finite-state network in Figure 9-1 and all sentences of 8 words or less that are parsed by the recursive network in Figure 9-3. Show the sentence that the hidden Markov model in Figure 9-2 predicts as most likely.

2. Draw the most specific finite-state network that will recognize the two sentences *The black cat chased the mouse* and *The cat caught the brown mouse*. Draw the most general finite-state network that will recognize these two sentences. Generate a sentence recognized by this general network that violates the rules of English grammar.

3. Draw two finite-state grammars that fall between the two networks from Exercise 2 in generality, neither more general than the other. Transform both grammars into hidden Markov models in which the first sentence in Exercise 2 is more likely than the second.

4. Trace the behavior of the HFS algorithm (Section 9.2.1) on the positive training sequences 10 and 1010, and on the negative sequences 1, 0, 11, 00, 101, and 1011. Start with a network that parses only the sequence 10. Draw the network selected at each step in the search process.

5. Trace the behavior of the KRG algorithm (Section 9.2.3) for inducing k reversible grammars on the positive training sequences *Mary bakes cakes*, *John bakes cakes*, *Mary eats pies*, and *Mary bakes pies*. For $k = 1$ and $k = 2$, draw the finite-state network after the algorithm has incorporated each sample sentence. Also show all unobserved sentences covered by the grammar at each stage.

6. Add the relative clause *that heard a mouse* to the parse tree in Figure 9-6 (a) as a component of the second noun phrase, then draw the corresponding recursive network for the entire parse tree.

7. Generate a plausible parse tree for the sentence *The dog that heard a cat saw a small mouse*, then generate a plausible modification of the transition network from Exercise 6 that parses this sentence, along the lines of the IPT algorithm (Section 9.3.2).

8. Generate a sentence and associated parse tree that could plausibly lead one to alter the network in Figure 9-6 (b) to let it parse arbitrary numbers of adjectives in the initial noun phrase.

9. Trace the behavior of the GLT′ algorithm (Section 9.3.3) on the positive training sentences *The dog heard a cat*, *A dog heard the cat*, *The cat heard a dog*, *A cat heard the dog*, *The dog heard the cat*, and *A cat saw a dog*. Show the best network after each step and its evaluation score. Note that the last three networks cover sentences that violate rules of English grammar. Generate negative training sentences that will keep the algorithm from overgeneralizing.

Historical and bibliographical remarks

Grammar induction has received attention from learning researchers since the first days of artificial intelligence and pattern recognition. Much of this work has been motivated by linguistic proposals about the nature of language learning (e.g., Chomsky, 1965) or diary studies about the stages observed in children's language acquisition (e.g., Brown, 1973). Other work has been influenced by theoretical results on formal languages, though negative results like those of Gold (1967) have not deterred researchers from devising heuristic approaches that work in many domains. Reviews of this work, with somewhat different emphases, can be found in McMaster, Sampson, and King (1976), Pinker (1979), Dietterich, London, Clarkson, and Dromey (1982), Langley and Carbonell (1987b), and Hill (1992).

Perhaps the first detailed algorithm in this area came from Solomonoff (1959), who described a method for inducing finite-state grammars from sample strings. Garvin (1967) and Feldman, Gips, Horning, and Reder (1969) describe other early work along these lines. More recently, Tomita (1982) presents a nonincremental hill-climbing approach that forms the basis for our HFS′ algorithm (Section 9.2.1). Stolcke and Omohundro (1993) explore a related approach that generates a hidden Markov network by successively merging nodes. Rabiner and Huang (1986) and Poritz (1988) provide useful reviews of the forward-backward algorithm for inducing the probabilities in a hidden Markov model, originally due to Baum, Petrie, Soules, and Weiss (1970).

In terms of incremental methods, Rivest and Schapire (1993) report a technique that takes advantage of an ordering on training strings to constrain finite-state induction, while Porat and Feldman (1991) use a similar approach. In contrast, Knobe and Knobe (1977) let their system query an oracle about the legality of candidate strings to distinguish among competing grammars. Angluin (1982) describes a method (the basis for our KRG algorithm) for the incremental induction of k reversible grammars, which Berwick and Pilato (1987) have used to acquire subsets of English grammar.

Early methods for the induction of phrase structure grammars (i.e., recursive transition networks) from sample strings are reported by Cook, Rosenfeld, and Aronson (1976) and by Wolff (1980). The GLT′ algorithm in Section 9.3.3 is based on Langley's (1994b) GRIDS, which shares many features with its predecessors. Stolcke and Omohundro (1994) use a similar approach to determine the structure of a context-free grammar, then invoke the inside-outside algorithm to determine the probabilities on rules. Poritz (1988) describes the operation of the latter technique, proposed originally by Baker (1979). VanLehn and Ball (1987) describe a quite different method that carries out breadth-first search.

Much of the work on learning recursive transition networks from pairs of sentences and parse trees has been psychologically motivated. Early work along these lines is reported by Klein and Kuppin (1970), Siklóssy (1972), and Reeker (1976). The IPT algorithm in Section 9.3.2 is based on Anderson's (1977) LAS system, which incrementally induces recursive networks from sentence-tree pairs. Anderson (1981a), Selfridge (1981), Langley (1982), Hill (1983), and Siskind (1990) have explored similar approaches to grammar acquisition.

Researchers have exploited a variety of methods to learn predictive structures. Cleeremans, Servan-Schreiber, and McClelland (1989) use backpropagation to learn weights in a recurrent network that predicts the next word in finite-state sentences as a function of previous ones, and Elman (1991) presents a similar approach to context-free grammar acquisition. Shen and Simon (1989) describe a technique for inducing action models, in the form of decision lists, for known actions, while Vere (1977) presents a related method that works when actions are unspecified.

CHAPTER 10

The Acquisition of
Search-Control Knowledge

In earlier chapters we focused on the acquisition of knowledge for performance tasks that involve recognition or classification. The previous chapter diverged from this focus somewhat by dealing with sequential and temporal domains, but with recognition and understanding still the basic task. However, another central facet of intelligence involves the ability to solve problems, and problem solving inherently requires search. Some of the knowledge organizations we have examined, particularly Horn clauses and state-transition graphs, hold the potential for search, but we have been concerned only with their accuracy and not with the details of the search process.

In this chapter we consider learning issues that arise in the context of problem-solving tasks. We will find that research on this topic draws heavily on learning methods originally designed for classification tasks, and that one can use any of the representations, organizational schemes, and induction algorithms we have explored in earlier chapters. We will also see that the sequential and generative nature of problem solving introduces additional issues that make the learning task both more interesting and more difficult.

We begin by addressing some general issues about the representation, use, and acquisition of problem-solving knowledge. After this, we examine four alternative frameworks for learning to control search that differ in the nature of the training data and in the initial knowledge of the learner. Finally, we consider some broader issues about the utility of learned search-control knowledge.

10.1 General issues in search control

As in classification domains, one cannot consider the acquisition of problem-solving knowledge without first considering more basic issues. Here we examine the representations upon which problem solvers operate, the knowledge structures they can acquire through learning, and the manner in which they can use that knowledge. With this as background, we then pose the task of learning search-control knowledge.

10.1.1 Representation of states, operators, and goals

Any problem-solving system requires some knowledge about the problem states it may encounter, the operators it can use to transform those states, and the goal state it hopes to achieve. However, the operator descriptions may be completely transparent (explicitly specifying both the conditions of application and the effects), partly transparent (giving only the legal conditions), opaque (specifying both aspects in procedural terms), or almost entirely absent (specifying only the name and arguments). Similarly, the goal state may be described explicitly as a set of features or literals, or it may be encoded implicitly in an evaluation function that the problem solver applies to determine the desirability of states (including the goal).

Let us consider an example domain that we will use throughout the chapter: the blocks world. Problem states in this domain involve a table and N blocks, any of which may be stacked on the table or on each other. Most formulations of the blocks world assume four operators – `pickup`, `unstack`, `putdown`, and `stack` – as shown in Table 10-1. Each operator has a name and arguments, a set of conditions for legal application, and a set of effects, usually stated as an add list and a delete list. For instance, one can `pickup` an object `?x` only if it is on the table, if it has nothing on it, and if the robot arm is empty. After applying this operator, the arm is holding the object, `?x` is no longer on the table, and the arm is no longer empty.

A problem solver does not need all of this information to find solutions to problems in the blocks world. Even without knowledge of operator conditions and effects, it can apply operators in the external world to generate new states and thus carry out forward-chaining search through the problem space. In other cases, the system may have access to transparent descriptions like those in Table 10-1, which let it employ

Table 10-1. Descriptions of operators for the blocks world.

```
(pickup (?x)
 (on ?x ?t) (table ?t) (clear ?x) (arm-empty) =>
 (<add> (holding ?x)) (<delete> (on ?x ?t) (arm-empty)))

(unstack (?x ?y)
 (on ?x ?y) (block ?y) (clear ?x) (arm-empty) =>
 (<add> (holding ?x) (clear ?y))
 (<delete> (on ?x ?y) (arm-empty)))

(putdown (?x)
 (holding ?x) (table ?t) =>
 (<add> (on ?x ?t) (arm-empty))
 (<delete> (holding ?x)))

(stack (?x ?y)
 (holding ?x) (block ?y) (clear ?y) (≠ ?x ?y) =>
 (<add> (on ?x ?y) (arm-empty))
 (<delete> (holding ?x) (clear ?y)))
```

more sophisticated problem-solving strategies that involve the creation of subproblems.

When combined with some constraints on possible states, such as the number of blocks, a set of operators implicitly generate a *state space* like that shown in Figure 10-1. This consists of a set of legal problem states connected by a set of links that correspond to one or more operators. In this case, the presence of three blocks leads to 22 states, 6 of which have only one neighbor, 12 of which have two neighbors, and 4 of which have three neighbors. Although the figure does not show it, each link corresponds to two operator instances that have inverse effects. For instance, the operator instance (`pickup b`) transforms the central state into the one to its immediate right, whereas the operator instance (`putdown b`) transforms the latter into the former.

Table 10-1 assumes that the problem solver represents each state as a set of literals. For example, it posits that the central state is described as {(on A T), (on B T), (on C T), (clear A), (clear B), (clear C), (arm-empty)}. This scheme also assumes a set of background literals

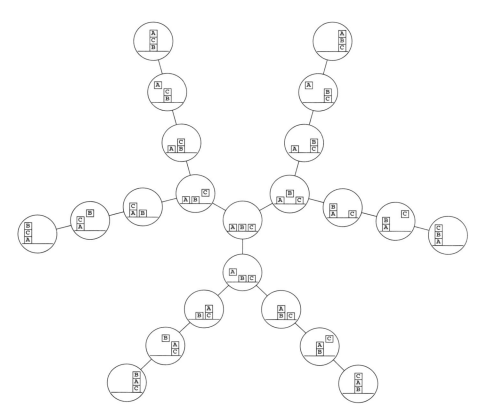

Figure 10-1. The state space for the three blocks world.

that are held in common across states: {(block A), (block B), (block C), (table T)}. Of course, other encodings are possible; one might describe each state as a set of Boolean features or a bit vector, with one bit for each literal that can occur in a state.

One can represent goals using the same language as for states. Typically, a goal specifies a desired state as a set of literals, which may completely describe a single state in the space or may provide only a partial description and thus correspond to a set of states. For many of the examples in this chapter, we will assume that the goal specification is {(on A B), (on B C), (on C T)}, which corresponds to the state in the upper right of Figure 10-1. In this case, only one legal state matches the specifications, even though they make no requirements about the predicates clear or arm-empty. However, if we had omitted the literal (on A B), then three states would have satisfied the goal description.

As with states, one can also encode goals as bit vectors, although this scheme is less common than the former approach.

One advantage of explicit goal descriptions is that they support the creation of subproblems, which let one decompose a problem-solving task into manageable parts. However, many search methods can operate with a procedural goal specification that simply returns `true` for a desired state and `false` otherwise, or with an evaluation function that returns only a numeric score. Naturally, the level of knowledge about goal descriptions has implications for learning, as we will see shortly.

10.1.2 Representation of search-control knowledge

Basic knowledge of states, operators, and goals is necessary for problem-solving activity, but it may not be enough to direct the search process. Fortunately, most problem-solving methods can take advantage of additional knowledge about one or more of these components. Although one can encode such knowledge by hand, there also exist algorithms for learning it from experience, as we will find later in the chapter.

One approach provides the problem solver with an evaluation function that returns the desirability of any given state. Typically, such a function estimates a state's distance from the goal description, although other interpretations are possible. A natural evaluation function for the blocks world returns the number of literals not shared with the desired state. For example, the central state in Figure 10-1 shares the literal (on C T) with the above goal specification, but not (on A B) or (on B C); thus, the function would return two for this state.

Although one can implement an evaluation metric as an opaque procedure, other alternatives also exist. One can encode such a function as a decision list or decision tree in which the tests inspect state features and the terminal nodes indicate scores. Another scheme would use a multi-layer neural network, in which input nodes correspond to state features and a single output node predicts the score. Yet another method would use an instance-based algorithm to infer a numeric value from the scores associated with stored prototypes. Each approach suggests ways of inducing evaluation functions from problem-solving experience.

An evaluation function assigns a numeric score to each state, but the actual scores are less important than their relative amount. This suggests the more general idea of *preference knowledge*, which specifies that the problem solver should prefer one state to another during search. One can extend this idea to handle classes of states, thus giving greater generality, and one can encode such preferences in explicit knowledge structures even more easily than numeric functions. For instance, a problem solver can use a logical rule to indicate that one class of states is preferable to another class, and it can use threshold and competitive schemes to achieve similar effects.

This idea extends beyond preferences among states. In some frameworks, the problem solver also makes decisions about which operator to apply and even which goal to process, and preference knowledge can deal with these situations as well. In some domains, the agent can also operate with simpler *selection knowledge*, which proposes the selection of a given state, operator, or goal independent of others that may be available. *Rejection rules*, which rule out consideration of an option, are also possible.

Another important dimension involves the organization of such knowledge in memory. One can view all problem-solving knowledge as an example of the state-transition graphs we considered in the previous chapter. However, there we saw that one can store connections between classes of states either in large, monolithic structures like grammars or in small, separate structures like production rules. We will reserve treatment of the monolithic approach for Chapter 11; in this chapter, we will focus on the alternative organization, which we refer to as *search-control knowledge*.

10.1.3 The use of problem-solving knowledge

Artificial intelligence has explored many varieties of problem solving and has developed many associated search strategies. Here we consider a few of the dimensions most important to research on learning in problem-solving domains. One central issue is whether search occurs internally, in the mind of the agent, or externally, in the world. The former allows a host of control strategies, including sequential processing with backtracking and 'parallel' methods that explore many paths at the same time. In contrast, external search allows only greedy or hill-climbing methods, since the problem solver cannot reverse actions already taken and it can only execute one of many alternatives. For example, an agent might explore the space of blocks-world states in Figure 10-1 either by applying operators in the world or by mentally projecting their effects.

A problem solver can also rely on different methods for controlling
internal search when this is possible. AI researchers have developed a
variety of heuristic methods that take advantage of domain knowledge
to direct search down profitable paths. These include heuristic depth-
first search, which pursues a single likely path but backtracks when it
encounters difficulties, beam search, which expands the best N nodes
at each level of the search tree, and best-first search, which retains a
set of unexpanded nodes and always expands the most attractive of
these. There also exist less systematic methods like greedy search and
hill climbing, which may halt at local optima but make fewer demands
on memory.

The organization of problem solving is even more important, since
this determines the nature of trace information used during learning.
The simplest scheme is forward-chaining, state-space search, in which
the problem solver considers only operators whose preconditions match
against the current state, applies one or more such operators, and iterates until reaching the goal or until forced to backtrack. Here search
occurs through an OR space, and a solution is a single path through the
state space. Another framework involves problem reduction, in which
the problem solver relies on domain knowledge about how to decompose complex problems into simpler ones. Here the search is through
an AND/OR space, and a successful solution takes the form of an AND
tree. Yet another problem-solving organization is means-ends analysis,
in which the agent selects some operator to aid in transforming the initial state into the desired one, then creates one subproblem to achieve
the operator's preconditions and another to transform its result into
the desired state. We will consider examples of each approach in the
sections that follow.

One can also distinguish between search through a *problem space* and
search through a *repair space*. In problem-space search, the problem
solver constructs a solution from scratch, composing states and operators until it achieves some path from the initial to the desired state. In
repair-space search, the agent begins with some possibly illegal but complete path and gradually transforms it into a more acceptable solution.
In this chapter and the following one, we will focus on problem-space
search, touching only briefly on repair-space search in Chapter 11 in the
context of analogy.

10.1.4 The task of acquiring search-control knowledge

Now that we have dealt with the representation and use of search-control knowledge, we can turn to the task of its acquisition. Briefly, we can state the problem as:

- *Given:* Partial knowledge of a problem-solving domain;
- *Given:* Experience with search through the problem space;
- *Acquire:* Knowledge that gives accurate decisions at choice points.

This formulation is intentionally vague; it does not specify any details about the nature of the initial knowledge, the experience, or the acquired control knowledge, or about the type of problem solver that uses it. Thus, the statement applies to any learning task requiring the improvement of search decisions, whether these occur in the mind of the agent or in the physical world.

The formulation also makes no commitment about the *source* of the learner's experience. Most work on this topic has assumed that the agent generates its own experiences through search on training problems. However, some researchers have developed *learning apprentices*, which glean their training instances from problem traces provided by a domain expert. One can use each scheme with any of the approaches we will consider; thus, our examples will make no assumptions about the source of path information. On yet another dimension, a system can acquire search-control knowledge from different *types* of experiences, including successful paths (e.g., problem solutions) and failures (e.g., dead ends and loops), as well as numeric information (e.g., the scores of an evaluation function).

As we noted in Chapter 1, learning attempts to improve performance on some dimension. For the classification tasks we addressed in previous chapters, the emphasis fell on improving the *accuracy* of decisions, even though one might also measure other aspects of classification. A number of alternative measures suggest themselves for problem-solving tasks. Most work on learning in problem solving has emphasized improving the *efficiency* of finding solutions,[1] but learning can also improve the *reliability* of plans when executed in the external world, and it can alter the *quality* of designs or other artifacts generated through problem solving. However, each type of improvement ultimately depends on

---

1. For this reason, researchers sometimes refer to it as *speedup learning*, even though learning in problem solving can focus on other issues.

making accurate decisions at choice points in the search process; it is for this reason that approaches to learning in problem solving borrow so many ideas from work on classification learning.

One important difference between problem solving and classification is that the former requires taking multiple steps before finding a solution. As a result, a problem solver seldom knows whether its decisions are accurate or inaccurate until long after it makes them. This leads to two central issues in learning for problem solving: assigning *credit* to desirable actions or decisions, and assigning *blame* to undesirable ones, in the absence of immediate feedback. Most of the methods we will examine are responses to these difficult problems. They are closely related to the view of learning in problem-solving domains as *test incorporation*, in which one takes the results of tests, evaluation functions, or similar information from late in a search tree and makes them available earlier in the search, where they can improve overall performance.

10.2 Reinforcement learning

One approach to the acquisition of problem-solving knowledge, *reinforcement learning*, focuses on preference knowledge for the selection of operators. Because this class of methods does not require information about operator effects, it is commonly applied to learning from sequences of external actions. However, many of the same issues arise in this context as with internal problem solving, and we will typically not distinguish between them.

In addition to a set of (possibly opaque) operators, a reinforcement learning system is provided with some *reward* function that evaluates states. Intuitively, states with high rewards are more desirable than ones with low or negative rewards, and the agent aims to approach the former and avoid the latter. Learning involves the acquisition of a control strategy that leads to states with high rewards, based on experience with the rewards produced by observed operator sequences.

10.2.1 Tabular approaches to reinforcement learning

The simplest approach to reinforcement learning stores knowledge in a table. Each entry describes a possible state-action pair, along with the expected reward that results from applying the action to that state.

Table 10-2. Reinforcement table for the blocks world, showing some possible states, operators applicable in those states, and the expected rewards for the state-operator combination.

States	Operators	Reward
(block a)(block b)(block c)(table t) (on b a)(on a c)(on c t)(arm-empty) (clear b)	(unstack b a)	0.1
(block a)(block b)(block c)(table t) (on a c)(on c t)(holding b)(clear a)	(putdown b) (stack b a)	0.2 0.0
. . .	. . .	. . .
(block a)(block b)(block c)(table t) (on b c)(on c t)(holding a)(clear b)	(stack a b) (putdown a)	0.9 0.0

Thus, a domain with p states and a actions would produce a $p \times a$ table, as in Table 10-2. However, if one knows the legal preconditions on operators, cells that correspond to illegal operator applications will be empty.

Typically, the problem solver uses this table to direct forward-chaining search. This involves finding the table entry for the current state, selecting the action that gives the highest expected score, and applying this action to produce a new state. The problem solver continues this cycle, producing a forward-chaining greedy search through the state space, until it reaches the desired state or some other halting condition, such as a local optimum. To encourage exploration of alternative paths, some systems use a stochastic scheme that, rather than selecting the best action, chooses actions as a probabilistic function of their predicted reward.

Reinforcement learning alters the predicted rewards stored in the state-action table on the basis of experience. The entries typically start with either random values or equal ones, but the score for a given state-action pair $<s, a>$ changes whenever the problem solver applies action a in state s. This produces a new state and a resulting reward, which the learner uses to revise the existing entry.

We will examine one updating scheme used in reinforcement learning systems. Let $Q(s, a)$ be the table entry for state s and action a. Let s' be the state resulting from applying this action in this state, and let $r(s, a)$ be the immediate reward that results. Furthermore, let $U(s')$ be $\max_{a'} Q(s', a')$, the maximum of the expected rewards for the actions one can apply in s'. Then a plausible updating method is

$$\Delta Q(s, a) \leftarrow \beta(r(s, a) + \gamma U(s') - Q(s, a)) \quad ,$$

where $0 < \gamma < 1$ is a discount factor and $0 < \beta < 1$ a correction rate.

This strategy, known as *Q learning*, computes the sum of the immediate reward and the discounted maximum reward expected for the following state, then subtracts the current entry for the state-action pair. It then multiplies this difference by the correction rate and modifies the entry in question by the resulting product. The discount factor γ specifies the importance of immediate versus delayed gratification, whereas the correction factor β determines the rate at which the learner revises table entries.

For example, assume that we store a table for the state space from Figure 10-1 and initialize all entries to 0. Further suppose that we want the learner to acquire a strategy for moving from any state in the space to the one in the upper right, and to this end we provide an immediate reward of 1 for this latter state but a reward of 0 for all others. Given a successful path from the bottom left state to the upper right state, Q learning would update the expected rewards for all state-action pairs along the path.

However, because both these and the immediate rewards are 0, the algorithm would only alter the score for the last step along the path, which led to 1 as the immediate reward. In this case, given $\beta = 0.1$ and $\gamma = 0.5$, it would increase the last entry $Q(s, a)$ by the amount $0.1 \times 1.0 + 0.0 = 0.1$, giving $0.0 + 0.1 = 0.1$ as the new entry. Given the same path with the same immediate rewards a second time, it would increase this pair's score by the same amount. However, first it would also modify the entry for the state-action pair one step earlier in the path. In this case, it would increase the expected reward by $(0.1 \times 0.0) + 0.5(0.1 - 0.0) = 0.05$, giving $0.0 + 0.05 = 0.05$ as the revised entry.

Given enough training cases, this learning scheme converges on the expression $Q(s, a) = r(s, a) + \gamma U(s')$ as the entry for each state-action pair <s, a> in the table. The overall effect is to transform the initial

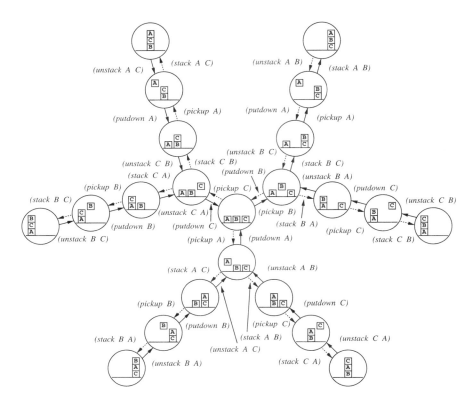

Figure 10-2. Search-control knowledge acquired by reinforcement learning, given an external reward that returns 1 for the goal state in the top right corner and 0 for all other states. Solid arrows indicate preferred actions that lead toward the goal state.

evaluation function (the external reward), which may be flat or non-monotonic with distance from the goal, into a revised function (the internal reward) that increases monotonically or nearly so. Thus, after sufficient experience, the problem solver can move toward the most desirable state from any location in the state space with little or no search, as Figure 10-2 indicates for the blocks world. One method used to increase the learning rate involves starting with a large value for β and gradually decreasing this parameter, which gives the algorithm a rough approximation during the early stages and allows fine tuning later in learning.

Another common algorithm for reinforcement learning, known as the *bucket brigade*, assumes that only some states provide external rewards.

As usual, each state-action pair <s, a> has an associated number reflecting the estimated desirability of action a in state s. Each time the problem solver applies the selected action, the bucket brigade decreases the score $Q(s, a)$ for the pair by some fraction f, but also increases the entry for the state-action pair that led to s by the same amount.[2] Upon reaching a state that gives some external reward, the algorithm increases the score for the pair that produced the state by $f \cdot r(s)$. The details differ from those in Q learning, as they do for another related method known as *temporal differences*, but the overall effect is similar.

This general approach to credit assignment has a number of attractive features. Reinforcement learning requires no knowledge of operators' effects, and its statistical flavor deals well with noisy domains in which one cannot predict these effects with certainty. Moreover, states and actions are more or less desirable, rather than good or bad, as assumed by some of the frameworks we will examine later. On the other hand, this simplistic, tabular approach to reinforcement learning can require very many training paths to arrive at reasonable entries for each state-action pair. In addition, since it stores at least one entry for each state, in most domains the size of memory grows exponentially with the length of problems.

10.2.2 Generalization in reinforcement learning

The basic problem with the above approach is that it does not generalize beyond specific states. To remedy this drawback, some work on reinforcement learning moves beyond simple tables to reduce memory loads and increase learning rates. For example, one approach represents each state as a feature vector and uses a multilayer threshold network to replace the table, with a different output that predicts the reward level for each possible action. Given a new state, one ships the state description through the network to predict a reward, then executes the action with the highest score. Figure 10-3 shows the partial structure of one possible network for the three blocks world.

For learning, one could use backpropagation or some other threshold induction method to modify weights in response to training instances.

---

2. The full algorithm is more complex, letting it deal with parallel applications of rules and characteristics of the rules themselves.

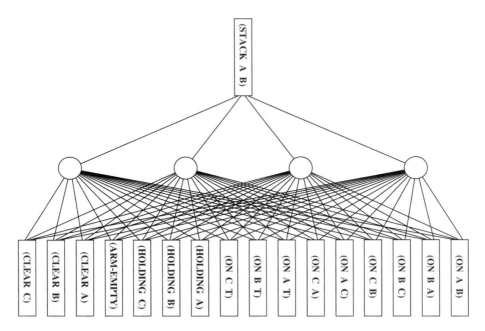

Figure 10-3. Partial structure of a multilayer network for predicting the expected reward of a given action (the output node) given different problem states (described by the input nodes). Other output nodes operate in parallel to predict scores for alternative actions.

This scheme would still use a routine like Q learning or the bucket brigade to update 'entries'. However, rather than retrieving $Q(s, a)$ and $U(s')$ from a table, the agent would instead send the state-action pair through the network to determine its score, compute the modified score, and use this score as the error that is passed to the threshold learning method. This scheme should encourage generalization across similar states and speed the learning process.

Another approach uses a concept hierarchy to organize similar sets of states in memory. As we saw in Chapter 7, such knowledge structures can predict numeric attributes in addition to class names. Thus, methods for decision-tree induction can incorporate state descriptors as predictive features in a 'regression tree' that associates expected rewards with its terminal nodes. Given a new state, the problem solver would sort this down a separate tree for each possible action, then select the action with the highest predicted reward.

A third common approach to generalization in reinforcement learning uses genetic algorithms; here the expected reward on production rules serves as their fitness, with more fit rules being selected for reproduction. The new rules are then evaluated by running them in the environment, with the best of them being selected to produce another generation, and so on. Such *classifier systems* are often used in conjunction with the bucket brigade algorithm for determining expected rewards.

10.2.3 Comments on reinforcement learning

The reinforcement learning approach to the acquisition of search-control knowledge has both advantages and disadvantages. On the positive side, it can handle uncertain and noisy domains, and it can interface with an external world more easily than the methods we examine in later sections. However, reinforcement approaches tend to have a slow learning rate even when combined with generalization techniques, particularly in the presence of lengthy solution paths.

One central problem with such methods is their reliance on gradual propagation of rewards backward through the search path. As a result, the problem solver needs to pass through early parts of the problem space many times before any rewards at all reach those locales. One response to this difficulty assumes that the programmer divides the state space into meaningful segments and trains the learning system separately on each segment. Because individual paths are shorter, this scheme lets rewards reach early states much sooner. However, one would rather have the problem solver itself decide how to segment problems, rather than relying on external aid.

Despite the apparent limitations of reinforcement learning, researchers have successfully applied the approach to a variety of interesting problems. Most of these focus on 'control' problems that involve closed-loop interaction with the external world. One commonly studied task involves balancing a pole on a cart. The state description includes information about the pole's angle and angular velocity, along with the cart's position and linear velocity, whereas the actions apply force to the cart in one direction or another. Another common testbed focuses on searching a two-dimensional grid for a cell that produces high reward. In a few cases, researchers have coupled reinforcement learning methods with physical robots to acquire useful behaviors.

10.3 Learning state-space heuristics from solution traces

Another approach to learning for state-space problem solving acquires control knowledge from traces of search on training problems. The framework does not rely on a reward function, but it does require a goal test to let it know when the problem solver has reached a desirable state or a failure test to determine when it has reached an undesirable state. Such methods can take advantage of explicit goal descriptions when available, but they do not require them. Given a solution trace that includes a sequence of operators that lead to a desired or undesired state, this class of methods learns heuristic conditions for the selection and/or rejection of operators. As we will see, this scheme reformulates the learning task in terms of supervised induction.

10.3.1 Inductive learning for state-space search

As we have seen, a state-space problem solver operates in a forward-chaining manner, selecting an operator that it can legally apply to the current state, generating a new state, and repeating the process according to some generic organization like depth-first, breadth-first, or best-first search. Alternatively, it can apply all operators to a given state, producing all possible successors, then select one of the new states for expansion. Thus, a learner can acquire state-space control knowledge that encodes decision strategies for operators, states, or both.

Table 10-3 gives pseudocode for LST (learning from solution traces), a nonincremental algorithm for inducing operator-selection knowledge from state-space solutions. Briefly, for each problem trace, the method treats each state along the solution path S as a positive instance of the operator that moves along S, whereas it treats the same state as a negative instance of operators that move one step off the path S.[3] After collecting this information from every solution trace for each operator O, LST invokes an induction algorithm to produce a concept description that discriminates the positive instances from the negatives. The resulting description constitutes the heuristic conditions under which selecting operator O will lead toward the desired state.

---

3. The full story is slightly more complicated. Because some operators take arguments, each instance must also include information about the bindings of these arguments in the state description.

Table 10-3. The LST algorithm: The acquisition of operator-selection knowledge from solution traces.

```
Procedure LST(PSET)

For each solution trace T in the problem set PSET,
    For each state S along T's solution path,
        Let P be an instantiation of operator O
            that leads along the trace T.
        Add the pair {S, P} to the positive instances of O.
        For each instantiation N of operator O
            that leads one step off T's solution path,
            Add the pair {S, N} to negative instances of O.
For each operator O,
    Induce an intensional description D that discriminates
        the positive cases of O from its negative cases.
    Store the selection knowledge 'If D, then select O'.
```

As with reinforcement learning, the LST framework can use any of the induction algorithms we examined in Chapters 2 through 7, since it transforms the task of learning search-control knowledge into a nonincremental supervised induction task. Thus, it can invoke methods for learning logical summaries, threshold concepts, and competitive descriptions. However, heuristic conditions for operator selection frequently require multiple decision regions, making methods from Chapters 5 through 7 most appropriate. Also, many formulations of state-space search involve relational languages, which indicate the relational methods discussed in Chapter 8. One can organize search-control knowledge into decision lists, inference networks, or concept hierarchies, but the use of state-transition networks raises issues that we delay until the following chapter.

Consider the solution path in Figure 10-4, which shows the positive and negative instances that LST generates for each operator based on the highlighted solution path. Table 10-4 presents the details of each training instance, specifying the description of each state and the arguments of each operator. Notice that a given state may serve as a positive case for one instantiation of an operator and a negative case for another instantiation. To these training data, LST applies an induction

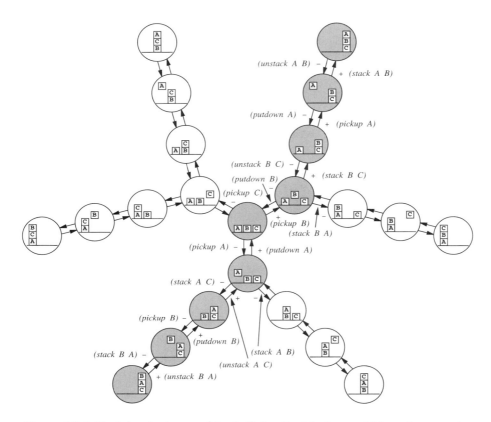

Figure 10-4. Training instances (shaded) for the blocks world based on a solution path that leads from the state in the lower left corner to the one in the upper right corner.

algorithm that generates an intensional description for the selection of each operator. One can view these as specializations of the legal preconditions on each operator.

For example, Table 10-5 shows a logical decision list that results when one applies an NSC-like algorithm (see Chapter 5) to the training instances generated by all paths that lead to the upper right state in Figure 10-4. For each operator (concept) O, the algorithm finds a description D that covers some positive instances but few negatives, then removes the instances covered by this new rule and repeats the process until it has covered all positive instances of O. The algorithm applies this strategy to each operator, generating a set of disjunctive rules for each one. Note that these rules are sensitive to the goal description, which

Table 10-4. Positive and negative instances for the blocks world operators produced from the solution trace in Figure 10-4.

States	Operators	Type
(block a)(block b)(block c)(table t) (on b a)(on a c)(on c t)(arm-empty) (clear b)	(unstack b a)	+
(block a)(block b)(block c)(table t) (on a c)(on c t)(holding b)(clear a)	(putdown b) (stack b a)	+ −
(block a)(block b)(block c)(table t) (on a c)(on b t)(on c t)(arm-empty) (clear a)(clear b)	(unstack a c) (pickup b)	+ −
(block a)(block b)(block c)(table t) (on b t)(on c t)(holding a) (clear b)(clear c)	(putdown a) (stack a b) (stack a c)	+ − −
(block a)(block b)(block c)(table t) (on a t)(on b t)(on c t)(arm-empty) (clear a)(clear b)(clear c)	(pickup b) (pickup a) (pickup c)	+ − −
(block a)(block b)(block c)(table t) (on a t)(on c t)(holding b) (clear a)(clear c)	(stack b c) (stack b a) (putdown b)	+ − −
(block a)(block b)(block c)(table t) (on b c)(on a t)(on c t)(arm-empty) (clear a)(clear b)	(pickup a) (unstack b c)	+ −
(block a)(block b)(block c)(table t) (on b c)(on c t)(holding a)(clear b)	(stack a b) (putdown a)	+ −

we did not include in Table 10-4; these constraints should let them recommend useful operators for problems with different goals than those encountered during training.

One can easily adapt the LST scheme to generate rejection knowledge rather than selection knowledge, simply by reversing the positive and negative instances for each operator. This approach gives rules that

Table 10-5. Operator-selection rules induced by an NSC-like algorithm from the instances generated by all solution paths that lead to the upper right state in Figure 10-4. Initial conditions on each operator are in parentheses, whereas new conditions are in brackets.

```
((on ?x ?t)(table ?t)(clear ?x)(arm-empty)
 [goal [on ?y ?x]][<not> [goal [on ?z ?y]]][[clear ?y]]
 [goal [on ?x ?w]][on ?x ?u][clear ?w] =>
 (select (pickup ?x)))
((on ?x ?t)(table ?t)(clear ?x)(arm-empty)
 [on ?x ?w][<not> [goal [on ?y ?x]]]
 [goal [on ?x ?z]][<not> [on ?z ?w]] =>
 (select (pickup ?x)))
((holding ?x)(table ?t)
 [goal [on ?x ?y]][<not> [clear ?y]] =>
 (select (putdown ?x)))
((holding ?x)(table ?t)
 [goal [on ?y ?x]][goal [on ?z ?y]] =>
 (select (putdown ?x)))
((holding ?x)(block ?y)(clear ?y)(≠ ?x ?y)
 [goal [on ?x ?y]][on ?y ?z][goal [on ?y ?z]] =>
 (select (stack ?x ?y)))
((on ?x ?y)(block ?y)(clear ?x)(arm-empty)
 [on ?y ?z][<not> [goal [on ?y ?z]]] =>
 (select (unstack ?x ?y)))
((on ?x ?y)(block ?y)(clear ?x)(arm-empty)
 [<not> [goal [on ?x ?y]]] =>
 (select (unstack ?x ?y)))
```

specify the conditions under which the problem solver should *not* select a given operator. In state spaces with few solutions, this scheme may lead to greater transfer and thus to more rapid learning. However, if the learning algorithm is generating its own solution traces on the basis of partly learned knowledge, it may ignore branches that lead to solutions and thus may deprive itself of useful training instances.

The induction of preference knowledge gives some aspects of both selection and rejection knowledge. Rather than generating positive and negative instances for each operator instantiation, the learner generates a training case for each pair of such instantiations, then induces a concept description that describes the conditions under which it should prefer one operator instantiation to another. This knowledge is more conservative than either selection or rejection descriptions, since it deals with combinations of particular operators. Thus, it should lead to slower learning than either of the other approaches, but it should also aid the problem solver in recovering from incorrect decisions based on faulty preferences.

One can also adapt this basic approach to acquire a different type of control knowledge represented as state preferences. In this case, the learner collects pairs of states, $<S_1, S_2>$, that have a common parent in a problem-solving trace, where S_1 falls on the solution path and S_2 falls one step off the path. The pair $<S_1, S_2>$ becomes a positive training instance for the concept 'preferable', whereas the pair $<S_2, S_1>$ becomes a negative instance for the same concept. The learner then uses some induction technique to determine an intensional description for this concept. Given new tasks, the problem solver can use this preference knowledge to control the order in which it expands states.

Although we have presented the LST algorithm and its relatives as delaying the induction step until they have collected instances from multiple solutions, one can also formulate versions that induce tentative control knowledge after each training problem and then use it to guide search for solutions to more difficult tasks. Fully incremental versions that learn after each problem-solving step are also possible, but these require some means for immediate assignment of credit and blame, such as the feedback from a domain expert available to a learning apprentice.

10.3.2 Analytic learning for state-space search

In some cases, the learner has access to transparent descriptions that accurately summarize each operator's preconditions and effects. When such knowledge is available, one can adapt methods like the ICE algorithm, which we discussed in Chapter 6, to the task of acquiring search-control knowledge. For each problem solution, the technique treats each state S along the solution path as a positive training instance of the operator selected in S; it then uses the remaining portion of the solution path to generate a 'proof' that this instantiated operator actually leads to the goal state. Thus, this approach constitutes a special case of the LST algorithm that we described above, although it ignores negative

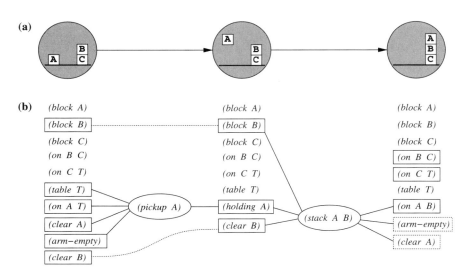

Figure 10-5. (a) Graphical description of a two-step solution path in the blocks world, and (b) a first-order description of the same path, with lines indicating dependencies in the explanation structure. The figure omits deleted literals for the sake of clarity.

instances when constructing control rules. Like other versions of LST, this analytic approach assumes some test for achievement of the goal, but this must be stated as an explicit 'target concept' that serves as the root for the proof tree.

At an intuitive level, the proof process involves chaining backward from all literals in the goal description, through the effects and preconditions of the operators along the remaining path. The terminal nodes in this proof are those literals in the state S that are required to reach the goal description through the observed sequence of operators. The algorithm keeps track of variable bindings in constructing this proof, which lets it replace the constants in the terminal literals with consistent variables. Finally, the algorithm constructs a selection rule that recommends the operator for state S whenever it encounters a state that matches this conjunction of generalized literals.

Consider the behavior of this approach on the two-step solution path in Figure 10-5, which transforms the initial state into one that matches the goal description {(on A B), (on B C), (on C T)}. The top part of the figure (a) presents the states along the solution path in visual terms, whereas the lower part (b) depicts the literals that constitute each state. The latter also shows the structure of the explanation or proof that this operator sequence will transform the initial state into the goal state. The literals in each pair of adjacent states are connected by the operator that transforms one into the other, with lines indicating the instantiated preconditions and the instantiated additions.

Because the explanation in the figure includes only those literals highlighted by boxes, the conditions of the acquired rule contain only those literals needed to produce the goal description when one applies the observed operator sequence. For the first decision in this solution path, the result of this process is the operator-selection rule

```
((on ?x ?t) (table ?t) (clear ?x) (arm-empty)
 [block ?y] [clear ?y] [≠ ?x ?y] =>
 (select (pickup ?x)))    ,
```

where the bracketed conditions are those not included in the original conditions on the `pickup` operator. The process of replacing constant terms with variables is not very interesting in this case, since the new conditions introduce only the term B (which becomes ?y), and this term does not even occur in the original conditions. However, note that the process does include a test to ensure that the two blocks are different, which is necessary for the success of the proof. The final rule recommends that one select the operator (pickup A) not only in the initial state in Figure 10-5, but also recommends analogous actions in other circumstances as well.

One can apply the same mechanism to more complex solution paths. For instance, the successful operator sequence

(unstack B A) → (putdown B) → (unstack A C) → (putdown A)
   → (pickup B) → (stack B C) → (pickup A) → (stack A B)

when combined with the operator descriptions in Table 10-1 leads the above method to produce the selection rule

```
((on ?x ?y) (block ?y) (clear ?x) (arm-empty)
 [table ?t] [block ?x] [on ?y ?z] [block ?z]
 [≠ ?x ?y] [≠ ?x ?z] [≠ ?y ?z] =>
 (select (unstack ?x ?y)))    .
```

This heuristic incorporates seven conditions beyond those in the original
unstack description, including three inequality tests to ensure that the
blocks involved are distinct.

Although the proofs we have examined have a different form than
those we saw in Chapter 6, one can easily transform them into a more
traditional notation. To achieve this, one rewrites each domain operator
as a set of inference rules, one for each literal that the operator adds or
deletes. Each such rule contains the legal conditions for the operator's
application, along with a test for whether the problem solver has applied
the operator to the current state. There must also exist one rule for each
known literal that infers this fact remains true in a given state, unless
the problem solver has applied an operator to the preceding state that
removes it. Finally, there must exist a single rule that detects when a
state satisfies the goal description. Like the inference rules in Chapter 6,
these produce an AND tree that one can compile into an intensional
concept description using the literals in a given state.

Note that the above learned rules assume that the target concept
focuses on achieving the literals generated by the final operator in the
solution sequence. Much of the work on analytic learning for state-
space search has made this assumption, but it seems most appropriate
for domains like the integral calculus, where the final state consists
of a single (unintegrated) literal. However, the goal specification for
domains like the blocks world can include many features, as we see in the
highlighted literals in the final state of Figure 10-5. Consider a similar
problem with the same goal description but with (on B C) missing from
the initial state. In this situation, the ideal operator instantiation is
(pickup B) rather than (pickup A), indicating that the pickup rule
shown above is overly general.

One response is to alter the target concept to include the *conjunction*
of literals specified in the goal description. For the training problem in
Figure 10-5, this scheme produces the rule

```
((on ?x ?t) (table ?t) (clear ?x) (arm-empty)
 (block ?y) (clear ?y) (≠ ?x ?y)
 [on ?y ?z] [on ?z ?t] =>
 (select (pickup ?x)))    ,
```

which includes two additional conditions. However, this rule seems inappropriate as well, as it will match even when the goal description is quite different. We could make the rule more specific by explicitly including the goal literals [goal [on ?x ?y]], [goal [on ?y ?z]], and [goal [on ?z ?t]], but this seems overly specific, since the action (pickup A) should still be preferred in cases where (goal (on B C)) and/or (goal (on C T)) are absent.

A more plausible scheme instead computes the *differences* between the initial state and the goal description, augments the state literals with these differences, and attempts to learn a target concept that does not contain any such differences. These observations do not detract from the usefulness of analytic approaches; they simply highlight the importance of specifying an appropriate target concept for the learning process.

Most analytic methods learn selection rules from successful paths, and the above approach works well in such cases. However, the target concept also plays a key role in analytic approaches to learning both *rejection rules* from failed paths and *preference rules* from goal interactions. These require different formulations of the target that let the learner prove that a given path is guaranteed to fail or to encounter some other difficulty. We do not have the space to consider such variations in detail, but they play an important role in some work on learning in problem solving.

Analytic methods for the acquisition of control knowledge have their strengths and weaknesses, as do the less knowledge-intensive methods like NSC that we examined earlier. The former are guaranteed to produce control rules that lead to the goal, but as we have seen, one must be careful in specifying the target concept; the latter require less background knowledge, but they also have the potential for acquiring inaccurate control knowledge. Analytic methods like ICE require knowledge of both operator preconditions and effects, whereas methods like NSC require only the former. The analytic approach can produce control rules that are more complex than necessary, but they do not require one to assume (perhaps incorrectly) that states just off the solution path are undesirable. Thus, the desirability of one approach over the other remains an empirical question, despite the claims of superiority for one method over the other that often appear in the literature.

10.4 Learning control knowledge for problem reduction

Another common framework for problem solving involves reducing complex tasks into simpler subproblems. There exist many instantiations of this basic idea. One approach, often called *problem reduction*, introduces a set of intermediate subgoals that the problem solver should attempt to achieve on the way to the original goal state. Another scheme, sometimes called *goal reduction*, replaces a goal specification with a set of other goal descriptions that, when satisfied, achieve the original goal. Yet another method defines high-level actions as sequences of simpler ones, which eventually terminate in primitive operators. The common feature is the decomposition of 'problems' into 'subproblems'; thus, we will refer to this generic approach as 'problem reduction' despite its more specific usage.

10.4.1 Problem reduction as search

As with forward-chaining methods, one can view problem-reduction techniques as carrying out search. However, in this case the process occurs through an AND/OR space rather than a simple state space, and a successful solution produces an AND tree rather than a simple path. Naturally, the problem solver can organize this search in various ways, using AND/OR versions of depth-first, breadth-first, and best-first search or less systematic methods such as hill climbing and greedy algorithms.

Table 10-6 presents a set of problem-reduction rules that solve tasks in the blocks world. The top-level operator, maketower, takes a list of objects as arguments and constructs a tower with the components in the specified order. This operator is recursively defined, calling on itself to construct a simpler tower, followed by the grasp operator and either stack or putdown, which are primitive operators. Maketower terminates when it attempts to construct a tower containing a single object that is the table or that it can successfully clear using makeclear. This operator is defined in turn using grasp and putdown, and it terminates when the block in question is clear. Grasp itself is defined with makeclear, followed by either pickup or unstack, but it can also terminate if the agent is already holding the block to be grasped.

Figure 10-6 presents the AND tree that results from using this set of decomposition rules to solve the second half of the problem we saw in

Table 10-6. Problem-reduction rules for the blocks world stated as Horn clauses. Each rule either decomposes a high-level operator into a sequence of lower-level ones or terminates in a state descriptor. Calls on the primitive operators from Table 10-1 alter the state description if their preconditions match but fail otherwise.

```
1. maketower([X]) :- table(X).
2. maketower([X]) :- makeclear(X).
3. maketower([X,Y|Z]) :- maketower([Y|Z]),grasp(X),stack(X,Y).
4. maketower([X,Y|Z]) :- grasp(W),putdown(W),maketower([X,Y|Z]).

5. grasp(X) :- holding(X).
6. grasp(X) :- makeclear(X),pickup(X).
7. grasp(X) :- makeclear(X),unstack(X,Y).

8. makeclear(X) :- clear(X).
9. makeclear(X) :- on(Y,X),grasp(Y),putdown(Y).
```

Figure 10-4. Thus, the top-level call is `maketower([A,B,C])` and the final state is a tower with block A on block B and with B on C. The initial state, not specified in the top-level call, is a tower with B on A and with A on C. Each node in the tree shows the name of the operator or state predicate, its arguments, and the number of the rule used to generate its children. The tree that solves the complete problem from the earlier figure has a similar form, but the reference to `makeclear(C)` becomes the root of a subtree that includes `grasp` and `putdown`, rather than pointing to the state descriptor `clear(C)`.

Of course, this figure does not reveal the search needed to generate the AND tree. Inspection of Table 10-6 reveals two important choice points: the problem solver must select between rules 3 and 4 when given a nontrivial `maketower` goal, and it must select between rules 6 and 7 when encountering a nontrivial `makeclear` problem. An incorrect choice can lead the problem solver to carry out significant unnecessary work, since each rule calls on nonprimitive operators before reaching the primitive ones at the end of the decomposition sequence. Only at this point can the problem solver determine whether the current state matches the operator's preconditions, and thus tell whether the entire rule will succeed or fail.

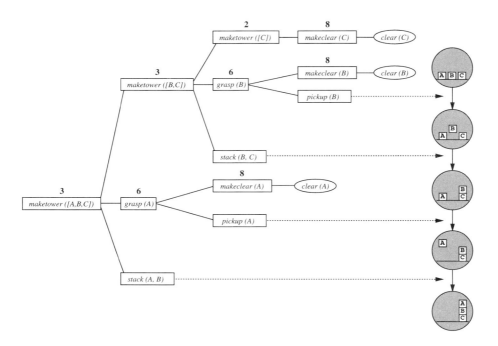

Figure 10-6. The AND tree that results from a problem reduction transformation of the blocks world state in the upper right to the one in the lower right. Rectangles denote instantiated clauses from Table 10-6, numbers indicate the rule responsible for each decomposition, and ellipses represent features of the current state. The order of operator application proceeds from top to bottom, generating the sequence of states on the right.

10.4.2 Inductive learning for problem-reduction search

As with state-space search, one can use inductive learning methods to acquire search-control knowledge that distinguishes desirable cases of each decomposition rule from undesirable ones. As before, the learner takes each node in the successful AND tree as a positive training instance of the rule applied at that point, whereas negative instances correspond to cases of different rules for the same predicate that it did not use there. Table 10-7 shows some positive training instances that result from the tree in Figure 10-6, along with some negative instances that might result from failed paths.

Table 10-7. Positive and negative instances of the problem-reduction rules from Table 10-6, with positive cases taken from nodes in Figure 10-6. Nonembedded literals describe the current problem state, and literals embedded in `goal` indicate the nonterminal goal that the problem solver is attempting to satisfy.

Problem descriptions	Rule number	Type
block(a), block(b), block(c), table(t)	1	–
on(a, t), on(b, t), on(c, t), arm-empty	2	–
clear(a), clear(b), clear(c)	3	+
goal(maketower([b, c]))	4	–
block(a), block(b), block(c), table(t)	1	–
on(a, t), on(b, t), on(c, t), arm-empty	2	+
clear(a), clear(b), clear(c)	3	–
goal(maketower([c]))	4	–
block(a), block(b), block(c), table(t)	8	+
on(a, t), on(b, t), on(c, t), arm-empty	9	–
clear(a), clear(b), clear(c)		
goal(makeclear(c))		
block(a), block(b), block(c), table(t)	5	–
on(a, t), on(b, t), on(c, t), arm-empty	6	+
clear(a), clear(b), clear(c)	7	–
goal(grasp(b))		

Given these data, an induction algorithm like NSC from Chapter 5 might generate a more selective version of the rule like

```
3.' maketower([X,Y|Z]) :- block(Y), maketower([Y|Z]),
                          grasp(X), stack(X,Y).
```

which will call on `maketower` recursively only when the second object in the tower is a block. Alternatively, the learner could incorporate the `block(Y)` condition into a separate rule that selects decomposition 3 with the appropriate arguments. Adding the condition `table(Y)` to rule 4 produces a similar effect, causing the rule to avoid calling on expensive operators when the overall rule is guaranteed to fail. Admittedly, we might have avoided the need for such a constraint by writing the decomposition rules in another way, but this example clarifies the basic point.

As with state-space search, one can adapt this basic approach to acquire other forms of search-control knowledge. For rejection rules, the learner treats positive instances as negative and vice versa, then induces rules that let the problem solver eliminate some candidates from competition. For preference rules, the learner uses pairs of states or reduction rules as training instances and induces the conditions under which the problem solver should prefer one over the other. We will not give examples of these methods, but they differ from those in Section 10.3 only in their emphasis on AND/OR rather than state-space search.

The use of incremental methods with problem reduction increases the chances for *within-trial learning*. Because each subproblem has a certain independence from other subproblems in the AND/OR tree, the learner need not wait for a complete solution before revising its knowledge base. Having generated positive and negative instances for a given nonprimitive operator, it can update the rules for that operator and then use the result in constraining search on later subproblems. In principle, such transfer can lead to more rapid learning than the more conservative nonincremental scheme we described above.

10.4.3 Analytic learning for problem-reduction search

Problem-reduction rules bear a close resemblance to the inference networks we examined in Chapter 6, suggesting the use of methods like ICE and IOE that take advantage of background knowledge. Recall that these algorithms propagate constraints through a proof tree to determine sufficient conditions for generating similar proofs. When applied to problem-reduction knowledge, the propagation occurs through the nodes in the AND tree, which has a form more like a traditional proof than the state-space solution paths we considered in the previous section. Given a successful AND tree, one natural use of analytic learning is to construct a single rule that connects the top-level goal to a sequence of primitive operators, and we discuss this approach in Chapter 11.

However, our focus in this chapter is on search-control knowledge, and one can also adapt this scheme to acquire a selection rule for each node in the AND tree. For example, consider how this method applies to the goal `maketower([B,C])` at the second level of Figure 10-6. The problem solver has decomposed this goal into `maketower([C])`, `grasp(B)`, and `stack(B,C)`. The subgoal `maketower([C])` has in turn been rewritten as `makeclear(C)`, which is satisfied because the initial state contains `clear(C)`. The subgoal `grasp(B)` has been broken into `makeclear(B)`, which is satisfied directly in the current state, and `pickup(B)`. The preconditions for this primitive operator – `on(B,T)`, `table(T)`, `clear(B)`, and `arm-empty` – also match, leading to its application and the creation of a new state. Having achieved the goal `grasp(B)`, the problem solver moves on to the second primitive operator, `stack(B,C)`. The current state also meets its preconditions – `holding(B)`, `block(B)`, and `clear(B)` – so the problem solver applies it and returns success for the original goal, `maketower([B,C])`.

Given this proof, an analytic method collects the state literals present in the initial state that were needed to complete the two `makeclear` goals – `clear(C)` and `clear(B)` – along with those needed to apply the two operators, not counting literals generated by the application of the first operator – `on(B,T)`, `table(T)`, `clear(B)`, `arm-empty`, and `block(B)`. The algorithm then unifies these with the variables in the original decomposition rules and operators, eliminating redundant literals and adding necessary inequality tests. In this case, the result would be the more specific decomposition rule

```
3." maketower([X,Y|Z]) :-
     clear(X),clear(Y),on(X,Y),table(Y),arm-empty, block(X),
     X≠Y,maketower([Y|Z]),grasp(X),stack(X,Y).
```

As before, an equivalent scheme would include the new conditions in a separate rule that selects decomposition 3 with the appropriate arguments. In either case, the problem solver would only select this particular goal if the current state met this set of preconditions, avoiding the need to call on itself and on `grasp` unless the entire rule was guaranteed to succeed.

In this approach, the acquired knowledge is much more specific than that learned with the NSC algorithm, which added only one new condition, `block(Y)`. However, the analytic approach adds a separate rule for each node in the final AND tree, thus guaranteeing the ability to solve the training problem with no search. Which method leads to more rapid reduction in search depends on the initial decomposition rules and on the training problems that the problem solver encounters during the learning process.

10.5 Learning control knowledge for means-ends analysis

Another approach to problem solving – means-ends analysis – also divides problems into subproblems, but does not require a programmer to specify a decomposition. Instead, a means-ends system selects an operator, typically one that reduces one or more differences between the current and the desired state, and then uses this operator to generate two subproblems. The first subproblem involves transforming the current state into one that matches the preconditions of the selected operator; the second involves transforming the state that would result from the operator's application into one that matches the original goal description. This scheme relies on transparent descriptions of the operators, since it uses the preconditions to generate the goal description for the first subproblem and the effects to generate the initial state of the second one.

10.5.1 Means-ends analysis as search

As with the other problem-solving methods we have examined, means-ends analysis also requires some basic organization – such as depth-first, breadth-first, or best-first – on its search. Most work on learning in this framework has assumed depth-first search as the default control technique. Consider the means-ends trace in Figure 10-7, which produces the operator sequence from Figure 10-4 when given the same problem. In this case, the problem solver selects the operator (stack B C) for the initial problem (labeled 1), but because the initial state does not satisfy its preconditions, it creates a subproblem (labeled 2) to transform the initial state into one that meets these conditions. For this subproblem the algorithm selects the operator (unstack A C), which also has unmet preconditions and leads to another subproblem (labeled 3). At this level, means-ends analysis selects (unstack B A), and since the initial state meets its preconditions, the problem solver mentally applies the operator, generating the second state in the solution path.

However, this transformation is not enough to let (unstack A C) apply, so the algorithm creates another subproblem (labeled 4) to deal with the remaining differences. Here it selects the operator (putdown B), which it can apply directly and which in turn lets it apply (unstack A C). More work remains before the problem solver can apply the originally selected operator, leading to two additional subproblems (labeled

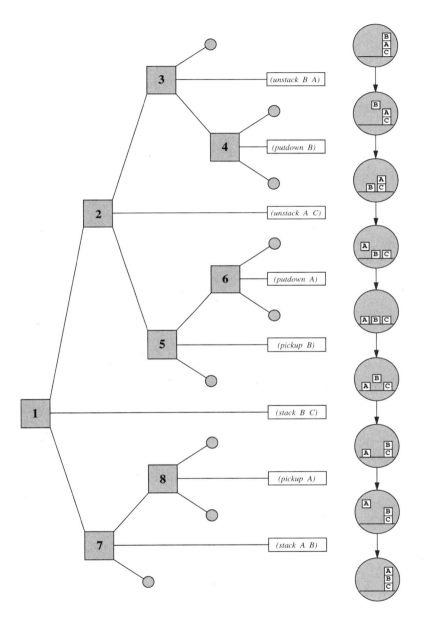

Figure 10-7. A means-ends trace that transforms the upper right problem state into the lower right state. Squares denote problems and subproblems, rectangles contain the operators selected for each problem, and small circles represent degenerate subproblems that involve no differences. Numbers indicate the order in which means-ends analysis generates each subproblem, which differs from the order in which the final solution sequence applies operators and generates states (from top to bottom).

5 and 6). Eventually the algorithm reaches the sixth state in the solution sequence, to which it can apply (stack B C). Unfortunately, some differences remain between the initial and the desired state, causing the creation of two more subproblems (labeled 7 and 8) before the problem solver can achieve the original desired state.

Of course, the trace in Figure 10-7 shows the end result of means-ends analysis, not the process itself, which involves AND/OR search. For each problem, the algorithm can consider selecting every possible operator instantiation, which in principle can lead to a much larger problem space than the state-space approach. However, most means-ends systems use simple heuristics that greatly reduce search, such as considering only those operators that eliminate some difference between the current and the desired state. If domain-specific knowledge is available, the problem solver can also use it to constrain search.

10.5.2 Learning from means-ends traces

Naturally, one can also induce control knowledge for means-ends analysis in much the same manner as with other problem-solving schemes. The basic idea involves adapting the LST algorithm to work with problem descriptions rather than with simple states. After arriving at a successful means-ends trace like that in Figure 10-7, the learner stores each subproblem P in the trace as a positive instance of the operator associated with P, and stores the same subproblem as a negative instance of operators that it considered but that did not lead to a successful trace. As before, the learner then runs some induction algorithm over the resulting training sets, producing intensional descriptions of the conditions under which it should select, reject, or prefer each operator.

Each training instance is a problem description that contains information about the current state, the differences between this state and the goal state, and possibly the stack of operators that have been selected but not yet applied. For example, Table 10-8 shows positive instances for the operator stack, based on problems 1 and 7 in Figure 10-7, and for unstack, based on problems 2 and 3 in the same figure. The table also includes negative instances that might plausibly be generated for each of these problems using an initial strategy that only selects operators that reduce existing differences.

Table 10-8. Positive and negative instances of operator selections for means-ends analysis, with the former taken from Figure 10-7. Nonembedded literals describe the current problem state, literals embedded in **goal** denote differences between the current and desired state, and literals embedded in **apply** indicate selected operators that have not yet applied due to unsatisfied preconditions.

Problem descriptions	Operators	Type
(on b a)(on a c)(on c t)(table t) (clear b)(arm-empty)(goal (on a b)) (goal (on b c))	(stack b c) (stack a b) (putdown b)	+ − −
(on a t)(on b c)(on c t)(table t) (clear a)(clear c)(arm-empty) (goal (on a b))	(stack a b) (putdown a)	+ −
(on b a)(on a c)(on c t) (table t)(clear b)(arm-empty) (goal (holding b))(goal (clear c)) (apply (stack b c))	(unstack a c) (pickup b)	+ −
(on b a)(on a c)(on c t) (table t)(clear b)(arm-empty) (goal (clear a))(apply (stack b c)) (apply (unstack a b))	(unstack b a)	+

Given training cases of this sort, an induction algorithm for finding logical descriptions might generate the rule

```
(goal (on ?x ?y))(<not> (goal (on ?y ?z))) =>
   (select (stack ?x ?y))  ,
```

which covers the first two problem descriptions in the table but not the latter two. Similarly, it might generate the rule

```
(goal (clear ?x))(on ?x ?y) => (select (unstack ?x ?y))  ,
```

which handles the last two subproblems but not the others. Given an appropriate set of such selection rules, a means-ends system can generate a trace like that in Figure 10-7 without search.

As with the other problem-solving frameworks we have seen, one can easily adapt this learning scheme to acquire rejection rules or preference rules. For example, the learner might acquire knowledge that lets it avoid selecting operators that lead to loops which reduce an existing problem to one of equal difficulty. Knowledge about preferences can come into play with versions of means-ends analysis that include an explicit step for selecting the difference to reduce. Such preferences can let the problem solver decide how to order its goals to minimize problem-solving effort.

Means-ends analysis shares with problem reduction the ability to decompose problems into parts, which means that a learner can acquire control knowledge whenever the problem solver decides it has succeeded or failed on one of these parts. The details of the process are somewhat different in the two frameworks, but both support the ability for learning early in problem solving to affect behavior later on the same task.

The analytic methods we have considered in earlier sections apply equally well to learning control knowledge for means-ends analysis. However, in this case the standard formulation of the target concept aims to eliminate differences between the current state and the goal description, as we suggested in the section on state-space search. Thus, the learned rules tend to emphasize such differences and their relation to literals in their condition sides. As in other approaches to problem solving, the control rules generated by analytic methods for means-ends analysis tend to be more specific than those found by other methods, but they are guaranteed to reproduce the solution paths from which they were learned.

10.6 The utility of search-control knowledge

In Section 10.1 we noted the close relationship between efficient problem solving and accurate decisions at choice points in the search process. For this reason, nearly all work on learning search-control knowledge relies on induction methods originally developed for classification domains. However, this treatment omits an important factor. If the aim of learning is to improve the efficiency of problem solving, rather than the quality of the resulting solutions, one must also deal with the *cost* of making the control decisions.

This issue can become a major concern when the conditions on control rules become complex. Given a relational or predicate logic representation of states and conditions, the match cost can grow exponentially with the number of literals involved, primarily because multiple literals in the state can match the same literal in the conditions, forcing the matcher to consider many partial instantiations before finding those with consistent bindings. Moreover, under the right conditions, some learning algorithms can produce search-control rules with many conditions that are very expensive to match.

The total effect is that, even when a control rule makes accurate decisions that actually reduce search, adding it to memory can sometimes *increase* the overall problem-solving time. This *utility problem* occurs whenever the savings $s(r)$ produced by a control rule r, which applies with probability $p(r)$, is offset by the match cost $m(r)$ for the rule. In particular, we can define the *utility* of a search-control rule r to be

$$u(r) = s(r) \times p(r) - m(r) \quad .$$

Given this definition, one should attempt to use a rule to control search only when its utility is greater than 0.

The utility problem is closely related to the problem of overfitting that we examined in Chapter 8, in that the addition of plausible knowledge worsens performance. Despite the emphasis on efficiency rather than accuracy, one can adapt the pruning methods designed for the latter to search-control rules. This analogy suggests three basic techniques: deciding not to add a control rule because it seems likely to hurt efficiency; deciding to remove an existing control rule for the same reason; and retaining a rule in memory but determining whether and how to use it in some dynamic fashion.

One can base such decisions on statistics about each rule's frequency of use, its match cost, and its ability to reduce problem-solving time. The first two factors are simple to update incrementally during problem solving, but to estimate the latter, one must either run the problem solver with and without the control rule or approximate it by other means. This approach to the utility problem treats control rules as being independent, but clearly interactions among rules are possible. For example, two rules may be much more effective together than in isolation, or the presence of one rule may decrease the utility of another. Nevertheless, considering all combinations of rules would be prohibitively expensive, so researchers typically rely on greedy methods that treat each rule separately.

Another response to the utility problem, with no analog to pruning in classification domains, attempts to limit the expressive power of learned control rules, thus ensuring low match cost. An extreme case of this scheme assumes Boolean features, as in much of the work on reinforcement learning. However, one can also incorporate this idea into more expressive languages that support pattern matching. The learner can also simplify the rules themselves to improve match cost, at the expense of accuracy but still improving the overall utility. Alternatively, the problem solver may use a heuristic matcher that examines only enough literals to make a plausible yet inexpensive decision. In general, the utility problem remains an important open issue in the acquisition of search-control knowledge.

10.7 Summary of the chapter

In this chapter, we focused on the acquisition of search-control knowledge for use in problem solving. We examined some typical representations for states, operators, and goals, as well as descriptions for selecting, rejecting, and preferring operators and states. We reviewed some basic approaches to problem solving, emphasizing the distinction between state-space search, problem reduction, and means-ends analysis. We also formulated the task of learning control knowledge for these search frameworks.

We noted that one common response to this task, reinforcement learning, assumes little knowledge about operators' conditions or effects, but requires that some reward be associated with each state. Based on experience with state-space search in an environment, reinforcement methods like Q learning use a table to store the expected reward for each state-operator pair, propagating later rewards back to earlier actions so that the learner eventually becomes able to approximate optimal behavior with only greedy search. We also found that one can increase the learning rate by replacing the table with an intensional description that predicts the expected reward and that one can use a variety of induction methods to generate this description.

Another approach to learning control knowledge for state-space search, the LST algorithm, uses solution paths to generate training instances for induction. States along each path become positive instances of operators that lead toward the goal and negative instances of those that lead away from the goal. We saw that one can use methods like NSC to formulate operator-selection rules from such data, and that one can adapt the scheme to induce rejection and preference rules. We also noted that one can use analytic methods, such as the ICE algorithm, to determine conditions on selection rules by regressing through solution paths.

The LST framework applies equally well to problem reduction and means-ends analysis. Here the decisions involve how to decompose problems and subproblems, but one can still use solution paths to identify positive and negative instances for use in learning. We saw that one can apply both inductive and analytic methods to both types of problem solving, and that again one can learn rules not only for selecting operators and states, but also for rejecting them or preferring one over another. The structure of the resulting control knowledge differs from that formed for state-space search, but the basic result is the same.

Finally, we considered the utility problem, in which the addition of search-control knowledge decreases the problem solver's efficiency rather than improving it. This can occur because the cost of matching learned knowledge can more than offset the savings in search. We noted the similarity between the utility problem and the problem of overfitting in classification learning, and we found that analogous solutions, akin to pruning, can guard against the problem.

Exercises

1. Assume an immediate reward of 1 for the central state in Figure 10-2 and a reward of 0 for all others. Initialize the state-action table to contain expected rewards of 0 for all entries. Given a path from the bottom left state to the center state, and assuming $\beta = 0.2$ and $\gamma = 0.1$, use Q learning to compute new entries for the four state-action pairs along the path. Also determine the revised entries if the path is traversed a second time.

2. Consider the blocks-world problem with a start state having B and C on the table and A on C, and with a goal state having A and B on the table and C on A. Use the LST algorithm (Table 10-3) to label state-operator pairs as positive or negative instances, based on the shortest path between these two states.

3. Construct one or more logical rules for selecting the `pickup` operator that might be formed through induction (as in Section 10.3.1) from the training cases in Exercise 2. Include conditions that refer to the goal state if you find them useful.

4. Based on the solution path from Exercise 2, construct the rule for selecting `pickup` that an analytic method (as in Section 10.3.2) would create. Assume that the target concept is to obtain the literals (`on A C`), (`clear A`), and (`arm-empty`). Show the proof structure used to generate this rule, as in Figure 10-6.

5. Extend Table 10-7 to include positive and negative instances generated from the top node in Figure 10-7. Does the modified rule 3′ make the right decision for these situations?

6. If the rules in Table 10-6 were run on a problem that involved transforming the leftmost state in Figure 10-1 into the top right state, search would eventually produce an AND tree with `maketower` nodes produced by rule 4 at the higher levels. Show a modified version of rule 4, such as might be generated by logical induction, that would select these decompositions when appropriate.

7. Show the modified version of rule 3 (analogous to 3″) from Table 10-6 that analytic learning would produce if given the entire AND tree in Figure 10-7.

8. Construct a control rule for selecting the `stack` operator that might plausibly be generated from instances for the top-level node in the means-ends trace from Figure 10-7. Show some form of justification structure to explain the origin of the rule's conditions.

9. For the `unstack` selection rule in Section 10.3.2, compute the match cost and savings (in terms of literals tested), along with the probability of application, over all problems that involve transforming one tower into another tower. Also, compute the overall utility of the rule for this set of problems and state whether it increases or decreases problem-solving time. Assume a depth-first search scheme that makes random choices in the absence of control knowledge. Reasoning by symmetry should simplify the computations.

Historical and bibliographical remarks

Research on learning search-control knowledge dates back to the earliest days of artificial intelligence, but it became an active research area only in the early 1980s. Minsky (1963) formulated the general issue of credit assignment in sequential behavior. Sleeman, Langley, and Mitchell (1982) proposed learning from solution paths (the LST algorithm from Section 10.3) as a general response to this problem, while Mitchell, Mahadevan, and Steinberg (1985) suggested using learning apprentices, which rely on expert feedback, to sidestep the matter. A collection by Minton (1993) includes a variety of papers on learning in problem solving. Early work in this area aimed at reducing the number of states generated during search. Minton (1990) reformulated the task as improving the speed of problem solving and showed that increased knowledge sometimes introduces a utility problem. His PRODIGY system incorporated techniques for rule pruning to overcome this problem, whereas Tambe, Newell, and Rosenbloom's (1990) SOAR instead limited the expressiveness of learned rules.

Although reinforcement learning is often treated separately from work on search control, it must deal with many of the same issues. Samuel's (1959) checker player constitutes the first work in this area, although Michie and Chambers' (1968) BOXES system, Barto, Sutton, and Anderson's (1983) adaptive heuristic critic, and Holland's (1986) bucket brigade algorithm are other early contributions. However, this topic received widespread attention only after Sutton's (1988) paper on temporal-difference learning and Watkins and Dayan's (1992) work on Q learning, which forms the basis of our treatment in Section 10.3.1. Work on generalization in reinforcement learning has often used neural network methods (e.g., Barto et al., 1983; Williams, 1992), but researchers have also used genetic algorithms (Grefenstette, Ramsey, & Schultz, 1990), nearest neighbor (Moore, 1990), and decision-tree induction (Chapman & Kaelbling, 1991). Recent proceedings of the annual conference on machine learning contain numerous papers on this topic, as does a special 1992 issue of the journal *Machine Learning*.

An early approach to learning state-space search heuristics, aimed at modeling human behavior, is reported by Anzai and Simon (1979). Brazdil (1978), Mitchell, Utgoff, and Banerji (1983), Ohlsson (1983), and Langley (1985) describe similar methods, all relying on versions of the LST algorithm and using subroutines for inducing logical decision lists. Langley (1985) reviews much of the work in this paradigm. Most systems focus on learning operator-selection rules, but some also support the creation of rejection rules, and Utgoff and Saxena (1987) suggest the induction of preference heuristics. Rendell (1986b) explores a quite different approach that induces an evaluation function to select among competing states. By the late 1980s, most work on state-space learning used analytic methods like those described in Section 10.3.2, following the appearance of Mitchell, Keller, and Kedar-Cabelli's (1986) LEX2 and Laird, Rosenbloom, and Newell's (1986) Soar.

Work on learning control knowledge for problem reduction and means-ends analysis developed somewhat later than for state-space schemes. Anderson (1981b) describes an inductive method for the former, while Zelle, Mooney, and Konvisser (1994) report an experimental comparison of inductive and analytic techniques for this task. Minton's (1990) Prodigy uses an analytic approach to learning selection, rejection, and preference rules for means-ends analysis. Jones and VanLehn's (1994) Gips takes a probabilistic approach to the same problem, while Jones and Langley's (1995) Eureka employs a method for structural analogy like that described in Chapter 8; both of these systems explain a variety of phenomena about human problem solving.

CHAPTER 11

The Formation of Macro-operators

In Chapter 10 we examined a variety of approaches to improving problem-solving ability with experience. Despite their differences, all of the methods rely on the idea that lowering the effective branching factor should reduce search and increase efficiency. However, the branching factor is not the only influence on the difficulty of problem-solving tasks. The *depth* of the desired state also plays an important role, and another natural approach to learning involves reducing the effective *length* of problem solutions.

In this chapter we consider this alternative approach to learning in problem solving, in which one stores *macro-operators* that let the problem solver apply many primitive operators at once. The basic assumption is that such knowledge structures can improve problem-solving efficiency by letting the problem solver take larger steps toward the desired state, thus requiring fewer overall decisions and ignoring choices within each sequence that might lead it astray.

In the sections that follow, we explore some variations on this basic approach to the acquisition of problem-solving knowledge. We begin by addressing some generic issues of representation, use, and learning. After this, we consider a straightforward class of methods that acquire simple linear macro-operators, then turn to more sophisticated techniques that provide additional flexibility. Next we consider the closely related methods for problem solving by analogy. We close with some observations about the utility of learned macro-operators that parallel our comments on the utility of search-control knowledge.

11.1 General issues related to macro-operators

Many of the basic issues concerning macro-operators are similar to those for search-control knowledge, and we will not repeat material in detail when we can avoid it. For instance, the standard representations for states, operators, and goals are the same in both frameworks, although work on macro-operators almost invariably assumes transparent operator descriptions. The techniques for using problem-solving knowledge are also similar, varying in the manner in which search is ordered (e.g., depth first vs. breadth first) and organized (e.g., state-space search vs. problem-reduction search). Macro-operator and search-control schemes differ primarily in their representation and organization of knowledge and in their formulation of the learning task. We discuss these issues below, along with the flexibility of macro-operators.

11.1.1 Representation and organization of macro-operators

The purpose of macro-operators is to let the problem solver take larger steps through the search space. Thus, they necessarily refer to a sequence of two or more simpler actions, typically primitive operators. In problem spaces involving operators that take arguments, the macro-operator must also specify the manner in which component operators share variables. In addition, a macro-operator must specify a set of preconditions that a state S must satisfy before the problem solver can apply it to S. Finally, a macro-operator typically includes a set of effects or actions that indicate the changes introduced by its application.

As an example, Table 11-1 presents three plausible macro-operators for the blocks world. The first of these, `moveupto`, consists of the primitive operator `pickup` followed by `stack`, where the block being picked up must be the same as that being stacked. The preconditions specify that the moved object must be on the table and clear, that the block on which it is being stacked is also clear, and that the arm is empty; these must hold for one to apply `pickup` and `stack` in sequence. The effects indicate that, after invoking `moveupto`, the moved block rests on the other, that the former is no longer on the table, and that the latter is no longer clear; these facts will result if one applies the two component operators in order. Similarly, the macro-operator `moveonto` contains the two operators `unstack` and `stack`, whereas `movedownto` includes

Table 11-1. Three two-step macro-operators for the blocks-world domain.

```
(moveupto (?x ?y)
 [(pickup ?x) → (stack ?x ?y)]
((on ?x ?t) (table ?t) (clear ?x) (arm-empty)
 (block ?y) (clear ?y) (≠ ?x ?y) =>
 (<add> (on ?x ?y)) (<delete> (on ?x ?t) (clear ?y)))

(moveonto (?x ?y)
 [(unstack ?x ?z) → (stack ?x ?y)]
((on ?x ?z) (block ?z) (clear ?x) (arm-empty)
 (block ?y) (clear ?y) (≠ ?x ?y) =>
 (<add> (on ?x ?y) (clear ?z))
 (<delete> (on ?x ?z) (clear ?y)))

(movedownto (?x ?t)
 [(unstack ?x ?y) → (putdown ?x)]
((on ?x ?y) (block ?y) (clear ?x) (arm-empty) (table ?t) =>
 (<add> (on ?x ?t) (clear ?y)) (<delete> (on ?x ?y)))
```

---

the primitives **unstack** and **putdown**. Again, their preconditions and effects are combinations of those for their component operators.

The careful reader will have noted the absence of certain preconditions that are required by a component operator but that are satisfied by the effects of an earlier component. There is a similar absence of certain effects that are introduced by an early component but removed by a later one. The literal (**holding ?x**) provides an example of both points in all three of the table's macro-operators. In each case, the first operator generates a state that includes an instantiated form of this literal, after which the second operator matches it against one of its preconditions and creates another state that lacks it. As a result, the literal (**holding ?x**) appears in neither the preconditions nor the effects of the various macro-operators.

The introduction of macro-operators introduces additional links into the state space. In particular, **moveupto** adds one link out of every node from which the sequence **<pickup, stack>** can start, and the other macro-operators have the same effect on states in which their sequences begin. Clearly, this increases the branching factor of the state space.

The process of creating macro-operators also causes redundancy, since it lets one move between certain pairs of states by at least two paths, one involving the macro-operator and the other using primitive steps. This means that there is the potential for increased search, but this can be offset if the learner stores useful macro-operators and if the problem solver considers them in the right order (which in itself is a difficult problem). We will return to these issues in Section 11.5.

We have been assuming that primitive operators constitute the components of a macro-operator, but there is no reason that other macro-operators cannot serve this function as well, provided that they ultimately ground out in primitives. For example, imagine that we have a macro-operator **unbuildtower** that takes a tower composed of three blocks and places all of them on the table. We can define this macro-operator using two calls to **movedownto** with different arguments, which we saw earlier is defined using the primitive operators **unstack** and **putdown**. Similarly, we could define the macro-operator **buildtower** in terms of two calls to **moveonto**; given the appropriate variables, this would create a tower from three blocks that are resting on the table. We will return to this example later in the chapter.

In this extended framework, the definitions of macro-operators place an organization on problem-solving knowledge. This form of organization is most similar to the inference networks we encountered in Chapter 6, in particular to Horn clauses. This organization provides an important source of constraints on the problem-solving process, specifying the order in which to apply operators. Typically, no search arises within the mental application of a defined macro-operator, but we will see some exceptions to this rule in Section 11.4.

11.1.2 The flexible use of macro-operators

Perhaps the most important dimension of variation among approaches to macro-operators lies in their flexibility. Much of the work on this topic assumes that the problem solver will treat them as monolithic structures that can be used in their entirety or not at all. This has the advantage of simplicity, but it restricts the usefulness of each macro-operator in terms of its transfer to new problems. Even when a macro-operator plays a role in solving novel tasks, its use can lead to a long solution path that, besides having high execution costs, can offset the reduction in problem-solving costs that results from taking larger steps. For instance, if the average macro-operator involves three primitive operators and the final solution contains three times as many steps as necessary, the problem solver must make just as many decisions as in the original space.

One response to these problems involves storing macro-operators in ways that provide greater flexibility. The basic idea is to maximize the use of macro-operator components on problems that differ but that have some aspects in common. As we discuss in Section 11.3, one scheme involves indexing macro-operators so that the problem solver can enter and exit them anywhere along their operator sequences. Another approach allows specification of disjunctive components in the operator sequence that apply in different situations. Yet another response introduces the notion of iterative or recursive macro-operators, which repeatedly apply a sequence of component operators until meeting some termination condition.

The extension of macro-operators to include disjuncts, conditional statements, and recursion is closely related to the problem-reduction approach to problem solving discussed in Chapter 10. In fact, the Horn clauses in Table 10-6 of that chapter can be reformulated as a set of flexible macro-operators that would have the same advantages in constraining search as the other notation. Of course, we assumed there that the reductions were given, whereas here the goal is to acquire useful macro-operators or problem-reduction rules from experience.

However, the dimension of flexibility does not stop at this point. An even more extreme approach lets the problem solver dynamically adapt the structure of a macro-operator as needed for the problem at hand. In some cases, this adaptation process requires the use of search. The literature refers to such methods as *analogical problem solving* or *case-based reasoning*, and usually treats them as unrelated to those methods that incorporate macro-operators. However, they share many features with the latter, and we discuss this variation on the macro-operator scheme in Section 11.4.

Of course, flexibility often comes at a price. As we saw above, the introduction of macro-operators increases the branching factor of the problem space, and more general macro-operators that support disjunction and recursion can exacerbate this effect. In principle, adaptation could require more search than would occur in the original space. Thus, in Section 11.5 we deal with the potential costs of flexibility, relating this issue to the notion of utility introduced in the previous chapter.

11.1.3 The task of creating macro-operators

With the above comments on representation and use as background, let us consider the task of learning macro-operators. We can formulate the problem as:

- *Given:* Knowledge of operators for a problem-solving domain;

- *Given:* Experience with solutions to problems in the domain;

- *Acquire:* Summaries of operator sequences that reduce the cost of finding solutions for novel problems.

As with search-control knowledge, we have been intentionally vague, although we will see many instantiations of the formulation in the following pages. As in Chapter 10, we will not concern ourselves with the source of experience, which may result from the problem solver's own search or from traces of an expert's decisions in the domain, or with the source of the training and test problems themselves. Again, the typical performance measure is the efficiency of finding solutions, but the quality of solutions can also be important. One difference from the search-control framework is that macro-operators typically result from successful paths rather than from failures. Another difference is that the issue of credit assignment plays a less central role in the macro-operator framework.

The process of creating macro-operators involves three basic steps. First, the learner must identify the operators or macro-operators in the problem-solving sequence that will serve as components of the new structure. Next, it must determine the internal structure of the macro-operator, including shared variables and conditional statements. Finally, the learner must generate the preconditions and effects associated with the new problem-solving entity. We consider examples of these three steps in the section that follows.

Typically, each step in the resulting macro-operator is based on experience gleaned from the solution to a single problem or subproblem, but we will also see some examples that rely on multiple training problems. Most work also depends on variants of the analytic methods we described in Section 10.3.2, but again we will refer to some examples of other approaches as well.

11.2 The creation of simple macro-operators

We are now ready to consider methods for the construction of simple 'fixed-sequence' macro-operators. In this section we examine the formation and use of such knowledge structures in three contexts that parallel those we considered in the previous chapter – state-space search, means-ends analysis, and problem-reduction search. There are many common features that hold across these frameworks, but there are also some important differences.

11.2.1 Macro-learning for state-space search

As we described in Chapter 10, a state-space problem solver can either select an operator to apply from among those that match the current state or, alternatively, it can select a state to expand, to which it applies all matching operators to generate successor states. In either case, it combines this process with some control scheme to generate a search tree in a forward-chaining manner. Let us consider how one might acquire macro-operators in the state-space framework. In particular, we will assume that the problem solver has found the solution path to the blocks-world problem shown in Figure 11-1, and that it uses the resulting trace in the learning process.[1]

IDENTIFYING COMPONENT OPERATORS

The first step involves determining the sequences of operators in the solution path to serve as components of the macro-operator. Clearly, one alternative is simply to construct a macro-operator based on the entire solution sequence. This would solve the training problem in a single step, but it would have minimal transfer to other problems that could arise in the space. Instead, one might prefer to identify operator sequences that solve useful subproblems.

Another approach bases a macro-operator on the last two operators in a solution path, replaces these operators with a call to the macro-operator, and repeats the process until it reaches the initial operator in the path. For the problem in Figure 11-1, it would define seven new

---

1. We will also assume that this process occurs only after one has found a solution to a given problem, although one can adapt some techniques to operate during problem solving, thus supporting within-problem transfer.

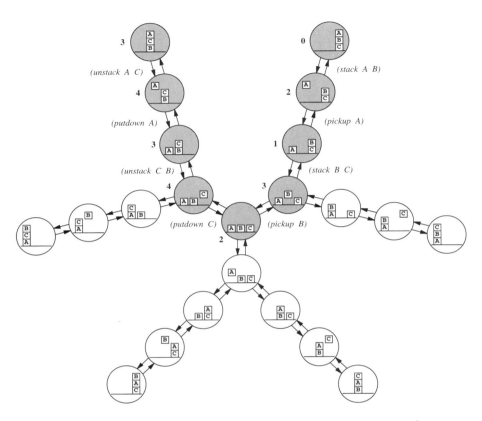

Figure 11-1. Experiences used in the formation of macro-operators for state-space search in the three blocks world. Shaded circles indicate states that fall along a solution path for the problem whose initial state lies at the upper left and whose goal state lies at the upper right. The numbers next to each state represent scores for an evaluation function (described in the text).

structures, each having two components. When expanded down to the level of primitive operators, the first refers to the last two steps in the solution path, the next to the last three steps, and so forth, with the final macro-operator expanding to the entire solution sequence.

This approach produces "tail transfer", giving macro-operators that are useful for domains in which problems have similar goal states. For example, this technique for selecting components would be appropriate for a blocks-world domain in which most problems aim at the construction of a three-block tower. In contrast, an alternative approach that forms pairwise macro-operators from the beginning of the solution path

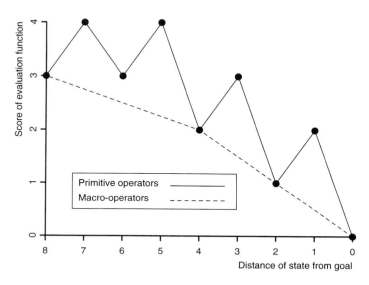

Figure 11-2. The scores of an evaluation function for states along the solution path in Figure 11-1 when only primitive operators are available (giving non-monotonic behavior) and when macro-operators are present (giving monotonic decrease with distance from the goal).

produces "head transfer". Such structures would be useful if most problems involve analogous initial states.

A more sophisticated approach uses the scores of an evaluation function to suggest useful sequences of operators. Note that the values of an ideal evaluation function increase or decrease monotonically with distance from the goal state. Unfortunately, most evaluation metrics are imperfectly correlated with distance, producing hills or valleys on the way to the goal and thus requiring search. However, carefully defined macro-operators can leap over these hills and valleys to states with higher values, giving the monotonicity needed to avoid search.

Given this insight, one can use the occurrence of valleys and hills in scores along a solution path to identify boundaries on useful macro-operators. For instance, suppose that the goal description for the problem in Figure 11-1 is {(on A B) (on B C) (on C T) (arm-empty)}, and that the evaluation function measures the number of these literals absent in a given state. The numbers shown next to states along the solution path indicate the scores generated by this function. Figure 11-2 graphs these scores as a function of distance from the goal state, showing the nonmonotonic nature of the metric with respect to this goal.

However, the figure also shows the functional behavior that results if one constructs macro-operators that leap over the hills and plateaus. In particular, this leads to macro-operators based on the first four operators in the solution path, the next two in the path, and the final two in the path. For the modified path produced by these macro-operators, which bypasses five of the states in the original path, the evaluation function decreases monotonically with distance from the goal. Naturally, different evaluation functions might identify different sequences, thus producing macro-operators with different transfer characteristics, but the basic idea holds considerable intuitive appeal.

Other parsing schemes are certainly possible, and later we will consider some of them in the context of other search organizations. Methods for identifying useful operator sequences remain one of the most significant open research problems in the acquisition of problem-solving knowledge.

Specifying internal structure

After the learner has parsed the solution sequence into a set of subsequences, it uses each subsequence as the basis for a new macro-operator. In the simplest case, the internal structure of this macro-operator is an ordered list of the component operators, along with shared arguments that reflect relationships among arguments of the operators used in the solution. For instance, consider the final subsequence in Figure 11-1, which is `<(pickup A), (stack A B)>`. Replacing A with `?x` and B with `?y`, we obtain the abstract sequence `<(pickup ?x), (stack ?x ?y)>`.

As we mentioned above, methods for parsing operator sequences lead to hierarchical structures. In this case, the component list of a macro-operator can refer not only to primitive operators but to other macro-operators, with the higher-level one passing arguments to its lower-level component. This can occur if macro-operators defined on one problem take part in the solution to a later problem. In Section 11.3, we will encounter more complex internal structures, but for now we assume they consist of a simple list of operators or macro-operators. Some work has extended this idea to identify partially ordered sets of components, but we will not use such structures in our examples.

Now let us turn to the final step in constructing a macro-operator. Consider the last subsequence in the solution from Figure 11-1, which includes the instantiated operators (pickup A) and (stack A B). These steps are the same as the example in Figure 10-6, which we discussed in the context of learning search-control knowledge.

The preconditions are straightforward to compute. One gathers all literals needed for the initial operator in the sequence, in this case (on A T), (table T), (clear A), and (arm-empty). Then one adds the literals needed by the second operator that are not generated during application of the first operator. Thus, (block B) and (clear B) are added to the set but not (holding A), since this was added by (pickup A) and thus is guaranteed to be present. If the macro-operator includes more components, this process continues until all are handled.

Having collected the literals that make the operator sequence possible, one next replaces the arguments with variables in a consistent manner.[2] As with search-control knowledge, one must also include tests to ensure that certain variables take on distinct bindings. However, the issues we raised about target concepts in the context of search control do not arise here, since the aim is to find conditions under which the problem solver *can* apply operators in the given sequence, not the conditions under which it *should* carry them out.

One can compute the macro-operator's actions using a very similar process. First one collects all actions carried out by the initial operator. In this case, (pickup A) adds the literal (holding A) and deletes (on A T) and (arm-empty), although Figure 10-6 does not show the deletions. Next one combines these with the actions carried out by the second operator, in this case (stack A B), but removing all actions of the first that are canceled by the second.

Here the additions (clear A) and (arm-empty) cancel the deletions of these literals by the first operator; thus, they are neither added nor deleted in the actions of the macro-operator. Similarly, the first operator's addition of (holding A) is countered through its deletion by the second, so this literal is also omitted from the overall effects. As with

---

2. This step is not strictly necessary. Some techniques place the specific literals in memory and generalize at retrieval time rather than at storage time. However, this scheme is usually associated with the methods described in Section 11.4 rather than with those under current discussion.

the preconditions, one iterates through all component operators, then replaces constant terms with variables in a consistent manner. In this example, the macro-operator retains only three effects: adding (on A B), deleting (on A T), and deleting (clear B).

Taken together, these steps produce a macro-operator that we introduced earlier in Table 11-1:

```
(moveupto (?x ?y)
  [(pickup ?x) → (stack ?x ?y)]
 ((on ?x ?t) (table ?t) (clear ?x) (arm-empty)
  (block ?y) (clear ?y) (≠ ?x ?y) =>
  (<add> (on ?x ?y)) (<delete> (on ?x ?t) (clear ?y)))
```

Briefly stated, this description specifies the conditions under which the problem solver can apply the operators pickup and stack in sequence (given the specified variable bindings) and the effects that result when they are applied.

In some cases, the abstraction process produces isomorphic macro-operators from different subsequences. In this example, the macro-operator resulting from the fifth and sixth operators is equivalent to the one above. In contrast, the structure based on the first four steps in the solution sequence is considerably more complex:

```
(unbuildtower (?x ?y ?z)
  [(unstack ?x ?y) → (putdown ?x) →
     (unstack ?y ?z) → (putdown ?y)]
 ((on ?x ?y) (block ?y) (clear ?x) (arm-empty) (table ?t)
  (on ?y ?z) (block ?z) (≠ ?x ?y) (≠ ?x ?z) (≠ ?y ?z) =>
  (<add> (on ?x ?t) (clear ?y) (on ?y ?t) (clear ?z))
  (<delete> (on ?x ?y) (on ?y ?z)))
```

This macro-operator matches against any state in which three blocks are stacked in a tower, and it produces a state in which these blocks are clear and in which the top two rest on the table. Taken together, the two macro-operators moveupto and unbuildtower let the problem solver complete the problem in Figure 11-1 (and its isomorphs) in three steps rather than eight. They should provide useful transfer on some other problems as well.

11.2.2 Macro-learning for means-ends analysis

Another problem-solving organization we encountered in Chapter 10 was means-ends analysis. In this framework, the problem solver selects an operator that reduces differences between the current and the desired state, then creates two subproblems – the first to transform the current state into one that matches the operator's preconditions, and the second to transform the resulting state into the originally desired one.

Macro-operators play the same role in means-ends analysis as they do in other search schemes, letting the problem solver take larger steps through the space and thus reducing effective solution length. Their form for this framework is the same as that for state-space search. Potentially, a means-ends problem solver can treat macro-operators in the same manner as any other operator, selecting them based on their ability to reduce differences between the current and the desired state. Thus, it can create subproblems based on macro-operator preconditions that have not been satisfied, as well as subproblems for macro-generated states that have not finished off the current problem.

However, this approach to problem solving has some interesting implications for the acquisition of macro-operators. Consider the means-ends trace in Figure 11-3, which depicts the result of search on a four-step blocks-world problem that involves building a tower. In addition to the top-level problem, this trace contains three subproblems, but only one of these (subproblem 3) involves two or more operators in the solution path. Note that the structure of a means-ends trace suggests another way to parse the solution sequence into macro-operators. In particular, each sequence of operators used in the solution of a problem or subproblem constitutes a potential macro-operator.

In this example, problem 1 in Figure 11-3 specifies the sequence of primitive operators `<(pickup B), (stack B C), (pickup A), (stack A B)>`, which one could use to generate the four-operator structure `buildtower` we mentioned earlier. Similarly, subproblem 3 indicates the operator sequence `<(pickup A), (stack A B)>`, which one could use to produce the `moveupto` macro-operator we encountered in Table 11-1. The structure of the means-ends trace for a given solution sequence determines the space of possible macro-operators, and means-ends analysis can produce different decompositions even for the same solution path, leading to macro-operators with different transfer characteristics.

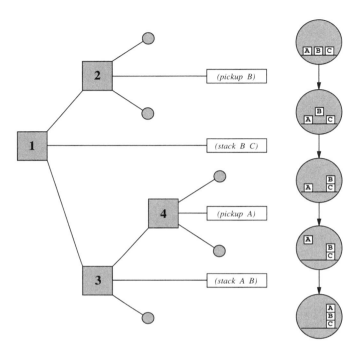

Figure 11-3. A means-ends trace that transforms the upper right problem state into the lower right state. Large squares denote problems and subproblems, rectangles contain the operators selected for each problem, and small circles represent degenerate subproblems that involve no differences. One can use the structure of this trace to parse the solution during the construction of macro-operators.

The hierarchical structure of means-ends traces means that some problems subsume others, so that there remains considerable choice about which macro-operators to define. For instance, the learner might construct a single macro-operator for the top-level problem (in this case problem 1), or one macro-operator for each of its nontrivial subproblems (in this case subproblem 3), and so forth. Another approach defines one macro-operator for each nontrivial problem and subproblem (here 1 and 3) in the means-ends trace, either in terms of primitive operators or in terms of lower-level macro-operators. This decision has clear implications for the resulting macro-operator's internal structure, and one can make intuitively plausible arguments in favor of either approach. For instance, defining macro-operators entirely in terms of primitive operators should cause less increase in the branching factor, whereas defining

Table 11-2. Two macro-operators generated from the means-ends trace in Figure 11-3. These have three components that reflect the structure of the problem-solving trace, with one based on the first subproblem, one based on the top-level operator, and one based on the last subproblem. Either the first or the last component are empty (`nil`) if degenerate subproblems occur, as in the last component of `moveupto`. Note that the presence of `moveupto` in the component list of `buildtower` reflects the relationship between problem 1 and subproblem 3 in the trace.

```
(buildtower (?x ?y ?z)
 [(pickup ?y) → (stack ?y ?z) → (moveupto ?x ?y)]
 ((on ?x ?t) (table ?t) (block ?y) (clear ?x) (clear ?y)
  (arm-empty) (on ?y ?t) (block ?z) (clear ?z) =>
  (<add> (on ?x ?y) (on ?y ?z))
  (<delete> (on ?x ?t) (clear ?x)
            (on ?y ?t) (clear ?z)))

(moveupto (?x ?y)
 [(pickup ?x) → (stack ?x ?y) → nil]
 ((on ?x ?t) (table ?t) (clear ?x) (arm-empty)
  (block ?y) (clear ?y) (≠ ?x ?y) =>
  (<add> (on ?x ?y)) (<delete> (on ?x ?t) (clear ?y)))
```

them in terms of other macro-operators seems more likely to produce at least some that will lead to useful transfer. The behavior of each approach in practice remains an open issue.

Table 11-2 shows the structures that result from a strategy that specifies macro-operators in terms of other macro-operators, given the means-ends trace in Figure 11-3. Here problem 1 has led to the top-level macro-operator **buildtower**, which is defined as the sequence **pickup**, **stack**, and **moveupto**. The final component, based on subproblem 3, has in turn been defined as the sequence **pickup** and **stack**. This scheme defines all macro-operators implicit in the structure of the means-ends trace, which lets the problem solver decompose similar problems in the same manner through macro-expansion.

The determination of preconditions and effects for a macro-operator is the same for means-ends analysis as for state-space search, which we described in Section 11.2.1. This process is unaffected by the parsing scheme used to determine the components, since it relies only on the sequence of operators, their preconditions, and their effects. Thus, the two frameworks generate macro-operators with similar forms, but they may construct them from different components.

11.2.3 Macro-learning for problem-reduction search

In Chapter 10 we also examined the acquisition of search-control knowledge in a problem-reduction framework. Here the problem solver carries out search through an AND/OR space, using domain knowledge stated as rewrite rules to decompose the top-level problem into subproblems, then to decompose these in turn, until it finds a solution connected to ground literals or primitive operators.

There is a strong sense in which the decomposition rules used during AND/OR search constitute macro-operators, in particular the type of disjunctive and recursive ones we will discuss in Section 11.3. Some of these rules are defined in terms of primitive operators, but we saw in the previous section that one can readily define macro-operators in terms of other macro-operators. Nevertheless, there are situations in which adding new macro-operators to an existing set of problem-reduction rules can improve their problem-solving performance. Let us examine how the process differs in this framework.

Table 11-3 replicates the decomposition rules from Table 10-6 for building towers in the blocks world, but with one additional clause. The new rewrite rule 3^a is a variant of rule 3 that succeeds precisely whenever the sequence <pickup(X), stack(X, Y)> will satisfy the maketower goal. Moreover, it achieves the goal in one step, without creating any new subproblems that might introduce search. In fact, this macro-operator would prove very useful in solving subproblem 3 in Figure 11-3, which requires exactly this operator sequence. Of course, it is essential that the problem solver consider this specialization before the more general rule, since the latter will eventually solve any problem that the former can, but at potentially greater cost.

One can generate a macro-operator like 3^a using analytic techniques[3] nearly identical to those we used to find search-control rules in Section 10.3.2. Briefly, the learner collects all literals in the initial state

---

3. Naturally, one could also invoke nonanalytic methods for this purpose, but such approaches are seldom used for work on macro-operators.

Table 11-3. Problem-reduction rules for the blocks world stated in a 'logic programming' syntax, repeated from Table 10-6, with an additional rule 3^a that constitutes a specialization of the original rule 3. Note that the original rules organize memory in much the same way as the defining of macro-operators in terms of other macro-operators.

```
1. maketower([X]) :- table(X).
2. maketower([X]) :- makeclear(X).
3ª maketower([X,Y]) :- clear(X),clear(Y),on(X,T),table(T),
               arm-empty,block(Y),X≠Y,pickup(X),stack(X,Y).
3. maketower([X,Y|Z]) :- maketower([Y|Z]),grasp(X),stack(X,Y).
4. maketower([X,Y|Z]) :- grasp(W),putdown(W),maketower([X,Y|Z]).

5. grasp(X) :- holding(X).
6. grasp(X) :- makeclear(X),pickup(X).
7. grasp(X) :- makeclear(X),unstack(X,Y).

8. makeclear(X) :- clear(X).
9. makeclear(X) :- on(Y,X),grasp(Y),putdown(Y).
```

that occur as terminal nodes in the solution, along with those needed to apply the primitive operators; it then replaces constant arguments with variables and adds the necessary inequality tests. This method is also nearly the same as the one we described in Section 11.2.1, which produces the rule **moveupto** from the same operator sequence. The only difference is that **moveupto** is expressed in terms of preconditions and effects, whereas the current scheme produces a problem-reduction rule that retains the head of the original clause to indicate the goal it achieves.

We should also consider the relationship between the macro-operator 3^a in Table 11-3 and the search-control rule that we introduced in Chapter 10. The two knowledge structures were generated from the same training experience using the same basic method, yet the macro-operator contains only ground literals and primitive operators, whereas the control rule refers to nonterminal symbols, including a recursive call. The macro-operator tells the problem solver how to handle a specific class of problems in one level; in contrast, the search-control rule covers a broader class but forces the problem solver to take multiple steps in generating a solution. In the following section we will examine a compromise that has some features of each approach.

11.3 The formation of flexible macro-operators

Although simple linear macro-operators let the problem solver handle complex problems in fewer steps, and thus potentially reduce search, they tend to be very specific. As a result, they typically apply only to a narrow range of problems that are nearly identical to the one that produced the macro-operator. This may be sufficient for highly regular domains in which only a few of the possible problems actually occur, but it means that they give little transfer to novel problems. Thus, in less regular domains where many of the possible problems do appear, the creation of linear macro-operators can lead to relatively slow learning. In this section we examine some approaches to representing, using, and acquiring more flexible macro-operators.

11.3.1 Triangle tables

Perhaps the simplest means to increase transfer to new problems is to store linear macro-operators in a flexible manner. One well-known knowledge structure of this sort, the *triangle table*, partitions the conditions and effects for each component operator so that the problem solver can easily access arbitrary subsequences of the macro-operator.

Table 11-4 shows the triangle table for a macro-operator based on the last four solution steps in Figure 11-1, a state-space operator sequence for building a tower analogous to the `unbuildtower` we saw in Section 11.2.1. For a macro-operator involving n component operators, the triangle table contains $n+1$ columns and $n+1$ rows, in this case giving five of each. Just above the last n columns, the table specifies the component operators in the order that they occur.

The leftmost column (labeled 0) differs slightly from the others, so we will consider it first. The initial row (labeled a) in this column specifies the initial state, with arguments replaced by variables. The second row (labeled b) indicates the literals from the initial state that remain after the problem solver has applied the first operator; thus, it shows the initial state minus any deletions by the first component. The third row

Table 11-4. A triangle table for the `buildtower` macro-operator based on the last four steps of the solution in Figure 11-1. Such knowledge structures provide flexibility by letting the problem solver enter and leave the macro-operator at any point. The union of literals marked "▷" specifies the preconditions for the operator in the following row.

	0	1	2	3	4
a	(block ?x) (block ?y) (block ?z) (table ?t)▷ (on ?x ?t)▷ (on ?y ?t) (on ?z ?t) (clear ?x)▷ (clear ?y) (clear ?z) (arm-empty)▷	(pickup ?x)			
b	(block ?x) (block ?y)▷ (block ?z) (table ?t) (on ?y ?t) (on ?z ?t) (clear ?x) (clear ?y)▷ (clear ?z)	(holding ?x)▷	(stack ?x ?y)		
c	(block ?x) (block ?y) (block ?z) (table ?t)▷ (on ?y ?t) (on ?z ?t)▷ (clear ?x) (clear ?z)▷		(arm-empty)▷ (on ?x ?y)	(pickup ?z)	
d	(block ?x)▷ (block ?y) (block ?z) (table ?t) (on ?y ?t) (clear ?x)▷ (clear ?z)		(on ?x ?y)	(holding ?z)▷	(stack ?z ?x)
e	(block ?x) (block ?y) (block ?z) (table ?t) (on ?y ?t) (clear ?z)		(on ?x ?y)		(arm-empty) (on ?z ?x)

of column 0 contains the literals in the initial state, less any removed by the first and second operators, and so forth. In this example, only six of the original eleven literals remain by the final step in the macro-operator.

The other columns contain similar material, but their entries are associated with the operator given above them. For instance, column 1 gives information about the first operator in the sequence and its generalized arguments, (pickup ?x). In particular, row b gives the literals added by this operator. The next cell down, in row c, repeats these added literals but removes any that are deleted by the second component operator (in this case all of them, leaving the cell empty). Similarly, the cell in row d specifies the literals added by the first operator, less any deleted by either the second or third operator. The pattern repeats in column 2, which provides information about the second operator, (stack ?x ?y). For instance, the cell in row c of column 2 specifies the literals added by this operator. Row d repeats these literals after subtracting any deleted by the third component, and row e does the same but removes literals deleted by either the third or fourth operator.

Thus, each column in the table contains explicit information about the literals that each operator adds (with the initial state generated by a condition-free operator), and implicit information about later operators' deletions. In contrast, each row contains information about the literals present after each step in the macro-operator. The union of literals in row b constitutes those present after the first action, the union for row c gives those present after the second, and so forth. Also, note that some literals are marked with "▷". The union of marked literals in a given row correspond to the preconditions for the operator next to that row.

Now we can consider how a state-space problem solver could use this memory structure to access the original macro-operator. Note that the preconditions for the macro-operator are simply the union of the marked literals in column 0. Thus, the problem solver need only collect these and match them against the current state to determine whether the macro-operator is applicable. Moreover, the literals added by the macro-operator are simply the union of those appearing in row e, less those present in the initial state. Similarly, its deletions are those literals of row a that do not appear in any column of row e.

However, the triangle table also lets the problem solver use portions of the original macro-operator, by exiting or leaving the structure at any point. For instance, suppose it encounters a state that matches the union of marked conditions in rows a and b of column 0, but not those in rows c and d. To determine the add list of this implicit macro-operator, which involves applying only the first two components, one simply takes the union of literals that appear in row c, columns 1 and 2 (i.e., beneath the two operators), less any present in the initial state. In this case, we get the single addition (on ?x ?y), which agrees with that for the equivalent two-step macro-operator moveupto from Table 11-1. Similarly, the delete list consists of those literals present in column 0 of row c that are not present in row a, less those occurring in the other columns of row c. Here we obtain two deletions, (on ?x ?t) and (clear ?y), which also agree with those for moveupto. This example shows how the table lets one exit the macro-operator at any point, giving the greatest possible head transfer.

Organizing knowledge in a triangle table also lets the problem solver *enter* the macro-operator at any step. For example, suppose it encounters a state in which the last three steps can apply in sequence.[4] It can test for the relevance of this subsequence by taking the union of marked literals in columns 0 and 1 within rows b, c, and d. If this set matches the current state, the problem solver can apply the final three operators in the table. In this case, it determines the add list of this implicit macro-operator by collecting the literals in columns 2, 3, and 4 of row e, except for those appearing in the initial state, giving both (arm-empty) and (on ?z ?x). Here the delete list includes those literals in columns 0 and 1 of rows b, c, and d that do not appear anywhere in row e; this time the result is the set {(holding ?x), (on ?z ?t), (clear ?x), (clear ?y)}. In this situation, we have a clear example of tail transfer.

Naturally, these two possibilities can occur in combination, which would lead the problem solver to use an implicit macro-operator that both begins and ends inside the original sequence. Although our examples have assumed state-space search, one can also use a triangle table in conjunction with a means-ends scheme. In this case, the problem solver examines the contents of each row to determine implicit macro-operators to select for application. The application of this approach to problem-reduction methods is less clear. The original formulation

---

4. We will not concern ourselves here with how the problem solver reached the initial state without using the pickup operator.

of triangle tables focused on their use in plan execution, in which the problem solver does not need add and delete lists. For this reason, some treatments of triangle tables show only the marked literals in column 0, which are sufficient for the match process.

In the previous section, we treated the decision about how to partition the solution sequence as central to the construction of useful macro-operators, but triangle tables make this decision moot. The learner can simply create a single macro-operator based on the entire sequence, then access any subsequence that seems relevant to a new problem. Effectively, the creation of a triangle table is equivalent to creating all possible linear macro-operators and considering them on each problem-solving step, but with a greatly reduced match cost. However, as we discuss in Section 11.5, even linear macro-operators increase the branching factor of the search process, and the ability to enter and exit macro-operators at any point can exacerbate this problem.

11.3.2 Disjunctive macro-operators

Although triangle tables let one enter and leave a macro-operator anywhere within the sequence, they remain limited in the flexibility they provide. In some cases, two solution subsequences may be nearly identical yet differ in a few of their components. One can construct separate macro-operators for each subsequence, but this leads to redundancy in terms of duplicated conditions; in turn, this can complicate the match process and increase the overall effort of problem solving. In such cases, it makes sense to merge the similar macro-operators into a knowledge structure that incorporates disjunctions.

A disjunctive macro-operator contains two types of information. *External* conditions and effects are associated with the entire knowledge structure, whereas *internal* conditions and effects are associated with each disjunction. Internal conditions specify when one should apply particular components that differ across the specific macro-operators, and internal effects indicate conditional actions. The problem solver matches external conditions only once on a given cycle, reducing computational costs, and always applies the external operators.

Table 11-5 shows a simple disjunctive macro-operator for the blocks world that combines the linear structures `moveupto` and `moveonto` from Table 11-1. As usual, the macro-operator includes a name (`moveto`) and arguments, along with a set of external preconditions and effects

Table 11-5. Two disjunctive macro-operators for the blocks world. Internal conditions and effects are enclosed in braces, whereas external conditions and effects occur at the end of each macro-operator.

```
(moveto (?x ?z)
  [{[(pickup ?x) ((table ?y) => nil)] ∨
    [(unstack ?x ?y) ((block ?y) => (<add> (clear ?y)))]}
      → (stack ?x ?z)]
 ((on ?x ?y) (clear ?x) (arm-empty)
  (block ?z) (clear ?z) (≠ ?x ?z) =>
  (<add> (on ?x ?z)) (<delete> (on ?x ?y) (clear ?z)))

(moveto' (?x ?z)
  [{[(pickup ?x) ((table ?y) => nil)] ∨
    [(unstack ?x ?y) ((block ?y) => (<add> (clear ?y)))]} →
   {[(putdown ?x) ((table ?z) => nil)] ∨
    [(stack ?x ?z) ((block ?z) => (<delete> (clear ?z)))]}]
 ((on ?x ?y) (clear ?x) (arm-empty)
  (clear ?z) (≠ ?x ?z) =>
  (<add> (on ?x ?z)) (<delete> (on ?x ?y)))
```

(at the end of the structure). Note that these preconditions and effects are precisely the ones that `moveupto` and `moveonto` hold in common.

Moreover, the internal conditions and effects, on which `moveupto` and `moveonto` differ, are embedded in the list of components. The second action in the component list is (stack ?x ?z), as in each of the linear macro-operators. However, the first component consists of a disjunction (enclosed in braces) specifying that one should apply (pickup ?x) if (table ?y) matches and instead apply (unstack ?x ?y) if (block ?y) matches. In the first case, no special effects result, but in the second, the literal (clear ?y) is added. The overall result is that the macro-operator `moveto` behaves like `moveupto` in the former situation and like `moveonto` in the latter.

The table also shows a more complex macro-operator, `moveto'`, that contains a disjunct for the second component as well as the first. This states that if ?x is being placed on the table, one should use the operator `putdown`, whereas `stack` is needed if ?x is being placed on another block. Conditional effects also occur in each of the components. Taken together, the two disjunctions cover four distinct configurations that produce similar but somewhat different effects.

The natural approach to using such disjunctive macro-operators, at least in a state-space framework, would be to test the external conditions and, if they match, to carry out the operator list, determining which member of each disjunct to apply as one proceeds. However, the external conditions are not sufficient to guarantee that the macro-operator will successfully apply all of its components. A more conservative scheme tests both external and internal conditions before invoking the macro-operator, setting flags to avoid the need for rematching to determine which member of each disjunct to use during the application process. A means-ends problem solver could use both external and internal effects to select macro-operators that will reduce existing differences.

Now we can consider how one might acquire macro-operators of the above sort. First the learner must decide that two or more existing macro-operators are worth merging.[5] This is an unsupervised task similar to those we discussed in Chapter 7 in the context of clustering. Most approaches involve detecting that two sequences involve many of the same operators, or that two macro-operators have similar conditions and effects.

Let us examine the behavior of FDM, a specific algorithm for the formation of disjunctive macro-operators. After selecting two or more macro-operators to merge, FDM matches the descriptions of the rules to find the conditions and effects that are common and those that differ. The former become external preconditions and effects for the disjunctive macro-operator; the latter become internal conditions, which are associated with the specific disjunctions in the component list for which they hold. Naturally, the algorithm must also formulate the component list, which involves simple string-matching operations if the original macro-operators have the same length.

As an example, suppose FDM has focused its attention on the two macro-operators moveupto and moveonto in Table 11-1. In this case, there are six shared conditions, with the only difference being that

---

5. In fact, this process may operate on similar subsequences rather than on linear macro-operators, but for the sake of simplicity we will assume that the learner first constructs specific macro-operators and then merges them. Note that detecting multiple occurrences of the same (or similar) operator sequence(s) constitutes another viable approach to determining the components of a macro-operator, which we addressed in Section 11.2.1.

(table ?t) occurs in moveupto and (block ?z) in moveonto. Similarly, there are three shared effects, with the only difference being that (<add> (clear ?z)) occurs in moveonto. The second elements of the component lists are identical after variable substitutions, but the first operators differ. Thus, FDM creates a disjunction for this action, storing (pickup ?x) with the (block ?x) condition and (stack ?x ?y) with the (table ?x) condition (after it has made variables consistent). The result is the disjunctive macro-operator moveto in Table 11-5.

If the lengths of the component lists differ, some search is required to determine the proper location for null components. In such situations, different choices produce quite different disjunctions. However, in many cases, one partial match will emerge as the best, producing an unambiguous disjunctive component list. As we will see shortly, disjunctive macro-operators with null components also have other implications.

11.3.3 Recursive and iterative macro-operators

We have seen that the inclusion of disjunctions adds considerable flexibility to macro-operators, but they do not cover all situations that a problem solver can encounter. For instance, consider a blocks-world problem in which all blocks are originally on the table and in which the aim is to put them all in a tower. The macro-operator buildtower in Table 11-2 solves this problem quite well for the three-block case, but it is not sufficient for variants that involve four or more blocks.

Humans recognize quite readily the cyclical nature of this task, which involves repeatedly applying pickup and stack until the tower is complete. Simple linear and disjunctive macro-operators must commit to a specific number of components, and thus cannot handle the general case of tower building. However, we can augment the notion of disjunctive macro-operators to support iteration or recursion. We will focus on the latter here, but the differences are mainly notational. Although recursion is more powerful than iteration, most work on recursive macro-operators has focused on situations in which iteration would also serve.

Table 11-6 (c) shows buildtower4, a recursive macro-operator that builds towers containing an arbitrary number of blocks. As with simple disjunctive macro-operators, the preconditions and effects specify structures that hold for all cases of the rule. The real power lies in the conditional list of components. The first component, (moveupto ?x

Table 11-6. Stages in the construction of a recursive macro-operator for building a blocks-world tower: (a) two simple macro-operators that handle the recursive and base cases in creating the tower; (b) a disjunctive macro-operator that
merges the two simple rules; and (c) a macro-operator that replaces `moveupto`
with a recursive call.

```
(a) (buildtower1 (?x ?y)
      [(moveupto ?x ?y) → (moveupto ?z ?x)]
      ((on ?x ?t) (table ?t) (block ?y)
       (clear ?x) (clear ?y) (arm-empty)
       (on ?z ?t) (clear ?z) =>
       (<add> (on ?x ?y)) (<delete> (on ?x ?t) (arm-empty)))

    (buildtower2 (?x ?y)
      [(moveupto ?x ?y) → nil]
      ((on ?x ?t) (table ?t) (block ?y)
       (clear ?x) (clear ?y) (arm-empty) =>
       (<add> (on ?x ?y)) (<delete> (on ?x ?t) (arm-empty)))
```

```
(b) (buildtower3 (?x ?y)
      [(moveupto ?x ?y) →
       {[(moveupto ?z ?x) ((on ?z ?t) (clear ?z) => nil)] ∨
        [nil ((<not> (on ?z ?t) (clear ?z)) => nil)]}]
      ((on ?x ?t) (table ?t) (block ?y)
       (clear ?x) (clear ?y) (arm-empty) =>
       (<add> (on ?x ?y)) (<delete> (on ?x ?t) (arm-empty)))
```

```
(c) (buildtower4 (?x ?y)
      [(moveupto ?x ?y) →
       {[(buildtower4 ?z ?x) ((on ?z ?t) (clear ?z) => nil)] ∨
        [nil ((<not> (on ?z ?t) (clear ?z)) => nil)]}]
      ((on ?x ?t) (table ?t) (block ?y)
       (clear ?x) (clear ?y) (arm-empty) =>
       (<add> (on ?x ?y)) (<delete> (on ?x ?t) (arm-empty))
```

?y), applies in all calls to the macro-operator and thus has no conditions, but the second component is more interesting.

If the conditions (`on ?z ?t`) and (`clear ?z`) match against the state
that results after the problem solver has applied the first component, it

calls on the macro-operator recursively, but this time with arguments ?z and ?x rather than ?x and ?y.[6] In contrast, if these conditions fail to match, the problem solver carries out the null action, effectively terminating its call to the macro-operator.

Thus, when applied to a state in which three blocks reside on the table, this macro-operator will recurse three levels (including the top one) and construct a tower of all three blocks; similarly, when called in a situation with four blocks, it will recurse four times and build a four-block tower. Note that, as stated, the macro-operator does not constrain the position of blocks in the resulting tower; the top-level conditions can match in many different ways, and the internal ones are nondeterministic as well. Thus, given a state involving n blocks on the table, the rule may build any of the $n!$ possible towers. This raises some issues about the use of recursive macro-operators in state-space and means-ends search, but we will not attempt to deal with them here.

The literature describes different approaches to formulating recursive and iterative macro-operators, but here we will focus on the most basic scheme, which we will call FRM. First, the algorithm identifies a potential recurrence by detecting a repeated application of an existing macro-operator. Next it constructs two temporary macro-operators, one in which the component list specifies the double application and one in which the second application is followed by the null action. FRM then merges these two structures into a disjunctive macro-operator, placing shared conditions outside the list of components and storing any disjunction-specific conditions with the appropriate components. Finally, it replaces the second occurrence of the original macro-operator with a recursive call to the new macro-operator.

Table 11-6 presents an example of this process. Suppose FRM notes that the operator sequence <(pickup B), (stack B C), (pickup A), (stack A B)> can be rewritten <(moveupto B C), (moveupto A B)>, which constitutes a repetition. From the definition of moveupto and the specific instances of its application, the algorithm creates two temporary macro-operators shown in Table 11-6 (a), then merges them into the single disjunction shown in (b), retaining the shared conditions out-

---

6. The external preconditions need not be matched again, only those that occur within the component list. At each level of recursion, variables in the argument list (e.g., ?x and ?y) are reset, ones bound in the external conditions (e.g., ?t) are retained, and ones bound in the component list are bound anew. No conditional effects are shown for the recursive case, as they are implicit in the external effects.

side the component list. At this point only one step remains: replacing the second occurrence of **moveupto** in the component list with a recursive call to **buildtower**. The result is the recursive macro-operator **buildtower4** in (c).

The approach embodied in FRM can be extended to handle situations involving multi-step patterns, as well more complex recursions that require more than two disjunctions (which might be added as the result of later experience). Note that the method could instead have formulated an alternative version of **buildtower2** that contained a null action followed by **moveupto**. When combined with **buildtower1**, this would have produced a final rule that involved head recursion rather than tail recursion. For this task, the resulting behavior would be the same, but in some cases such differences can generate quite different effects.

Our treatment has assumed that the problem-solving experience used in learning is unstructured, but this is true only for state-space search. Consider again the means-ends trace in Figure 11-3, which solves an analogous problem to the one we considered in Table 11-6. Note that the problem decomposition has the same structure as the definition of our recursive macro-operator, suggesting that one could use the decomposition itself to determine the exact form that the recursion should take. One can also imagine how this framework might support central embedding (in which the recursive call occurs in the center rather than in the head or tail) and multiple calls to the same recursive structure.

Much of the research on recursive macro-operators has taken place in the context of problem-reduction formalisms. Here the issues are somewhat different, in that the knowledge base begins with both disjunctive and recursive definitions, often stated as sets of Horn clauses. Thus, one can determine when recursion is appropriate by checking whether a subgoal unifies with the supergoal in a solved problem. However, early work ignored this possibility and formed simple macro-operators that contained a fixed number of subgoals consisting of primitive operators or ground literals. Advances in this area have been based on the realization that problem solving may be more efficient if one does not replace recursive calls with their definitions but retains them instead. One can view this approach as a compromise between fixed-sequence macro-operators and search-control rules.

Although the aim of learning flexible macro-operators is to improve performance during problem solving, where a main concern is efficiency,

the task holds much in common with work on grammar induction, where
the goal is to improve accuracy. Both types of problems involve the
detection of recurring and repeated sequences, and both concern the
creation of disjunctive classes and recursive descriptions that summarize sequential experience in useful ways. The literature on automatic
programming from examples traces, and more recent work on inductive
logic programming that involves recursive definitions, also address many
related issues.

11.4 Problem solving by analogy

Another framework attempts to use macro-operators in an even more
flexible manner. The basic idea involves retaining those components of
the macro-operator that are appropriate to the problem at hand and
adapting the remaining portions in ways that aid its solution. This
approach is sometimes referred to as *analogical problem solving* and
sometimes as *case-based reasoning*. In this context, macro-operators
typically go by other names, such as *plans*, *problem-solving traces*, or
cases, but we will continue with our previous usage, as the knowledge
structures are essentially the same. Below we examine some issues that
are specific to this framework. After this, we consider the use of analogical reasoning in the context of state-space search, means-ends analysis,
and problem reduction.

11.4.1 Special issues in analogical problem solving

As with the other methods we have seen in this chapter, analogical
approaches to problem solving involve the retrieval of a stored macro-
operator, which is then used to guide solution of a new problem. However, analogy allows greater transfer to new situations because it can
adapt the macro-operator by omitting, inserting, or substituting component operators where appropriate. Omission requires little effort, as one
can view it as associating an implicit null disjunction with each component. However, insertion and substitution typically require search to fill
in the necessary operators. In principle, this means that the adaptation
process can introduce as much computation as problem solving in the
original space, but sensible constraints can reduce this risk. In addition, false analogies can lead the problem solver astray, causing more
work than if it had not used the macro-operator. Appropriate retrieval

strategies can reduce the potential for such negative transfer, but we will not focus on them here.

In general, analogical problem solving relies on macro-operators that incorporate information about the structure of the solutions that led to them. In order to remove, substitute, or expand any portion of the original solution, the analogical process must know that solution's internal structure to produce appropriate transfer. This requires no changes for state-space search, since the only structure concerns the order of operator selection, but later we will see differences in representation for the means-ends and problem-reduction frameworks.

We should distinguish between analogical *problem solving*, the current topic, and analogical *prediction*, which we considered in Section 5.6 and in Section 8.5.3. The goal of the former is typically to improve the efficiency of problem solving, whereas the concern of analogical prediction is to improve the accuracy of classification. Thus, analogy in problem solving uses a stored solution to a training problem, or a macro-operator based on that solution, to reduce effort on a new test problem, usually falling back on search for portions that do not transfer. In contrast, analogy for prediction uses a stored training instance to predict missing features or literals in a test instance. Usually this prediction occurs without any fallback method to handle features that differ in the two cases, as in other methods for instance-based prediction.

The literature on analogy often treats these two tasks together because both typically involve partial matching of structural or relational descriptions. This matching process constitutes nearly the entire content of analogical prediction, whereas it resides mainly in the retrieval stage for analogical problem solving. Once the problem solver has selected a macro-operator from memory, it usually relies on complete matching to determine the appropriateness of component operators. Nor is partial matching strictly necessary even during retrieval; some methods index macro-operators by only a few goal literals and decide during use whether to continue with an ongoing analogy or to abandon it. Nevertheless, indexing and retrieval remain major open problems in this approach, and we will not emphasize them here.

Methods for analogical problem solving can also vary in the relative amount of effort they expend during learning and performance. At one extreme, they can simply store entire problem descriptions for use in retrieval and successful solution traces for use in replay, requiring maxi-

Table 11-7. A four-step macro-operator for the blocks world used in the examples of problem solving by analogy.

```
(movedownthenstack (?x ?y)
  [(unstack ?x ?y) → (putdown ?x) →
    (pickup ?y) → (stack ?y ?x)]
 ((on ?x ?y) (block ?y) (clear ?x) (arm-empty)
  (table ?t) (on ?y ?t) (block ?x) (≠ ?x ?y) =>
  (<add> (on ?x ?t) (on ?y ?x) (clear ?y))
  (<delete> (on ?x ?y) (clear ?x) (on ?y ?t))))
```

mum effort during the problem-solving process. In another scheme, the learning process stores the same abstractions that are usually associated with macro-operators, using analytic or alternative techniques. We will focus on the analytic approach in our examples, since it is the most representative. At the far end of the spectrum lie methods that store abstract conditions with each component operator, further reducing the work needed during performance.

In this chapter we have been concerned with the acquisition and use of macro-operators, which summarize solutions to entire problems, rather than control knowledge about individual problem-solving steps. Of course, one can use instance-based or analogical prediction methods to store and make decisions about each choice point in the search process, but this topic fits more properly with our discussions of search control in Chapter 10. To distinguish this approach from other work that uses analogy in problem solving, we will refer to it as *analogical search control*. Here we will focus exclusively on the analogical use of larger-scale knowledge structures.

11.4.2 Analogy in state-space search

Although the literature contains few examples of analogy used to direct state-space search, we will begin with that framework because of its simplicity. Table 11-7 shows the stored four-step solution trace that we will use in our examples. This has the same form as a linear macro-operator, including a list of component operators with arguments, a set of conditions that guarantee applicability of the entire sequence,

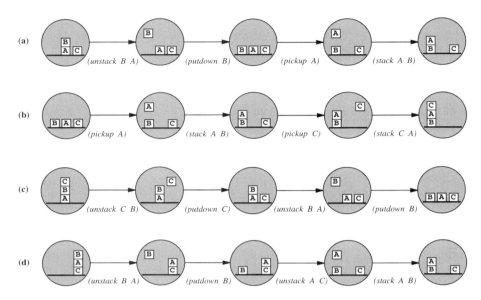

Figure 11-4. Four problems that can be solved by analogy with the macro-operator in Table 11-7. Problem (a) can be solved using the same operator sequence; (b) requires omissions at the front and additions at the end; (c) requires additions at the front and omissions at the end; and (d) requires the substitution of a single component operator.

and a set of effects stated as additions and deletions. One can use the mechanisms described in Section 11.2.1 to construct this structure from a solution trace. Here we will focus on its use by APS, an algorithm for analogical problem solving in state-space search. Table 11-8 presents pseudocode for this technique, which attempts to apply operators in the order that the macro-operator specifies, and which diverges from this path only when necessary.

Figure 11-4 depicts the solutions to four related problems in the three blocks world that illustrate different aspects of the analogical reasoning process. Note that the first problem (a) corresponds directly to the situation described by the macro-operator in Table 11-7, the second (b) requires the problem solver to omit the first two steps in the macro-operator but to add two additional ones at the end, the third (c) involves the insertion of two new steps at the beginning but omits the final two stored components, and the final problem (d) requires only substitution of the third component operator. Each example shows the final solution, but not the search necessary to find this path.

Table 11-8. The APS algorithm: Analogical reasoning for state-space problem solving adapts a retrieved macro-operator to a new problem, invoking state-space search to handle differences between the expected and the actual situation.

```
Inputs: M is a macro-operator;
        P is the position of a component operator.
        S is the current state;
        G is a set of goal conditions;
        B is a set of variable bindings.
Top-level call: APS(M, 1, Initial state, G, Initial bindings).

Procedure APS(M, P, S, G, B)

If the goal G matches state S, then return S.
Else if P is greater than the length of M,
    Then return SSS(M, P, S, G, B).
Else let (P', B') be AMatch(M, P, S, G, B).
    If P' is not Failed,
    Then let Op be the operator in position P' of M.
        Apply Op to S to generate state S'.
        Return APS(M, P' + 1, S', G, B').
    Else let (S', P', B') be SSS(M, P', S, G, B).
        If P' is Failed, then return Failed.
        Else if P' is Done, then return S'.
            Else let Op be the operator in position P' of M.
                Apply Op to S' to generate state S''.
                Return APS(M, P' + 1, S'', G, B').

Procedure AMatch(M, P, S, G, B)

If P is greater than the length of M,
Then return Failed.
Else let Op be the operator in position P of M.
    Let C be Op's preconditions partly instantiated with B.
    If C matches state S with bindings B',
    Then return (P, B').
    Else return AMatch(M, P + 1, S, G, B).
```

Note: The procedure SSS carries out some form of state-space search. If it finds a state S' that satisfies the goal G, it returns (S', Done, Nil); if it finds a state S' that satisfies the conditions of the operator in position P with bindings B', it returns (S', P, B').

We will start with the first problem, which involves the least work for an analogical method. In some versions of analogy, the problem solver detects that the initial state perfectly matches the conditions on the macro-operator and simply applies its operators in sequence. However, we will assume otherwise, since the resulting behavior also covers variants that do not store weakest preconditions. In this case, APS considers applying the first operator in the sequence, (unstack ?x ?y), using the variable bindings generated during matching of the external conditions to constrain the match of this component. Because the operator's conditions successfully match, the problem solver mentally applies it. APS then compares the conditions of the second operator, (putdown ?x), to the resulting state; these also match, leading the problem solver to apply it as well. Similar events occur with the third and fourth operators. However, APS must still determine whether it has reached the desired state. In this case, the fifth state matches the goal description, and problem solving halts.

The initial state for the second problem (b) does not match the conditions of the operator perfectly, but it does constrain the bindings on the components of the macro-operator. Naturally, different partial matches are possible; for each of the four problems, we will assume that the retrieval process selects the bindings ?x -> B and ?y -> A. In this case, APS finds that the first component's conditions fail to match the initial state, so it considers the second component. This operator's conditions mismatch as well, but the third component's conditions succeed. Thus, the problem solver applies (pickup ?y) and generates a new state, which satisfies the conditions of the fourth macro-operator component. Applying this operator leads to a third state, but one that does not satisfy the goal conditions.

At this point, APS has used up the components in the macro-operator without reaching the goal, so it invokes state-space search to find the remaining steps. In this case there is only one operator it can apply without cycling, (pickup C), and this leads to another state with only one choice, (stack C A), which produces the desired state. However, in some cases, diverging from the steps in the macro-operator can lead to considerable search. Note that APS operates in a greedy manner, in that it never considers backtracking over successful applications of macro-operator steps. More sophisticated versions of this algorithm would be required to recover from selected macro-operators that cannot be adapted to the current problem.

Figure 11-4 (c) shows the converse type of situation. Again the initial state does not match the conditions of the macro-operator's first component, but in this case none of the later components' conditions match either. Thus, APS must turn to search at the beginning of the problem, reconsidering the relevance of each component each time it generates a new state. The only applicable operator in this state is (unstack C B), which the components also fail to match, but the next operator produced by state-space search[7] is (putdown C), which produces a state that is matched by the first component of the macro-operator. The state resulting from its application is matched by the second component, which produces a fifth state. At this point, APS notes that the state matches the goal conditions, so it halts without bothering to apply the remaining components in its macro-operator.

The algorithm's behavior on problem (d) produces a somewhat different effect. In this case the first state satisfies the preconditions of the first component, as does the second state for the following operator. The third component does not match the third state, leading the problem solver to invoke state-space search. However, the only operator that does not lead to cycling here is (unstack A C). Upon applying this operator, APS finds that it appears to be back on track, in that the new state satisfies the preconditions of the final component. Application of this operator produces a state that meets the goal specifications, and problem solving ends. In this case, analogy combined with search leads to replacement of a stored component with another that fortuitously produces the desired result.

A simpler variant of the APS algorithm would check only whether the current state meets the preconditions of the next unapplied operator in the macro-operator or satisfies the goal description, rather than skipping on to successive component operators. This approach involves less matching, and it produces identical behavior when the test problem only requires extra steps at the beginning of the solution path, as in Figure 11-4 (c). However, it causes extra search in cases appropriate for tail transfer, as in problem (b), or substitution, as in problem (d). Moreover, the resulting solution path may contain more operators than are generated by the full algorithm.

---

7. As in Figure 11-4 (b), this task involves only one alternative at each decision point handled by the state-space mechanism, but other situations can produce actual search.

The above formulation of state-space analogy assumes that the problem solver must check the applicability of each component as it moves through the macro-operator. We have seen that if the learner takes the effort to determine the weakest preconditions for the macro-operator, it can avoid the checks in the special case where these conditions match the initial state. At the cost of additional processing at storage time, the learner can also determine conditions that guarantee the applicability of each component in the macro-operator. Using such knowledge, the problem solver can identify, at the outset of a problem, the components it can apply without modification and those it cannot. In addition, such analyses can detect situations in which only a partial ordering among the operators is important. Thus, storage of direct dependencies lets the problem solver infer that it can reuse some components even if earlier ones cannot be used.

11.4.3 Analogy in means-ends analysis

One can use a similar approach to analogical reasoning in combination with means-ends analysis. Recall that this problem-solving method selects an operator to reduce differences between the current and the desired states, then recurses on the two subproblems that result. This strategy imposes a hierarchical structure on the solution that is reflected in the resulting macro-operators. This in turn requires some additional tests during the analogical use of macro-operators, but it also provides some greater opportunities.

Let us return to the sample means-ends trace in Figure 11-3, which solves problems similar to the one in Figure 11-4 (b). As we saw earlier, one scheme for storing the knowledge in this trace is to create a macro-operator for the solution of the top-level problem that refers to macro-operators for solutions to its subproblems. In this case there exists only one nontrivial subproblem, so only two macro-operators would result, `buildtower` and `moveupto` from Table 11-2.

We can modify the APS algorithm to operate within a means-ends framework. Suppose the new method, which we will call APM, encounters problem (a) from Figure 11-4 and somehow retrieves the macro-operator `buildtower` from Table 11-2 in an attempt to solve it, with bindings `?x -> C`, `?y -> A`, and `?z -> B`. Using the definition of this macro-operator to constrain the means-ends process, APM would select (stack A B) as its top-level operator and it would create two associated subproblems, which we will refer to as P1 and P2.

The subproblem P1 involves transforming the initial state into one that meets the preconditions of (stack A B). Following the macro-operator, APM would select (pickup A) as the operator for this sub-problem. In the source problem from Figure 11-3, the initial state satisfied the preconditions of this operator, leading to its immediate application. However, more remains to be done in the current problem, since (clear A) is not present, producing a subproblem of P1, say P3.

Because the macro-operator does not provide any guidance in this unexpected situation, APM would resort to regular means-ends analysis to handle the subproblem. In this case, the strategy would select (unstack B A) as the associated operator, which it would immediately apply because it matches the initial state. However, the preconditions of (pickup A) remain unsatisfied in that (arm-empty) is now absent. This leads to a subproblem of P3, which we will call P4. Let us suppose that, in this case, means-ends analysis selects (putdown B) as its operator.[8] The current state satisfies its preconditions, producing a new state that solves both subproblems P4 and P3. This in turn allows application of (pickup A), which generates a state that solves subproblem P1 and lets APM apply (stack A B).

The macro-operator expects the resulting state to contain differences from the goal description, and thus to require invocation of the macro-operator moveupto to solve subproblem P2. However, inspection reveals that the state generated by (stack A B) already satisfies the goal description. Thus, APM would omit this step in buildtower and halt its efforts, since it has already solved the problem.

The events in this scenario are very similar to those we saw in the state-space examples. In this case, APM needed to insert additional sub-problems at the beginning of the top-level macro-operator and needed to omit a subproblem at the end. However, similar events can also occur within any of the lower-level macro-operators that are generated from a means-ends trace. This can lead to splicing in arbitrary operator sequences in the middle of a solution or to the removal of any expected subproblems that need not be solved.

---

8. Another option is (stack B C), which solves the subproblem P4 but eventually leads to a plan with many unnecessary steps.

Table 11-9. Problem-reduction rule representation of a macro-operator, learned from the AND tree in Figure 10-6, that augments the rules in Table 11-3. A bracketed number preceding a subgoal in the right-hand side indicates the rule to use in achieving that subgoal. Encoding the structure of the solution lets analogy remove, substitute, or expand any subtree in solving a new problem.

3^b `maketower([X,Y,Z]) :- on(X,T),table(T),block(Y),clear(X),`
`                          clear(Y),arm-empty,on(Z,T),clear(Z),`
`                          [`3^c`]maketower([Y,Z]),[`6^a`]grasp(X),stack(X,Y).`
3^c `maketower([X,Y]) :-`
`                          [`2^a`]maketower([Y]),[`6^a`]grasp(X),stack(X,Y).`
2^a `maketower([X]) :- [8]makeclear(X).`
6^a `grasp(X) :- [8]makeclear(X),pickup(X).`

11.4.4 Analogy in problem-reduction search

In some ways, problem-reduction approaches are even better suited to analogy than the other frameworks we have examined. This results from their use of rewrite rules to constrain the problem-solving process. These rules are effectively clustered by common literals in the clause heads, and this grouping can significantly constrain the analogical mechanism.

Consider again the AND tree from Figure 10-6, which results from the solution of a problem isomorphic to the one in Figure 11-4 (b), using the problem-reduction rules in Table 11-3. One could transform this tree into a single monolithic macro-operator, but this would not reflect the internal structure of the solution, which can be important in analogy. Instead, suppose that this solution led to the four rules in Table 11-9, which do specify this structure. Note that references to subgoals in the right-hand side include a prefix that indicates the number of the rule to be invoked. Using this information, a modified analogical problem solver, APR, can replay the entire solution without search, since each subgoal states the rules to use in its decomposition. The top-level macro-operator 3^b also contains a set of ground literals that must hold in the current state for it to succeed without modification. The retrieval mechanism can use these conditions to select among alternative rules for satisfying a goal.

Suppose APR encounters a more difficult problem involving the initial state of Figure 11-4 (a) and the desired state of Figure 11-4 (b), and further suppose the retrieval process decides to invoke macro-operator 3^b with bindings X -> C, Y -> A, and Z -> B. As its first step, APR would use rule 3^b to decompose the top-level goal into three subgoals: $[3^c]$maketower([A,B]), $[6^a]$grasp(C), and stack(C,A). It would then rewrite the first subgoal as $[2^a]$maketower([B]), $[6^a]$grasp(A), and stack(A,B). Next APR would transform the first of these subgoals into [8]makeclear(B), which it successfully grounds in the literal clear(B). This satisfies the goal makeclear(B) and maketower(B), so the algorithm would move on to the subgoal grasp(A), which it decomposes into [8]makeclear(A) and pickup(A). As before, it would try to ground the first of these in clear(A), but this literal is not true for the current state.

In response, the APR algorithm would invoke standard AND/OR search in an attempt to satisfy the subgoal another way. The only other decomposition available for makeclear is rule 9 from Table 11-3. Upon creating the subgoals on(Y,A), grasp(Y), and putdown(Y), APR would find that the first subgoal matches only if it binds Y to B. After further decomposition of grasp(B), it would apply the operator unstack(B,A) and finally putdown(B), which achieves the subgoal makeclear(A). The rest of the replayed solution would proceed as planned, without the need for additional search. The resulting AND tree differs from that shown in Figure 10-6 only in the arguments and in the substitution of a subtree for the second clear literal; the final solution path contains two additional operators at the beginning of the sequence.

In this example, the analogical problem solver had to descend to terminal nodes before realizing the need to adapt the retrieved macro-operator. The difficulty was detected fairly early and corrected in a relatively local area, but in some problems the surprise may not come until much later in the macro-operator expansion. However, one can use an idea similar to that in Section 11.4.2 to more directly identify difficulties with an analogy. Briefly, one stores conditions for guaranteed success not only with the top-level macro-operator, but with the macro-operators created from each subproblem in the AND tree, then determines whether the new problem satisfies any one of them. If the conditions for any of these macro-operators match, the problem solver can expand that portion of the solution down to the terminal nodes. If the problem does not satisfy the conditions of any macro-operator, then the problem solver must inspect each one to determine the source of the difficulty, down to the level of ground literals. Each such mismatch identifies a potential site for search to replace the stored decomposition with another that, if successful, will let the analogical process continue.

In summary, the hierarchical structure of an AND tree (which one can store as a set of constrained reduction rules) simplifies the identification of difficulties during analogical transfer to a new problem, and the grouping of rules by the goals they achieve constrains the adaptation process used to correct such difficulties. These factors may explain the literature's bias toward the problem-reduction framework for work on analogical reasoning.

11.5 The utility of macro-operators

In the previous chapter we noted that learned search-control knowledge, even when accurate, is not guaranteed to improve the efficiency of problem solving, and in some cases can actually decrease it. A similar utility problem can occur with macro-operators, both for related reasons and for additional ones. Thus, this approach to the acquisition of problem-solving knowledge also requires additional mechanisms to increase the chances of performance improvement.

As we have seen, macro-operators reduce the effective length of any given solution path by letting the problem solver take larger steps. But in many domains, their preconditions tend to be complex because they compose the preconditions of their components; this can produce high match costs, offsetting the reduction in cost that results from less search. Moreover, the addition of macro-operators increases the branching factor of the search space; the reduction in effective solution length must offset this increase to produce an overall decrease in problem-solving effort. Finally, the use of macro-operators can sometimes lead to lower-quality solutions that involve more primitive steps than those produced by search in the original space, making them expensive to execute.

As before, there are three basic responses to such utility problems that may improve the average-case efficiency of problem solving. First, the learner can selectively *store* macro-operators, adding to memory only those that pass some criterion when they are first proposed. Since many approaches generate each macro-operator from a single solution path, this response typically involves some static analysis of the new structure's potential.

Alternatively, the learner can selectively *remove* macro-operators after it has stored them in memory. This gives the system an opportunity to collect statistics about the structure's effect on efficiency, letting it keep only those macro-operators that have reduced the cost of problem solving for some period after their introduction. Naturally, the same comments we made in Chapter 10, about interactions among search-control rules, hold for macro-operators.

A third scheme involves the selective *use* of learned macro-operators. For instance, the learner can collect ongoing statistics on stored structures, removing them from active consideration if they appear to harm performance and reactivating them if they appear to improve it. A simpler scheme uses all acquired macro-operators, but in limited ways. For example, the problem solver might consider them in attempting to solve the top-level problem, but not allow their use in subproblems. This approach reduces the increased branching factor and match costs while retaining the ability to solve some problems very rapidly. One can also attempt to learn heuristic conditions for selecting each macro-operator, but this introduces the same utility issues we discussed in Chapter 10.

11.6 Summary of the chapter

In this chapter we examined an approach to reducing search in problem solvers by decreasing the effective length of solution paths. We found that macro-operators, which are stated as sequences of primitive operators or other macro-operators, can implement this idea. We also saw that one can apply such macro-operators in a fixed sequence or in more flexible ways that apply to more problems. We formulated the task of learning macro-operators as involving three subtasks: identifying the operators that will serve as components of the macro-operator, determining its internal structure, and specifying its preconditions and effects. The first of these steps is the most challenging, and the one in which methods most differ.

We instantiated this framework in some detail for state-space search, showing how one can use peaks of an evaluation function to partition a solution sequence and how one can use analytic methods to transform each subsequence into a linear macro-operator. We saw how analogous methods apply for means-ends analysis and problem-reduction search, but we also also saw that these problem-solving frameworks suggest different schemes for partitioning solutions into macro-operators.

We then examined three approaches to the creation and use of flexible macro-operators. Triangle tables provide an efficient storage scheme for linear macro-operators that let one enter or leave at any point. Disjunctive macro-operators let one specify alternative operators at each point in the sequence, along with conditional preconditions and effects. Recursive macro-operators extend this idea to let macro-operators invoke themselves, giving them the ability to handle problems with varying numbers of steps. The creation of both disjunctive and recursive macro-operators requires inductive steps that go beyond the analytic methods used for simple linear structures.

Analogical problem-solving methods extend flexibility of macro-operators even further, letting one remove operators, replace them with others, or introduce additional ones that are required to solve the current problem. We saw examples of the usefulness of this approach in the context of state-space search, means-ends analysis, and problem reduction. However, we also saw that the adaptation process that is central to analogical reasoning can sometimes require as much search as problem solving in the original space.

Finally, we addressed the general issue of the utility of learned macro-operators. Because macro-operators increase the branching factor of the problem space, they are not guaranteed to reduce search even when they lead to a shorter solution path. Moreover, the cost of matching the potentially complex preconditions of macro-operators can increase problem-solving time even if they do reduce search. The responses to these utility problems are similar to those for search-control knowledge: one can selectively store macro-operators that seem likely to improve performance, one can selectively retain some structures after storage, and one can selectively use macro-operators that appear useful. As with search control, the utility problem remains a central open issue in work on macro-operators.

Exercises

1. Consider the blocks-world problem with a start state having B and C on the table and A on C, and with a goal state having A and B on the table and C on A. Using an evaluation function that measures the number of literals shared with the goal state, graph the scores of states along the solution path, as in Figure 11-2. Show the fixed-sequence macro-operators that result from the "valley-to-valley" scheme in Section 11.2.1.

2. Show the fixed-sequence macro-operators that can be constructed, as described in Section 11.2.2, from the means-ends trace in Figure 10-7 in Chapter 10.

3. Use the problem-reduction rules in Table 11-3 to generate a solution to the problem solved in Figure 11-3. Show the macro-operator (a specialization of rule 3) that results from the trace of this solution.

4. Construct a triangle table based on the solution from Exercise 1. List three additional problems one can solve with this structure.

5. Consider the blocks-world problem with a start state having A and B on the table and C on B, and with the same goal state as in Exercise 1. Create a disjunctive macro-operator based on the shortest solution to this problem and on the solution to Exercise 1.

6. Define a fixed-sequence macro-operator movedown that takes the top block from a stack and puts it on the table. Given the solution sequence <(unstack A B), (putdown A), (unstack B C), (putdown B)>, generate a recursive macro-operator for unbuilding a tower, showing the same steps as in Table 11-6.

7. Explain the steps through which the APS algorithm (Table 11-8) can solve the problem in Exercise 5 by analogy with the macro-operator shown in Table 11-7. Also show how APS can use a macro-operator based on the solution to Exercise 5 to solve the problem in Figure 11-4 (c).

8. Show the learned rules (like those in Table 11-9) that result from the proof tree in Exercise 3. Show a proof tree based on these rules for the simpler, two-step problem in Figure 10-5, along with the numbers of the rules (learned and original) used to generate the solution. Show a similar proof tree for a more difficult problem, with the same goal state, in which the initial state has A on B, with B and C on the table.

Historical and bibliographical remarks

Research on the formation of macro-operators to improve problem solving goes back to Fikes, Hart, and Nilsson's (1972) STRIPS, a means-ends planner that used triangle tables (Section 11.3.1) to support flexible use of the stored structures, and Nilsson (1985) provides a more recent treatment of this idea. However, most of the ensuing work has focused on fixed-sequence macro-operators. Lewis (1978) first proposed the composition of production rules, a mechanism closely related to macro formation, to explain certain psychological findings, while Neves and Anderson (1981) implemented this idea within the ACT architecture. Shrager, Hogg, and Huberman (1988) show mathematically that improvement with such methods generally follows a power law. However, Minton (1985) found that, because macro-operators increase the branching factor, adding them can sometimes decrease the speed of a means-ends planner, with Markovitz and Scott (1989) reporting similar results. Iba's (1989) MACLEARN incorporates heuristics (including the scheme described in Section 11.2.1) to create and retain only useful macro-operators.

Much of the literature on explanation-based learning has focused on the creation of fixed-sequence macro-operators for problem-reduction search. DeJong and Mooney (1986) present an early formulation of this approach; their treatment is aimed at plan understanding rather than plan generation, but Shavlik (1990) describes a related approach designed to increase the speed of problem solvers. Mooney (1989) compares different strategies for using fixed-sequence macro-operators in a problem-reduction framework; he reports utility problems with some schemes but not with others.

The potential for utility problems provided an important motivation for exploring more flexible notions of macro-operators. Our FDM algorithm (Section 11.3.2) comes from Shell and Carbonell's (1989) work on this topic, while our FRM method (Section 11.3.3) borrows loosely from Shavlik's (1990) BAGGER2 system. Cheng and Carbonell (1986) report a similar scheme that forms iterative macro-operators rather than recursive ones. All of these methods are closely related to algorithms for grammar induction (see Chapter 9), although only VanLehn's (1987) SIERRA takes much advantage of this mapping. Mooney (1988) takes a different approach to achieving flexibility by storing macro-operators with actions that are only partially ordered.

Although we presented analogical problem solving as a flexible approach to using macro-operators, the more typical view is that analogy is an entirely separate area. Hall (1989) reviews early work on this topic, including but not limited to problem-solving methods, while Mostow (1989) focuses on the latter topic. Kling (1971) reports an initial use of analogy in theorem proving, but Carbonell (1983) popularized the idea within the machine learning community and introduced the distinction between transformational and derivational analogy (Carbonell, 1986). The APS algorithm in Section 11.4.2 borrows from his work on the former approach. Veloso and Carbonell (1993) describe an implementation of derivational analogy in PRODIGY, a means-ends planner; Hickman and Larkin (1990) report a similar approach in FERMI, a problem-reduction architecture, and Kambhampati's (1990) PRIAR incorporates analogous ideas into a least-commitment framework. The literature on analogical problem solving is closely related to that for case-based planning, as represented by Alterman (1986), Sycara (1988), Hammond (1990), and others.

CHAPTER 12

Prospects for Machine Learning

In the previous chapters, we have attempted to provide a coherent survey of machine learning, giving both the details of specific algorithms and a conceptual framework for organizing them. However, any organization has limits, and the price is that we have been forced to omit some important aspects of the discipline. Moreover, our focus on algorithms has directed attention away from equally central methodological developments in the study of learning. In this chapter we briefly consider closely related areas of research and discuss some broader trends in the field. We close with comments on the future of machine learning.

12.1 Additional areas of machine learning

The majority of learning research can be assigned to one of the categories covered in earlier chapters, and we have made efforts to provide as broad coverage as possible. Nevertheless, our framework has ignored some important areas that deserve more attention than we have given them. We have also neglected to mention connections between machine learning and other disciplines. In this section we acknowledge these oversights and attempt to mitigate them.

12.1.1 Research on machine discovery

Learning involves the detection of regularities in data that are useful in new situations, and scientists appear to engage in similar activity in their discovery of laws and theories. This analogy has led many researchers in the machine learning community to adapt their ideas to scientific domains, with considerable success. Most work has focused on examples taken from the history of science, but recent tests have included unsolved problems of active interest in physics, chemistry, biology, and other branches of science.

Research on machine discovery falls into two broad categories that parallel distinctions in the history of science. Empirical discovery attempts to uncover regularities that summarize or describe observations. This activity includes the induction of numerical relations (e.g., Kepler's laws of planetary motion), the formation of qualitative laws (e.g., chemical reactions), and the construction of taxonomic hierarchies (e.g., classification schemes for living organisms). A second category aims to formulate scientific theories that explain laws or data by the introduction of unobservable terms. This activity includes the construction of both structural models (e.g., the quark theory) and process theories (e.g., the kinetic theory of gases).

In general, these tasks are viewed as distinct from the typical problems addressed in machine learning research. Work on taxonomy formation is an exception, in that it draws on unsupervised methods for constructing of concept hierarchies (Chapter 7), and work on numeric discovery can be seen as one approach to handling regression problems (Chapter 8). However, methods for finding qualitative laws seldom appear in the machine learning literature outside of their use on discovery tasks, and work on scientific theory formation has a quite different flavor from the approaches to 'theory revision' we saw in Chapter 6. Nevertheless, the common concern with induction from observations has led many members of the machine learning community to address discovery problems, so that work on this topic remains an important part of the field.

12.1.2 Research on experimentation and exploration

Most research on machine learning assumes that training cases are randomly selected from the space of possible instances or problems. However, we have seen that the behavior of incremental methods often depends on the order of training cases, and even nonincremental techniques are sensitive to the particular training sets they observe. Some work has assumed the presence of a benevolent tutor who gives informative instances, such as near misses, or provides ideal training sequences, such as the lexicographic orders in Chapter 9.

However, a more robust approach involves letting the learning system select its own training cases. Some algorithms of this sort effectively design critical experiments to distinguish among competing hypotheses, letting them eliminate competitors and thus reduce the complexity of the learning task. Others incorporate strategies for exploring portions of the instance space that have not yet been encountered to obtain more representative information about the domain. Both approaches can considerably increase learning rates over random presentations.

As in other parts of machine learning, much of the research on experimentation and exploration has focused on classification tasks, but some efforts have dealt with problem-solving domains. Also, most work has been associated with incremental algorithms in which order effects play an important role, but one can use similar ideas to ensure representative data for nonincremental schemes. The move toward more autonomous systems is encouraging, and progress in this area should produce increasingly reliable learning algorithms.

12.1.3 Research on knowledge compilation

We have examined methods for improving the efficiency of problem solving through the acquisition of search-control knowledge and macro-operators. Both can be viewed as forms of knowledge compilation, in which learning transforms an initial knowledge base into one that operates more effectively on novel problems. However, work in this area is not limited to the approaches we presented in Chapters 10 and 11, and we should briefly consider some alternatives.

Clearly, the aims of knowledge compilation are similar to those of compilers for traditional programming languages. Some researchers in machine learning have adapted this idea to the compilation of knowledge for problem solving, and related ideas have emerged in the knowledge representation community, in work on data base queries, and in research on automated software design.

The central idea behind these approaches is the reformulation of an initial specification in more efficient terms, typically using transformations that preserve the correctness of the original knowledge. Some versions take advantage of training cases or user interactions to direct search through the space of transformations, but most techniques are purely analytical. Nevertheless, they typically rely on the same criteria for success as methods that take advantage of experience, measuring the effect of compilation on processing efficiency.

12.1.4 Relationship to other disciplines

Although machine learning is commonly viewed as part of artificial intelligence and, to a lesser extent, cognitive science, it clearly has strong connections to other disciplines as well. For example, many of the techniques for inducing threshold and competitive concepts, which we considered in Chapters 3 and 4, originated in pattern recognition, a field that diverged from AI in the 1960s. Research in this paradigm emphasizes numeric rather than symbolic techniques and focuses on problems of perceptual classification. However, the two fields share numerous concerns, and many algorithms and problems from pattern recognition have found their way into the machine learning literature.

Machine learning and statistics also have many common interests. Both concern induction from sample data, both make domain assumptions for the sake of tractability, and both must address issues of noise and overfitting. Historically, statistics has emphasized numeric rather than symbolic representations and algorithmic rather than heuristic methods, but these biases have lessened in recent years. In fact, some techniques have been independently invented within the two communities, the most important example being algorithms for the induction of decision trees (Chapter 7). Moreover, statistical methods for exploratory data analysis have always been heuristic in nature, with early work on clustering directly influencing later research efforts on unsupervised machine learning.

Finally, developments in control theory have dealt with issues similar to those arising in machine learning approaches to problem solving, in that both areas focus on determining actions that will achieve some environmental objectives. As in pattern recognition and statistics, research in control theory has concentrated primarily on numeric and algorithmic schemes, but many of its insights remain relevant. The methods designed by control theorists are most closely related to the reinforcement learning techniques that we examined in Chapter 10, but they have implications for all work on learning in problem-solving domains.

12.2 Methodological trends in machine learning

In this book, we have focused on well-defined learning problems and on the algorithms that researchers have developed to address them. This reflects a bias in the machine learning community itself, which has long been oriented toward the identification of new problems and the development of new algorithms. However, this perspective ignores some recent methodological trends that have proven very important to the field. In this section we note these advances and their implications.

12.2.1 Experimental studies of learning algorithms

Early research in machine learning relied on idealized, hand-crafted examples, and researchers often tested their systems on only a few cases. This has changed drastically in recent years, and papers in the literature now commonly report results on realistic learning tasks that involve many test cases. Moreover, researchers now typically present findings on a number of different data sets, to show the robustness and generality of their algorithms. The average number of test domains should increase as the standards of the field become even higher.

Another encouraging sign is that different researchers now often test their algorithms on the *same* task domains, allowing comparisons between algorithms. This trend has been aided by the collection and distribution of standard data sets. A major repository has emerged at the University of California, Irvine, that includes over 70 data sets available to the public, and the set continues to grow.[1] Many of the UCI domains deal with classification tasks, but standard problem-solving and reasoning tasks are also beginning to emerge.

Changes in the nature of testing have been equally important. Early work in machine learning simply examined an algorithm's output to determine its plausibility. However, papers now regularly present the results of scientific experiments, in which changes in one or more independent variables affect dependent measures. Some studies even report the evaluation of explicit hypotheses using statistical tests. The most common independent variables concern characteristics of the learning al-

---

1. The UCI data sets and their associated documentation are available by `ftp` from `ics.uci.edu` using the account and password `anonymous`. The various domains reside in the directory `pub/machine-learning-databases`.

gorithm, whereas the natural dependent measures focus on performance (e.g., accuracy or efficiency) after learning.

Researchers have also started to examine carefully the aspects of domains that affect learning behavior. Some experimental studies have focused on naturalistic data in order to show real-world relevance, but others have constructed synthetic domains to allow control of problem characteristics. Two obvious features include the complexity of the knowledge to be learned and the amount of noise in the data, and we discussed others in Chapter 1. The important point is that many researchers now realize that, in order to make progress, the field requires some explicit methods for evaluating alternative algorithms and for identifying the conditions under which they will work well.

12.2.2 Theoretical analyses of learning

Formal studies of inductive inference have a long history in theoretical computer science. However, only recently have theorists started to address issues of concern to researchers who actually build machine learning systems. Early work focused on whether learning algorithms would eventually converge on the target concept or grammar, and on the classes of induction tasks that allow convergence. This approach constituted an important first step, but it afforded little insight into realistic learning problems.

A major advance came when researchers turned their attention to the quality of the induced knowledge. Work on *probably approximately correct* (PAC) learning advanced the idea that learned knowledge should usually be relatively accurate when applied in novel situations. Coupling this idea with computational feasibility yielded a definition of *polynomially learnable* problems that do not require too many instances to learn and that allow efficient methods for both learning and performance. When studying the learnability of a particular problem, one common research tactic is to show that one of these criteria cannot be met. The initial PAC analyses dealt with the induction of logical, Boolean concepts from supervised data, but researchers have since extended the basic framework to both other representations (e.g., threshold units) and other tasks (e.g., unsupervised learning). They have also addressed learning in the presence of noise and the role of background knowledge.

However, most work in the PAC framework has remained disconnected from practical algorithms, and its worst-case predictions about learning rates have been strikingly different from experimental results. Recently, a few researchers have reported average-case formulations of simple induction algorithms, obtaining close fits between predicted and observed learning curves on synthetic domains. Closer interaction of this sort between theory and experimentation will be necessary before machine learning can develop into a mature scientific discipline.

12.2.3 Applications of machine learning

We have noted the encouraging progress in experimental evaluation, but it is important to distinguish between experiments with learning algorithms on realistic problems and applications of such software for use outside the research community. Testing a machine learning system on a challenging real-world problem does not necessarily constitute a successful application; the result must be used by others whose main interest lies in the system's output, rather than in its mechanisms.

Such fielded applications of machine learning have been rare, but the number has increased rapidly in recent years. The methods used in these efforts run the gamut of learning techniques we have examined in previous chapters. Most recent successes have focused on classification or prediction tasks, but impressive examples also exist in the areas of configuration and layout, planning and scheduling, and execution and control.

These applications provide existence proofs that machine learning can make a difference on problems of interest to industry and commerce. However, many more examples will be necessary before automated learning methods become significant competitors for more traditional knowledge engineering approaches to the acquisition of domain-specific knowledge, and the field would do well to concentrate a substantial portion of its energies toward developing additional applications.

12.2.4 Computational models of human learning

Much of the early work on machine learning was motivated by concerns with modeling human behavior. Moreover, some of the earliest and most influential learning algorithms were developed by psychologists. Research in this tradition continues, but as machine learning has developed its own identity, the proportion of systems cast as serious psychological models has decreased.

This trend is unfortunate. Humans constitute our best example of a robust learning system, and using knowledge of their behavior to constrain the design of learning algorithms makes good heuristic sense. Progress in machine learning requires some evaluation metric to direct search through the space of algorithms, but the ability to explain psychological phenomena is as valuable a measure as careful experimental studies, elegant formal analyses, or successful applications.

An important obstacle to the development of computational learning models is lack of knowledge. Few system builders are familiar with the established findings on human learning, and few experimental psychologists have the skills needed to construct running systems. One response would involve collecting stimuli and results from pivotal experiments in the psychological literature, similar to the data bases currently used for experimental studies of learning systems. Such a repository would make it much easier for machine learning researchers to evaluate their systems' abilities to account for important phenomena in human learning, and thus would encourage increased activity in this area.

12.2.5 Unified frameworks for machine learning

As the previous chapters attest, machine learning includes a broad class of techniques that come from a variety of backgrounds. Thus, it should come as little surprise that the literature often emphasizes differences among the various approaches rather than similarities. Some reported distinctions are legitimate, but many result from variations in metaphors and notation, and others exist primarily for rhetorical purposes.

For instance, research on analytic learning emphasizes an analogy with logic and describes knowledge in terms of Horn clauses. In contrast, work on multilayer neural networks draws on a neurological metaphor and presents knowledge as nodes and weighted links. Moreover, at times researchers in both paradigms have made strong claims about the distinctive nature of their approaches, many of them rhetorical in nature and not backed by evidence. However, in Chapter 6 we saw that these two approaches have important common features, and that many of the claimed differences are more apparent than real.

Distinctions are important, but an ultimate goal of any scientific field should be a unified framework that explains superficially different processes in terms of common underlying mechanisms. Fortunately, many researchers in the machine learning community now seem concerned

with developing such a framework. The chapters in this book take
some preliminary steps in this direction, and an increasing number of
papers describe hybrid learning systems that incorporate aspects of previously separate techniques. Examples include methods that combine
probabilistic and instance-based algorithms, that use decision trees to
organize linear threshold units, and that use threshold learning methods
to revise logical networks. These trends are encouraging, and we hope
that more researchers will focus their energies toward unifying the field.

12.2.6 Integrated cognitive architectures

Another change in research style, cutting across the entire AI community, relates to the development of integrated architectures for cognition. Early researchers commonly implemented a separate system for
each new task they encountered. These systems incorporated only minor theoretical commitments about the nature of intelligent behavior,
and thus provided few constraints on work in other domains. This trend
has changed in recent years, with many researchers now turning to integrated architectures that make strong assumptions about the control
structures needed to support intelligence.

We mention this work here because many of these architectures include learning algorithms as one of their central components. Such integrated frameworks will be necessary if the field ever hopes to construct
intelligent artifacts that can interact with the physical world, or to move
beyond isolated systems that are developed anew for each specific task.
Moreover, we predict that learning will continue to play an important
role in the development of such cognitive architectures, since acquiring
knowledge from the environment would seem necessary for long-term
adaptive behavior.

12.3 The future of machine learning

Over the last decade, the development of improved learning algorithms
and the methodological advances described in the previous section have
transported machine learning from the periphery of artificial intelligence
into one of its central areas. Along with this shift has come increased
contact with other AI subcommunities, and as methods for machine
learning become more robust, they are gaining increased attention from
researchers concerned with planning, diagnosis, natural language, and

other problem-oriented areas of the parent field. In turn, these domains provide significant challenges for scientists who have traditionally been concerned with abstract issues and artificial learning tasks.

Without doubt, attempts to adapt machine learning to more challenging problems will reveal limitations of the existing paradigms and suggest novel directions for automating the acquisition of knowledge. Thus, researchers will be forced to devise new representations, search frameworks, and control schemes to support the learning process. The resulting approaches may initially be domain specific, inefficient, and inelegant, but they will respond to issues that have been ignored previously. Such learning methods may not fit nicely into existing organizations, like the one presented in this book, but that is often the nature of scientific progress.

At the same time, theoretical concerns will continue to drive some of the research in machine learning. Scientists will explore hybrids of existing algorithms, propose frameworks that unify apparently different techniques, and carry out studies to identify the behavior of alternative methods under varying conditions. Hopefully, they will also begin to relate experimental results to those predicted by theory, revising the theory when necessary. Finally, they will attempt to identify new dimensions and new themes that have emerged from applications efforts, idealizing them enough to make them amenable to experimental study and theoretical analysis.

Taken together, basic and applied research should continue to improve the range and capabilities of learning algorithms, and to increase our understanding of this intriguing class of mechanisms. These advances in turn will have far-ranging implications for the rest of artificial intelligence, letting the field move beyond static systems to ones that improve performance over time as they acquire and refine knowledge in the light of experience.

Historical and bibliographical remarks

Research on automating scientific discovery has played a role in machine learning since it first emerged as a distinct field. Early work in this area included Lenat's (1978) AM, which discovered concepts and conjectures in mathematics, and Langley's (1981) BACON, which found empirical laws in physics (Chapter 8). Langley, Simon, Bradshaw, and

Zytkow (1987) describe additional work on discovering both empirical laws and structural models in physics, chemistry, and biology, while Jones (1986), Rose and Langley (1986), and Kocabas (1991) report extensions to this approach. Falkenhainer (1990), O'Rorke, Morris, and Schulenberg (1990), and Rajamoney (1990) present a different line of discovery research, aimed at adapting and revising process theories of observed phenomena. Shrager and Langley (1990) contains a representative sample of work on scientific discovery, special issues of *Machine Learning* and workshop proceedings report additional work, and Thagard (1988) discusses the relations between this paradigm and the philosophy of science.

Because experimentation plays an important role in scientific reasoning, there has been some overlap on these two topics. Kulkarni and Simon's (1990) KEKADA and Rajamoney's (1990) COAST both design critical experiments to distinguish among competing hypotheses in scientific domains, and some work outside machine discovery takes a very similar approach. For instance, Sammut and Banerji (1986) and Gross (1991) adapt this idea to supervised concept learning, while Scott and Markovitz (1991) take much the same approach to unsupervised induction. Gil (1993) explores the uses of experimentation in learning action models for use in planning, and Knobe and Knobe's (1977) approach to grammar induction also relied on careful selection of training sentences. In addition, many methods for reinforcement learning include a bias toward exploring unfamiliar parts of the state space (e.g., Lin, 1992).

We considered some approaches to knowledge compilation, notably the construction of search-control knowledge and macro-operators, in Chapters 10 and 11. Kibler (1978) presents an alternative approach that involves the transformation of programs into more efficient forms, and Mostow (1983) considers another scheme that involves the progressive refinement of high-level advice. Dietterich (1986) contains representative research on the topic of knowledge compilation, covering a variety of techniques for improving the efficiency of software, only some of which require experience with training problems.

The disciplines of pattern recognition, statistics, and control theory have much longer histories than machine learning. Nilsson (1965) surveys early work in the former area, while Duda and Hart (1973) cover somewhat later developments. Breiman, Friedman, Olshen, and Stone's (1984) book on decision-tree induction contains references to earlier statistical work on nonparametric statistics. Gale (1986) contains a variety of chapters at the intersection of artificial intelligence and statistics, and proceedings of the annual conference on this topic have additional reports. Dean and Wellman (1991) provide an introduction to control theory from the perspective of artificial intelligence and give references to earlier work in this tradition.

There have been relatively few papers written on the methodology of machine learning, although individual research papers often treat this matter implicitly. Kibler and Langley (1988) provide arguments for the experimental study of learning algorithms, illustrated by examples of different approaches, and a few critiques of specific experimental methods also exist (e.g., Rendell & Cho, 1990; Segre, Elkan, & Russell, 1991). Surveys of computational learning theory (e.g., Angluin & Smith, 1983; Haussler, 1990) provide some insight into formal approaches to induction, but tend to focus on results rather than methodology. The same comments hold for reviews of psychological models (e.g., Billman et al., 1990) and applications of machine learning (e.g., Widrow, Rumelhart, & Lehr, 1994), although Langley and Simon (in press) discuss some broader issues for the latter. Only a few scientists (e.g., Laird, 1991; Newell, 1990) discuss the issues that arise in developing and evaluating integrated architectures. Occasional editorials stress the need for unified learning frameworks (e.g., Langley, 1989a, 1989b) or cross-paradigm comparisons (Mooney, Shavlik, Towell, & Gove, 1989), but these are rare as well. This seems reasonable, as any field that is overly concerned with its own methodology has little attention to focus on substantive progress.

References

Ackley, D. H., Hinton, G. E., & Sejnowski, T. J. (1987). A learning algorithm for Boltzmann machines. *Cognitive Science*, *9*, 147–169.

Aha, D. W. (1990). *A study of instance-based algorithms for supervised learning tasks: Mathematical, empirical, and psychological evaluations*. Doctoral dissertation, Department of Information & Computer Science, University of California, Irvine.

Aha, D. W. (1992). Tolerating noisy, irrelevant and novel attributes in instance-based learning algorithms. *International Journal of Man-Machine Studies*, *36*, 267–287.

Aha, D. W., & Bankert, R. L. (1994). Feature selection for case-based classification of cloud types. *Working Notes of the AAAI94 Workshop on Case-Based Reasoning* (pp. 106–112). Seattle, WA: AAAI Press.

Aha, D. W., Kibler, D., & Albert, M. K. (1991). Instance-based learning algorithms. *Machine Learning*, *6*, 37–66.

Ahmad, S., & Tresp, V. (1993). Some solutions to the missing feature problem in vision. In C. L. Giles, S. J. Hanson, & J. D. Cowan (Eds.), *Advances in neural information processing systems* (Vol. 5). San Francisco, CA: Morgan Kaufmann.

Allen, B. P. (1994). Case-based reasoning: Business applications. *Communications of the ACM*, *37*, March, 40–42.

Almuallim, H., & Dietterich, T. G. (1991). Learning with many irrelevant features. *Proceedings of the Ninth National Conference on Artificial Intelligence* (pp. 547–552). San Jose, CA: AAAI Press.

Alterman, R. (1986). An adaptive planner. *Proceedings of the Fifth National Conference on Artificial Intelligence* (pp. 65–69). Philadelphia, PA: Morgan Kaufmann.

Anderson, J. R. (1977). Induction of augmented transition networks. *Cognitive Science*, *1*, 125–157. Reprinted in J. W. Shavlik & T. G. Dietterich (Eds.) (1990), *Readings in machine learning*. San Francisco, CA: Morgan Kaufmann.

Anderson, J. R. (1981a). A theory of language acquisition based on general learning principles. *Proceedings of the Seventh International Joint Conference on Artificial Intelligence* (pp. 97–103). Vancouver, Canada: Morgan Kaufmann.

Anderson, J. R. (1981b). Tuning of search of the problem space for geometry proofs. *Proceedings of the Seventh International Joint Conference on Artificial Intelligence* (pp. 165–170). Vancouver, Canada: Morgan Kaufmann.

Anderson, J. R. (Ed.). (1981c). *Cognitive skills and their acquisition*. Hillsdale, NJ: Lawrence Erlbaum.

Anderson, J. R., & Kline, P. J. (1979). A learning system and its psychological implications. *Proceedings of the Sixth International Joint Conference on Artificial Intelligence* (pp. 16–21). Tokyo, Japan: Morgan Kaufmann.

Anderson, J. R., & Matessa, M. (1992). Explorations of an incremental, Bayesian algorithm for categorization. *Machine Learning*, *9*, 275–308.

Angluin, D. (1982). Inference of reversible languages. *Journal of the ACM*, *29*, 741–765.

Angluin, D., & Smith, C. (1983). Inductive inference: Theory and methods. *Computing Surveys*, *15*, 237–269.

Annenberg, M. R. (1973). *Cluster analysis for applications*. New York: Academic Press.

Anzai, Y., & Simon, H. A. (1979). The theory of learning by doing. *Psychological Review*, *86*, 124–140.

Asker, L. (1994). Improving accuracy of incorrect domain theories. *Proceedings of the Eleventh International Conference on Machine Learning* (pp. 19–27). New Brunswick, NJ: Morgan Kaufmann.

Baffles, P. T., & Mooney, R. J. (1993). Symbolic revision of theories with M-of-N rules. *Proceedings of the Thirteenth International Joint Conference on Artificial Intelligence* (pp. 1134–1140). Chambéry, France: Morgan Kaufmann.

Baker, J. K. (1979). *Trainable grammars for speech recognition*. Paper presented at the 97th Meeting of the Acoustical Society of America. Cambridge, MA.

Barto, A. G., Sutton, R. S., & Anderson, C. W. (1983). Neuronlike elements that can solve difficult learning control problems. *IEEE Transactions on Systems, Man, and Cybernetics*, *13*, 834–846.

Baum, L. E., Petrie, T., Soules, G., & Weiss, N. (1970). A maximization technique occurring in the statistical analysis of probabilistic functions of Markov chains. *Annals of Mathematical Statistics*, *41*, 164–171.

Berwick, R. C. (1980). Computational analogues of constraints on grammars: A model of syntactic acquisition. *Proceedings of the 18th Annual Meeting of the Association for Computational Linguistics* (pp. 49–53). Philadelphia, PA: ACL.

Berwick, R. C., & Pilato, S. (1987). Learning syntax by automata induction. *Machine Learning*, *2*, 9–38.

Biggs, D., de Ville, B., & Suen, E. (1991). A method of choosing multiway partitions for classification and decision trees. *Journal of Applied Statistics*, *18*, 49–62.

Billman, D., Fisher, D., Gluck, M., Langley, P., & Pazzani, M. (1990). Computational models of category learning. *Proceedings of the Twelfth Annual Conference of the Cognitive Science Society* (pp. 989–996). Cambridge, MA: Lawrence Erlbaum.

Blumer, A., Ehrenfeucht, A., Haussler, D., & Warmuth, M. K. (1987). Occam's razor. *Information Processing Letters*, *24*, 377–380. Reprinted in J. W. Shavlik & T. G. Dietterich (Eds.) (1990), *Readings in machine learning*. San Francisco, CA: Morgan Kaufmann.

Booker, L. B. (1988). Classifier systems that learn internal world models. *Machine Learning*, *3*, 161–192.

Booker, L. B., Goldberg, D. E., & Holland, J. H. (1989). Classifier systems and genetic algorithms. *Artificial Intelligence*, *40*, 235–282. Reprinted in J. W. Shavlik & T. G. Dietterich (Eds.) (1990), *Readings in machine learning*. San Francisco, CA: Morgan Kaufmann.

Bower, G. H. (1981). *Theories of learning*. Englewood Cliffs, NJ: Prentice-Hall.

Bradshaw, G. (1987). Learning about speech sounds: The NEXUS project. *Proceedings of the Fourth International Workshop on Machine Learning* (pp. 1–11). Irvine, CA: Morgan Kaufmann.

Bratko, I., & Muggleton, S. (in press). Applications of inductive logic programming. *Communications of the ACM*.

Brazdil, P. (1978). Experimental learning model. *Proceedings of the Third AISB/GI Conference* (pp. 46–50). Hamburg, West Germany.

Breiman, L., Friedman, J. H., Olshen, R. A., & Stone, C. J. (1984). *Classification and regression trees*. Belmont, CA: Wadsworth.

Brown, R. (1973). *A first language: The early stages*. Cambridge, MA: Harvard University Press.

Bruner, J. S., Goodnow, J. J., & Austin, G. A. (1956). *A study of thinking*. New York: John Wiley.

Buntine, W. (1990). *A theory of learning classification rules*. Doctoral dissertation, Department of Computer Science, University of Technology, Sydney, Australia.

Buntine, W., & Niblett, T. (1992). A further comparison of splitting rules for decision-tree induction. *Machine Learning*, *8*, 75–86.

Carbonell, J. G. (1983). Learning by analogy: Formulating and generalizing plans from past experience. In R. S. Michalski, J. G. Carbonell, & T. M. Mitchell (Eds.), *Machine learning: An artificial intelligence approach*. San Francisco, CA: Morgan Kaufmann. Reprinted in J. W. Shavlik & T. G. Dietterich (Eds.) (1990), *Readings in machine learning*. San Francisco, CA: Morgan Kaufmann.

Carbonell, J. G. (1986). Derivational analogy: A theory of reconstructive problem solving and expertise acquisition. In R. S. Michalski, J. G. Carbonell, & T. M. Mitchell (Eds.), *Machine learning: An artificial intelligence approach* (Vol. 2). San Francisco, CA: Morgan Kaufmann. Reprinted in J. W. Shavlik & T. G. Dietterich (Eds.) (1990), *Readings in machine learning*. San Francisco, CA: Morgan Kaufmann.

Carbonell, J. G., Michalski, R. S., & Mitchell, T. M. (1983). An overview of machine learning. In R. S. Michalski, J. G. Carbonell, & T. M. Mitchell (Eds.), *Machine learning: An artificial intelligence approach*. San Francisco, CA: Morgan Kaufmann.

Cardie, C. (1993). Using decision trees to improve case-based learning. *Proceedings of the Tenth International Conference on Machine Learning* (pp. 25–32). Amherst, MA: Morgan Kaufmann.

Caruana, R. A., & Freitag, D. (1994). Greedy attribute selection. *Proceedings of the Eleventh International Conference on Machine Learning* (pp. 28–36). New Brunswick, NJ: Morgan Kaufmann.

Cestnik, G., Kononenko, I., & Bratko, I. (1987). Assistant-86: A knowledge-elicitation tool for sophisticated users. In I. Bratko & N. Lavrac (Eds.), *Progress in machine learning*. London: Sigma Press.

Chapman, D., & Kaelbling, L. P. (1991). Input generalization in delayed reinforcement learning: An algorithm and performance comparisons. *Proceedings of the Twelfth International Joint Conference on Artificial Intelligence* (pp. 726–731). Sydney, Australia: Morgan Kaufmann.

Cheeseman, P., Kelly, J., Self, M., Stutz, J., Taylor, W., & Freeman, D. (1988). Autoclass: A Bayesian classification system. *Proceedings of the Fifth International Conference on Machine Learning* (pp. 54–64). Ann Arbor, MI: Morgan Kaufmann. Reprinted in J. W. Shavlik & T. G. Dietterich (Eds.) (1990), *Readings in machine learning*. San Francisco, CA: Morgan Kaufmann.

Cheng, P. W., & Carbonell, J. G. (1986). Inducing iterative rules from experience: The Fermi experiment. *Proceedings of the Fifth National Conference on Artificial Intelligence* (pp. 490–495). Philadelphia, PA: Morgan Kaufmann.

Chomsky, N. (1965). *Aspects of the theory of syntax*. Cambridge, MA: MIT Press.

Clark, P., & Niblett, T. (1989). The CN2 induction algorithm. *Machine Learning*, *3*, 261–284.

Cleeremans, A., Servan-Schreiber, D., & McClelland, J. (1989). Finite state automata and simple recurrent networks. *Neural Computation*, *1*, 372–381.

Cohen, W. (1988). Generalizing number and learning from multiple examples in explanation-based learning. *Proceedings of the Fifth International Conference on Machine Learning* (pp. 256–269). Ann Arbor, MI: Morgan Kaufmann.

Connolly, D. (1993). Constructing hidden variables in Bayesian networks via conceptual clustering. *Proceedings of the Tenth International Conference on Machine Learning* (pp. 65–72). Amherst, MA: Morgan Kaufmann.

Cook, C. M., Rosenfeld, A., & Aronson, A. (1976). Grammatical inference by hill climbing. *Informational Sciences, 10*, 59–80.

Cooper, G. F., & Herskovits, E. (1992). A Bayesian method for the induction of probabilistic networks from data. *Machine Learning, 9*, 309–347.

Cost, S., & Salzberg, S. (1994). A weighted nearest neighbor algorithm for learning with symbolic features. *Machine Learning, 10*, 57–78.

Cover, T. R., & Hart, P. E. (1967). Nearest neighbor pattern classification. *IEEE Transactions on Information Theory, 13*, 21–27.

Craw, S., & Sleeman, D. (1990). Automating the refinement of knowledge-based systems. *Proceedings of European Conference on Artificial Intelligence* (pp. 167–172). Stockholm, Sweden: Pitman.

Dasarathy, B. W. (Ed.). (1990). *Nearest neighbor (NN) norms: NN pattern classification techniques*. Los Alamitos, CA: IEEE Computer Society Press.

Dean, T. L., & Wellman, M. P. (1991). *Planning and control*. San Francisco, CA: Morgan Kaufmann.

DeJong, G. F., & Mooney, R. (1986). Explanation-based learning: An alternative view. *Machine Learning, 1*, 145–176. Reprinted in J. W. Shavlik & T. G. Dietterich (Eds.) (1990), *Readings in machine learning*. San Francisco, CA: Morgan Kaufmann.

De Jong, K. A., & Spears, W. M. (1991). Learning concept classification rules using genetic algorithms. *Proceedings of the Twelfth International Joint Conference on Artificial Intelligence* (pp. 651–656). Sydney, Australia: Morgan Kaufmann.

Devijver, P. A., & Kittler, J. (1982). *Pattern recognition: A statistical approach*. New York: Prentice-Hall.

Dietterich, T. G. (Ed.). (1986). *Proceedings of the Workshop on Knowledge Compilation* (Technical Report). Corvallis: Oregon State University, Department of Computer Science.

Dietterich, T. G. (1987). Learning at the knowledge level. *Machine Learning, 1*, 287–316. Reprinted in J. W. Shavlik & T. G. Dietterich (Eds.) (1990), *Readings in machine learning*. San Francisco, CA: Morgan Kaufmann.

Dietterich, T. G. (1989). Machine learning. In J. F. Traub (Ed.), *Annual review of computer science* (Vol. 3). Palo Alto, CA: Annual Reviews, Inc.

Dietterich, T. G., Hild, H., & Bakiri, G. (1990). A comparative study of ID3 and backpropagation for English text-to-speech mapping. *Proceedings of the Seventh International Conference on Machine Learning* (pp. 24–31). Austin, TX: Morgan Kaufmann.

Dietterich, T. G., London, B., Clarkson, K., & Dromey, G. (1982). Learning and inductive inference. In P. R. Cohen & E. A. Feigenbaum (Eds.), *The handbook of artificial intelligence* (Vol. 3). San Francisco, CA: Morgan Kaufmann.

Drastal, G., Raatz, S., & Czako, G. (1989). Induction in an abstraction space: A form of constructive induction. *Proceedings of the Eleventh International Joint Conference on Artificial Intelligence* (pp. 708–712). Detroit, MI: Morgan Kaufmann.

Duda, R. O., & Hart, P. E. (1973). *Pattern classification and scene analysis*. New York: John Wiley.

Elio, R., & Watanabe, L. (1991). An incremental, deductive strategy for controlling constructive induction in learning from examples. *Machine Learning*, *7*, 7–44.

Elman, J. L. (1991). Distributed representations, simple recurrent networks, and grammatical structure. *Machine Learning*, *7*, 195–225.

Etzioni, O. (1990). Why PRODIGY/EBL works. *Proceedings of the Eighth National Conference on Artificial Intelligence* (pp. 916–922). Boston, MA: AAAI Press.

Evans, T. G. (1968). A program for the solution of a class of geometric analogy intelligence test questions. In M. Minsky (Ed.), *Semantic information processing*. Cambridge, MA: MIT Press.

Everitt, B. (1980). *Cluster analysis* (2nd ed.). New York: Halsted Press.

Fahlman, S. E. (1988). Faster-learning variations on back-propagation: An empirical study. *Proceedings of the 1988 Connectionist Models Summer School* (pp. 38–51). Pittsburgh, PA: Morgan Kaufmann.

Fahlman, S. E., & Lebiere, C. (1990). *The cascade-correlation learning architecture* (Tech. Rep. No. CMU-CS-90-100). Pittsburgh, PA: Carnegie Mellon University, School of Computer Science.

Falkenhainer, B. C. (1990). A unified approach to explanation and theory formation. In J. Shrager & P. Langley (Eds.), *Computational models of scientific discovery and theory formation*. San Francisco, CA: Morgan Kaufmann. Reprinted in J. W. Shavlik & T. G. Dietterich (Eds.) (1990), *Readings in machine learning*. San Francisco, CA: Morgan Kaufmann.

Falkenhainer, B., Forbus, K. D., & Gentner, D. (1989). The structure-mapping engine: Algorithm and examples. *Artificial Intelligence*, *41*, 1–63.

Falkenhainer, B. C., & Michalski, R. S. (1986). Integrating quantitative and qualitative discovery: The ABACUS system. *Machine Learning*, *1*, 367–422.

Falkenhainer, B. C., & Rajamoney, S. (1988). The interdependencies of theory formation, revision, and experimentation. *Proceedings of the Fifth International Conference on Machine Learning* (pp. 353–366). Ann Arbor, MI: Morgan Kaufmann.

Feigenbaum, E. A. (1961). The simulation of verbal learning behavior. *Proceedings of the Western Joint Computer Conference* (pp. 121–132). Reprinted in J. W. Shavlik & T. G. Dietterich (Eds.) (1990), *Readings in machine learning*. San Francisco, CA: Morgan Kaufmann.

Feldman, J. A., Gips, J., Horning, J. J., & Reder, S. (1969). *Grammatical complexity and inference* (Tech. Rep. No. CS 125). Stanford, CA: Stanford University, Computer Science Department.

Fikes, R. E., Hart, P. E., & Nilsson, N. J. (1972). Learning and executing generalized robot plans. *Artificial Intelligence, 3*, 251–288. Reprinted in J. W. Shavlik & T. G. Dietterich (Eds.) (1990), *Readings in machine learning*. San Francisco, CA: Morgan Kaufmann.

Fisher, D. H. (1987). Knowledge acquisition via incremental conceptual clustering. *Machine Learning, 2*, 139–172. Reprinted in J. W. Shavlik & T. G. Dietterich (Eds.) (1990), *Readings in machine learning*. San Francisco, CA: Morgan Kaufmann.

Fisher, D. H. (1989). Noise-tolerant conceptual clustering. *Proceedings of the Eleventh International Joint Conference on Artificial Intelligence* (pp. 825–830). Detroit, MI: Morgan Kaufmann.

Fisher, D., & Langley, P. (1986). Methods of conceptual clustering and their relation to numerical taxonomy. In W. Gale (Ed.), *Artificial intelligence and statistics*. Reading, MA: Addison Wesley.

Fisher, D. H., & Langley, P. (1990). The structure and formation of natural categories. In G. H. Bower (Ed.), *The psychology of learning and motivation: Advances in research and theory* (Vol. 26). Cambridge, MA: Academic Press.

Fisher, D., & McKusick, K. B. (1989). An empirical comparison of ID3 and back-propagation. *Proceedings of the Eleventh International Joint Conference on Artificial Intelligence* (pp. 788–793). Detroit, MI: Morgan Kaufmann.

Fisher, D. H., Pazzani, M. J., & Langley, P. (Eds.). (1991). *Concept formation: Knowledge and experience in unsupervised learning*. San Francisco, CA: Morgan Kaufmann.

Fisher, R. A. (1936). The use of multiple measurements in taxonomic problems. *Annals of Eugenics, 7*, 179–188.

Fix, E., & Hodges, J. L. (1951). *Discriminatory analysis. Nonparametric discrimination: Consistency properties* (Report No. 4, Project No. 21-49-004). Randolph Field, TX: USAF School of Aviation Medicine.

Flann, N. S., & Dietterich, T. G. (1989). A study of explanation-based methods for inductive learning. *Machine Learning*, *4*, 187–226. Reprinted in J. W. Shavlik & T. G. Dietterich (Eds.) (1990), *Readings in machine learning*. San Francisco, CA: Morgan Kaufmann.

Friedman, J. H. (1977). A recursive partitioning decision rule for nonparametric classification. *IEEE Transactions on Computers*, *C-26*, 404–408.

Friedman, J. H. (1991). Multivariate adaptive regressive splines. *Annals of Statistics*, *19*, 1–141.

Friedman, J. H., Bentley, J., & Finkel, R. (1977). An algorithm for finding best matches in logarithmic expected time. *ACM Transactions on Mathematical Software*, *3*, 209–226.

Gale, W. (Ed.). (1986). *Artificial intelligence and statistics*. Reading, MA: Addison Wesley.

Garvin, P. I. (1967). The automation of discovery procedure in linguistics. *Language*, *43*, 172–178.

Gennari, J. H., Langley, P., & Fisher, D. H. (1989). Models of incremental concept formation. *Artificial Intelligence*, *40*, 11–61.

Gentner, D., & Forbus, K. (1991). MAC/FAC: A model of similarity-based retrieval. *Proceedings of the Thirteenth Annual Conference of the Cognitive Science Society* (pp. 504–509). Chicago: Lawrence Erlbaum.

Gerwin, D. (1974). Information processing, data inferences, and scientific generalization. *Behavioral Science*, *19*, 314–325.

Gil, Y. (1993). Efficient domain-independent experimentation. *Proceedings of the Tenth International Conference on Machine Learning* (pp. 128–134). Amherst, MA: Morgan Kaufmann.

Ginsberg, A., Weiss, S., & Politakis, P. (1988). Automatic knowledge base refinement for classification systems. *Artificial Intelligence*, *35*, 197–226.

Gluck, M. A., & Bower, G. H. (1988). Evaluating an adaptive network model of human learning. *Journal of Memory and Language*, *27*, 166–195.

Glymour, C., Scheines, R., Spirtes, P., & Kelly, K. (1987). *Discovering causal structure: Artificial intelligence, philosophy of science, and statistical modeling*. New York: Academic Press.

Gold, E. M. (1967). Language identification in the limit. *Information and Control*, *10*, 447–474.

Goldberg, D. E. (1990). *Genetic algorithms in search, optimization, and machine learning*. Reading, MA: Addison-Wesley.

Goldberg, D. E. (1994). Genetic and evolutionary algorithms come of age. *Communications of the ACM*, *37*, March, 113–119.

Good, I. J. (1950). *Probability and the weighing of evidence*. London: Charles Griffin.

Grefenstette, J. J., Ramsey, C. L., & Schultz, A. C. (1990). Learning sequential decision rules using simulation models and competition. *Machine Learning*, *5*, 355–381.

Greiner, R. (1988). Learning by understanding analogies. *Artificial Intelligence*, *35*, 81–125.

Greiner, R. (in press). PALO: A probabilistic hill-climbing algorithm. *Artificial Intelligence*.

Gross, K. P. (1991). *Concept acquisition through attribute evolution and experiment selection*. Doctoral dissertation, School of Computer Science, Carnegie Mellon University, Pittsburgh, PA.

Grossberg, S. (1987). Competitive learning: From interactive activation to adaptive resonance. *Cognitive Science*, *11*, 23–63.

Hadzikadic, M., & Yun, D. (1989). Concept formation by incremental conceptual clustering. *Proceedings of the Eleventh International Joint Conference on Artificial Intelligence* (pp. 831–836). Detroit, MI: Morgan Kaufmann.

Hall, R. P. (1989). Computational approaches to analogical reasoning: A comparative analysis. *Artificial Intelligence*, *39*, 39–120.

Hammond, K. J. (1990). Case-based planning: A framework for planning from experience. *Cognitive Science*, *14*, 385–443.

Hanson, S. J. (1990). Meiosis networks. In D. S. Touretzky (Ed.), *Advances in neural information processing systems* (Vol. 2). San Francisco, CA: Morgan Kaufmann.

Hanson, S. J., & Bauer, M. (1989). Conceptual clustering, categorization, and polymorphy. *Machine Learning*, *3*, 343–372.

Hassibi, B., & Stork, D. G. (1993). Second-order derivatives for network pruning. In C. L. Giles, S. J. Hanson, & J. D. Cowan (Eds.), *Advances in neural information processing systems* (Vol. 5). San Francisco, CA: Morgan Kaufmann.

Haussler, D. (1988). Quantifying inductive bias: AI learning algorithms and Valiant's learning framework. *Artificial Intelligence*, *36*, 177–222. Reprinted in J. W. Shavlik & T. G. Dietterich (Eds.) (1990), *Readings in machine learning*. San Francisco, CA: Morgan Kaufmann.

Haussler, D. (1990). Probably approximately correct learning. *Proceedings of the Eighth National Conference on Artificial Intelligence* (pp. 1101–1108). Boston: AAAI Press.

Hayes-Roth, F., & McDermott, J. (1978). An interference matching technique for inducing abstractions. *Communications of the ACM*, *21*, 401–410.

Heckerman, D. (1995). *A tutorial on learning Bayesian networks* (Technical Report MSR-TR-95-06). Redmond, WA: Microsoft Research.

Heckerman, D., Geiger, D., & Chickering, D. M. (1994). Learning Bayesian networks: The combination of knowledge and statistical data. *Proceedings of the Tenth Conference on Uncertainty in Artificial Intelligence* (pp. 293–301). Seattle, WA: Morgan Kaufmann.

Helmbold, D., Sloan, R., & Warmuth, M. K. (1990). Learning nested differences of intersection-closed concept classes. *Machine Learning, 5*, 165–196.

Hertz, J. A., Palmer, R. G., & Krogh, A. S. (1991). *Introduction to the theory of neural computation*. Redwood City, CA: Addison-Wesley.

Hickman, A. K., & Larkin, J. H. (1990). Internal analogy: A model of transfer within problems. *Proceedings of the Twelfth Annual Conference of the Cognitive Science Society* (pp. 53–60). Cambridge, MA: Lawrence Erlbaum.

Hill, J. A. C. (1983). A computational model of language acquisition in the two-year old. *Cognition and Brain Theory, 6*, 287–317.

Hill, J. A. C. (1992). Language acquisition. In S. Shapiro (Ed.), *Encyclopedia of artificial intelligence* (2nd ed.). New York: John Wiley & Sons.

Hinton, G. E. (1986). Learning distributed representations of concepts. *Proceedings of the Eighth Annual Conference of the Cognitive Science Society* (pp. 1–12). Amherst, MA: Lawrence Erlbaum.

Hinton, G. E. (1989). Connectionist learning procedures. *Artificial Intelligence, 40*, 185–234. Reprinted in J. W. Shavlik & T. G. Dietterich (Eds.) (1990), *Readings in machine learning*. San Francisco, CA: Morgan Kaufmann.

Holland, J. H. (1975). *Adaptation in natural and artificial systems*. Ann Arbor, MI: University of Michigan Press.

Holland, J. H. (1986). Escaping brittleness: The possibilities of general-purpose learning algorithms applied to parallel rule-based systems. In R. S. Michalski, J. G. Carbonell, & T. M. Mitchell (Eds.), *Machine learning: An artificial intelligence approach* (Vol. 2). San Francisco, CA: Morgan Kaufmann.

Holte, R. (1993). Very simple classification rules perform well on most commonly used domains. *Machine Learning, 11*, 63–91.

Hume, D. (1748). *An inquiry concerning human understanding*. Reprinted 1955. New York: Liberal Arts Press.

Hunt, E. B. (1962). *Concept learning: An information processing problem*. New York: John Wiley & Sons.

Hunt, E. B., Marin, J., & Stone, P. J. (1966). *Experiments in induction*. New York: Academic Press.

Iba, G. A. (1989). A heuristic approach to the discovery of macro-operators. *Machine Learning, 3*, 285–317.

Iba, W., Wogulis, J., & Langley, P. (1988). Trading off simplicity and coverage in incremental concept learning. *Proceedings of the Fifth International Conference on Machine Learning* (pp. 73–79). Ann Arbor, MI: Morgan Kaufmann.

John, G. H., Kohavi, R., & Pfleger, K. (1994). Irrelevant features and the subset selection problem. *Proceedings of the Eleventh International Conference on Machine Learning* (pp. 121–129). New Brunswick, NJ: Morgan Kaufmann.

Jones, R. (1986). Generating predictions to aid the scientific discovery process. *Proceedings of the Fifth National Conference on Artificial Intelligence* (pp. 513–522). Philadelphia, PA: Morgan Kaufmann.

Jones, R. M., & Langley, P. (1995). Retrieval and learning in analogical problem solving. *Proceedings of the Seventeenth Annual Conference of the Cognitive Science Society* (pp. 466–471). Pittsburgh, PA: Lawrence Erlbaum.

Jones, R. M., & VanLehn, K. (1994). Acquisition of children's addition strategies: A model of impasse-free, knowledge-level learning. *Machine Learning*, *16*, 11–36.

Jordan, M. I., & Jacobs, R. A. (1993). Supervised learning and divide-and-conquer: A statistical approach. *Proceedings of the Tenth International Conference on Machine Learning* (pp. 159–166). Amherst, MA: Morgan Kaufmann.

Kambhampati, S. (1990). Mapping and retrieval during plan reuse: A validation structure based approach. *Proceedings of the Eighth National Conference on Artificial Intelligence* (pp. 170–175). Boston, MA: AAAI Press.

Kearns, M. J., & Vazirani, U. V. (1994). *An introduction to computational learning theory*. Cambridge, MA: MIT Press.

Keller, R. M. (1988). Defining operationality for explanation-based learning. *Artificial Intelligence*, *35*, 227–241. Reprinted in J. W. Shavlik & T. G. Dietterich (Eds.) (1990), *Readings in machine learning*. San Francisco, CA: Morgan Kaufmann.

Kibler, D. (1978). *Power, efficiency, and correctness of transformation systems*. Doctoral dissertation, Department of Information & Computer Science, University of California, Irvine.

Kibler, D., & Aha, D. W. (1987). Learning representative exemplars of concepts: An initial case study. *Proceedings of the Fourth International Workshop on Machine Learning* (pp. 24–30). Irvine, CA: Morgan Kaufmann. Reprinted in J. W. Shavlik & T. G. Dietterich (Eds.) (1990), *Readings in machine learning*. San Francisco, CA: Morgan Kaufmann.

Kibler, D., Aha, D. W, & Albert, M. K. (1989). Instance-based prediction of real-valued attributes. *Computational Intelligence*, *5*, 51–57.

Kibler, D., & Langley, P. (1988). Machine learning as an experimental science. *Proceedings of the Third European Working Session on Learning* (pp. 81–92). Glasgow, Scotland: Pittman. Reprinted in J. W. Shavlik & T. G. Dietterich (Eds.) (1990), *Readings in machine learning*. San Francisco, CA: Morgan Kaufmann.

Kira, K., & Rendell, L. (1992). A practical approach to feature selection. *Proceedings of the Ninth International Conference on Machine Learning* (pp. 249–256). Aberdeen, Scotland: Morgan Kaufmann.

Kittler, J. (1986). Feature selection and extraction. In T. Y. Young & K. S. Fu (Eds.), *Handbook of pattern recognition and image processing*. Orlando, FL: Academic Press.

Klahr, D., Langley, P., & Neches, R. (Eds.) (1987). *Production system models of learning and development*. Cambridge, MA: MIT Press.

Klein, S., & Kuppin, M. A. (1970). *An interactive, heuristic program for learning transformational grammars* (Tech. Rep. No. 97). Madison: University of Wisconsin, Computer Sciences Department.

Kling, R. (1971). A paradigm for reasoning by analogy. *Artificial Intelligence*, *2*, 147–178.

Knerr, S., Personnaz, L., & Dreyfus, G. (1990). Single-layer learning revisited: A stepwise procedure for building and training a neural network. In F. F. Soulié & J. Hérault (Eds.), *Neurocomputing*. Berlin: Springer-Verlag.

Knobe, B., & Knobe, K. (1977). A method for inferring context-free grammars. *Information and Control*, *31*, 129–146.

Kocabas, S. (1991). Conflict resolution as discovery in particle physics. *Machine Learning*, *6*, 277–309.

Kohavi, R. (1994). Bottom-up induction of oblivious read-once decision graphs: Strengths and limitations. *Proceedings of the Twelfth National Conference on Artificial Intelligence* (pp. 613–618). Seattle, WA: AAAI Press.

Kohonen, T. (1982). Self-organized formation of topologically correct feature maps. *Biological Cybernetics*, *43*, 59–69. Reprinted in J. W. Shavlik & T. G. Dietterich (Eds.) (1990), *Readings in machine learning*. San Francisco, CA: Morgan Kaufmann.

Kolodner, J. L. (1993). *Case-based reasoning*. San Francisco, CA: Morgan Kaufmann.

Kononenko, I. (1991). Semi-naive Bayesian classifier. *Proceedings of the Sixth European Working Session on Learning* (pp. 206–219). Porto, Portugal: Pittman.

Koza, J. R. (1989). Hierarchical genetic algorithms operating on populations of computer programs. *Proceedings of the Eleventh International Joint Conference on Artificial Intelligence* (pp. 768–774). Detroit, MI: Morgan Kaufmann.

Kruschke, J. K. (1992). ALCOVE: An exemplar-based connectionist model of category learning. *Psychological Review*, *99*, 22–44.

Kulkarni, D., & Simon, H. A. (1990). Experimentation in machine discovery. In J. Shrager & P. Langley (Eds.), *Computational models of scientific discovery and theory formation*. San Francisco, CA: Morgan Kaufmann.

Laird, J. E. (1991). Preface for special section on integrated cognitive architectures. *SIGART Bulletin*, *2*, 12–123.

Laird, J. E., Rosenbloom, P. S., & Newell, A. (1986). Chunking in SOAR: The anatomy of a general learning mechanism. *Machine Learning*, *1*, 11–46. Reprinted in J. W. Shavlik & T. G. Dietterich (Eds.) (1990), *Readings in machine learning*. San Francisco, CA: Morgan Kaufmann.

Langley, P. (1981). Data-driven discovery of physical laws. *Cognitive Science*, *5*, 31–54.

Langley, P. (1982). Language acquisition through error recovery. *Cognition and Brain Theory*, *5*, 211–255.

Langley, P. (1985). Learning to search: From weak methods to domain-specific heuristics. *Cognitive Science*, *9*, 217–260.

Langley, P. (1987). A general theory of discrimination learning. In D. Klahr, P. Langley, & R. Neches (Eds.), *Production system models of learning and development*. Cambridge, MA: MIT Press.

Langley, P. (1989a). Toward a unified science of machine learning. *Machine Learning*, *3*, 253–259.

Langley, P. (1989b). Unifying themes in empirical and explanation-based learning. *Proceedings of the Sixth International Workshop on Machine Learning* (pp. 2–4). Ithaca, NY: Morgan Kaufmann.

Langley, P. (1993). Induction of recursive Bayesian classifiers. *Proceedings of the 1993 European Conference on Machine Learning* (pp. 153–164). Vienna: Springer-Verlag.

Langley, P. (1994a). Selection of relevant features in machine learning. *Proceedings of the AAAI Fall Symposium on Relevance* (pp. 140–144). New Orleans, LA: AAAI Press.

Langley, P. (1994b). *Simplicity and representation change in grammar induction*. Unpublished manuscript, Robotics Laboratory, Computer Science Department, Stanford University, Stanford, CA.

Langley, P., & Allen, J. A. (1991). Learning, memory, and search in planning. *Proceedings of the Thirteenth Annual Conference of the Cognitive Science Society* (pp. 364–369). Chicago: Lawrence Erlbaum.

Langley, P., Bradshaw, G. L., & Simon, H. A. (1983). Rediscovering chemistry with the BACON system. In R. S. Michalski, J. G. Carbonell, & T. M. Mitchell (Eds.), *Machine learning: An artificial intelligence approach*. San Francisco, CA: Morgan Kaufmann.

Langley, P., & Carbonell, J. G. (1984). Approaches to machine learning. *Journal of the American Society for Information Science*, *35*, 306–316.

Langley, P., & Carbonell, J. G. (1987a). Language acquisition and machine learning. In B. MacWhinney (Ed.), *Mechanisms of language acquisition*. Hillsdale, NJ: Lawrence Erlbaum.

Langley, P., & Carbonell, J. G. (1987b). Machine learning. In S. Shapiro (Ed.), *Encyclopedia of artificial intelligence*. New York: John Wiley & Sons.

Langley, P., Drastal, G., Rao, R. B., & Greiner, R. (1994). Theory revision in fault hierarchies. *Proceedings of the Fifth International Workshop on Principles of Diagnosis*. New Paltz, NY.

Langley, P., Gennari, J. H., & Iba, W. (1987). Hill-climbing theories of learning. *Proceedings of the Fourth International Workshop on Machine Learning* (pp. 312–323). Irvine, CA: Morgan Kaufmann.

Langley, P., Iba, W., & Thompson, K. (1992). An analysis of Bayesian classifiers. *Proceedings of the Tenth National Conference on Artificial Intelligence* (pp. 223–228). San Jose, CA: AAAI Press.

Langley, P., & Sage, S. (1994a). Induction of selective Bayesian classifiers. *Proceedings of the Tenth Conference on Uncertainty in Artificial Intelligence*. (pp. 399–406). Seattle, WA: Morgan Kaufmann.

Langley, P., & Sage, S. (1994b). Oblivious decision trees and abstract cases. *Working Notes of the AAAI94 Workshop on Case-Based Reasoning* (pp. 113–117). Seattle, WA: AAAI Press.

Langley, P., & Simon, H. A. (1981). The central role of learning in cognition. In J. R. Anderson (Ed.), *Cognitive skills and their acquisition*. Hillsdale, NJ: Lawrence Erlbaum.

Langley, P., & Simon, H. A. (in press). Applications of machine learning and rule induction. *Communications of the ACM*.

Langley, P., Simon, H. A., Bradshaw, G. L., & Zytkow, J. M. (1987). *Scientific discovery: Computational explorations of the creative processes*. Cambridge, MA: MIT Press.

Langley, P., & Zytkow, J. M. (1989). Data-driven approaches to empirical discovery. *Artificial Intelligence*, *40*, 283–312.

Lavrac, N., & Dzeroski, S. (1993). *Inductive logic programming: Techniques and applications*. New York: Ellis Horwood.

Lebowitz, M. (1987). Experiments with incremental concept formation: UNIMEM. *Machine Learning*, *2*, 103–138.

Lenat, D. B. (1978). The ubiquity of discovery. *Artificial Intelligence*, *9*, 257–285. Reprinted in J. W. Shavlik & T. G. Dietterich (Eds.) (1990), *Readings in machine learning*. San Francisco, CA: Morgan Kaufmann.

Lewis, C. (1978). *Production system models of practice effects*. Doctoral dissertation, Department of Psychology, University of Michigan, Ann Arbor.

Lin, L. J. (1992). Self-improving reactive agents based on reinforcement learning, planning, and teaching. *Machine Learning*, *8*, 293–321.

Ling, X. C., & Narayan, M. A. (1991). A critical comparison of various methods based on inverse resolution. *Proceedings of the Eighth International Workshop on Machine Learning* (pp. 173–177). Evanston, IL: Morgan Kaufmann.

Lippman, R. P. (1987). An introduction to computing with neural nets. *IEEE ASSP Magazine*, April, 4–22.

Littlestone, N. (1987). Learning quickly when irrelevant attributes abound: A new linear threshold algorithm. *Machine Learning*, *2*, 285–318.

Marchand, M., & Golea, M. (1993). On learning simple neural concepts: From halfspace intersections to neural decision lists. *Network*, *4*, 67–85.

Markovitz, S., & Scott, S. D. (1989). Utilization filtering: A method for reducing the inherent harmfulness of deductively learned knowledge. *Proceedings of the Eleventh International Joint Conference on Artificial Intelligence* (pp. 738–743). Detroit, MI: Morgan Kaufmann.

Martin, J. D. (1989). Focusing attention for observational learning: The importance of context. *Proceedings of the Eleventh International Joint Conference on Artificial Intelligence*. Detroit, MI: Morgan Kaufmann.

Martin, J. D., & Billman, D. O. (1994). Acquiring and combining overlapping concepts. *Machine Learning*, *16*, 121–155.

Matheus, C. J., & Rendell, L. A. (1989). Constructive induction on decision trees. *Proceedings of the Eleventh International Joint Conference on Artificial Intelligence* (pp. 645–650). Detroit, MI: Morgan Kaufmann.

McKusick, K. B., & Langley, P. (1991). Constraints on tree structure in concept formation. *Proceedings of the Twelfth International Joint Conference on Artificial Intelligence* (pp. 810–816). Sydney, Australia: Morgan Kaufmann.

McMaster, I., Sampson, J. R., & King, J. E. (1976). Computer acquisition of natural language: A review and prospectus. *International Journal of Man–Machine Studies*, *8*, 367–396.

Michalski, R. S. (1980). Pattern recognition as rule-guided inductive inference. *IEEE Transactions on Pattern Analysis and Machine Intelligence*, *2*, 349–361.

Michalski, R. S. (1983). A theory and methodology of inductive learning. In R. S. Michalski, J. G. Carbonell, & T. M. Mitchell (Eds.), *Machine learning: An artificial intelligence approach*. San Francisco, CA: Morgan Kaufmann. Reprinted in J. W. Shavlik & T. G. Dietterich (Eds.) (1990), *Readings in machine learning*. San Francisco, CA: Morgan Kaufmann.

Michalski, R. S., Carbonell, J. G., & Mitchell, T. M. (Eds.). (1983). *Machine learning: An artificial intelligence approach* (Vol. 1). San Francisco, CA: Morgan Kaufmann.

Michalski, R. S., Carbonell, J. G., & Mitchell, T. M. (Eds.). (1986). *Machine learning: An artificial intelligence approach* (Vol. 2). San Francisco, CA: Morgan Kaufmann.

Michalski, R. S., & Chilausky, R. L. (1980). Learning by being told and learning from examples: An experimental comparison of two methods of knowledge acquisition in the context of developing an expert system for soybean disease diagnosis. *International Journal of Policy Analysis and Information Systems, 4.*

Michalski, R. S., Mozetic, I., Hong, J., & Lavrac, N. (1986). The multi-purpose incremental learning system AQ15 and its testing application to three medical domains. *Proceedings of the Fifth National Conference on Artificial Intelligence* (pp. 1041–1045). Philadelphia, PA: Morgan Kaufmann.

Michalski, R. S., & Stepp, R. (1983). Learning from observation: Conceptual clustering. In R. S. Michalski, J. G. Carbonell, & T. M. Mitchell (Eds.), *Machine learning: An artificial intelligence approach.* San Francisco, CA: Morgan Kaufmann.

Michie, D., & Chambers, R. A. (1968). BOXES: An experiment in adaptive control. In E. Dale & D. Michie (Eds.), *Machine intelligence* (Vol. 2). Edinburgh, Scotland: Oliver & Boyd.

Mingers, J. (1989a). An empirical comparison of selection measures for decision-tree induction. *Machine Learning, 3,* 319-342

Mingers, J. (1989b). An empirical comparison of pruning methods for decision-tree induction. *Machine Learning, 4,* 227-243

Minsky, M. (1963). Steps toward artificial intelligence. In E. A. Feigenbaum & J. Feldman (Eds.), *Computers and thought.* New York: McGraw-Hill.

Minsky, M., & Papert, S. (1967). *Perceptrons.* Cambridge, MA: MIT Press.

Minton, S. N. (1985). Selectively generalizing plans for problem solving. *Proceedings of the Ninth International Joint Conference on Artificial Intelligence* (pp. 596–599). Los Angeles, CA: Morgan Kaufmann.

Minton, S. N. (1990). Quantitative results concerning the utility of explanation-based learning. *Artificial Intelligence, 42,* 363–391. Reprinted in J. W. Shavlik & T. G. Dietterich (Eds.) (1990), *Readings in machine learning.* San Francisco, CA: Morgan Kaufmann.

Minton, S. (Ed.). (1993). *Machine learning methods for planning.* San Francisco, CA: Morgan Kaufmann.

Mitchell, T. M. (1977). Version spaces: A candidate elimination approach to rule learning. *Proceedings of the Fifth International Joint Conference on Artificial Intelligence* (pp. 305–310). Cambridge, MA: Morgan Kaufmann.

Mitchell, T. M. (1980). *The need for biases in learning generalizations* (Technical Report No. CBM-TR-117). New Brunswick, NJ: Rutgers University, Department of Computer Science. Reprinted in J. W. Shavlik & T. G. Dietterich (Eds.) (1990), *Readings in machine learning*. San Francisco, CA: Morgan Kaufmann.

Mitchell, T. M. (1982). Generalization as search. *Artificial Intelligence, 18*, 203–226. Reprinted in J. W. Shavlik & T. G. Dietterich (Eds.) (1990), *Readings in machine learning*. San Francisco, CA: Morgan Kaufmann.

Mitchell, T. M., Keller, R. M., & Kedar-Cabelli, S. (1986). Explanation-based generalization: A unifying view. *Machine Learning, 1*, 47–80. Reprinted in J. W. Shavlik & T. G. Dietterich (Eds.) (1990), *Readings in machine learning*. San Francisco, CA: Morgan Kaufmann.

Mitchell, T. M., Mahadevan, S., & Steinberg, L. (1985). LEAP: A learning apprentice for VLSI design. *Proceedings of the Ninth International Joint Conference on Artificial Intelligence* (pp. 573–580). Los Angeles, CA: Morgan Kaufmann.

Mitchell, T. M., Utgoff, P., & Banerji, R. B. (1983). Learning problem solving heuristics by experimentation. In R. S. Michalski, J. G. Carbonell, & T. M. Mitchell (Eds.), *Machine learning: An artificial intelligence approach*. San Francisco, CA: Morgan Kaufmann. Reprinted in J. W. Shavlik & T. G. Dietterich (Eds.) (1990), *Readings in machine learning*. San Francisco, CA: Morgan Kaufmann.

Moody, J., & Darken, C. (1991). Fast learning in networks of locally-tuned processing units. *Neural Computation, 1*, 281–294.

Mooney, R. (1988). Generalizing the order of operators in macro-operators. *Proceedings of the Fifth International Workshop on Machine Learning* (pp. 270–283). Ann Arbor, MI: Morgan Kaufmann.

Mooney, R. (1989). The effect of rule use on the utility of explanation-based learning. *Proceedings of the Eleventh International Joint Conference on Artificial Intelligence* (pp. 725–730). Detroit, MI: Morgan Kaufmann.

Mooney, R., Shavlik, S., Towell, G., & Gove, A. (1989). An experimental comparison of symbolic and connectionist learning algorithms. *Proceedings of the Eleventh International Joint Conference on Artificial Intelligence* (pp. 775–780). Detroit, MI: Morgan Kaufmann. Reprinted in J. W. Shavlik & T. G. Dietterich (Eds.) (1990), *Readings in machine learning*. San Francisco, CA: Morgan Kaufmann.

Moore, A. W. (1990). Acquisition of dynamic control knowledge for a robot manipulator. *Proceedings of the Seventh International Conference on Machine Learning* (pp. 244–252). Austin, TX: Morgan Kaufmann.

Moore, A. W., & Lee, M. S. (1994). Efficient algorithms for minimizing cross validation error. *Proceedings of the Eleventh International Conference on Machine Learning* (pp. 190–198). New Brunswick, NJ: Morgan Kaufmann.

Mostow, J. (1983). Machine transformation of advice into a heuristic search procedure. In R. S. Michalski, J. G. Carbonell, & T. M. Mitchell (Eds.), *Machine learning: An artificial intelligence approach.* San Francisco, CA: Morgan Kaufmann.

Mostow, J. (1989). Design by derivational analogy: Issues in the automated replay of design plans. *Artificial Intelligence, 40*, 119–184.

Mozer, M., & Bachrach, J. (1991). Slug: A connectionist architecture for inferring the structure of finite-state environments. *Machine Learning, 7*, 139–160.

Muggleton, S. (1987). Duce: An oracle-based approach to constructive induction. *Proceedings of the Tenth International Joint Conference on Artificial Intelligence* (pp. 287–292). Milan, Italy: Morgan Kaufmann.

Muggleton, S., & Buntine, W. (1988). Machine invention of first-order predicates by inverting resolution. *Proceedings of the Fifth International Conference on Machine Learning* (pp. 339–352). Ann Arbor, MI: Morgan Kaufmann.

Muggleton, S., & Feng, C. (1992). Efficient induction of logic programs. In S. Muggleton (Ed.), *Inductive logic programming.* New York: Academic Press.

Murphy, P. M., & Aha, D. W. (1992). *UCI Repository of machine learning databases* [Machine-readable data repository]. Irvine: University of California, Department of Information & Computer Science.

Murphy, P. M., & Pazzani, M. J. (1991). ID2-of-3: Constructive induction of M-of-N concepts for discrimination in decision trees. *Proceedings of the Eighth International Workshop on Machine Learning* (pp. 173–177). Evanston, IL: Morgan Kaufmann.

Murthy, S., Kasif, S., Salzberg, S., & Beigel, R. (1993). OC1: Randomized induction of oblique decision trees. *Proceedings of the Eleventh National Conference on Artificial Intelligence* (pp. 322–327). Washington, DC: AAAI Press.

Natarajan, B. K. (1991). *Machine learning: A theoretical approach.* San Francisco, CA: Morgan Kaufmann.

Neves, D. M., & Anderson, J. R. (1981). Knowledge compilation: Mechanisms for the automatization of cognitive skills. In J. R. Anderson (Ed.), *Cognitive skills and their acquisition.* Hillsdale, NJ: Lawrence Erlbaum.

Newell, A. (1990). *Unified theories of cognition.* Cambridge, MA: Harvard University Press.

Nilsson, N. J. (1965). *Learning machines*. New York: McGraw-Hill.

Nilsson, N. J. (1985). *Triangle tables: A proposal for a robot programming language* (Technical Note 347). Menlo Park, CA: SRI International.

Nordhausen, B., & Langley, P. (1990). A robust approach to numeric discovery. *Proceedings of the Seventh International Conference on Machine Learning* (pp. 411–418). Austin, TX: Morgan Kaufmann.

Norton, S. W. (1989). Generating better decision trees. *Proceedings of the Eleventh International Conference on Artificial Intelligence* (pp. 800–805). Detroit, MI: Morgan Kaufmann.

Ohlsson, S. (1983). A constrained mechanism for procedural learning. *Proceedings of the Eighth International Joint Conference on Artificial Intelligence* (pp. 426–428). Karlsruhe, West Germany: Morgan Kaufmann.

Oliver, J. J. (1993). Decision graphs – An extension of decision trees. *Proceedings of the Fourth International Workshop on Artificial Intelligence and Statistics* (pp. 343–350). Fort Lauderdale, FL.

O'Rorke, P., Morris, S., & Schulenberg, D. (1990). Theory formation by abduction: A case study based on the chemical revolution. In J. Shrager & P. Langley (Eds.), *Computational models of scientific discovery and theory formation*. San Francisco, CA: Morgan Kaufmann.

Ourston, D., & Mooney, R. (1990). Changing the rules: A comprehensive approach to theory refinement. *Proceedings of the Eighth National Conference on Artificial Intelligence* (pp. 815–820). Boston: AAAI Press.

Pagallo, G. (1989). Learning DNF by decision trees. *Proceedings of the Eleventh International Joint Conference on Artificial Intelligence* (pp. 639–644). Detroit, MI: Morgan Kaufmann.

Patterson, A., & Niblett, T. B. (1982). *ACLS manual*. Edinburgh, Scotland: Intelligent Terminals, Ltd.

Pazzani, M. J. (1988). Integrated learning with incomplete and incorrect theories. *Proceedings of the Fifth International Conference on Machine Learning* (pp. 291–297). Ann Arbor: Morgan Kaufmann.

Pazzani, M. J. (1995). Searching for attribute dependencies in Bayesian classifiers. *Proceedings of the Fifth International Workshop on Artificial Intelligence and Statistics* (pp. 424–429). Fort Lauderdale, FL.

Pinker, S. (1979). Formal models of language learning. *Cognition, 7*, 217–283.

Platt, J. (1991). A resource-allocating network for function interpolation. *Neural Computation, 3*, 213–225.

Plotkin, G. (1970). A note on inductive generalization. In B. Meltzer & D. Michie (Eds.), *Machine intelligence* (Vol. 5). New York: Elsevier North-Holland.

Porat, S., & Feldman, J. A. (1991). Learning automata from ordered examples. *Machine Learning, 7*, 109–138.

Poritz, A. B. (1988). Hidden Markov models: A guided tour. *Proceedings of the International Conference on Acoustics, Speech, and Signal Processing* (pp. 7–13). IEEE.

Provan, G. M., & Singh, M. (1995). Learning Bayesian networks using feature selection. *Proceedings of the Fifth International Workshop on Artificial Intelligence and Statistics* (pp. 450–456). Fort Lauderdale, FL.

Quinlan, J. R. (1983). Learning efficient classification procedures and their application to chess end games. In R. S. Michalski, J. G. Carbonell, & T. M. Mitchell (Eds.), *Machine learning: An artificial intelligence approach*. San Francisco, CA: Morgan Kaufmann.

Quinlan, J. R. (1986). Induction of decision trees. *Machine Learning*, *1*, 81–106. Reprinted in J. W. Shavlik & T. G. Dietterich (Eds.) (1990), *Readings in machine learning*. San Francisco, CA: Morgan Kaufmann.

Quinlan, J. R. (1987). Generating production rules from decision trees. *Proceedings of the Tenth International Joint Conference on Artificial Intelligence* (pp. 304–307). Milan, Italy: Morgan Kaufmann.

Quinlan, J. R. (1990). Learning logical definitions from relations. *Machine Learning*, *5*, 239–266.

Quinlan, J. R. (1993a). Combining instance-based and model-based learning. *Proceedings of the Tenth International Conference on Machine Learning* (pp. 236–243). Amherst, MA: Morgan Kaufmann.

Quinlan, J. R. (1993b). *C4.5: Programs for machine learning*. San Francisco, CA: Morgan Kaufmann.

Quinlan, J. R., & Rivest, R. L. (1989). Inferring decision trees using the minimum description length principle. *Information and Computation*, *80*, 227–248.

Rabiner, L. R., & Huang, B. H. (1986). An introduction to hidden Markov models. *IEEE ASSP Magazine*, *3*, 4–16.

Rajamoney, S. (1990). A computational approach to theory revision. In J. Shrager & P. Langley (Eds.), *Computational models of scientific discovery and theory formation*. San Francisco, CA: Morgan Kaufmann.

Rao, R. B., Greiner, G., & Hancock, T. (1994). Exploiting the absence of irrelevant information: What you don't know can help you. *Proceedings of the AAAI Fall Symposium on Relevance* (pp. 178–182). New Orleans, LA: AAAI Press.

Rao, R. B., & Lu, S. C.-Y. (1992). Learning engineering models with the minimum description length principle. *Proceedings of the Tenth National Conference on Artificial Intelligence* (pp. 717–722). San Jose: AAAI Press.

Reeker, L. H. (1976). The computational study of language acquisition. In M. Yovits & M. Rubinoff (Eds.), *Advances in computers* (Vol. 15). New York: Academic Press.

Rendell, L. A. (1986a). A general framework for induction and a study of selective induction. *Machine Learning*, *1*, 177–226.

Rendell, L. A. (1986b). A new basis for state-space learning systems and a successful implementation. *Artificial Intelligence*, *20*, 369-392.

Rendell, L. A., & Cho, H. (1990). Empirical learning as a function of concept character. *Machine Learning*, *1*, 177–226.

Richman, H. (1991). Discrimination net models of concept formation. In D. H. Fisher, M. J. Pazzani, & P. Langley (Eds.), *Concept formation: Knowledge and experience in unsupervised learning*. San Francisco, CA: Morgan Kaufmann.

Rissanen, J. (1978). Modeling by shortest data description. *Automatica*, *14*, 465–471.

Rivest, R. L. (1987). Learning decision lists. *Machine Learning*, *2*, 229–246.

Rivest, R. L., & Schapire, R. E. (1993). Inference of finite automata using homing sequences. *Information and Computation*, *103*, 299–347.

Rose, D., & Langley, P. (1986). Chemical discovery as belief revision. *Machine Learning*, *1*, 423–451.

Rosenblatt, F. (1958). The perceptron: A probabilistic model for information storage and organization in the brain. *Psychological Review*, *65*, 386-408. Reprinted in J. W. Shavlik & T. G. Dietterich (Eds.) (1990), *Readings in machine learning*. San Francisco, CA: Morgan Kaufmann.

Rosenblatt, F. (1962). *Principles of neurodynamics*. New York: Spartan Books.

Rumelhart, D. E., Hinton, G., & Williams, R. J. (1986). Learning internal representations by error propagation. In D. E. Rumelhart & J. L. McClelland (Eds.), *Parallel distributed processing: Explorations in the microstructure of cognition* (Vol. 1). Cambridge, MA: MIT Press. Reprinted in J. W. Shavlik & T. G. Dietterich (Eds.) (1990), *Readings in machine learning*. San Francisco, CA: Morgan Kaufmann.

Rumelhart, D. E. & McClelland, J. L. (Eds.) (1986). *Parallel distributed processing: Explorations in the microstructure of cognition* (Vol. 1). Cambridge, MA: MIT Press.

Rumelhart, D. E., & Zipser, D. (1985). Feature discovery by competitive learning. *Cognitive Science*, *9*, 75–112. Reprinted in J. W. Shavlik & T. G. Dietterich (Eds.) (1990), *Readings in machine learning*. San Francisco, CA: Morgan Kaufmann.

Sammut, C., & Banerji, R. B. (1986). Learning concepts by asking questions. In R. S. Michalski, J. G. Carbonell, & T. M. Mitchell (Eds.), *Machine learning: An artificial intelligence approach* (Vol. 2). San Francisco, CA: Morgan Kaufmann.

Sammut, C., Hurst, S., Kedizer, D., & Michie, D. (1992). Learning to fly. *Proceedings of the Ninth International Conference on Machine Learning* (pp. 385–393). Aberdeen, Scotland: Morgan Kaufmann.

Samuel, A. L. (1959). Some studies in machine learning using the game of checkers. *IBM Journal of Research and Development*, *3*, 210–229. Reprinted in J. W. Shavlik & T. G. Dietterich (Eds.) (1990), *Readings in machine learning*. San Francisco, CA: Morgan Kaufmann.

Samuelson, C., & Rayner, M. (1991). Quantitative evaluation of explanation-based learning as an optimization tool for a large-scale natural language system. *Proceedings of the Twelfth International Joint Conference on Artificial Intelligence* (pp. 609–615). Sydney, Australia: Morgan Kaufmann.

Schlimmer, J. C. (1987). Efficiently inducing determinations: A complete and efficient search algorithm that uses optimal pruning. *Proceedings of the Tenth International Conference on Machine Learning* (pp. 284–290). Amherst, MA: Morgan Kaufmann.

Schlimmer, J. C., & Fisher, D. (1986). A case study of incremental concept induction. *Proceedings of the Fifth National Conference on Artificial Intelligence* (pp. 496–501). Philadelphia, PA: Morgan Kaufmann.

Schlimmer, J. C., & Langley, P. (1992). Machine learning. In S. Shapiro (Ed.), *Encyclopedia of artificial intelligence* (2nd ed.). New York: John Wiley & Sons.

Scott, P. D., & Markovitz, S. (1991). Representation generation in an exploratory learning system. In D. H. Fisher, M. J. Pazzani, & P. Langley (Eds.), *Concept formation: Knowledge and experience in unsupervised learning*. San Francisco, CA: Morgan Kaufmann.

Segre, A., Elkan, C., & Russell, A. (1991). A critical look at experimental evaluations of EBL. *Machine Learning*, *6*, 183–195.

Selfridge, M. (1981). A computer model of child language acquisition. *Proceedings of the Seventh International Joint Conference on Artificial Intelligence* (pp. 92–96). Vancouver, B.C., Canada: Morgan Kaufmann.

Shapiro, E. Y. (1981). An algorithm that infers theories from facts. *Proceedings of the Seventh International Joint Conference on Artificial Intelligence* (pp. 446–451). Vancouver, BC, Canada: Morgan Kaufmann.

Shavlik, J. W. (1990). Acquiring recursive and iterative concepts with explanation-based learning. *Machine Learning*, *5*, 39–70. Reprinted in J. W. Shavlik & T. G. Dietterich (Eds.) (1990), *Readings in machine learning*. San Francisco, CA: Morgan Kaufmann.

Shavlik, J. W., & Dietterich, T. G. (Eds.). (1990). *Readings in machine learning*. San Francisco, CA: Morgan Kaufmann.

Shell, P., & Carbonell, J. G. (1989). Towards a general framework for composing disjunctive and iterative macro-operators. *Proceedings of the Eleventh International Joint Conference on Artificial Intelligence* (pp. 596–602). Detroit, MI: Morgan Kaufmann.

Shen, W. M., & Simon, H. A. (1989). Rule creation and rule learning through environmental exploration. *Proceedings of the Eleventh International Joint Conference on Artificial Intelligence* (pp. 675–680). Detroit, MI: Morgan Kaufmann.

Shrager, J., Hogg, T., & Huberman, B. A. (1988). A graph-dynamic model of the power law of practice and the problem-solving fan effect. *Science, 242*, 414–416.

Shrager, J., & Langley, P. (1990). Computational approaches to scientific discovery. In J. Shrager & P. Langley (Eds.), *Computational models of scientific discovery and theory formation.* San Francisco, CA: Morgan Kaufmann.

Shrager, J., & Langley, P. (Eds.). (1990). *Computational models of scientific discovery and theory formation.* San Francisco, CA: Morgan Kaufmann.

Siklóssy, L. (1972). Natural language learning by computer. In H. A. Simon & L. Siklóssy (Eds.), *Representation and meaning: Experiments with information processing systems.* Englewood Cliffs, NJ: Prentice-Hall.

Simon, H. A., & Lea, G. (1974). Problem solving and rule induction: A unified view. In L. W. Gregg (Ed.), *Knowledge and cognition.* Hillsdale, NJ: Lawrence Erlbaum. Reprinted in J. W. Shavlik & T. G. Dietterich (Eds.) (1990), *Readings in machine learning.* San Francisco, CA: Morgan Kaufmann.

Siskind, J. M. (1990). Acquiring core meanings of words, represented as Jackendoff-style conceptual structures, from correlated streams of linguistic and non-linguistic input. *Proceedings of the Twenty-Eighth Annual Meeting of the Association for Computational Linguistics* (pp. 143–156). Pittsburgh, PA: ACL.

Sleeman, D., Langley, P., & Mitchell, T. (1982). Learning from solution paths: An approach to the credit assignment problem. *AI Magazine, 3*, 48–52.

Smith, E. E., & Medin, D. L. (1981). *Categories and concepts.* Cambridge, MA: Harvard University Press.

Smith, S. F. (1983). Flexible learning of problem solving heuristics through adaptive search. *Proceedings of the Eighth International Joint Conference on Artificial Intelligence* (pp. 422–425). Karlsruhe, Germany: Morgan Kaufmann.

Solomonoff, R. (1959). A new method for discovering the grammars of phrase structure languages. *Proceedings of the International Conference on Information Processing.*

Sonquist, J. A., Baker, E., & Morgan, J. (1977). *Searching for structure*. Ann Arbor, MI: University of Michigan, Institute for Social Research.

Spackman, K. A. (1988). Learning categorical criteria in biomedical domains. *Proceedings of the Fifth International Conference on Machine Learning* (pp. 36–46). Ann Arbor, MI: Morgan Kaufmann.

Stanfill, C. W. (1987). Memory-based reasoning applied to English pronunciation. *Proceedings of the Sixth National Conference on Artificial Intelligence* (pp. 577–581). Seattle, WA: AAAI Press.

Stolcke, A., & Omohundro, S. (1993). Hidden Markov model induction by Bayesian model merging. In C. L. Giles, S. J. Hanson, & J. D. Cowan (Eds.), *Advances in neural information processing systems* (Vol. 5). San Francisco, CA: Morgan Kaufmann.

Stolcke, A., & Omohundro, S. (1994). Inducing probabilistic grammars by Bayesian model merging. *Proceedings of the Second International Conference on Grammatical Inference and Applications* (pp. 106–118). Alicante, Spain: Springer-Verlag.

Sutton, R. S. (1988). Learning to predict by the methods of temporal differences. *Machine Learning*, *3*, 9–44.

Sycara, K. (1988). Patching up old plans. *Proceedings of the Tenth Annual Conference of the Cognitive Science Society* (pp. 405–411). Montreal, Quebec, Canada: Lawrence Erlbaum.

Tambe, M., Newell, A., & Rosenbloom, P. S. (1990). The problem of expensive chunks and its solution by restricting expressiveness. *Machine Learning*, *5*, 299–348.

Thagard, P. (1988). *Computational philosophy of science*. Cambridge, MA: MIT Press.

Thagard, P., Holyoak, K., Nelson, G., & Gochfield, D. (1990). Analogical retrieval by constraint satisfaction. *Artificial Intelligence*, *46*, 259–310.

Thrun, S. B., & Mitchell, T. M. (1993). Explanation-based learning: A comparison of symbolic and neural network approaches. *Proceedings of the Eleventh International Conference on Machine Learning* (pp. 197–204). New Brunswick, NJ: Morgan Kaufmann.

Tomita, M. (1982). Dynamic construction of finite-state automata from examples using hill climbing. *Proceedings of the Fourth Annual Conference of the Cognitive Science Society* (pp. 105–108). Ann Arbor, MI: Lawrence Erlbaum.

Towell, G., Shavlik, J., & Noordeweier, M. O. (1990). Refinement of approximate domain theories by knowledge-based neural networks. *Proceedings of the Eighth National Conference on Artificial Intelligence* (pp. 861–866). Boston: AAAI Press.

Utgoff, P. E. (1988). Perceptron trees: A case study in hybrid concept representations. *Proceedings of the Seventh National Conference on Artificial Intelligence* (pp. 601–606). St. Paul, MN: AAAI Press.

Utgoff, P. E. (1989). Incremental induction of decision trees. *Machine Learning*, *4*, 161–186.

Utgoff, P. E., & Brodley, C. E. (1990). An incremental method for finding multivariate splits for decision trees. *Proceedings of the Seventh International Conference on Machine Learning* (pp. 58–65). Austin, TX: Morgan Kaufmann.

Utgoff, P. E., & Saxena, S. (1987). Learning a preference predicate. *Proceedings of the Fourth International Workshop on Machine Learning* (pp. 115–121). Irvine, CA: Morgan Kaufmann.

Valdes-Perez, R. E., Zytkow, J. M., & Simon, H. A. (1993). Scientific model building as search in matrix spaces. *Proceedings of the Eleventh National Conference on Artificial Intelligence* (pp. 472–478). Washington, DC: AAAI Press.

Valiant, L. G. (1984). A theory of the learnable. *Communications of the ACM*, *27*, 1134–1142. Reprinted in J. W. Shavlik & T. G. Dietterich (Eds.) (1990), *Readings in machine learning*. San Francisco, CA: Morgan Kaufmann.

VanLehn, K. (1987). Learning one subprocedure per lesson. *Artificial Intelligence*, *31*, 1–40. Reprinted in J. W. Shavlik & T. G. Dietterich (Eds.) (1990), *Readings in machine learning*. San Francisco, CA: Morgan Kaufmann.

VanLehn, K., & Ball, W. (1987). A version space approach to learning context-free grammars. *Machine Learning*, *2*, 39–74.

Veloso, M. M., & Carbonell, J. G. (1993). Derivational analogy in PRODIGY: Automating case acquisition, storage, and utilization. *Machine Learning*, *10*, 249–278.

Vere, S. A. (1975). Induction of concepts in the predicate calculus. *Proceedings of the Fourth International Joint Conference on Artificial Intelligence* (pp. 281–287). Tbilisi, USSR: Morgan Kaufmann.

Vere, S. (1980). Multilevel counterfactuals for generalization of relational concepts and productions. *Artificial Intelligence*, *14*, 139–164.

Watkins, C. J. C. H., & Dayan, P. (1992). Q learning. *Machine Learning*, *8*, 279–292.

Weigend, A. S., Huberman, B. A., & Rumelhart, D. E. (1990). Predicting the future: A connectionist approach. *International Journal of Neural Systems*, *1*, 193–209.

Weiss, S. M., & Indurkhya, N. (1993). Rule-based regression. *Proceedings of the Thirteenth International Joint Conference on Artificial Intelligence* (pp. 1072–1078). Chambéry, France: Morgan Kaufmann.

Weiss, S. M., & Kapouleas, I. (1989). An empirical comparison of pattern recognition, neural nets, and machine learning classification methods. *Proceedings of the Eleventh International Joint Conference on Artificial Intelligence* (pp. 781–787). Detroit, MI: Morgan Kaufmann. Reprinted in J. W. Shavlik & T. G. Dietterich (Eds.) (1990), *Readings in machine learning*. San Francisco, CA: Morgan Kaufmann.

Wharton, R. M. (1977). Grammar enumeration and inference. *Information and Control*, *33*, 253–272.

Widrow, B., & Hoff, M. E. (1960). Adaptive switching circuits. *Institute of Radio Engineers, Western Electronic Show and Convention, Convention Record*, *4*, 96–194.

Widrow, B., Rumelhart, D. E., & Lehr, M. A. (1994). Neural networks: Applications in industry, business, and science. *Communications of the ACM*, *37*, March, 93–105.

Widrow, B., & Winter, R. G. (1988). Neural nets for adaptive filtering and adaptive pattern recognition. *IEEE Computer*, *21*, March, 25–39.

Williams, R. J. (1992). Simple statistical gradient-following algorithms for connectionist reinforcement learning. *Machine Learning*, *8*, 229–256.

Wilson, S. W. (1987). Classifier systems and the animat problem. *Machine Learning*, *2*, 199–228.

Winston, P. H. (1975). Learning structural descriptions from examples. In P. H. Winston (Ed.), *The psychology of computer vision*. New York: McGraw-Hill.

Wogulis, J., & Pazzani, M. (1993). A methodology for evaluating theory revision systems: Results with Audrey II. *Proceedings of the Thirteenth International Joint Conference on Artificial Intelligence* (pp. 1128–1134). Chambéry, France: Morgan Kaufmann.

Wolff, J. G. (1980). Language acquisition and the discovery of phrase structure. *Language and Speech*, *23*, 255–269.

Zelle, J. M., Mooney, R. J., & Konvisser, J. B. (1994). Combining top-down and bottom-up methods in inductive logic programming. *Proceedings of the Eleventh International Conference on Machine Learning* (pp. 343–351). New Brunswick, NJ: Morgan Kaufmann.

Zytkow, J. M., Zhu, J., & Hussam, A. (1990). Automated discovery in a chemistry laboratory. *Proceedings of the Eighth National Conference on Artificial Intelligence* (pp. 889–894). Boston, MA: AAAI Press.

Index